British Foreign Policy, 1918–1945
A Guide to Research and Research Materials

Guides to European Diplomatic History
Research and Research Materials

Series Editor
Christoph M. Kimmich

British Foreign Policy, 1918–1945
By Sidney Aster
ISBN: 0-8420-2176-0

French Foreign Policy, 1918–1945
By Robert J. Young
ISBN: 0-8420-2178-7

German Foreign Policy, 1918–1945
By Christoph M. Kimmich
ISBN: 0-8420-2167-1

International Organizations, 1918–1945
By George W. Baer
ISBN: 0-8420-2179-5

Italian Foreign Policy, 1918–1945
By Alan Cassels
ISBN: 0-8420-2177-9

Available from Scholarly Resources Inc.
Wilmington, Delaware

British Foreign Policy
1918–1945

A Guide to Research and Research Materials

Compiled and Edited
by
Sidney Aster

Scholarly Resources Inc.
Wilmington, Delaware

© 1984 by Scholarly Resources Inc.
All rights reserved
First published 1984
Printed and bound in the United States of America

Scholarly Resources Inc.
104 Greenhill Avenue
Wilmington, Delaware 19805

Library of Congress Cataloging in Publication Data

Aster, Sidney , 1942–
    British foreign policy, 1918–1945.

    Includes bibliographies and indexes.
    1. Great Britain—Foreign relations—1910–1936—
Library resources—Great Britain.   2. Great Britain—
Foreign relations—1936–1945—Library resources—
Great Britain.   3. Great Britain—Foreign relations—
1910–1936—Archival resources—Great Britain.
4. Great Britain—Foreign relations—1936–1945—
Archival resources—Great Britain.   I. Title.
Z6465.G7A85   1984   [DA578]   327.41'0072041   84–533
ISBN 0-8420-2176-0

To my children

Andrea Zoe and Dylan Mark

INTRODUCTION TO THE SERIES

This handbook on Great Britain is one in a series of research guides on European diplomatic history between 1918 and 1945. It is intended for scholars doing research on seminar papers, dissertations, and books, who want information to help them plan their work and to guide them on their visits to archives and libraries. It will enable them to find their way quickly and efficiently through the voluminous research and research materials that have become available in recent years and will point them toward solutions to the problems they will encounter in the course of their work.

The handbook is organized to serve the researcher's needs. The introductory chapter provides an overview of the entire field. The second chapter describes how foreign policy was made in Great Britain--how the foreign office was organized and how it functioned, how it affected the conduct of foreign affairs and diplomacy, and how it was influenced by bureaucratic politics, domestic developments, and public opinion. This information will help the reader determine where to concentrate his research, how to allot research time, and, not least, how best to approach the materials in the archives. The third chapter brings together the most current information on public and private archives, on newspaper collections, libraries, and research institutes. It indicates what work can be undertaken on this side of the Atlantic and what has to be left for a visit to Europe, and further, given the frequent duplication of source material, what repository will be most useful and rewarding. The remainder of the volume is bibliography. Sections on general and bibliographical reference works are followed by a survey of the literature in the field, ranging from documentary series to memoirs to significant secondary sources. Arranged topically within a broadly chronological framework, largely annotated, this bibliography permits ready reference to specific books and articles, historic personalities, and diplomatic events. Together with the archival information, the bibliography will suggest areas for further research or reassessment.

There are five volumes in the series. Besides Great Britain, they cover France, Germany, Italy, and International Organizations. Each has its own distinctive features, for of course the archival holdings and the research based on these holdings vary considerably. They are, however, meant to be complementary. They focus on materials relevant to different subject areas, and, within the limits set by the history of international relations, avoid needless duplication. They are organized along similar lines, and researchers who need to consult several volumes should have no trouble.

Each volume is edited by an authority in the field. Each reflects experience gained on the spot in archives and libraries as well as knowledge shared by colleagues, archivists, and librarians. The volumes therefore are as current and reliable as possible.

The editors hope that these handbooks will prove to be valuable companions to all who are interested in international affairs and diplomacy.

Christoph M. Kimmich
Series Editor

CONTENTS

PREFACE

"I have not read all these books myself, but I have read more of them than it would be good for any one to read again", was how John Maynard Keynes prefaced a bibliography in 1921. Such sentiment is certainly dear to the heart of any bibliographer. However, there are others. It is equally pertinent, for example, that any bibliography is obsolete the moment compilation ends. But that is not a definition of despair. For the function of bibliography, among many others, is to act as an occasional sieve. The outdated, the irrelevant and the slipshod are discarded, hopefully without too many errors of judgement. Likewise it must also be acknowledged that the problem of selection ultimately is personal. It is one individual's attempt to take stock, assess the best, indicate the gaps, and point to the road ahead.

The process of gathering information, selecting and annotating was an individual one. Consequently, my few acknowledgements are deeply intended. Over a period of many months, Kathie Hill typed the manuscript on a word processor. She carried out this exacting task with enormous skill, patience and even good humour. In the latter stages, she was joined by Clara Stewart, who applied her expertise at a crucial time. Together they saw the manuscript through to completion. I am very grateful and indebted to them. Stella Gora and Margaret Byrne of Erindale College Library never baulked at my massive requests for inter-library loans. Wolfgang Arnold very kindly gave of his time to proof-read some of the foreign language titles. As always, Joyce deserves more thanks than I can possibly offer in print.

Erindale College   Sidney Aster
University of Toronto
December 1983

I. INTRODUCTION

Nothing succeeds like failure as far as the historian of international history is concerned. And nowhere is this more applicable than in the case of British foreign policy from 1918 to 1945. At the end of the second world war, Britain did of course emerge as a member of a victorious coalition of major powers. But to prescient observers, few as they were, Britain's former great power status and prestige were in question, and her resources seriously depleted. The dynamics of decline and failure, therefore, form the themes of British foreign policy in the first half of the twentieth century.

This experience has proved naturally to be a windfall for the historian. Rarely can a similar span of about twenty-five years have been subjected to such scalpel-like dissection by both the scholarly and popular historian, not to speak of the media itself. And the corpse continues to invite further attention and examination.

While the mystery remains why this should be so, given the obsession with failure, there are other possible explanations. One must begin with the fact that the archival documentation for the period is massive, to say the least. In May 1967 the Labour government of Harold Wilson reduced the rule of secrecy governing British state records from fifty to thirty years. Two years later, he announced that the records for the second world war, occupying nearly seven miles of shelving, would be released as a whole in 1972. In a very short time, therefore, the available material surpassed the ability of any one historian to examine in an entire working lifetime. In other words, there is adequate documentation and research topics for generations of historians to come.

Another possible suggestion is that the period under consideration contains questions about the conduct of foreign policy which might never be conclusively answered. For example, were there alternative and viable policies which British diplomats, politicians and the military could have pursued? A final suggestion, closely related, is largely

historiographical. The first commentators on the inter-war
period set up an inviting target. British foreign policy
makers, pursuing a policy of appeasement, were passionately
condemned as "guilty men." The attempt to undo that verdict
subsequently became the raison d'être of virtually every
historian entering the Public Record Office in London. The
effort to set the record straight, therefore, and with the
evidence available to reopen the trial, emerged as the
obsession of historians from the early 1960s to the early
1980s. The net result of about twenty years of historical
investigation, if generalisation is possible, has been
fragmentation rather than synthesis, analysis without
perspective, comment instead of value judgement.

The process of returning to the archives for intensive
investigation has had certain beneficial effects. The mono-
dimensional view of diplomatic history as a recital of
correspondence between the Foreign Office and embassies abroad
has mercifully been abandoned. Instead, investigation has
focused on vital, but previously neglected areas. For example,
publicity, propaganda and the media are proving of increasing
interest. Wartime intelligence, particularly relating to Ultra
matters, has found abundant investigators. Despite clever
conclusions based on insufficient evidence, inter-war
intelligence matters will always be problematic until the
relevant material is released, if ever. The military and strategic dimension, and its close relationship to diplomatic dis-
cussions, has drawn numerous students. Diplomacy during the
second world war is only beginning to attract attention. There
may of course prove to be very little to revise in this area.
Finally, there has been no scarcity of contributors to the
continuing debate about appeasement. The discussion has now
widened to include the research methodology of the social
sciences in an attempt to produce a model oriented approach to
the problem. Other investigators insist on the necessity of
relating domestic political, cultural, financial and social
considerations to foreign policy. Still others search for the
roots of appeasement in a "tradition of appeasement" in British
foreign policy. While the area of debate and research has no
doubt widened, the great breakthrough, let alone the final
word, remains as elusive as ever. Perhaps it is about time to
return to the "guilty men" thesis.

For the historian looking to the future, the requirement
must surely be synthesis. No doubt studies of particular
events and issues will continue. But the preliminary research,
combined with the available documents, has adequately prepared
the ground for a new generation of synthetical works. Possible

areas include a thorough history of Britain's relation with the
League of Nations, a study of economic foreign policy, a
comprehensive analysis of public opinion, and a history of the
Foreign Office (a task which the present writer is now engaged
upon). Bilateral or area studies still show gaps, particularly
with regard to Eastern Europe, Scandinavia and South America as
a whole, or Portugal, Spain, Czechoslovakia, Greece and South
Africa to name but a few. The 1920s remain largely
unexplored. While it lacks the perverse glamour of the 1930s,
the post-Versailles decade has yet to find its historian. Last
but not least, it is indicative that there exists no
satisfactory history of British foreign policy from 1918 to
1945.

Such are the considerations that have moulded the shape of
this bibliography. Its objective, among many others, is to
point the way towards greater synthesis in future research.
Following an account of the development of the Foreign Office,
chapter three has been designed to present, as clearly as
possible, the major British resources for research in libraries
and archives. Chapter four begins with a breakdown of the
rich, existing reference guides and bibliographies. One
section in this chapter, a rather long one, is intended to
emphasise the extensive range of British memoirs and
biographies. The following section specifically highlights
various dimensions of foreign policy, bilateral and area
studies, and the appeasement debate. The concluding section
takes a chronological approach to the entire period, indicating
research accomplished and specific aspects yet to be explored.

In the final analysis, the burden of bibliography is about
selection. The materials considered in this volume are merely
a sampling from a vast field. But those choices have been
deliberately fashioned by several general guidelines. Emphasis
has been placed on monographs and articles produced with the
benefit of documents released under the thirty year rule of
secrecy. As a result, work produced prior to the 1960s is
generally under-represented. Secondly, it has not been
considered feasible or desirable to divorce entirely foreign
from imperial policy. The inter-action of both areas of
concern was a pressing problem at the time. While not
emphasised as strongly as foreign policy, therefore, imperial
questions form part of the bibliography. For the same reason,
military, economic foreign policy, foreign service, propaganda
and media, intelligence, and League of Nations aspects are also
included. Thirdly, annotations have been designed to provide
information of value to the researcher. They indicate sources

used, contents, where this is unclear, and sometimes other
works of a closely related nature. Judgemental comments have
largely been omitted, despite the obvious temptation, on the
assumption that one historian's dross is another's gold.
Lastly, the emphasis throughout has been on British and British
related research. That in itself is more than enough for the
lifetime, or interest, of any one historian.

II. THE FOREIGN OFFICE AND FOREIGN POLICY

A. History and Background

The Foreign Office, as so many other British departments
of state, enjoyed no orderly line of historical development. [1]
Until 1640 the fiction was maintained that foreign policy,
like religion, marriage and the succession in the previous
century - "matters of state" as Elizabeth I's lord keeper
described them - was a subject suitable for treatment only by
the crown alone. The office of secretary of state for Foreign
Affairs dates only from 1782, as does the formation of a
separate department for the subject. The term "Foreign
Office" does not occur before 1807. It was not until 1868
that the Foreign Office building in Downing Street, still
occupied to this day, was opened. An amalgamated Foreign
Office and foreign service at long last became a reality in
1943. In many ways, the Foreign Office and foreign policy
have been a prisoner of this evolution, a combination of
"organic development and conscious planning." [2]

Although foreign policy had traditionally been regarded
as a matter of royal prerogative, advice on the subject,
particularly from the Privy Council, was not viewed as below
the dignity of the crown. As early as 1253, during the reign
of Henry III, there is evidence of a secretary to the crown.
The expansion of royal business, occasioned in no small part
by the reformation, led to the appointment of two secretaries
between 1539 and 1540. A hundred years later, a division of
foreign business was arranged. The "King's Principal Secretary" had his work divided with one other colleague. A rough
line appears to have been drawn across the map of Europe,
separating a more protestant north from a largely catholic
south. Generally, by the eighteenth century the senior secretary presided over the southern department, that is France,
Spain, Italy, Portugal and Turkey. The other concerned himself with the northern department which covered the rest of
Europe. This dual secretariat, a very flexible operation,
worked efficiently, though hardly as a system. Foreign
affairs was limited in terms of geography and capable of being
handled by one or two individuals, while the sovereign, as
previously, was still powerful enough to impart overall
coherence and unified direction.

Implementation, as distinct from formulation, of foreign
policy required a diplomatic service. A memorable comment,
from an otherwise unmemorable diplomat, defined for posterity
the role of the early ambassador. Sir Henry Wooton, ambassador of James I, once wrote in a hotel visiting book while on
his way to Vienna, "an Ambassador is an honest man sent to lie
abroad for the good of his country." That flippant observa-
tion, when reported to James I, led to the dismissal of
Wooton. Nonetheless, it effectively epitomised the status and
function of the earliest diplomats. "They lied, they spied,
they stole", Sir Harold Nicolson aptly noted. [3]

Membership of this early diplomatic coterie, for it was
not yet a service, was very much a family affair. There was
no system of training, selection or promotion. Crown patronage usually guaranteed appointment to a foreign post, and
politics led to a recall. Ambassadors were without
privileges, except the sometimes useful one of immunity from
arrest for excessive debt abroad. They tended to be
professional meddlers in the internal affairs of their host
state, dispensing bribery, planning internal opposition, and
ferreting out what little intelligence was available. Staff
at the British embassy, a privately rented home with the royal
coat of arms hanging over the door, was recruited by the
ambassador himself, dispensing largesse to relatives or
cronies. This imprint of a family embassy was to survive with
little change until the first world war.

Crown prerogative, rudimentary organisation and an aristocratic diplomatic class served the purposes of state until
the late eighteenth century. Then, on 29 March 1782, Charles
James Fox sent a circular to British diplomats abroad. It
informed them that George III had appointed him as "One of His
Majesty's Principal Secretaries of State" entrusted "with the
sole Direction of the Department for Foreign Affairs". The
exact functions of the new department were thus described
three years later:

> The business of the Secretary of State's Office for the
> Foreign Department, consists in conducting the correspon-
> dence with all Foreign Courts, negotiating with the
> Ambassadors or Ministers of all the Foreign Courts in
> Europe, as well as of the United States of America, and
> receiving and making representations and applications to
> and from the same, and in corresponding with other prin-
> cipal Departments of the State thereupon. [4]

Few subsequent definitions have so succinctly summarised the
nature of the work entrusted to the newly created Foreign
Office.

FOREIGN OFFICE AND FOREIGN POLICY

Throughout the course of the nineteenth century the
Foreign Office expanded structurally, yet at the same time
successfully resisted external pressure to change. The number
of despatches received and sent, for example, swelled from
6,193 in 1821 to 101,515 in 1900. In the course of the
century, too, the number and size of the "political" departments tended to increase. By 1899 there was a Western, Far
Eastern, American and Eastern department handling respective
geographic areas. Yet the staff responsible for this work
hardly expanded, numbering forty-three in 1858 compared to
forty-one in 1902-1903.[5] One possible explanation was sounded
in a typically Victorian note of self-deprecation by a Foreign
Office official who observed: "The immense number of
despatches which come from agents to Foreign Courts are piled
up in large presses, but no note of them is taken, nor is
there even an index to them; so that, if anything is wanted,
the whole year's accumulation must be rummaged over before it
can be found...."[6]

The autonomy of the nineteenth century Foreign Office,
zealously guarded by a whole series of influential foreign
secretaries, did not go unchallenged. In the 1850s the entire
civil service came under the scrutiny of the Treasury.
Recruitment and organisation were the focus of attention,
emphasis being placed on the need for competitive entrance
examinations and for a distinction between intellectual and
mechanical functions for officials. During the next forty
years the Foreign Office successfully fought the Treasury,
maintaining that the nature of its work, largely confidential,
and the necessity for absolute integrity among its officials
obviated large scale reforms. The maximum concession allowed
by the Foreign Office was the introduction by 1871 of a system
of limited competitive examination. For the most part, however, the nineteenth century Foreign Office remained a "family
system". The need for nomination continued to ensure that
candidates came from families known to the foreign secretary,
usually from the aristocratic and gentry ranks. And all
candidates were still required to have a guaranteed personal
income of £400 a year for the initial two years of service.

While the Foreign Office resisted the demands of its
critics, the diplomatic service did in fact respond to the
mid-Victorian trend towards professionalism in the civil
service.[7] Senior diplomatic appointments were gradually
removed from the realm of political patronage. The amateur
was replaced by the career diplomat, with a salary, allowances, rank, promotion and from 1883 a competitive entrance
examination. The £400 a year income qualification remained.
The Ridley Commission on the Civil Service, which sat between
1886 and 1890, recommended the amalgamation of the Foreign
Office with the diplomatic service, and the removal of the

7

income qualification. Both suggestions met with complete dis-
approval. Nonetheless, temporary exchanges between the two,
permitted from the early 1860s, resulted in some movement at
the lower levels. By 1914 such changeovers were beginning to
appear at the higher ranks. In most ways, however, the
Foreign Office and the diplomatic service retained the imprint
of the family system. Both were socially exclusive, drawn
from the titled and the political elite, and with the per-
sisting aura of patronage. John Bright's view in 1858 that
foreign affairs was "a gigantic system of outdoor relief for
the aristocracy of Great Britain" still rang true.

By the turn of the twentieth century, the Foreign Office
was more prepared to admit that its critics might be talking
sense. In quick succession a series of reforms were phased in
between 1900 and 1907. The so-called mechanical functions,
which included clerical work, cyphering and decyphering,
registering correspondence and filing, were handed over to
junior clerks. Senior clerks began the practice of writing
minutes for the consideration of the foreign secretary, a task
which has proved to be the contemporary historian's great
delight. Boards of selection were introduced to assist the
foreign secretary on individual nominations. The diplomatic
service was left relatively untouched by these reforms.

On the eve of the first world war, therefore, the Foreign
Office was opening its corridors to the winds of change. The
cobwebs and dust of the Victorian regime may have been
partially shaken off. But it was indeed a minimum
concession. For it was still an imperfect machine on the
verge of an era where Britain's competitive advantage was no
longer automatic.

B. Inter-War, 1919-1939

"In war ... diplomacy is the handmaid of the necessities
of the War Office and the Admiralty," Sir Edward Grey noted in
his memoirs. Another foreign secretary, Anthony Eden, echoed
this view, writing that "In War ... diplomacy is strategy's
twin."[8] Such a loss of influence by the Foreign Office was to
some extent inevitable in wartime. It was worsened by a
streamlined war cabinet, a prime minister, David Lloyd George,
with independent views on foreign policy, and a private
secretariat which had his ear. This decline was one from
which the Foreign Office was never to recover.

The pre-war momentum for continued structural reforms had
been side-tracked, as so much else in British life, by the
outbreak of the war. By 1918 the pressure returned, more in
the form of a public crusade than an in-house quarrel. A
vociferous, if not entirely accurate, case was made that the

8

"old diplomacy" had contributed to the outbreak of war. It
was alleged that secret negotiations monopolised by an
irresponsible elite should be replaced in a post-war world by
"open diplomacy," with "open covenants, openly arrived at."
Part of this "open diplomacy," it was argued, should be a
foreign policy structure which was more responsive to
parliamentary control and more representative of all sections
of British society.

The 1919-1920 reforms of the Foreign Office were only in
part a response to the public mood. In essence, they implemented some of the recommendations of the Macdonnell Commission on the Civil Service which had reported in December
1914. The Foreign Office and the diplomatic service were
amalgamated into a single "foreign service." A promotions
committee was established to advise the foreign secretary.
The private means qualification was abolished and new recruits
were to be placed on a joint seniority list.

It was grandly proclaimed at the time that these reforms
were an admission that "Diplomacy, once a question between
Court and Court, had now become a question between People and
People".⁹ In practice, the reforms were not quite so sharp a
break with the past. Recruitment still tended to come from
the aristocracy. Interchangeability encouraged some transfer,
at the lower level, between Foreign Office desk jobs and
foreign posts. But senior Foreign Office positions were still
zealously coveted, and supply and demand worked to disastrous
effect. While there were perhaps three senior Foreign Office
jobs, at least forty to fifty ambassadors and ministers could
easily qualify. The impediments to democratisation still
remained. In the Foreign Office, at least, there was no
lasting impression made of any difference between the "old"
and the "new" diplomacy.

Far more serious were the problems which the 1919-1920
reforms failed to resolve. It is surprising, but not un-
typical, that for a nation of shopkeepers economic foreign
policy had suffered from inadequate attention and a divided
command structure. Prior to the first world war commercial
affairs obeyed different masters in London. There existed a
commercial department of the Board of Trade, a separate commercial department of the Foreign Office since 1872, commercial attachés abroad appointed in the 1880s, separate trade
commissioners for the dominions overseas, and from 1917 a
Department of Overseas Trade. Instead of a massive rationali-
sation, a new commercial diplomatic service was established in
1920, under the joint control of the Foreign Office and the
Board of Trade. In a period when the economic and financial
dimensions of diplomacy were to become as important a battle-

field as foreign policy, the Foreign Office was left without
its own commercial service.

The problem of British consuls overseas, it could hardly
be termed a service, was also not resolved. In the early
nineteenth century, it had been intended to convert this
hotchpotch of semi-public officials into salaried civil
servants, paid by parliamentary vote. None of these intentions were realised by the turn of the twentieth century.
Consuls remained a mixture of independent individuals, without
systematic recruitment, with inadequate prospects or rewards,
and socially ostracised by their diplomatic colleagues.
Periodic suggestions for amalgamation were always rejected.
At the end of 1936, the three consular branches, the General,
Levant and Far Eastern, were finally integrated with the
Foreign Office and diplomatic service, at least as far as new
entrants were concerned. Complete integration lay in the not
too distant future.

Propaganda, publicity and news information was the last
difficulty swept under the carpet in 1919-1920. The pre-war
Foreign Office cultivated very little press contact, with the
exception of employees of The Times. Under the impact of the
war, however, the British proved resilient and even innova-
tive, building up sophisticated propaganda and information
services. The entire structure, in which Britain had a commanding lead, was unfortunately dismantled after 1918.
Temporary wartime departments and ministries, such as for
political intelligence and information, were wound up. They
were regarded as a regrettable and temporary expedient. The
sole survivor was the news department. It was reconstituted,
severely restricted in scope, and delegated to maintain peacetime contacts with the press. The prevailing attitude, which
so handicapped British foreign policy in the inter-war years,
was that publicity and propaganda were "diplomatically
dangerous and anyhow quite unworthy of Great Britain".[10]

The consequences of this limited reorganisation became
increasingly apparent as the influence of the Foreign Office
continued to decline from 1919 to 1939. With regard to structure and organisation, personnel remained fairly static.
After the recruitment explosion of the war, the number of
civil servants in the foreign service in 1938 stood at 902, a
very small increase over the 1920 figure of 885. Yet the
sheer physical demands sharply increased. The number of
despatches handled by the Foreign Office, for example in 1926,
had been 145,169. In 1938 the comparable figure was
223,879.[11] The political departments tried to accommodate
this increased pressure of work. Between 1920 and 1939 these
comprised the following: American and African (from 1930
American); Far Eastern; Eastern; Central; Western (from 1922

League of Nations and Western); Northern; Egyptian (formed in 1924); and Southern (formed in 1933). It is little wonder that in 1939 the permanent under-secretary of state for Foreign Affairs complained in his diary, "Life is hell."[12]

The news department of the Foreign Office continued to struggle for recognition in its own little backwater. Only in the mid-1930s, with the establishment of the British Council, the appointment of a chief press liaison officer at No. 10, and increased funding, did the "projection of Britain" finally begin to recover some ground. Even then the suspicion remained that somehow publicity, not to speak of propaganda, was incompatible with appeasement.

Economic foreign policy fared little better in the 1919-1939 period. Throughout that time the Foreign Office and the Treasury were at loggerheads. One aspect of the difficulty concerned the degree of control, if not outright interference, exercised by the secretary to the Treasury and head of the civil service upon the Foreign Office and foreign policy. The other concerned the question of reparations in the 1920s. The Foreign Office and the Treasury held diametrically opposing views on this most difficult aspect of foreign economic policy. The former argued the case for linking reparations and disarmament; the latter contended that reparations and war debts posed the greatest threat to stability and peace. The fact, too, that the Foreign Office had to communicate its policy to the Bank of England via the Treasury led to an almost complete breakdown of co-ordination.

The economic foreign problems of the 1930s changed, but the structural ones persisted. There existed no single department with overall control over the collection, assessment and dissemination of politico-economic intelligence. In December 1930 precisely such a proposal was floated in the Foreign Office. It evoked little reaction. What resulted was neither a compromise nor a concession, but a token gesture. An economic section within the western department was formed. Frank Ashton-Gwatkin, a former consular official, was put in charge of what he later described as "a one-man liaison bureau."[13] In its overall aim of sharpening the appreciation of foreign economic policy, the experiment proved an almost complete failure.

Structural and organisational weaknesses, vital as they were, do not in the final analysis illuminate the course of British foreign policy in the inter-war years. It is highly doubtful whether a fully amalgamated and democratised foreign service, effective news and propaganda organs, a less authoritarian Treasury, and effective politico-economic intelligence would have made any great difference, other than timing, in

the final outcome of the period, that is, a renewal of war
with Germany. Of far greater importance, for example, was the
failure to distinguish between Weimar and Nazi Germany, the
constraints imposed on foreign policy by domestic economic
problems, the stark realities of military weakness peddled by
the chiefs of staff, and profound divisions of opinion within
the Foreign Office itself about policy towards the dictators.
Equally relevant is the lead given by strong prime ministers
and avoided by ineffective foreign secretaries. Of the five
inter-war prime ministers, only David Lloyd George, James
Ramsay MacDonald and Neville Chamberlain held decisive views,
right or wrong, on foreign affairs. Only Sir Austen
Chamberlain, of the eight inter-war foreign secretaries,
served long and effectively enough to return the Foreign
Office temporarily to a position of some influence. These
then are some of the factors one must examine for the continuing eclipse of the Foreign Office and the diplomatic
failures of the inter-war years.

C. The Second World War and the Eden Reforms

The second world war proved to be among the greatest
tests ever faced by the Foreign Office, but it was thoroughly
met. In common with other ministries, there was the
experience of the previous world war to draw upon. In
addition, the foreign secretary was invited to join the war
cabinet, and from December 1940 the Anthony Eden-Winston
Churchill relationship must be taken into account. While not
as special as both later pretended, it guaranteed a pivotal
role for the Foreign Office in wartime diplomatic
negotiations, particularly involving the grand alliance.

What served further to reinvigorate the Foreign Office
was the introduction of the most daring reorganisation of the
foreign services ever attempted. Anthony Eden's Proposals for
the Reform of the Foreign Service, the White Paper (Cmd. 6420)
of January 1943, declared that it was the intention of the
government to create a new service which, by its composition,
recruitment, training and organisation,

> shall be better able not merely to represent the inter-
> ests of the nation as a whole, but also to deal with the
> whole range of international affairs, political, social
> and economic, and so constitute an adequate instrument
> for the maintenance of good relations and mutual under-
> standing between the United Kingdom and other coun-
> tries.[14]

This statement, in essence, acknowledged the failures of
the Foreign Office and overseas services since 1919, if not
earlier. At the heart of the proposals was the recommendation

12

to amalgamate completely the Foreign Office and the diplomatic, commercial and consular services into a new foreign service. Subsidiary proposals included grants and allowances for complete mobility, proper personnel management and control, power to retire, on pension, unsuitable officers before the age of sixty, complete interchangeability, and consideration for the question of recruiting women. The Eden reforms became law through an order-in-council on 20 May 1943.

By the mid-1950s most of these recommendations had been implemented. The ideal of a generalist service, with mobility, interchangeability and open recruitment, was at last realised. But the Foreign and Commonwealth Office, as the Foreign Office was renamed in 1968, continued to invite investigation. The 1964 Plowden report had been followed by the 1969 Duncan report, the 1977 cabinet think tank (Central Policy Review Staff) report, and the resignation of the foreign secretary and his two senior Foreign Office ministers in the wake of the Falkland Islands war of 1982. In that year, too, on the 200th anniversary of its foundation, the Foreign and Commonwealth Office stood accused of acting as a "spokesman in Britain for foreign governments rather than for Britain to foreign governments".[15]

D. APPENDIX

1. The Foreign Office

Secretaries of State for Foreign Affairs

Dec. 1916   Arthur James Balfour, 1st Earl of Balfour
Oct. 1919   1st Earl Curzon, Marquess Curzon of Kedleston
Jan. 1924   James Ramsay MacDonald
Nov. 1924   Sir Austen Chamberlain
June 1929   Arthur Henderson
Aug. 1931   Sir Rufus D. Isaacs, 1st Marquess of Reading
Nov. 1931   Sir John Simon, 1st Viscount Simon
June 1935   Sir Samuel Hoare, 1st Viscount Templewood
Dec. 1935   Anthony Eden, 1st Earl of Avon
Feb. 1938   Sir Charles Lindley Wood, 1st Earl of Halifax
Dec. 1940   Anthony Eden
July 1945   Ernest Bevin

Permanent Under-Secretaries of State

1916-20   1st Baron Hardinge of Penshurst
1920-25   Sir Eyre Crowe
1925-28   Sir William G. Tyrrell, 1st Baron Tyrrell
1928-30   Sir Ronald C. Lindsay
1930-38   Sir Robert Vansittart, Baron Vansittart
1938-46   Sir Alexander G.M. Cadogan

2. The Diplomatic Service

Ambassadors, Ministers, etc. to Select Powers

Argentina
Sir R.T. Tower, 1910-19
Sir J.W.R. Macleay, 1919-22,
 1930-33
Sir B.F. Alston, 1923-25
Sir M.A. Robertson, 1925-30
Sir H.G. Chilton, 1933-35
Sir N.M. Henderson, 1935-37
Sir E. Ovey, 1937-42
Sir D.V. Kelly, 1942-46

Austria
Sir F.O. Lindley, 1919-20
A. Akers-Douglas, 2nd
 Viscount Chilston, 1921-27
Sir E.C.E. Phipps, 1928-33
Sir W.H.M. Selby, 1933-37
Sir C.M. Palairet, 1937-38

Belgium
Sir F.H. Villiers, 1911-20
Sir G.D. Grahame, 1920-28
3rd Earl Granville, 1928-33
Sir G.R. Clerk, 1933-34
Sir E. Ovey, 1934-37
Sir R.H. Clive, 1937-39
Sir L. Oliphant, 1939-40,
 1941-44
A.F. Aveling, 1940-41
Sir H.M. Knatchbull-
 Hugessen, 1944-47

Brazil
Sir A.R. Peel, 1915-19
Sir R.S. Paget, 1919-20
Sir J.A.C. Tilley, 1921-25
Sir B.F. Alston, 1925-29
Sir W. Seeds, 1930-35
Sir H. Gurney, 1935-39
Sir G.G. Knox, 1939-41
Sir N.H.H. Charles, 1941-44
Sir D.St.C. Gainer, 1944-47

Bulgaria
Sir H.G. Dering, 1919-20
Sir A.R. Peel, 1920-21
Sir W.A.F. Erskine, 1921-27

Bulgaria, contd.
Sir R.A.C. Sperling, 1928-29
Sir S.P. Waterlow, 1929-33
Sir C.H. Bentinck, 1934-36
Sir M.D. Peterson, 1936-38
Sir G.W. Rendel, 1938-41
Sir W.E. Houstoun-Boswall,
 1944-46

Chile
Sir F.W. Stronge, 1913-19
Sir J.C.T. Vaughan, 1919-22
Sir A.C. Grant-Duff, 1923-24
Sir T.B. Hohler, 1924-27
Sir A.J.K. Clark Kerr, 1st
 Baron Inverchapel, 1928-30
Sir H.G. Chilton, 1930-33
Sir R.C. Michell, 1933-37
Sir C.H. Bentinck, 1937-40
Sir C.W. Orde, 1940-45

China
Sir J.N. Jordan, 1906-20
Sir B.F. Alston, 1920-22
Sir J.W.R. Macleay, 1922-26
Sir M.W. Lampson, 1st Baron
 Killearn, 1926-33
Sir A.G.M. Cadogan, 1933-36
Sir H.M. Knatchbull-Hugessen,
 1936-38
Sir A.J.K. Clark Kerr, 1st
 Baron Inverchapel, 1938-42
Sir H.J. Seymour, 1942-46

Czechoslovakia
Sir G.R. Clerk, 1919-26
Sir J.W.R. Macleay, 1927-29
Sir J. Addison, 1930-36
Sir C.H. Bentinck, 1936-37
Sir B.C. Newton, 1937-39
Sir R.H. Bruce Lockhart,
 1940-41
Sir F.K. Roberts, 1941
Sir P.B.B. Nichols, 1942-47

14

Denmark
Sir R.S. Paget, 1916-18
Sir C.M. Marling, 1919-21
3rd Earl Granville, 1921-26
Sir M. Cheetham, 1926-28
Sir T.B. Hohler, 1928-33
Sir H. Gurney, 1933-35
Sir P.W.M. Ramsay, 1935-39
C.H. Smith, 1939-40
Sir A.W.G. Randall, 1945-52

Egypt
Gen. Sir F.R. Wingate,
  1917-19
Field Marshal 1st Viscount
  Allenby, 1919-25
1st Baron Lloyd, 1925-29
Sir P.L. Loraine, 1929-33
Sir M.W. Lampson, 1st Baron
  Killearn, 1934-46

France
Sir F. Bertie, 1st Viscount
  Bertie of Thame, 1905-18
17th Earl of Derby, 1918-20
1st Baron Hardinge of
  Penshurst, 1920-22
1st Marquess of Crewe,
  1922-28
Sir W.G. Tyrrell, 1928-34
Sir G.R. Clerk, 1934-37
Sir E.C.E. Phipps, 1937-39
Sir R.H. Campbell, 1939-40
A. Duff Cooper, 1st Viscount
  Norwich, 1944-48

Germany
Baron Kilmarnock, 21st Earl
  of Erroll, 1920
1st Viscount D'Abernon,
  1920-26
Sir R.C. Lindsay, 1926-28
Sir H.G.M. Rumbold, 1928-33
Sir E.C.E. Phipps, 1933-37
Sir N.M. Henderson, 1937-39

Greece
3rd Earl Granville, 1917-21
Sir F.O. Lindley, 1922-23
Sir M. Cheetham, 1924-26
Sir P.L. Loraine, 1926-29

Greece, contd.
Sir P.W.M. Ramsay, 1929-33
Sir S.P. Waterlow, 1933-39
Sir C.M. Palairet, 1939-43
Sir R.W.A. Leeper, 1943-46

Hungary
Sir T.B. Hohler, 1920-24
Sir C.A. Barclay, 1924-28
A. Akers-Douglas, 2nd
  Viscount Chilston, 1928-33
Sir P.W.M. Ramsay, 1933-35
Sir G.G. Knox, 1935-39
Sir O.St.C. O'Malley, 1939-41
Sir A.D.F. Gascoigne, 1945-46

Iran (Persia)
Sir P.Z. Cox, 1918-20
H.C. Norman, 1920-21
Sir P.L. Loraine, 1921-26
Sir R.H. Clive, 1926-31
Sir R.H. Hoare, 1931-34
Sir H.M. Knatchbull-Hugessen,
  1934-36
Sir H.J. Seymour, 1936-39
Sir R.W. Bullard, 1939-46

Iraq
Sir H.W. Young, 1932
Sir F.H. Humphrys, 1932-35
Sir A.J.K. Clark Kerr, 1st
  Baron Inverchapel, 1935-38
Sir M.D. Peterson, 1938-39
Sir B.C. Newton, 1939-41
Sir K. Cornwallis, 1941-45

Italy
Sir J. Rennell Rodd, 1st
  Baron Rennell of Rodd,
  1908-19
Sir G.W. Buchanan, 1919-21
Sir R.W. Graham, 1921-33
Sir J.E. Drummond, 16th Earl
  of Perth, 1933-39
Sir P.L. Loraine, 1939-40
Sir N.H.H. Charles, 1944-47

Japan
Sir W. Conyngham Greene,
  1912-19
Sir C.N.E. Eliot, 1920-26

Japan, contd.
Sir J.A.C. Tilley, 1926-31
Sir F.O. Lindley, 1931-34
Sir R.H. Clive, 1934-37
Sir R.L. Craigie, 1937-41

Mexico
H.A.C. Cummins, 1917-24
Sir N. King, 1925
Sir E. Ovey, 1925-29
Sir E.St.J.D.J. Monson, 1929-34
J. Murray, 1935-37
Sir O.St.C. O'Malley, 1937-38
T.I. Rees, 1941
Sir C.H. Bateman, 1941-47

Netherlands
Sir W.B. Townley, 1917-19
Sir R.W. Graham, 1919-21
Sir C.M. Marling, 1921-26
3rd Earl Granville, 1926-28
Sir O.W.T. Russell, 1928-33
Sir C.H. Montgomery, 1933-38
Sir G.N.M. Bland, 1938-48

Norway
Sir M.de C. Findlay, 1911-23
Sir F.O. Lindley, 1923-29
Sir C.J.F.R. Wingfield, 1929-34
Sir C.F.J. Dormer, 1934-40
Sir L. Collier, 1941-50

Poland
Sir H.G.M. Rumbold, 1919-20
Sir W.G. Max-Muller, 1920-28
Sir W.A.F. Erskine, 1928-34
Sir H.W. Kennard, 1935-41
Sir C.F.J. Dormer, 1941-43
Sir O.St.C. O'Malley, 1943-45

Portugal
Sir L.D. Carnegie, 1913-28
Sir C.A. Barclay, 1928-29
Sir F.O. Lindley, 1929-31
Sir C.F.W. Russell, 1931-35
Sir C.J.F.R. Wingfield, 1935-37

Portugal, contd.
Sir W.H.M.Selby, 1937-40
Sir R.H. Campbell, 1940-45

Rumania
Sir G.H. Barclay, 1912-19
Sir A.R. Peel, 1919-20
Sir H.G. Dering, 1920-26
Sir R.H. Greg, 1926-29
Sir C.M. Palairet, 1929-35
Sir R.H. Hoare, 1935-41
Sir J.H. Le Rougetel, 1944-46

Russia, and the Soviet Union
Sir G.W. Buchanan, 1910-18
Sir R.M. Hodgson, 1924-27
Sir E. Ovey, 1929-33
2nd Viscount Chilston, 1933-38
Sir W. Seeds, 1939-40
Sir R. Stafford Cripps, 1940-42
Sir A.J.K. Clark Kerr, 1st Baron Inverchapel, 1942-46

Saudi Arabia
W.L. Bond, 1929-30
Sir A. Ryan, 1930-36
Sir R.W. Bullard, 1936-39
Sir F.H.W. Stonehewer-Bird, 1939-43
S.R. Jordan, 1943-45

Spain
Sir A.H. Hardinge, 1913-19
Sir E.W. Howard, 1st Baron Howard of Penrith, 1919-24
Sir H.G.M. Rumbold, 1924-28
Sir G.D. Grahame, 1928-35
Sir H.G. Chilton, 1935-38
Sir O.St.C. O'Malley, 1938-39
Sir R.M. Hodgson, 1939
Sir M.D. Peterson, 1939-40
Sir S. Hoare, 1st Viscount Templewood, 1940-44

Sweden
Sir E.W. Howard, 1st Baron Howard of Penrith, 1913-19

Sweden, contd.
Sir C.A. Barclay, 1919-24
Sir A.C. Grant-Duff, 1924-27
Sir J.C.T. Vaughan, 1927-29
Sir H.W. Kennard, 1929-31
Sir A.J.K. Clark Kerr, 1st
  Baron Inverchapel, 1931-35
Sir C.M. Palairet, 1935-37
Sir E.St.J.D.J. Monson,
  1938-39
Sir V.A.L. Mallet, 1940-45

Switzerland
Sir H.G.M. Rumbold, 1916-19
Sir O.W.T. Russell, 1919-22
Sir M. Cheetham, 1922-24
Sir R.A.C. Sperling, 1924-27
Sir C.F.W. Russell, 1928-31
Sir H.W. Kennard, 1931-35
Sir G.R. Warner, 1935-39
Sir D.V. Kelly, 1940-42
Sir C.J. Norton, 1942-46

Turkey
Sir H.G.M. Rumbold, 1920-24
Sir R.C. Lindsay, 1924-26
Sir G.R. Clerk, 1926-33
Sir P.L. Loraine, 1933-39
Sir H.M. Knatchbull-Hugessen,
  1939-44
Sir M.D. Peterson, 1944-46

United States of America
Sir C.A. Spring-Rice, 1913-18
Sir R.D. Isaacs, 1st Marquess
  of Reading, 1918
Sir E. Grey, 1st Viscount
  Grey of Falloden, 1919
Sir A.C. Geddes, 1st Baron
  Geddes, 1920-24
Sir E.W. Howard, 1st Baron
  Howard of Penrith, 1924-30
Sir R.C. Lindsay, 1930-39
11th Marquess of Lothian,
  1939-40
1st Earl of Halifax, 1941-46

Yugoslavia
Sir C.A. Young, 1919-25
Sir H.W. Kennard, 1925-29

Yugoslavia, contd.
Sir N.M. Henderson, 1929-35
Sir R.H. Campbell, 1935-39
Sir R.I. Campbell, 1939-41
Sir G.W. Rendel, 1941-43
Sir R.C.S. Stevenson, 1943-46

3. The Foreign Office circa 1930

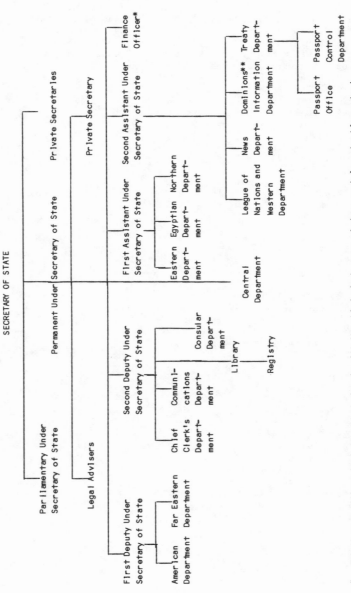

*   The finance officer in fact worked closely with the chief clerk, some of whose work is under his control.
** In 1933 the dominions information department reverted to its original status as a part of the treaty department, and a new southern department was formed.

18

FOREIGN OFFICE AND FOREIGN POLICY

END NOTES

1.   This analysis of the Foreign Office and foreign policy is
based on the sources indicated in the section below entitled
"The Foreign Office"; additional material on the pre-1919
period has been gathered from D.B. Horn, The British Diplomatic Service, 1689-1789 (London, 1961); Charles Ronald
Middleton, The Administration of British Foreign Policy, 1782-
1846 (Durham, NC, 1977); Raymond A. Jones, The Nineteenth
Century Foreign Office: An Administrative History (London,
1971); his The British Diplomatic Service, 1815-1914
(Waterloo, Ontario, 1983); and Zara Steiner, The Foreign
Office and Foreign Policy, 1898-1914 (London, 1969).

2.   Lord Plowden, Report of the Committee on Representational
Services Overseas, Cmd. 2276 (London, 1964), 1.

3.   Sir Harold Nicolson, Diplomacy (London, 1963), 20-21.

4.   Quoted in The Records of the Foreign Office, 1782-1939,
Public Record Office Handbooks, no. 13 (London, 1969), 2-3.

5.   Frank T.A. Ashton-Gwatkin, The British Foreign Service
(Syracuse, NY, 1950), 11-12; Sir John A.C. Tilley and Stephen
Gaselee, The Foreign Office (London, 1933), 48-49; Valerie
Cromwell, "The Foreign and Commonwealth Office", in 'The
Times' Survey of Foreign Ministries of the World, edited by
Zara Steiner (London, 1982), 546.

6.   Quoted in Tilley and Gaselee, 34-35.

7.   Cf. Horn, 13; and Jones, British Diplomatic Service, 215.

8.   Viscount Grey, Twenty-Five Years, 1892-1916, vol. 2
(London, 1925), 166; Earl of Avon, The Eden Memoirs, vol. 3,
The Reckoning, 183.

9.   Algernon Cecil, "The Foreign office", in The Cambridge
History of British Foreign Policy, 1783-1919, vol. 3, edited
by Sir Adolphus Ward and G.P. Gooch (London, 1923), 619.

10. Ashton-Gwatkin, British Foreign Service, 20.

11. David Butler and Jennie Freeman, British Political Facts,
1900-1967 (London, 1968), 174; Documents on British Foreign
Policy, 1919-1939, 1st Series, vol. 1, edited by Sir Llewellyn
Woodward, et al., iii.

12. Sir Alexander Cadogan, The Diaries of Sir Alexander
Cadogan, O.M., 1938-1945, edited by David Dilks (London,
1971), 86.

19

13. Frank Ashton-Gwatkin, "Thoughts on the Foreign Office, 1918-1939", Contemporary Review, 188(1955), 378.

14. Proposals for the Reform of the Foreign Service, Cmd. 6420 (London, 1953), xi.

15. Quoted in "Britain's Foreign Office", The Economist, 27 Nov. 1982, 20.

III.   RESEARCH LIBRARIES AND ARCHIVES

A.   Information and Publications

The material for the study of British foreign policy from
1918 to 1945 is scattered throughout the United Kingdom. There
is hardly a national or local record office and library,
university library, or special archive supported by a privately
endowed society which does not contain some relevant material.
Record Repositories in Great Britain: A Geographical Directory
(7th ed., London, 1982), compiled by the Royal Commission on
Historical Manuscripts, lists no less than 215 repositories
"whose objectives include the systematic collection and
preservation of written records, other than those of its own
administration, and which also makes regular provision for
their public use." A comprehensive list therefore is
impossible. What follows is a selection of libraries, record
offices and archives which are known to contain useful material
for the study of British foreign policy.

1. ABERDEEN UNIVERSITY, Library, Manuscripts and Archives
   Section, King's College, Aberdeen AB9 2UB (M-F 9.15-4.30).
   Founded in 1495, Aberdeen University contains six library
   buildings. The majority of books in the humanities are in
   King's College. The collection numbers about 750,000
   volumes, with 6,000 periodicals.

   Aberdeen University, Library. Guide to Sources of Information: Manuscripts and Archives. Aberdeen, 1979.

2. BANK OF ENGLAND, Historical Research Section, Threadneedle
   Street, London EC2R 8AH (by appointment only). The
   Library is primarily concerned with materials dealing with
   banking and finance. Its holdings include central banking
   reports, trade statistics, economic tracts, acts of
   parliament, etc. The records of the Bank cover the
   principal activities, including advice to governments,
   economic intelligence and relations with financial
   institutions abroad. Consideration is given to specific
   research enquiries, such as access to the Montagu Norman
   diaries. Descriptive lists can be seen of those
   department records transferred to the archive.

3. BIRMINGHAM UNIVERSITY, The Library, Special Collections Department, Main Library, PO Box 363, Birmingham B15 2TT (M-F 9-5). The main library of the University of Birmingham, opened in 1960 and extended in 1971, houses more than one million volumes and 7,700 current periodicals. The political archives are centred around the Chamberlains' papers and those of Anthony Eden.

University of Birmingham, The Library. Guide to the Chamberlain Collection. Compiled by B.S. Benedikz. Birmingham, 1978.

For the papers of Joseph, Austen and Neville Chamberlain and their families.

4. BRITISH BROADCASTING CORPORATION, Written Archives Centre, Caversham Park, Reading RG4 8TZ (M-F, 9.45-5.15). The BBC archives contain material relevant to history, politics, biography and broadcasting. Beside internal BBC documentation, correspondence files, radio and television scripts, and publications form the bulk of the collection. There is additionally an extensive and classified collection of press cuttings relating to broadcasting.

BBC. Written Archives: Reference and Registry Services. Reading, 1980.

5. BRITISH LIBRARY. The British Library was formed in 1973 with the amalgamation of the British Museum Library, the National Central Library, the National Lending Library for Science and Technology, and the British National Bibliography. The British Library, not part of the British Museum, is organised into three main divisions: Reference, Lending and Bibliographical Services. The Reference Division is further organised into departments: Printed Books, Manuscripts, Oriental Manuscripts and Printed Books, and the Science Reference Library. The Newspaper Library is a branch of the Department of Printed Books. The Department of Printed Books, Great Russell Street, London WC1B 3DG (M-F, Sat. 1-5, T,W,Th 9-9), is a vast storehouse of worldwide materials, numbering about ten million volumes. It enjoys the privilege of copyright deposit, that is, a copy of any book, sheet music, map or plan published in the United Kingdom must be deposited with the Library if a written demand is made within twelve months of publication. British and foreign government publications are available in its Official Publications Library (M,F, Sat. 9.30-4.45, T,W,Th 9.30-8.45), with numerous reference books on open access shelves. The Department of Manuscripts (M-Sat. 10-4.45), which requires a special pass, contains over 81,000 volumes of

manuscripts. A persons and places card index is
available. Details of current accessions are published in
the British Library Journal, while earlier accessions are
in the British Museum Quarterly. The Newspaper Library,
Colindale Avenue, London NW9 5HE (M-Sat. 10-5),
established in 1905 as a storage library for post-1800
newspapers, is the principal legal deposit library for
newspapers in the United Kingdom. It contains over half a
million volumes and parcels of British daily and weekly
newspapers and periodicals, as well as a vast collection
of Commonwealth and foreign newspapers. Newspapers
published in Oriental languages are held in the Department
of Oriental Manuscripts and Printed Books, Great Russell
Street, London WC1B 3DG (M-F 10-5, Sat. 10-1).

British Library, Department of Manuscripts. Catalogue of
Additions to the Manuscripts in the British Museum,
1916-1920. London, 1933-.

Supplements for 1921-45, 5 vols. (1950-70); 1946-1950, 3
vols. (1980); 1951-55, 2 vols. (1982).

British Library, Department of Manuscripts. Register of
Microfilms and Other Photocopies in the Department of
Manuscripts. London, 1976.

Published by the List and Index Society for the British
Library; vol. 9 of the "Special Series".

British Library, Department of Printed Books. General
Catalogue of Printed Books: Photolithographic Edition
to 1955. 263 vols. London, 1976.

Basically, the working catalogue of the Reading Room; in
all languages except the Oriental; an indispensable
bibliographic source; mainly an author catalogue; ten-year
supplement, 1956-65, 50 vols. (1968); five-year
supplements, 1966-70, 26 vols. (1971-72); 1971-75, 13
vols. (1978); 1976-82, 50 vols. (1983); subject index
published in five-year cumulations, 1946-60; and 1960-70,
12 vols. (1982).

British Library, Lending Division. BLL Conference Index,
1964-1973. Boston Spa, 1974.

British Library, Lending Division. Current British
Journals. Boston Spa, 1982.

British Library, Lending Division. A Union Catalogue of
United States Studies Periodicals in the United
Kingdom. London, 1982.

British Library, Newspaper Library. Catalogue of the
Newspaper Collections in the British Library. 8 vols.
Compiled by P.E. Allen. London, 1975.

Vols. 1-4 by place of publication; vols. 5-8 for alphabetical listing by titles; see also Microfilms of
Newspapers and Journals for Sale, 1979 (London, 1979).

British Library, Official Publications Library. Checklist of British Official Serial Publications. 12th ed.
London, 1983.

British Library, Reference Division. Catalogue of Books
and Periodicals on Estonia in the British Library
Reference Division. Compiled by Salme Pruuden. London,
1981.

British Library, Reference Division. Catalogue of Printed
Maps, Charts and Plans. 15 vols. London, 1967.

Volume of "Corrections and Additions" (1968); ten-year
supplement, 1965-74 (1978).

British Library, Reference Division. Information Guide:
A Survey of Subject Guides to Sources of Information
Produced by Library and Information Services in the
United Kingdom. Compiled by P.J. Taylor. London, 1978.

British Library, Science Reference Library. Guide to
Government Department, and Other Libraries and
Information Bureaux. Edited by John W. Burchell. 25th
ed. London, 1982.

British Museum. The British Museum: A Guide to its
Public Services. London, 1970.

List and Index Society. 'Rough Register' of Acquisitions
of the Department of Manuscripts, British Museum,
1961-1965. London, 1966.

Vol. 7 of the "Special Series"; supplements, vols. 8, 10
and 15 for acquisitions, 1966-80.

Nickson, M.A.E. The British Library: Guide to the
Catalogues and Indexes of the Department of
Manuscripts. 2nd rev. ed. London, 1982.

For a more detailed survey see T.C. Skeat, The Catalogues
of the Manuscript Collections, rev. ed. (London, 1962).

RESEARCH LIBRARIES AND ARCHIVES

6. BUSINESS ARCHIVES COUNCIL, Library, Denmark House, 15
Tooley Street, London Bridge, London SE1 2QF (M-F 10-4).
The Council, formed in 1934, is concerned with the preservation and location of business records for historical
research. It houses a collection of business histories,
some privately printed, and a register of business
archives. Its annual Business Archives contains articles
in the field, reviews, information about accessions and
bibliographies. The Council publishes as well a quarterly
Newsletter. Similar functions are performed by the
Business Archives Council of Scotland, Glasgow University
Archives, The University, Glasgow G12 8QQ.

British Archives Council. The First Five Hundred: A
Duplicated List of Chronicles and House Histories of
Companies and Organisations in the BAC Library. London,
1959.

British Archives Council. Shipping: A Survey of Historical Records. Edited by Peter Mathias and A.W.H.
Pearsall. London, 1971.

7. CAMBRIDGE UNIVERSITY, University Library, West Road,
Cambridge CB3 9DR (M-F 9-6.45, Sat. 9-12.30). The
University Library serves the needs of the University and
visiting scholars. Since 1709 it has had the privilege of
copyright deposit. It contains nearly 2,750,000
monographs and bound serials, 600,000 maps and over 15,000
volumes of manuscript materials. The Official
Publications Room contains British and Commonwealth
publications, as well as being the depository for United
Nations and other international agency publications.
Unpublished handlists of the papers of the Crewe and
Templewood papers are available in the Department of
Manuscripts.

Munby, A.N.L. Cambridge College Libraries: Aids for
Research Students. Cambridge, 1962.

Peek, H.E., and Hall, C.P. The Archives of the University
of Cambridge. Cambridge, 1962.

University Library. A Catalogue of the German Naval
Archives Microfilmed at the Admiralty, London, for the
University of Cambridge and the University of Michigan.
Directed by F.H. Hinsley and H.M. Ehrmann. London,
1959.

Additional catalogue of selected files (1964).

University Library. Current Serials. 2 vols. London, 1976.

University Library. Handlist of the Hardinge Papers at the University Library Cambridge. Compiled by N.J. Hancock. Cambridge, 1968.

University Library. Handlist of the Political Papers of Stanley Baldwin, First Earl Baldwin of Bewdley. Compiled by A.E.B. Owen. Cambridge, 1973.

University Library. Libraries Directory. Cambridge, 1977.

University Library. Microfilm Series. Cambridge, 1977.

Supplement: Microform Accessions, 1977-79 (1979).

University Library. Summary Guide to Accessions of Western Manuscripts Other than Medieval, since 1867. Compiled by A.E.B. Owen. Cambridge, 1966.

7a. Centre of South Asian Studies, University of Cambridge, Laundress Lane, Cambridge CB2 1SD (M-F 9.30-5.30). The Centre of South Asian Studies, established in 1964, promotes study and research in south Asian subjects, including southeast Asia. The Cambridge South Asian Archive has a large subject-related collection of documentary materials, including private papers, film and tape recordings.

Centre of South Asian Studies. Cambridge South Asian Archive. 3 vols. Edited by Mary Thatcher. Cambridge, 1974-83.

Details of the holdings of the Centre.

Centre of South Asian Studies. Guide to South Asian Material in the Libraries of London, Oxford and Cambridge. Edited by Rajeshwari Datta. Cambridge, 1966.

Centre of South Asian Studies. Principal Collections of Papers in the Cambridge South Asian Archive. Cambridge, 1983.

Centre of South Asian Studies. South Asian Government Bibliographies. Microfiche. Cambridge, 1980.

Centre of South Asian Studies. Records of the British Period in South Asia Relating to India, Pakistan,

Ceylon, Burma, Nepal and Afghanistan Held in the Centre of South Asian Studies, University of Cambridge. Compiled by Mary Thatcher. Microfiche. Cambridge, 1979.

Centre of South Asian Studies. Union Catalogue of the Government of Pakistan Publications Held by Libraries in London, Oxford and Cambridge. Cambridge, 1967.

7b. Churchill College, Archives Centre, Cambridge CB3 ODS (M-F 9-12.30, 1.30-5). The Archives Centre was founded in 1960 as a memorial to Winston Churchill. Its objective is to acquire private papers of individuals associated with, or contemporary to, Churchill. These now number over 170. However, the heart of the collection remains the papers of Churchill himself.

Churchill College, Archives Centre. A Guide to the Holdings of Churchill College Archives Centre. Cambridge, 1980.

Alphabetical listing of holdings with brief annotations.

8. DURHAM UNIVERSITY, University Library, Oriental Section, Elvet Hill, Durham DH1 3TH (M-F 9-5, Sat. 9-12.30). The Oriental Section of the Library houses the Sudan Archive. Established in 1957, the Sudan Archive acquires the papers of former officials, soldiers, missionaries and businessmen who served or lived in the Sudan during the Anglo-Egyptian Condominium period, 1899-1955. Papers relating to Egypt, Arabia, Palestine, Ethiopia, Syria and bordering states are also preserved. The Centre for Middle Eastern and Islamic Studies encourages and co-ordinates activities in this field, including the publication of monographs and bibliographies.

Durham University, Centre for Middle Eastern and Islamic Studies. A Bibliography of Saudi Arabia. Compiled by J.H. Stevens and R. King. Durham, 1973.

See also the same authors' A Bibliography of Oman (Durham, 1973).

Durham University, Centre for Middle Eastern and Islamic Studies. Current British Research in Middle Eastern and Islamic Studies, nos. 1-4. Durham, 1971-83.

9. FOREIGN AND COMMONWEALTH OFFICE LIBRARY. The FCO Library is based on the collections of the former libraries of the Colonial Office and Foreign Office. It is administered by the Library and Records Department, part of a library

system which provides services to the FCO and the ministry
of Defence. The FCO Library is also responsible for
transferring official documents to the Public Record
Office. The main library, Sanctuary Buildings, Great
Smith Street, London, SW1P 3BZ (M-F 9.30-5.30) contains
the primary collection of books and periodicals. A
secondary branch, Cornwall House, Stamford Street, London
SE1 9NS (M-F 9.30-4.45), houses the FCO collection of
reference materials and captured German foreign ministry
and naval documents.

Colonial Office, Library. Catalogue of the Colonial
 Office Library, London. 15 vols. Boston, MA, 1964.

Supplement for 1963-67 (1967); 2nd supplement, 1968-71, 2
vols. (1972); 3rd supplement, 1971-77, 4 vols. (1979).

Foreign Office, The Library. Catalogue of the Printed
 Books in the Library of the Foreign Office. London,
 1926.

Continued in Catalogue of the Foreign Office Library,
1926-1968, 8 vols. (London, 1972); after the merger in
1968 of the Foreign Office and the Commonwealth Office,
accessions to the merged Library from 1969-71 included in
the Second Supplement to the Catalogue of the Colonial
Office Library (London, 1972); and then in Accessions to
the Library, 1971-1977, 4 vols. (Boston, MA, 1979).

Parry, Clive. "The Foreign Office Archives."
 International Relations, 2(1961), 211-19.

9a. India Office Library and Records, Orbit House, 197
 Blackfriars Road, London SE1 8NG (M-F 9.30-6, Sat.
 9.30-1). The basis of the Library is an amalgamation in
 1967 of the India Office Records and the India Office
 Library. The main collection of documents, derived from
 the India Office (1858-1947) and the Burma Office
 (1937-1948), comprises over 170,000 volumes and files.
 Departmental records include the "Political and Secret,
 1778-1950" and the "Private Office, c. 1916-1947". The
 latter contains the private and personal files of the
 secretaries of state for India. The Newspaper Reading
 Room is housed separately in the Centre Block of Bush
 House, Aldwych, London WC2 (T-Th 10-5).

Baxter, Ian A. A Guide to Biographical Sources. London,
 1979.

28

Farrington, A.J. Guide to the Records of the India Office
Military Department. London, 1982.

Griffin, Andrew. A Brief Guide to Sources for the Study
of Burma in the India Office Records. London, 1979.

See also Lesley Hall, A Brief Guide to Sources for the
Study of Afghanistan (London, 1981).

India Office Library. Catalogue of European Printed
Books. 10 vols. Boston, MA, 1964.

India Office Library. Index of Post-1937 European Manuscript Accessions, India Office Library. Boston, MA,
1964.

India Office Records. Accessions of Private Collections,
1937-1977. Compiled by Rosemary Seton. London, 1978.

For manuscripts received before 1937 see C.O. Blagden, et
al., Catalogue of Manuscripts in European Languages, 2
vols. (London, 1916-37).

Lancaster, Joan C. A Guide to the Lists and Catalogues of
the India Office Records. London, 1966.

See also her "The India Office Records", Archives,
9(1970), 130-41; and "The Scope and Uses of the India
Office Library and Records with Particular Reference to
the Period 1600-1947", Asian Affairs, 9(1978), 31-43.

Sutton, S.C. A Guide to the India Office Library. 2nd
ed. London, 1971.

Tuson, Penelope. The Records of the British Residency and
Agencies in the Persian Gulf. London, 1979.

Walker, Dorothy. Catalogue of the Newspaper Collection in
the India Office Library. London, 1977.

10. HISTORICAL MANUSCRIPTS COMMISSION: NATIONAL REGISTER OF
ARCHIVES, Quality House, Quality Court, Chancery Lane,
London WC2A 1HP (M-F 9.30-5). The Royal Commission on
Historical Manuscripts, established in 1869, acts as a
central clearing-house for information about the nature
and location of historical manuscripts and papers outside
the public records. Since 1945 the Historical Manuscripts
Commission has also maintained the National Register of
Archives, a vital source of information on public and
private records. Its search room in Chancery Lane
contains over 21,000 reports on collections of papers,

accumulating at the rate of about 1,000 a year, including those of the National Register of Archives (Scotland). All these reports are numbered and catalogued and their contents are gradually indexed. The reports can be searched through various finding aids, including an index of persons and subjects. Copies of the principal lists are distributed to the copyright libraries and the Institute of Historical Research, among other locations. However, the only complete set is maintained in the Search Room. The Bulletin of the National Register of Archives (London, 1948-) provides news about private collections and accessions.

HMSO. Publications of the Royal Commission on Historical Manuscripts: Government Publications Sectional List, no. 17. London, 1983.

Historical Manuscripts Commission. Guide to the Location of Collections Described in the Reports and Calendars Series, 1870-1980. London, 1982.

Vol. 3 of Guides to Sources of British History.

Historical Manuscripts Commission. A Guide to the Reports on Collections of Manuscripts of Private Families, Corporations and Institutions in Great Britain and Ireland Issued by the Royal Commissioners for Historical Manuscripts. 2 parts. London, 1914-73.

Part 1, vol. 2, for index of places, 1911-57; part 2, 3 vols., for reports issued 1911-57, for index of persons.

Historical Manuscripts Commission. Accessions to Repositories and Reports Added to the National Register of Archives, 1972. London, 1973-.

Previously entitled List of Accessions to Repositories; until 1961 published in the Bulletin of the Institute of Historical Research.

Historical Manuscripts Commission: National Register of Archives. Sources of Business History in the National Register of Archives. London, 1964-.

Irregular lists of contents and locations; 1st five-year cumulation (1971).

Ranger, Felicity. "The National Register of Archives, 1945-1969." Journal of the Society of Archivists, 3(1969), 452-62.

The entire issue was devoted to the centenary of the Royal Commission on Historical Manuscripts.

11. HOUSE OF LORDS, RECORD OFFICE, London SW1A 0PW (M-F 9.30-5.30). The records of both houses of parliament are preserved in the Victoria Tower at the palace of Westminster. These records are accessible to the public in the search room of the House of Lords Record Office. Of major interest is the collection of modern political papers acquired in 1975 after the closure of the Beaverbrook Library. Accessions since 1971 are published in the House of Lords Record Office Memoranda.

Bond, Maurice F. Guide to the Records of Parliament. London, 1971.

By a former Clerk of the Records; printed and manuscript sources.

House of Lords, Record Office. A Guide to Historical Collections of the Nineteenth and Twentieth Centuries Preserved in the House of Lords Record Office, Memorandum no. 60. Compiled by H.S. Cobb. London, 1978.

House of Lords, Record Office. A Guide to the Political Papers, 1874-1970, Deposited by the First Beaverbrook Foundation: House of Lords Record Office Memorandum no. 54. Compiled by Katharine V. Wheeler. London, 1975.

12. IMPERIAL WAR MUSEUM, Lambeth Road, London SE1 6HZ (M-F 10-5). The Imperial War Museum, founded in 1917, is concerned with documenting the two world wars and other military operations involving Britain and the Commonwealth since 1914. The Museum's organisation includes the Departments of Printed Books, Documents, Photographs, Film, Sound Records, and Information Retrieval. The Department of Printed Books is a national reference library with a very large collection of books, pamphlets, periodicals and maps. It issues monthly accessions lists by subject and compiles short bibliographies on some 500 aspects of military history. The Department of Documents collects military archives of the twentieth century. It contains some captured German material and a large collection of British private, military and political, papers. Established in 1972, the Department of Sound Records has an extensive oral history programme, about 7,000 hours of material, which includes taped reminiscences of service personnel and broadcast

recordings. Catalogues of oral history recordings are
available from the Museum.

Imperial War Museum. A Catalogue of the Records of the
   Reichsministerium für Rüstung und Kriegsproduktion.
   London, 1969.

Imperial War Museum. List of Current Journals, Corrected
   to August, 1980. London, 1980.

See also Subject Guide to Booklists, Corrected to the End
   of June 1976 (London, 1976).

Imperial War Museum, Foreign Documents Centre.
   Provisional Reports, no. 1-. London, 1966-.

Contents: no. 1 provides information on 13 British
repositories holding unpublished records of former enemy
powers; nos. 2-6 respectively describe various archives in
the German Federal Republic, Italy, the German Democratic
Republic, Austria and Poland.

Imperial War Museum. Handbook. London, 1976.

13. LABOUR PARTY, Archives, 150 Walworth Road, London SE17 1JT
   (M-F 10-5). The Library contains resources covering party
   politics in all fields of home and foreign affairs. The
   archives of the Labour party include press cuttings from
   1918, party and committee documents, such as the minutes
   of the National Executive Committee and the International
   department, and personal and special collections.

   Labour Party. Guide to the Archives. Compiled by Stephen
      Bird. London, 1982.

   Labour Party. Labour Party: A Bibliography. London,
      1967.

14. LEEDS UNIVERSITY, BROTHERTON LIBRARY, Leeds LS2 9JT (M-F
   9-5). The Brotherton Library contains the main collection
   of materials for the study of international history. The
   Library continues to add to its extensive holdings of
   source materials, mainly published documents and extensive
   microfilms from the PRO, but including an expanding
   collection of manuscripts relating to international
   history in the twentieth century.

   Brotherton Library. Some Source Materials in the
      Brotherton Library of Interest to Students of
      International History. Leeds, 1980.

15. LONDON UNIVERSITY, Library, Senate House, Malet Street,
WClE 7HU (M-F 9.30-9, Sat. 9.30-5.30). The main library
serves all the constituent institutions of the University
of London and contains predominantly research
collections. There are over one million monographs and
serials and about 5,500 periodical titles. Holdings of
the Library are incorporated into the London Bibliography
of the Social Sciences (London, 1931-).

Guide to Admission to Libraries in the University of
London. London, 1977.

Percival, Janet, ed. A Guide to Archives and Manuscripts
in the University of London. 2 vols. London, 1983-84.

Vol. 1 covers the six major institutions; vol. 2 will
include material in other colleges and institutions of the
University.

15a. British Library of Political and Economic Science, 10
Portugal Street, London WC2A 2HD (M-F 10-9.20, Sat. 10-5;
July, M-F 10-9.20, Aug., M-F 10-5). Founded in 1896 on
the initiative of Sidney Webb, the British Library of
Political and Economic Science is both the working library
of the London School of Economics and Political Science
and a national collection of research materials. It
encompasses the social sciences in the widest sense and
holds an estimated two and a half million separate items.
The Library is also a depository for United States federal
documents, and materials from the United Nations and the
Organisation of American States. The Manuscript Section
(M-F 10-6.30, Sat. 10-5; Aug. M-F 10-5) is particularly
rich in twentieth century political and economic private
papers. The Library has been the base of the Political
Archives Investigation Committee. In 1980 the British
Oral Archive of Political and Administrative History was
established at the Library. The pilot stage of this
archive resulted in transcript interviews with twenty-nine
individuals.

Allen, C.G. "Manuscript Collections in the British
Library of Political and Economic Science." Journal of
the Society of Archivists, 2(1960), 52-60.

British Library of Political and Economic Science. A
London Bibliography of the Social Sciences. Compiled by
B.M. Headicar and C. Fuller. 4 vols. London, 1931-32.

Based on the holdings of the Library; the largest subject
bibliography of its kind; supplements, in progress,

1st-17th, for publications 1929-82, 36 vols. (London, 1934-83).

British Library of Political and Economic Science. Guide to the Library. 2nd ed. London, 1979.

See also Outline of the Resources of the Library (London, 1976).

Seldon, Anthony. "'Elite' Oral History at the London School of Economics." Oral History Journal, 10(1982), 12-15.

15b. Institute of Commonwealth Studies, 27 Russell Square, London WC1B 5DS (M-W 9.30-7, Th-F 9.30-6). The Institute, established in 1949, promotes the study of Commonwealth history and social sciences. As a research centre of the University of London, it organises seminars, publishes, and contains a major reference library. Relevant documents and manuscripts are also actively acquired. The Library maintains a register of research in British universities on Commonwealth topics and publishes a quarterly Accessions List.

Institute of Commonwealth Studies. Guide to Resources for Commonwealth Studies in London, Oxford and Cambridge, with Bibliographical and other Information. Compiled by Arthur Reginald Hewitt. London, 1957.

15c. Institute of Historical Research, Senate House, London WC1E 7HU (M-F 9-9, Sat. 9-5). The Institute functions as the University's centre for advanced research in history. The Library, arranged as a series of seminar rooms, emphasises the acquisition of primary materials, reference works, bibliographies, guides to archives and manuscripts, etc. A copy of each higher degree thesis in history is received at the Institute. Its publications include a bibliography of historical works issued in the United Kingdom, the Bulletin, and an annual compilation of theses completed and theses in progress.

Institute of Historical Research. A Guide to the Library. London, 1976.

15d. Liddell Hart Centre for Military Archives, King's College, Strand, London WC2R 2LS (M-F 9.30-5.30). Military affairs have been a subject of specialisation at King's College since 1927. Facilities for study have been vastly intensified since 1953. In 1964 the Centre for Military Archives was established at the College to act as a repository for twentieth century

private papers relating to military matters. The Centre
was renamed the Liddell Hart Centre for Military Affairs
after the acquisition of his papers and library in 1973.
It has a large collection of diaries, letters, etc. of
statesmen, service officers, civil servants and others,
all relating to defence policy since 1900 and the two
world wars.

Brooks, Stephen. "Liddell Hart and his Papers", in War
   and Society: A Yearbook of Military History. Vol. 2.
   Edited by Brian Bond and Ian Roy. London, 1977.

Liddell Hart centre for Military Archives. Consolidated
   List of Accessions, 1981. London, 1981.

Liddell Hart Centre for Military Archives. Notes for
   Readers. London, 1979.

Sheppard, Julia. "The Liddell Hart Centre for Military
   Archives at King's College, London." Archives, 13(1978)
   190-95.

15e. School of Oriental and African Studies, Library, Malet
Street, London WC1E 7HP (M-F 9-8.30, vacations, M-F 9-5,
Sat. 9.30-12.30). Founded in 1917, the Library has a
major specialist collection of over 500,000 volumes, and
2,350 manuscripts, including twenty-five major archives,
in 109 languages. Since 1961 it is the national lending
library for Oriental and African Studies. A union
catalogue of Asian publications is maintained by the
Library. The British in India Oral Archive Committee has
deposited a number of tapes and transcripts.

School of Oriental and African Studies. Library
   Catalogue of the School of Oriental and African
   Studies. 28 vols. Boston, MA, 1963.

Supplements published in 1968, 1973, 1979.

School of Oriental and African Studies. Library Guide.
   London, 1980.

A thorough guide, divided by geographic sections, with
bibliographies of relevant reference books.

School of Oriental and African Studies. Papers Relating
   to the Chinese Maritime Customs, 1860-1943 in the
   Library. London, 1973.

School of Oriental and African Studies. Union Catalogue of Asian Publications, 1965- 1970. Edited by David E. Hall. 4 vols. London, 1971.

Supplement (1973); lists Asian publications acquired by sixty-four British libraries since 1964.

Yasumura, Y. List of Japanese Periodicals in the Library of the School of Oriental and African Studies. London, 1974.

15f. School of Slavonic and East European Studies, Library, Senate House, Malet Street, London WC1E 7HU (M-F 10-7). Founded in 1915 as a part of King's College, the School of Slavonic and East European Studies became a university institute in 1932. The Library supports teaching and research into the languages, literature, history and social conditions of the USSR and Eastern Europe. The library collection of over 220,000 monographs and 1200 current periodicals also includes some manuscript materials.

School of Slavonic and East European Studies. A Guide to the Library. London, 1971.

School of Slavonic and East European Studies. Guide to Reference Material in the Library on Finland. Edited by J.E.O. Screen. London, 1977.

16. MANCHESTER UNIVERSITY, John Rylands University Library, Special Collections Division, Deansgate, Manchester M3 3EH (M-F 9.30-5.30, Sat. 9.30-1). The John Rylands University Library was formed in 1972 by merging the John Rylands Library and the Manchester University Library. The immense resources of this merger include over two and a half million volumes, 8,000 current periodicals and 16,000 manuscripts.

John Rylands University Library. Handlist of English Manuscripts ... 1928; and Handlist of Additions ... 1928-1934 Onwards. Manchester, 1928-.

17. MINISTRY OF DEFENCE LIBRARIES. Several libraries now come under the aegis of the ministry of Defence. These include the Air Library, Adastral House, Theobald's Road, London WC1X 8RU (M-F 9-5); the RUSI Building Library, Whitehall, London SW1A 2ET; Whitehall Library, Old War Building, Whitehall, London SW1A 2EU (M-F 9-5.15); and the Naval Historical Library, Empress State Building, Lillie Road, Fulham, London SW6 1TR (M-F 10-5). Limited access, mainly

for reference purposes, is available at the discretion of the librarians.

Ministry of Defence, Naval Library, London. Author and Subject Catalogue of the Naval Library. 5 vols. Boston, MA, 1967.

War Office, Library. Catalogue of the War Office Library. 3 vols. London, 1906-12.

Annual supplements, 1913-40.

18. NATIONAL ARMY MUSEUM, Department of Records, Royal Hospital Road, London SW3 4HT (T-Sat. 10-4.30). The collection includes substantial holdings of books, periodicals and manuscripts on the history of the British army (1550-1914) and the Indian army to 1947. The post 1914 period is covered by the Imperial War Museum.

Chandler, D.G. "The National Army Museum." History Today, 22(1972), 664-68.

19. NATIONAL LIBRARY OF SCOTLAND, Department of Manuscripts, George IV Bridge, Edinburgh EH1 1EW (M-F 9.30-8.30, Sat. 9.30-1). The Library is a national institution for research on all aspects of Scottish history, a copyright deposit library since 1910, and with special responsibility for Scottish bibliography. Its Lending Services are the result of a merger in 1974 between the Scottish Central Library and the National Library. The entire collection numbers over three million books, with additional periodicals and newspapers. There are over 20,000 manuscript collections in the Library, many relevant to the wider context of British history. Accessions are noted in the Annual Report of the National Library of Scotland.

National Library of Scotland. Catalogue of Manuscripts Acquired since 1925. 3 vols. Edinburgh, 1938-68.

National Library of Scotland. A Guide to the Reference Services. Compiled by J.R. Seaton. Edinburgh, 1976.

20. NATIONAL LIBRARY OF WALES, Department of Manuscripts and Records, Aberystwyth, Dyfed SY23 3BU (M,Th,F 9.30-5, T,W 2-8.30, first and third Sat. of month 9.30-5). The National Library of Wales was founded in 1907 by Royal Charter and began operation in 1909. As well as a copyright deposit library, it is a national library specialising in Welsh materials, but with a good

collection of private papers of Welshmen prominent in
British public life.

National Library of Wales. Handlist of Manuscripts in
the National Library of Wales. 3 vols. Aberystwyth,
1943-61.

Supplementary listings in the National Library of Wales
Journal and in the Annual Reports.

21. NATIONAL MARITIME MUSEUM, Manuscripts Section, Romney
Road, Greenwich, London SE10 9NF (M-F 10-5, Sat. 10-1,
2-5). The Museum was established in 1934 for the study
and illustration of British maritime history, art,
literature, science and archaeology. Particular attention
is paid to the areas of the administrative history of the
Royal Navy, strategical and tactical developments, the
economics of transportation and the management of merchant
shipping in peace and war. As a recognised repository for
public documents, the Manuscripts Section holds about
9,000 volumes of Admiralty records and maritime related
private papers.

National Maritime Museum. Catalogue of the Library.
London, 1968-.

In progress; vol. 2 for biography; vol. 5 for naval
history.

National Maritime Museum. Guide to the Manuscripts in
the National Maritime Museum. Edited by R.J.B. Knight.
2 vols. London, 1977-80.

Vol. 1 entitled: The Personal Collections; vol. 2:
Public Records, Business Records and Artificial
Collections.

22. OXFORD UNIVERSITY, Bodleian Library, Department of Western
Manuscripts, Oxford OX1 3BG (M-F 9-10 term, 9-7 vacation,
Sat. 9-1). The Bodleian Library, dating back to the
seventeenth century, is a copyright library, second only
in size to the British Library. The collection numbers
about three and a half million volumes, with particularly
rich manuscript holdings for twentieth century public
figures in the Department of Western Manuscripts.
Manuscript accessions after 1915 are listed in the
Bodleian Quarterly Record (later the Bodleian Library
Record).

Current Foreign and Commonwealth Periodicals in the
Bodleian Library and in other Oxford Libraries.
London, 1953.

Addenda and Corrigenda (1958); two supplements (1956-62);
current material on cards in the Bodleian Library.

Madan, F., et al. Summary Catalogue of Western Manuscripts in the Bodleian Library.... 7 vols. Oxford,
1895-1953, repr. 1980.

Morgan, Paul, comp. Oxford Libraries Outside the
Bodleian. Oxford, 1980.

Listing by college, faculty, departmental and institute
libraries; includes an appendix of manuscript collections.

22a. Nuffield College, The Library, Oxford OX1 1NF (M-F 9.30-1,
2-6, Sat. 9.30-1). Nuffield College, endowed in 1937 by
1st Viscount Nuffield, concentrates on post-graduate
research. The Library actively collects the private
papers of twentieth century figures prominent in British
political, economic and social life. Included are many
collections relevant to the study of foreign policy, such
as the papers of Sir Stafford Cripps and F.A. Lindemann
(1st Viscount Cherwell).

22b. Rhodes House Library, South Parks Road, Oxford OX1 3RG
(M-F 9-7, Sat. 9-1). Opened in 1929, Rhodes House Library
concentrates on the history, politics, economics and
social conditions of the Commonwealth (excluding India),
the United States and sub-Saharan Africa. Relevant
copyright materials are deposited at the Library. It
contains a vast collection of about 500,000 books,
manuscripts, journals, maps and some 5,000 reels of
microfilm. Since the inception of the Oxford Colonial
Records Project in 1963, the amount of manuscript
materials in the Library has dramatically increased. Over
2,500 former colonial administrators have deposited
private papers at Rhodes House Library.

Frewer, Louis B. Rhodes House Library, Oxford. Revised
by F.E. Leese. Oxford, 1976.

Rhodes House Library. Manuscript Collections of Africana
in Rhodes House Library, Oxford. Compiled by Louis B.
Frewer. Oxford, 1971.

Rhodes House Library. Manuscript Collections (Excluding
Africana) in Rhodes House Library, Oxford. Compiled by
Louis B. Frewer. Oxford, 1970.

Supplementary Accessions to the End of 1977 and
Cumulative Index, compiled by Wendy S. Byrne (Oxford,
1978).

Rhodes House Library. Papers of Charles Roden Buxton ...
Rhodes House Library. Oxford, 1973.

22c. St. Antony's College, Library, Middle East Centre, 68
Woodstock Road, Oxford OX2 6HR (M-F 9.30-1, 2-5.15).
Since 1962 the Library has collected the private papers of
individuals who either served in the Middle East or whose
main concern, as bankers, businessmen, etc., was with the
Middle East.

Middle East Centre, St. Antony's College. A Catalogue
of the Private Papers Collection in the Middle East
Centre, St. Antony's College, Oxford. Edited by Diana
Grimwood-Jones. London, 1979.

23. PUBLIC RECORD OFFICE, (i) Chancery Lane, London WC2A 1LR;
(ii) Ruskin Avenue, Kew, Richmond, Surrey TW9 4DU (M-F
9.30-5, closed first two weeks in October). The Public
Record Office in Chancery Lane was established by an act
of parliament in 1838. Prior to that time documents had
been collected by individual government departments, but
storage facilities were poor and limited. In order to
establish some control over these numerous repositories of
public records, the government appointed a royal
commission in 1800. Then, in 1838, the Public Record
Office Act provided for the centralisation of "all rolls
records writs books proceedings decrees bills warrants
accounts papers and documents whatsoever of a public
nature" in one office. A new repository was erected in
1850-53 and records were slowly gathered together, with
terms of preservation and public access gradually defined.

The national archives preserved at the PRO, consisting of
many millions of documents, derive from two main sources.
The first are the nation's judicial and administrative
records: those of Chancery, the Exchequer, the Courts of
Common Law and other courts. The second are those of the
public departments: the State Paper Office, the
Admiralty, the Treasury, the Home, the Colonial, the
Foreign and the War Offices, among many others. The
records now remaining at Chancery Lane comprise all those
described in volume one of the Guide to the Contents of
the Public Record Office (see below), except the Copyright
Office, those of some other departments with quasi-legal
or related functions, the records of the State Paper
Office, the Probate and Census Records and some gifts and
deposits. Most materials relevant to the study of foreign

policy from 1918 to 1945 are stored at Kew. Records are
available for consultation only in the building in which
they are stored. It is also important to remember that
not all official records are in the PRO. The lord
chancellor has designated certain local repositories as
places of deposit. Some government departments, such as
the India Office Library and Records, maintain their own
records. Others not covered by the Public Records Act
include the House of Lords Record Office, the Office of
Population Censuses and Surveys, and the record offices of
Scotland and Northern Ireland. Finally, some collections
remain in private hands, or have been given, sold or lent
to institutions, most notably the British Library.
Departmental records are generally available for public
inspection thirty years after their creation. A list of
documents retained for longer periods is available in the
search rooms.

The records themselves are arranged into major divisions,
called 'groups', which generally correspond to the
administrative department of origin. Groups are
designated by an abbreviation, such as FO for Foreign
Office. Within each record group are 'classes' of
material, such as general correspondence, minutes of
committees, etc., which are designated by a number. Thus
FO371 represents the class of Political Correspondence in
the Foreign Office record group. The next division after
classes is 'pieces', which represent a specific volume,
box, bundle or file. The piece number is usually set off
by an oblique stroke, for example, FO371/23015. Each
record group has a class list, printed, typed or in
manuscript. Some are further provided with indexes or
calendars, which may contain extracts from the documents.

There is in fact no overall general index to the entire
body of the records. However, the researcher is extremely
fortunate in having a multiplicity of extensive finding
aids. The Guide to the Contents of the Public Records in
its printed and new, computer produced, forms is the basic
tool for research about a specific person, subject or
place. The class lists and indexes, both published and
available at the search rooms, are another valuable tool.
These are gradually becoming more widely available through
the arrangements for reprints reached between the PRO and
the Kraus Reprint Organisation. Photographic copies of
many other unpublished lists are issued periodically to
libraries and subscribers by the List and Index Society.
Finally, the PRO itself publishes an ongoing handbook
series. This is an extremely valuable research tool and
every intending researcher should be thoroughly familiar

with the relevant volumes to derive the greatest benefit
from a visit to the PRO.

Galbraith, Vivian Hunter. Introduction to the Use of the
    Public Records. London, 1952.

A practical handbook for the beginner; contains a useful
bibliography.

Public Record Office. The Cabinet Office to 1945.
    Compiled by S.S. Wilson. London, 1975.

PRO handbook, no. 17; an account of the evolution of the
Cabinet Office and an explanation of surviving records in
the various cabinet classes; twelve annexes of related
information.

Public Record Office. Catalogue of Microfilm, 1976.
    London, 1977.

Only records of which the PRO retains master negatives on
microfilm; large collections of Foreign Office and other
PRO documents have been reproduced in microform by such
publishers as Scholarly Resources, Kraus Microform,
Harvester Microform and Garland Publishing.

Public Record Office. Classes of Department Papers for
    1906-1939. London, 1966.

Alphabetical listing of government departments with
classes of departmental records transferred to the PRO
before the middle of 1965; in effect, an addendum to vol.
2 of the Guide to the Contents of the Public Record Office
(London, 1963).

Public Record Office. Guide to the Contents of the
    Public Record Office. 3 vols. London, 1963-68.

Vol. 1 for legal records, etc.; vol. 2 for state papers
and departmental records as of 31 Aug. 1960; vol. 3
describes records transferred up to 31 Dec. 1966, with
corrections and additions to vols. 1-2; descriptions of
classes added from Jan. 1967 are entered in typed
supplements, known as the "Current Guide", in the search
rooms of the PRO; as are amendments to vols. 1-3 of the
Guide to the Contents of the Public Record Office; brief
details of new classes and additions to existing classes
are given in the "Summary of Records Transmitted" as an
appendix to the Annual Report of the Keeper of Public
Records; for materials prior to 1923 see M.S. Giuseppi,

Guide to the Manuscripts Preserved in the Public Record
Office, 2 vols. (London, 1923-24).

Public Record Office. The Records of the Cabinet Office
to 1922. London, 1966.

PRO handbook, no. 11; detailed description of the
organisation of the Cabinet Office from 1916-22 and
contents of 44 classes of records transferred to the PRO.

Public Record Office. The Records of the Colonial and
Dominions Office. Compiled by R.B. Pugh. London,
1964.

PRO handbook, no. 3; section 1 describes the organisation
of the Colonial Office since 1801 and the Dominions
Office since 1925; section 2 analyses the records; section
3 gives an annotated list of record classes by colonies
and subjects.

Public Record Office. The Records of the Foreign Office,
1782-1939. London, 1969.

PRO handbook, no. 13, an indispensable guide to research
in the Foreign Office papers; introduces the researcher to
about 900 classes of papers in the Foreign Office group
and related records; part 1 provides a history of the
administrative machinery of the Foreign Office between
1782 and 1939; part 2 analyses the records developed in
this process; part 3 describes four specimen searches;
part 4 is an annotated list of all the classes making up
the Foreign Office group, including classes created after
1939; appendixes detail signs and codes used in the
Foreign Office registers and indexes, private collections
in the PRO bearing on foreign affairs, and the location of
papers of secretaries of state for Foreign Affairs.

Public Record Office. Records of Interest to Social
Scientists, 1919 to 1939: Introduction. Compiled by
Brenda Swann and Maureen Turnbull. London, 1971.

A useful subject guide to PRO material; includes sections
on 'central direction', finance, foreign affairs, industry
and defence.

Public Record Office. The Second World War: A Guide to
Documents in the Public Record Office. London, 1972.

PRO handbook, no. 15; covers the main military, political
and administrative aspects of the second world war
released to the public in 1972; explains the workings of

government departments and other bodies that produced the records; describes classes, with glossaries of wartime code names, abbreviations and cabinet committees.

Public Record Office, Foreign Office. Foreign Office Confidential Papers Relating to China and her Neighbouring Countries, 1840-1914, with an Additional List, 1915-1937. Compiled by Hui-Min Lo. London, 1970.

See also Carol Reynolds, A Guide to British Foreign Office, Confidential Print: China, 1848-1922 (New York, 1970).

Public Record Office, Foreign Office. Index to Foreign Office Correspondence, 1920-. Nendeln, 1969-.

In progress; complete for 1920-45; 4 vols. per annual index; all papers identified are available at the PRO.

Public Record Office, Lists and Indexes. Alphabetical Guide to War Office and Other Military Records Preserved in the Public Record Office. London, 1931.

Vol. 53 of the PRO Lists and Indexes.

Public Record Office, Supplementary Lists and Indexes. List of Admiralty Records. Vols. 3-9. Millwood, NY, repr. 1975-80.

No. VI in the PRO Supplementary Lists and Indexes; reprinted by agreement between the PRO and the Kraus Reprint Division of Kraus-Thompson Organization Ltd.; other series reprinted from the Supplementary Lists and Indexes include no. VIII, List of War Office Records, 2 vols. (1969-75); no. XIII, List of Foreign Office Records, 23 vols. (1964-75); these include General Correspondence (Political) volumes for 1914-46; and no. XVI, List of Colonial Office Records, 3 vols. (1976-).

23a. List and Index Society, c/o Public Record Office, Chancery Lane, London WC2A 1LR. The Society was formed in 1965 to distribute, to members only, bound copies of unpublished PRO search room lists and indexes, issued by photographic process. The choice of volumes is made by the Council, which attempts to give equitable representation to all periods and interests. The first 202 volumes of PRO class lists and indexes have been published. About fifteen of these volumes deal with the cabinet office and the prime minister's office. The sixteen volumes of the "Special Series" reproduce lists in archives other than the PRO.

List and Index Society. Publications, 1966-1983.
London, 1983.

24. READING UNIVERSITY, The Library, Department of Archives
and Manuscripts, Whiteknights, Reading RG6 2AE (M-F 9-1,
2-5). The Library contains about 550,000 volumes and
5,400 current periodicals, as well as housing the European
Documentation Centre and a fairly extensive collection of
foreign newspapers. The growing collection of manuscript
material is divided into five main groups. The most
relevant are the archive of modern political papers and
the archive of British publishing and printing.

Edwards, J.A. A Brief Guide to Archives and Manuscripts
in the Library, University of Reading. Reading, 1980.

25. ROYAL AIR FORCE MUSEUM. Department of Archives and
Aviation Records, Aerodrome Road, Hendon, London NW9 5LL
(M-F 10-4). Established in 1963, the Royal Air Force
Museum is concerned with aviation, in all its aspects. In
addition to displays, the museum is also a research centre
with a growing collection of books, periodicals,
manuscripts, etc. The Department of Printed Books
contains over 70,000 volumes and subscribes to almost 300
periodicals. The Archives and Aviation Records Department
contains thousands of archival and documentary items,
including log books, private papers of airmen and records
of commercial aviation companies.

Royal Air Force Museum. Periodicals Catalogue. London,
1975.

Royal Air Force Museum. Royal Air Force Museum,
1972-1975. London, 1976.

26. ROYAL COMMONWEALTH SOCIETY, Library, 18 Northumberland
Avenue, London WC2N 5BJ (M-F 10-5.30). The Royal
Commonwealth Society, founded in 1868, has one of the
largest collections of material on the Commonwealth. The
Library, with a bookstock of over 400,000 items, contains
monographs, an extensive collection of periodicals,
official publications, manuscripts, and the collections of
the Royal African Society, the Kipling Society and the
British Association of Malaysia among others.

Reese, Trevor R. The History of the Royal Commonwealth
Society, 1868-1968. London, 1968.

Royal Commonwealth Society, Library. Biography
Catalogue. Compiled by Donald H. Simpson. London,
1961.

Royal Commonwealth Society, Library. The Manuscript
Catalogue of the Library of the Royal Commonwealth
Society. Compiled by Donald H. Simpson. London, 1975.

About 600 entries arranged alphabetically by author within
geographic areas; supplementary lists in the Society's
Library Notes.

Royal Commonwealth Society, Library. Subject Catalogue
of the Royal Commonwealth Society. 7 vols. Boston,
MA, 1971.

Extensive card catalogue arranged by geographical areas,
subdivided by subject; within these headings the order is
chronological; 1st supplement, 2 vols., for additions from
1971-76, published 1977.

27. ROYAL INSTITUTE OF INTERNATIONAL AFFAIRS, Chatham House,
10 St. James's Square, London SW1Y 4LE (M-F 10-6, Th
10-7). The Royal Institute of International Affairs was
established in 1920 to advance the study of international
relations, economics and jurisprudence, and to provide
information on these subjects. The Institute organises
lectures, sponsors research projects, issues various
publications and maintains two libraries. The main
library is a leading specialist collection in the field,
with monographs, pamphlets and official documents. It
also maintains a classified card index to periodicals
since 1950 and issues fortnightly Articles in Periodicals,
as well as a Classified List of Books and Pamphlets Added
to the Library. The Chatham House Press Library,
established in 1924, contains over eight million cuttings
on all aspects of international affairs. Arrangement of
this massive archive is by country and subject, further
subdivided by topic or area. The Press Library is open
only to bona fide researchers at the post-graduate level.
Files for the 1920s and 1930s are microfilmed; those for
the period 1940-1969 are to be transferred to the British
Library, Newspaper Library. In 1976 the Council of the
RIIA agreed that the Institute's archives, subject to
certain exclusions, would be open after thirty years for
study by researchers.

Morgan, Roger. "'To Advance the Sciences of
International Politics...': Chatham House's Early
Research." International Affairs, 55(1979), 140-51.

Royal Institute of International Affairs. Index to
Periodical Articles, 1950-1964, in the Library of the
Royal Institute of International Affairs. 2 vols.
Boston, MA, 1964.

Index to over 30,000 articles taken from the wide range of periodicals received by the Institute; supplements for periodical articles 1965-72 and 1973-78 published in 1973 and 1979 respectively.

28. SCOTTISH RECORD OFFICE, PO Box 36, H.M. General Register House, Edinburgh EH1 3YY (M-F 9-4.45). Primarily a repository for the Public Records of Scotland, the Scottish Record Office also holds the private papers of individuals and organisations with a wider influence on British foreign affairs. The National Register of Archives (Scotland) is maintained at West Register House.

   List of Gifts and Deposits in the Scottish Record Office. 2 vols. Edinburgh, 1971-76.

29. SOCIAL SCIENCE RESEARCH COUNCIL DATA ARCHIVE, University of Essex, Wivenhoe Park, Colchester, Essex CO4 3SQ. The SSRC Data Archive is the largest national repository of machine-readable social science data in Britain. It was set up in 1967 with a brief to collect, preserve and disseminate machine-readable data relating to social and economic affairs from academic, commercial and government sources. Over 2,500 data sets are currently held by the Data Archive. Acquisitions are listed in the triannual Data Archive Bulletin.

   SSHRC Data Archive. Data Catalogue: Guide to the Survey Archive's Social Science Data Holdings and Allied Services. Colchester, n.d.

30. SUSSEX UNIVERSITY, Library, Falmer, Brighton BN1 9QL (M-F 9-5.15). The University of Sussex Library contains over 500,000 volumes and 3,500 current periodicals. It houses the East Africa collection, the European Documentation Centre, and the Tom Harrison Mass-Observation Archive, established in 1974 as a charitable trust. Mass-Observation functioned between 1937 and 1950 as a social survey movement.

   Sussex University, Library, Manuscript Section. List of Papers of Kingsley Martin, 1897-1969. Brighton, 1976.

   Sussex University, Library, Manuscript Section. Vernon Bartlett Papers, 1913-1973. Brighton, 1975.

31. THE TIMES, Archives, PO Box 7, 200 Gray's Inn Road, London WC1X 8EZ (M-F 10-1, 2-5). The collection includes information relating to the history of The Times within the context of British political, social and economic life. The holdings contain private papers, diaries and

correspondence, official and private, of editors and
correspondents.

Phillips, Gordon. "The Archives of 'The Times'."
Business Archives, 41(1976), 20-24.

32. WARWICK UNIVERSITY LIBRARY, Modern Records Centre,
Coventry CV4 7AL (M-Th 9-1, 1.30-5, F 9-1, 1.30-4). The
Modern Records Centre was established within the
University of Warwick Library in 1973. Its object is to
collect and make available for research primary sources
for British political, social and economic history.
Particular attention is paid to labour history and
industrial relations. New accessions are described in the
biannual Information Bulletin (no. 1, 1974-). Check-lists
or catalogues are compiled for each accession, and a set
of these is held in the Centre.

Guide to the Modern Records Centre, University of Warwick
Library. Occasional Publications No. 2. Compiled by
Richard Storey and Janet Druker. Warwick, 1977.

For accessions from 1973 to 1977; supplement, Occasional
Publications No. 9 (1981), includes details of the
predecessor archive of the Confederation of British
Industry.

33. WIENER LIBRARY AND INSTITUTE OF CONTEMPORARY HISTORY, 4
Devonshire Street, London W1N 2BH (M-F 10-5.30). The
Library is a major resource for the study of twentieth
century totalitarianism and antisemitism. It contains
material on Nazism, fascism, Germany since 1914, Middle
East history, particularly Israel, Palestine and Zionism,
and a large Nuremberg Trials collection. The press
cutting archive, organised by subject, holds over one
million items. As of 1980 most of the books have been
transferred to Tel Aviv University, but all material
needed for research is available, mostly on microfilm.

Kehr, Helen, and Langmaid, Janet. The Nazi Era,
1919-1945: A Select Bibliography of Published Works
from the Early Roots to 1980. London, 1982.

Based on the holdings of the Wiener Library; see also the
earlier From Weimar to Hitler: Germany, 1918-1933
(London, 1974).

Wiener Library. Catalogue of Nuremberg Documents.
London, 1961.

Supplements 1-2 (1962-63); register of documents related
to the holocaust and index of persons interrogated.

Wiener Library. Persecution and Resistance under the
Nazis. Edited by Ilse R. Wolfe. 2nd ed. London,
1960.

B. General Guides, Directories and Union Lists

34. Association of Special Libraries and Information Bureaux.
Aslib Directory. Edited by Ellen M. Codin. 4th. ed.
2 vols. London, 1977-80.

Vol. 2 for the humanities and social sciences.

35. Auchterlonie, Paul, and Safadi, Yasin H., eds. Union
Catalogue of Arabic Serials and Newspapers in British
Libraries. London, 1977.

36. Bloomfield, Valerie. Guide to Resources for Canadian
Studies in Britain. Ottawa, 1979.

37. Burkett, Jack, ed. Special Library and Information
Services in the United Kingdom. 2 vols. London, 1974.

Vol. 2: Government and Related Library and Information
Services in the United Kingdom.

38. Clark, G. Kitson, and Elton, G.R. Guide to Research
Facilities in History in the Universities of Great
Britain and Ireland. 2nd ed. Cambridge, 1965.

39. Collison, Robert. Published Library Catalogues: An
Introduction to their Content and Use. London, 1974.

A useful subject guide to the many published library
catalogues; see also his Directory of Libraries and
Special Collections on Asia and North Africa (Hamden, CT,
1970).

40. Datta, Rajeshwari, ed. Union Catalogue of the Government
of Pakistan Publications Held by Libraries in London,
Oxford and Cambridge. London, 1967.

See also the same author's Union Catalogue of the Central
Government of India Publications Held by Libraries in
London, Oxford and Cambridge (London, 1970); and Teresa
Macdonald, Union Catalogue of the Government of Ceylon
Publications Held by Libraries in London, Oxford and
Cambridge (London, 1970).

41. Directory of British Associations, 1965-. Beckenham,
1965-.

4th ed., 1974; brief listing of national associations, societies, organisations, institutes, etc.

42. Downs, Robert Bingham, and Downs, Elizabeth C. British and Irish Library Resources: A Bibliographical Guide. London, 1981.

A valuable record of library catalogues, checklists, guides and directories.

43. Guide to the Historical Publications of the Societies of England and Wales. 13 vols. London, 1930-48.

Supplements 1-13, 1929-1942/46, to the Bulletin of the Institute of Historical Research; see also Edward Lindsay Carson Mullins, A Guide to the Historical and Archaeological Publications of Societies in England and Wales, 1903-1933 (London, 1968); and Cyril Matheson, Catalogue of the Publications of Scottish Historical and Kindred Clubs and Societies...1908-1927 (Aberdeen, 1928).

44. HMSO. British National Archives: Government Public-ations Sectional List, no. 24. London, 1983.

A list of publications of the Public Record Office, the Public Record Office of Northern Ireland, the Scottish Record Office and the House of Lords Record Office.

45. Harcup, Sara E. Historical, Archaeological and Kindred Societies in the British Isles: A List. 2nd ed. London, 1968.

46. Hewitt, Arthur Reginald, comp. Union List of Common-wealth Newspapers in London, Oxford and Cambridge. London, 1960.

Based on the holdings of the British Museum; details of 2,426 newspapers in sixty-two libraries and newspaper offices.

47. Irwin, Raymond, and Staveley, Ronald, eds. The Libraries of London. 2nd ed., rev. London, 1964.

Describes in detail history, purpose and collections of various libraries.

48. Lambert, Jean. The Bibliography of Museum and Art Gallery Publications and Audio-Visual Aids in Great Britain and Ireland 1977. London, 1978.

49. Libraries, Museums and Art Galleries Year Book, 1978-1979. Edited by Adrian Brink. Cambridge, 1981.

50. Library Association. Libraries in the United Kingdom and the Republic of Ireland. 10th ed. London, 1983.

    A list of public library authorities and addresses.

51. The London Union List of Periodicals: Holdings of the Municipal and County Libraries of Greater London. Edited by H.J. Rengert. 3rd ed. London, 1969.

52. Mandahl, S.M., and Carnell, R.W. Checklist of Japanese Periodicals Held in British University and Research Libraries. Sheffield, 1971.

53. Moon, Brenda E., comp. Periodicals for South-East Asian Studies: A Union Catalogue of Holdings in British and Selected European Libraries. London, 1979.

54. Mullins, E.L.C. Texts and Calendars: An Analytical Guide to Serial Publications. London, 1958.

    As issued by various Record Commissions, Public Record Offices and record societies.

55. Naylor, B., et al. Directory of Libraries and Special Collections on Latin America and the West Indies. London, 1975.

56. Philip, Alexander J. An Index to the Special Collections in Libraries, Museums and Art Galleries (Public, Private and Official) in Great Britain and Ireland. London, 1949.

    Arranged by subject, with location and description.

57. Record Depositories in Great Britain: A Geographical Directory. 7th ed. London, 1982.

    HMSO for the Royal Commission on Historical Manuscripts.

58. Roberts, Stephen, et al., comps. Research Libraries and Collections in the United Kingdom: A Selective Inventory and Guide. London, 1978.

59. Snow, Peter, comp. The United States: A Guide to Library Holdings in the United Kingdom. London, 1982.

A guide to printed, microform and audio-visual materials
in 350 libraries in Britain.

60. Standing Conference on Library Materials on Africa. The
SCOLMA Directory of Libraries and Special Collections on
Africa. Compiled by Robert Collison. 2nd ed. London,
1967.

61. Tait, James A., and Tait, Heather. Library Resources in
Scotland, 1976-1977. Glasgow, 1978.

See also Library Resources in Wales, edited by M. June
Maggs (London, 1976).

62. Travis, Carole, and Alman, Miriam. Periodicals from
Africa: A Bibliography and Union List of Periodicals
Published in Africa. Boston, MA, 1977.

Holdings of about sixty libraries, representing the major
African collections in the United Kingdom.

63. Walker, Gregory, ed. Directory of Libraries and Special
Collections on Eastern Europe and the U.S.S.R. London,
1971.

Material in Britain relating to the USSR and Eastern
Europe; see also his Sources for Soviet, East European and
Slavonic Studies in British Libraries (London, 1981).

64. Wise, Terence, comp. A Guide to Military Museums.
Hemel Hempstead, 1971.

65. World of Learning, 1947-. London, 1947-.

Annual; international listing, by country, of learned
societies, research organisations and libraries.

C. Manuscript Research

66. Baldock, Robert W. A Survey of Southern African Manuscripts in the United Kingdom. London, 1976.

67. Bill, E.G.W. A Catalogue of Manuscripts in Lambeth Palace
Library, MSS 2341-3119. London, 1983.

Including material on Anglo-German relations in the 1930s
and 1940s.

68. Clark, Sir George. "British Business Archives,
1935-1948." Business Archives, 34(1971), 7-9.

69. Cook, Chris, et al., comps. <u>Sources in British Political History, 1900-1951</u>. 5 vols. London, 1975-78.

The researcher's vade mecum; a project of the Political Archives Investigation Committee carried out under the auspices of the British Library of Political and Economic Science; vol. 1 subtitled: <u>A Guide to the Archives of Selected Organisations and Societies</u>; vol. 2: <u>A Guide to the Private Papers of Selected Public Servants</u>; vol. 3: <u>A Guide to the Private Papers of Members of Parliament, A-K</u>; vol. 4: <u>A Guide to the Private Papers of Members of Parliament, L-Z</u>; vol. 5: <u>A Guide to the Private Papers of Selected Writers, Intellectuals and Publicists</u>; numerous useful appendices in each volume.

70. Crick, Bernard R., and Alman, Miriam. <u>A Guide to Manuscripts Relating to America in the United Kingdom</u>. London, 1978.

Revised edition, edited by John W. Raimo (1979); for the British Association for American Studies; see also Carnegie Institution, Washington, <u>Guides to Manuscript Materials for the History of the United States</u>, 23 vols. (Washington, DC, 1906-43); includes several volumes on British materials.

71. Emmison, F.G., and Smith, W.J., comps. <u>Material for Theses in Local Record Offices and Libraries</u>. London, 1980.

Historical Association Helps for Students, no. 87; a geographic listing of manuscript sources, further subdivided by subject; useful for out of the way manuscripts; persons and subject index.

72. Forster, Janet, and Sheppard, Julia, eds. <u>British Archives: A Guide to Archive Resources in the United Kingdom</u>. London, 1982.

A thorough list of repositories, with archives and manuscript collections of historical interest; an essential starting point for manuscript research.

73. <u>Guides to Materials for West African History in European Archives</u>. Nos. 1-5. London, 1962-73.

No. 5 for archives of the United Kingdom; by Noel Matthews (1973).

74. Hazlehurst, Cameron, and Woodland, Christine. A Guide to
    the Papers of British Cabinet Ministers, 1900-1951.
    London, 1974.

    For the Royal Historical Society; an indispensable
    research tool; alphabetical listing with detailed
    information as to career and papers, both in archives and
    privately held; index of collections in institutions; also
    useful for careers spanning the nineteenth and twentieth
    century is Historical Manuscripts Commission, Papers of
    British Cabinet Ministers, 1782-1900 (London, 1982); vol.
    1 of Guides to Sources for British History.

75. Hepworth, Philip. Select Biographical Sources: The
    Library Association Manuscript Survey. London, 1971.

    Information on biographical research and location of about
    3,500 select biographical manuscript repositories; see
    also his Archives and Manuscripts in Libraries (London,
    1964).

76. Higham, Robin. "Aeronautical History: Some Offbeat
    British Archives." American Archivist, 26(1963), 63-65.

77. Historical Manuscripts Commission. Private Papers of
    British Diplomats, 1782-1900. London, 1984.

    Vol. 4 of Guides to Sources for British History.

78. Jones, Charles A. Britain and the Dominions: A Guide to
    Business and Related Records in the United Kingdom
    Concerning Australia, Canada, New Zealand and South
    Africa. Boston, MA, 1978.

79. Jones, Philip. Britain and Palestine, 1914-1948.
    London, 1979.

    For the British Academy; locates unpublished records and
    papers of organisations and individuals based in Britain,
    and involved in any manner with Palestine during this
    period.

80. Keen, Rosemary. A Survey of the Archives of Selected
    Missionary Societies. London, 1968.

    For the Historical Manuscripts Commission.

81. Lenz, Wilhelm, ed. Manuscript Sources for the History
    of Germany since 1500 in Great Britain. Boppard, 1975.

82. MacLeod, Roy, and Friday, James R. Archives of British
    Men of Science. London, 1972.

    By a Sussex University study group; traces papers of 3,500
    scientists who were active between 1850 and 1939; in
    microfiche, with accompanying index and guide; see also
    Historical Manuscripts Commission, The Manuscript Papers
    of British Scientists, 1600-1940 (London, 1982); vol. 3 of
    Guides to Sources for British History.

83. Manchester Studies Unit. The Directory of British Oral
    History Collections. Colchester, 1981.

84. Mander-Jones, Phyllis, ed. Manuscripts in the British
    Isles Relating to Australia, New Zealand and the
    Pacific. Honolulu, 1972.

    Arranged by country, with London holdings analysed first.

85. Matthews, Noel, and Wainwright, M. Doreen. A Guide to
    Manuscripts and Documents in the British Isles Relating
    to the Far East. London, 1977.

    Includes public depositories and some papers privately
    held; see also the same authors' A Guide to Manuscripts
    and Documents in the British Isles Relating to Africa
    (London, 1971); for Africa south of the Sahara; and A
    Guide to Western Manuscripts and Documents in the British
    Isles Relating to South and South East Asia (London,
    1965); collections of India Office Library excluded.

86. Mayer, Sydney L., and Koenig, William J. The Two World
    Wars: A Guide to Manuscript Collections in the United
    Kingdom. London, 1976.

    Details of military, naval and diplomatic materials.

87. Meckler, Alan M., and McMillan, Ruth. Oral History
    Collections. New York, 1975.

88. Netton, I.R., comp. Middle East Materials in United
    Kingdom and Irish Libraries: A Directory. London,
    1983.

89. Pearson, J.D. Guide to Manuscripts and Documents in the
    British Isles Relating to the Middle East and North
    Africa. London, 1980.

90. Pemberton, John E. European Materials in British
    University Libraries: A Bibliography and Union
    Catalogue. London, 1972.

91. Pritchard, R. John. "A Survey of Tokyo War Trial
    Records in Britain", in Proceedings of the British
    Association for Japanese Studies, vol. 1, part 1:
    History and International Relations. Edited by Peter
    Lowe. Sheffield, 1976.

    A publication of the Centre of Japanese Studies,
    Sheffield University.

92. Sturges, R.P. Economists' Papers, 1750-1950: A Guide
    to Archive and Other Manuscript Sources for the History
    of British and Irish Economic Thought. London, 1975.

    Alphabetical listing of over 150 prominent economists.

93. Tapsell, Alan. A Guide to the Materials for Swedish
    Historical Research in Great Britain. Stockholm, 1958.

94. Thomas, Daniel H., and Case, Lynn M. The New Guide to
    the Diplomatic Archives of Western Europe.
    Philadelphia, PA, 1975.

    With a chapter on Britain, describing history and content
    of various archives.

95. Walne, Peter, ed. A Guide to Manuscript Sources for the
    History of Latin America and the Caribbean in the
    British Isles. London, 1973.

IV.   BIBLIOGRAPHY

A. GENERAL

The information explosion of the mid-twentieth century is
a very mixed blessing for the historian. The guides to this
information are inordinately abundant and sometimes complex.
But the benefits to be derived are likewise enormous, limited
only by the enthusiasm and energy of the researcher. What
follows in this reference section can only be a mere sampling
of the abundance and variety of such reference guides. The
selection is designed on two basic principles. The first is
to indicate the variety of guides that are available. The
second principle is to cite, as far as possible, British
produced and British related materials.

1. Bibliographies

Bibliographies of Bibliographies

96. Besterman, Theodore. A World Bibliography of Biblio-
    graphies and of Bibliographical Catalogues, Calendars,
    Abstracts, Digests, Indexes, and the Like. 4th ed.
    5 vols. Lausanne, 1965-66.

    Standard and comprehensive work for bibliographies
    published through 1963; about 117,000 items divided by
    about 16,000 headings; decennial supplement, 1964-74,
    compiled by Alice F. Toomey (Totowa, NJ, 1977).

97. Bibliographic Index: A Cumulative Bibliography of
    Bibliographies, 1937-. New York, 1938-.

    From 1970 published in April and August, with annual
    cumulation; subject list of bibliographies found in books
    and periodicals, including foreign languages; on-line
    access available 1984.

98. Collison, Robert. Bibliographies, Subject and
    National: A Guide to their Contents, Arrangement and
    Use. 3rd ed., rev. London, 1968.

57

Bibliographies of Bibliographies

About 500 annotated bibliographies; index of subjects and names.

99. Gray, Richard A., and Villmow, Dorothy. Serial Bibliographies in the Humanities and Social Sciences. Ann Arbor, MI, 1969.

Reference Guides

100. American Reference Books Annual, 1970-. Vol. 1-. Edited by Bohdan S. Wynar. Littleton, CO, 1970-.

Annotated annual of reference books; five-year cumulative index.

101. Conover, Helen F., comp. A Guide to Bibliographical Tools for Research in Foreign Affairs. 2nd ed. Washington, DC, 1958.

Mainly English language materials; reprinted with supplement in 1968.

102. Day, Alan Edwin. History: A Reference Book. London, 1977.

A basic guide to reference books for the historian.

103. Hepworth, Philip. How to Find Out in History: A Guide to Sources of Information for All. London, 1966.

A research guide and bibliographic essay; with emphasis on British materials.

104. Higgens, Gavin, ed. Printed Reference Material. 2nd ed. London, 1983.

For the Library Association; a standard work with various contributors.

105. Krikler, Bernard, and Laqueur, Walter, eds. A Reader's Guide to Contemporary History. London, 1972.

106. Levine, Herbert M., and Owen, Dolores B. An American Guide to British Social Science Resources. Metuchen, NJ, 1976.

Details of British information services in the United States, major British libraries and associations.

BIBLIOGRAPHIES

Reference Guides

107. Mason, John Brown. <u>Research Resources: Annotated Guide to the Social Sciences</u>. 2 vols. Santa Barbara, CA, 1968.

     Vol. 1 annotates various indexing and abstracting services, bibliographies, directories, etc.; vol. 2 is a guide to statistical sources and official publications.

108. Poulton, Helen J. <u>The Historian's Handbook: A Descriptive Guide to Reference Works</u>. Norman, OK, 1972.

     Introductory bibliographic guide to reference works.

109. Sheehy, Eugene P., comp. <u>Guide to Reference Books</u>. Chicago, IL, 1976.

     Supplements (1980, 1982); large section on general reference books; special section on history; see also Carl M. White, et al., <u>Sources of Information in the Social Sciences: A Guide to the Literature</u>, 2nd ed. (Chicago, IL, 1973).

110. Walford, Albert John. <u>Guide to Reference Material</u>. 3 vols. Vols. 1–2, 4th ed. London, 1982.

     A standard reference guide, well annotated; emphasis on items published in Britain; vol. 2 for social and historical sciences; condensed version <u>Walford's Concise Guide to Reference Material</u> (London, 1981).

General Bibliographies

111. Boehm, Eric H. <u>Bibliographies on International Relations and World Affairs: An Annotated Directory</u>. Santa Barbara, CA, 1965.

     Lists twenty best bibliographies and eighty-three publications with regular bibliographies.

112. <u>Commonwealth National Bibliographies: An Annotated Directory</u>. London, 1977.

     For the Commonwealth Secretariat; listing by country.

113. Coulter, Edith M., and Gerstenfeld, Melanie. <u>Historical Bibliographies: A Systematic and Annotated Guide</u>. Berkeley, CA, 1965.

General Bibliographies

114. Council on Foreign Relations. Foreign Affairs Biblio-
     graphy: A Selected and Annotated List of Books on
     International Relations, 1919/32-1962/72. 5 vols. New
     York, 1935-76.

     Revised and enlarged bibliography based on quarterly ones
     appearing in Foreign Affairs; see also Foreign Affairs
     50-Year Bibliography: New Evaluations of Significant
     Books on International Relations, 1920-1970, edited by
     Byron Dexter (New York, 1972).

115. International Committee of Historical Sciences. Biblio-
     graphie internationale des travaux historiques publiés
     dans les volumes de "Mélanges", 1880/1939-1940/50. 2
     vols. Paris, 1955-65.

     Divided by country, with subject and name index; see also
     Internationale Jahresbibliographie der Festschriften,
     vol. 1- (London, 1981-); Otto Leistner, ed.,
     Internationale Bibliographie der Festschriften
     (Osnabrück, 1976); and New York, Public Library, Research
     Libraries, Guide to Festschriften, 2 vols. (Boston, MA,
     1977).

116. Roach, John Peter Charles, ed. A Bibliography of Modern
     History. London, 1968.

     Intended as an independent reference work and companion
     to the New Cambridge Modern History, vol. 1- (London,
     1957-).

Current Bibliographies

117. Bibliography of Historical Works Issued in the United
     Kingdom, 1940/45-1966/70. 5 vols. London, 1947-72.

     In progress; sponsor and editor varies; volumes exclude
     periodical articles; strong emphasis on British history.

118. Bindoff, Stanley Thomas, and Boulton, James T. Research
     in Progress in English and History in Britain, Ireland,
     Canada, Australia and New Zealand. London, 1976.

119. British Books in Print: The Reference Catalogue of
     Current Literature, 1874-. London, 1874-.

     Irregular; beginning 1971 a computer-produced annual with
     alphabetical author and title sequence.

60

BIBLIOGRAPHIES

Current Bibliographies

120. British National Bibliography, 1950-. London, 1950-.

The basic national bibliography prepared for the Council
of the British National Bibliography at the British
Library; periodical listings excluded; published weekly
with cumulations at intervals; cumulated subject volumes
published every four years; since 1977 carries advance
cataloguing information; for publications before 1950 see
The English Catalogue of Books (London, 1906-); and The
Bookseller (London, 1858-); which cumulates annually into
Whitaker's Cumulative Book List (1924-).

121. Current Research in British Studies by North American
Scholars. Edited by Robert Kent Donovan. 8th ed.
Manhattan, KS, 1980.

Previous editions published irregularly from 1953;
produced for the Conference on British Studies.

122. Historical Association, London. Annual Bulletin of
Historical Literature. Vol. 1-, 1911-. London, 1912-.

Survey articles by specialists on the annual
publications; mainly British emphasis.

123. International Bibliography of Historical Sciences.
Edited for the International Committee of Historical
Sciences. Vol. 1-, 1926-. New York, 1930-.

Historical sciences widely interpreted to include
international relations, political, economic and social
aspects, etc.; no volumes for 1940-46; this gap partially
remedied by Pier Fausto Palumbo, Bibliografia storica
internazionale, 1940-1947 (Rome, 1950).

124. Royal Historical Society Annual Bibliography of British
and Irish History: Publications of 1975-. Edited by
G.R. Elton. Hassock, 1976-.

In progress; chronological approach with subject
subdivisions; author and subject indexes.

125. Writing on British History, 1901-1933: A Bibliography on
the History of Great Britain from about 400 A.D. to
1914, Published during the Years 1901-1933 Inclusive,
with an Appendix Containing a Select List of
Publications in these Years on British History since
1914. 5 vols. London, 1968-70.

Current Bibliographies

Annual (irregular) series of same title thereafter,
compiled by A.T. Milne, et al., for years 1934-45, in 8
vols., published 1937-60; vols. covering 1946/48-1965/66,
9 vols. (1973-81); selective for post-1914 period.

Subject Bibliographies

126. Amstutz, Mark R. Economics and Foreign Policy: A guide
to Information Sources. Detroit, MI, 1977.

Annotated bibliography on the political economy of
international relations; other examples of such
bibliographies relevant to this guide include Gerard L.
Alexander, Guide to Atlases: World, Regional, National,
Thematic; An International Listing of Atlases Published
Since 1950 (Metuchen, NJ, 1971); supplement for 1971 to
1975 published in 1977; Hardin Craig, comp., A Biblio-
graphy of Encyclopaedias and Dictionaries Dealing with
Military, Naval and Maritime Affairs, 1577-1970, 4th ed.
(Houston, TX, 1970); Henry Oliver Lancaster, Bibliography
of Statistical Bibliographies (London, 1968); S. Padraig
Walsh, Anglo-American General Encyclopaedias, 1703-1967:
A Historical Bibliography (New York, 1968); Lora Jeanne
Wheeler, International Business and Foreign Trade:
Information Sources (Detroit, MI, 1968); Robert B.
Slocum, Biographical Dictionaries and Related Works
(Detroit, MI, 1967, 2nd suppl., 1978); British Council,
Public Administration: A Select List of Books and
Periodicals (London, 1964); Max Arnim, Internationale
Personalbibliographie, 1800-1959, 3 vols. (Leipzig,
1944-63); and Mitsuzo Masui, A Bibliography of Finance
(Kobe, 1935).

127. Anderson, Martin, and Bloom, Valerie, comps.
Conscription: A Select and Annotated Bibliography.
Stanford, CA, 1976.

1,385 fully annotated entries; separate chapter on
bibliographies.

128. Bayliss, Gwyn M. Bibliographic Guide to the Two World
Wars: An Annotated Survey of English-Language
Reference Materials. London, 1977.

Arranged by type of reference work; author, title and
subject indexes; see also E. David Cronon and Theodore
Rosenof, The Second War and the Atomic Age, 1940-1973
(Northbrook, IL, 1975); A.G.S. Enser, comp., A Subject
Bibliography of the Second World War: Books in English,

BIBLIOGRAPHIES

Subject Bibliographies

1939-1974 (Boulder, CO, 1977); James E. O'Neill and
Robert W. Krauskopf, eds., World War II: An Account of
its Documents (Washington, DC, 1976); Myron J. Smith,
World War II at Sea: A Bibliography of Sources in
English (Metuchen, NJ, 1975); Marty Bloomberg and Hans
H. Weber, World War II and its Origins: A Select
Annotated Bibliography of Books in English (Littleton,
CO, 1975); Arthur L. Funk, et al., comps., A Select
Bibliography of Books on the Second World War, in
English, Published in the United States, 1966-1975
(Manhattan, KS, 1975); Janet Ziegler, comp., World War
II: Books in English, 1945-1965 (Stanford, CA, 1971).

129. Böttcher, Winfried, et al. Britische Europaideen,
     1940-1970: Eine Bibliographie. 2 vols. Düsseldorf,
     1971-73.

     Vol. 1 is a chronological list of books published in
     Britain on integration; vol. 2 concentrates on individual
     European countries; see also the same authors' Das
     britische Parlament und Europa, 1940-1972: Eine
     Fachbibliographie (Baden-Baden, 1975).

130. Boulding, Elise, et al. Bibliography on World Conflict
     and Peace. Boulder, CO, 1979.

     See also Berenice A. Carroll, et al., Peace and War: A
     Guide to Bibliographies (Santa Barbara, CA, 1983); and
     Blanche Wiesen Cook, ed., Bibliography on Peace Research
     in History (Santa Barbara, CA, 1969).

131. The British Labour Movement to 1970: A Bibliography.
     Compiled by Harold Smith. London, 1981.

     Covers all aspects; almost 4,000 entries, arranged by
     subject, published between 1945 and 1970; see also Ruth
     and Edmund Frow and Michael Katanka, The History of
     British Trade Unions: A Select Bibliography (London,
     1969).

132. Chaloner, William Henry, and Richardson, R.C. British
     Economic and Social History: A Bibliographical Guide.
     Totowa, NJ, 1976.

133. Christie, Ian R. British History Since 1760: A Select
     Bibliography. London, 1970.

63

Subject Bibliographies

Historical Association, Helps for Students of History,
no. 81; about five pages devoted to the twentieth
century.

134. Collison, Robert. Broadcasting in Britain: A Bibliography. London, 1961.

135. Elton, G.R. Modern Historians on British History,
1485-1945: A Critical Bibliography, 1945-1969.
London, 1970.

A bibliographic essay, with a chapter devoted to the
twentieth century; author and subject index.

136. Flint, John E. Books on the British Empire and Commonwealth: A Guide for Students. London, 1968.

See also Robin W. Winks, ed., Historiography of the
British Empire-Commonwealth: Trends, Interpretations and
Resources (Durham, NC, 1966).

137. Ghebali, Victor-Yves, comp. Bibliographical Handbook of
the League of Nations. 3 vols. Geneva, 1980.

Special Bibliographies, Repertoires and Indexes, no. 3,
of the United Nations Library, Geneva; comprehensive
subject bibliography; provisional edition.

138. Gunzenhäuser, Max, ed. Die Pariser Friedenskonferenz
1919 und die Friedensverträge, 1919-1920.
Frankfurt/M., 1970.

Long introductory essay with over 200 page bibliography;
see also Nina Almond and Ralph H. Lutz, An Introduction
to a Bibliography of the Paris Peace Conference
(Stanford, CA, 1935).

139. Havighurst, Alfred F., comp. Modern England, 1901-1970:
A Bibliography. London, 1976.

For the Conference on British Studies; 2,500 entries
divided by subject; separate chapter on foreign
relations.

140. Higham, Robin, ed. A Guide to the Sources of British
Military History. Berkeley, CA, 1971.

BIBLIOGRAPHIES

Subject Bibliographies

> For the Conference on British Studies; six chapters on period from 1918-45; detailed bibliographic essays; see also Robert Greenhalgh Albion, Maritime and Naval History: An Annotated Bibliography, 4th ed., rev. (London, 1973); Alan C. Aimone, Bibliography of Military History: A Selected and Annotated History of Reference Sources, 3rd ed. (West Point, NY, 1978).

141. Hill, Richard Leslie. A Bibliography of the Anglo-Egyptian Sudan, from the Earliest Times to 1937.... London, 1939.

> Supplemented by Abdel Rahman el Nasri, A Bibliography of the Sudan, 1938-1958 (London, 1962).

142. Lloyd, Lorna, and Sims, Nicholas A. British Writing on Disarmament from 1914 to 1978: A Bibliography. London, 1979.

> See also Richard Dean Burns, Arms Control and Disarmament: A Bibliography (Santa Barbara, CA, 1977); and League of Nations, Annotated Bibliography on Disarmament and Military Questions (Geneva, 1931).

143. Matthews, William. British Diaries: An Annotated Bibliography of British Diaries Written Between 1442 and 1942. Berkeley, CA, 1950.

> Lists both published and manuscript diaries in chronological order by date of first entry; author index; see also his British Autobiographies: An Annotated Bibliography of British Autobiographies Published or Written before 1951 (Berkeley, CA, 1955).

144. Michel, Henri. Bibliographie critique de la résistance. Paris, 1964.

> Updated in each issue of the Revue d'histoire de la deuxième guerre mondiale.

145. Mowat, Charles Loch. British History since 1926: A Select Bibliography. Revised by Peter Lowe. London, 1977.

> Historical Association, Helps for Students of History, no. 61; includes sections on biography, memoirs, foreign policy and defence; see also his Great Britain since 1914 (London, 1971); part of "The Sources of History: Studies in the Use of Historical Evidence" series.

Subject Bibliographies

146. Olson, William Joseph. <u>Britain's Elusive Empire in the Middle East, 1900-1921: An Annotated Bibliography</u>. New York, 1982.

    Introductory essay; lists both Middle East reference books and those dealing with British policy in particular.

147. Sainsbury, Keith. <u>International History, 1939-1970: A Select Bibliography</u>. London, 1973.

    Historical Association, Helps for Students of History, no. 86; chronological listing, subdivided by areas.

148. Smith, Bruce Lannes, et al. <u>Propaganda, Communication and Public Opinion: A Comprehensive Reference Guide</u>. Princeton, NJ, 1946.

    About 2,500 titles of books and articles appearing between 1934 and 1943; continued in Bureau of Social Science Research, Washington, DC, <u>International Communication and Public Opinion: A Guide to the Literature</u>, compiled by Bruce Lannes Smith and Chitra M. Smith (Princeton, NJ, 1956).

149. Smith, Myron J. <u>The Secret Wars: A Guide to Sources in English</u>. 3 vols. Santa Barbara, CA, 1980.

    Vol. 1 entitled: <u>Intelligence, Propaganda and Psychological Warfare, Resistance Movements, and Secret Operations, 1939-1945</u>; see also Marjorie W. Cline, et al., eds., <u>Scholar's Guide to Intelligence Literature</u> (Frederick, MD, 1983); Paul W. Blackstock and Frank L. Schaf, eds., <u>Intelligence, Espionage, Counterespionage and Covert Operations: A Guide to Information Sources</u> (Detroit, MI, 1978); and Max Gunzenhäuser, <u>Geschichte des geheimen Nachrichtendienstes (Spionage, Sabotage und Abwehr): Literaturbericht und Bibliographie</u> (Frankfurt/M., 1968).

150. Spiers, John, et al. <u>The Left in Britain: A Checklist and Guide</u>. Hassocks, 1976.

    Subtitled: <u>With Historical Notes to 37 Left-Wing Political Movements and Groupings Active in Britain between 1904-1972 whose Publications Comprise the Harvester/Primary Sources Microfilm Collection</u>.

BIBLIOGRAPHIES

Subject Bibliographies

151. Stephens, Lester D. Historiography: A Bibliography. Methuchen, NJ, 1975.

    Covers historical theory and methods, historiography and reference works.

152. Watson, Charles A. The Writing of History in Britain: A Bibliography of Post-1945 Writings about British Historians and Biographers. New York, 1982.

153. Woods, Frederick, ed. Bibliography of the Works of Sir Winston Churchill. London, 1979.

154. Wright, Moorhead, et al. Essay Collections in International Relations: A Classified Bibliography. New York, 1977.

    Over 1,600 essays, from 240 books published between 1945 and 1975, listed by subject; author and subject index.

155. Wrigley, Chris. A.J.P. Taylor: A Complete Annotated Bibliography and Guide to His Historical and Other Writings. Brighton, 1980.

Dissertations

156. ASLIB. Index to Theses Accepted for Higher Degrees in the Universities of Great Britain and Ireland, vol. 1-, 1950/51-. London, 1953-.

    Annual classified arrangement, and alphabetically by university with subject categories; for previous period see Retrospective Index to Theses of Great Britain and Ireland, 1716-1950, edited by Roger R. Bilboul, 5 vols. (Santa Barbara, CA, 1975-77); vol. 1 for the social sciences and humanities; other useful guides are Michael M. Reynolds, ed., A Guide to Theses and Dissertations: An Annotated, International Bibliography of Bibliographies (Detroit, MI, 1975); and Marc Chaveinc, Guide to the Availability of Theses (Groningen, 1978).

157. Bloomfield, Barry Cambray. Theses on Asia Accepted by Universities in the United Kingdom and Ireland, 1877-1964. London, 1967.

    Updated in the Bulletin of the Association of British Orientalists.

Dissertations

158. Dissertation Abstracts International, Section C:
European Abstracts, vol. 37-, no. 1-. Ann Arbor, MI,
1976-.

Part of Dissertations Abstracts International (Ann
Arbor, MI, 1938-); quarterly list of mainly western
European theses available on microfilm from University
Microfilm, Inc.; for data base on-line searching by
computer see also Comprehensive Dissertation Index,
1861-1972, 1973-77, 1978 (Ann Arbor, MI, 1973-).

159. Labour and Social History Theses: American, British and
Irish University Theses and Dissertations in the Field
of British and Irish Labour History, Presented between
1900 and 1978. Compiled by Victor F. Gilbert. London,
1982.

160. London University, Institute of Commonwealth Studies.
Theses in Progress in Commonwealth Studies: A
Cumulative List. London, 1950-.

161. London University, Institute of Historical Research.
Historical Research for University Degrees in the
United Kingdom, 1931/32-52. London, 1933-53.

Bulletin of the Institute of Historical Research, Theses
Supplement, no. 1-14; information on theses completed and
in progress; follows on lists published annually in
History from 1920-29; and in the Bulletin from 1930-32;
superseded by the Institute's Theses Completed, 1953-
(London, 1954-) and Theses in Progress, 1954- (London,
1954-); issues for 1954-66 published as Theses
Supplement, no. 15-27 to the Bulletin; from 1967 lists
appear as separate publications of the Institute; for a
definitive retrospective list see Phyllis M. Jacobs,
comp., History Theses, 1901-1970: Historical Research
for Higher Degrees in the Universities of the United
Kingdom (London, 1976).

162. London University, Institute of Latin American Studies.
Theses in Latin American Studies at British
Universities in Progress and Completed, 1966/67-.
London, 1967-.

Annual listing by university; author and subject indexes.

163. Sharp, Tony. Unpublished Doctoral Dissertations Relating
to the Historical Period 1939-1949. London, 1979.

BIBLIOGRAPHIES

Dissertations

    Association of Contemporary Historians, Bulletin no. 8; diplomatic and military aspects largely omitted.

164. Sluglett, Peter. Theses on Islam, the Middle East and North-West Africa, 1880-1978, Accepted by Universities in the United Kingdom and Ireland. London, 1983.

    See also F.J. Shulman, ed., American and British Doctoral Dissertations on Israel and Palestine in Modern Times (Ann Arbor, MI, 1973).

165. United Kingdom Publications and Theses on Africa, 1963. Cambridge, 1966-.

    Irregular; thesis section is supplement to Theses on Africa Accepted by Universities in the United Kingdom and Ireland (Cambridge, 1964); see also J.H. McIlwaine, Theses on Africa, 1963-1975, Accepted by Universities in the United Kingdom and Ireland (London, 1978).

Reproductions and Data Bases

166. Dodson, Suzanne Cates. Microform Research Collections: A Guide. Westport, CT, 1978.

    Listing of about 200 microform research collections.

167. Guide to Microforms in Print, Incorporating International Microforms in Print, 1977-. Westport, CT, 1977-.

    Archive materials, monographs, journals, newspapers, government publications, etc., available on microform; see also the companion Subject Guide to Microforms in Print, 1962/63- (Washington, DC, 1962-).

168. Hall, James Logan. On-line Information Retrieval Sourcebook. London, 1977.

    See also his On-line Bibliographic Data Bases: 1979 Directory (London, 1979); and Data Bases in Europe: A Directory to Machine-Readable Data Banks in Europe, edited by Alex Tomberg, 3rd ed. (London, 1977).

169. Library and Information Science Abstracts, no. 1-, Jan./Feb. 1969-. London, 1969-.

Reproductions and Data Bases

Bimonthly; international coverage of information in hard copy, microfilm and computer-readable form; computer data base from 1969-.

170. Microlist: An International Record of New Micropublications. Vol. 1-, Jan. 1977-. Westport, CT, 1977-.

171. Williams, Martha E., and O'Donnell, R. Computer-Readable Data Bases: A Directory and Data Sourcebook. Washington, DC, 1979.

Covers over 500 data bases.

2. Reference Works

Biographical Dictionaries, Lists and Directories

172. Bellamy, Joyce M., and Saville, John, eds. Dictionary of Labour Biography. London, 1972-.

In progress; intended period of coverage from about 1790.

173. Bidwell, Robin, comp. and ed. Bidwell's Guide to Government Ministers. 3 vols. London, 1973.

Vol. 1: The Major Powers and Western Europe, 1900-1971; vol. 3: The British Empire and Successor States, 1900-1972; see also C.G. Allen, ed., Rulers and Governments of the World, 2 vols. (New York, 1977-78).

174. Biography Index: A Cumulative Index to Biographical Material in Books and Magazines. Vol. 1-. New York, 1947-.

Quarterly with annual cumulation; index by name, profession and dates of birth and death.

175. Boylan, Henry. A Dictionary of Irish Biography. London, 1978.

See also Dictionary of Welsh Biography Down to 1940 (Oxford, 1959); and Gordon Donaldson and Robert S. Morpeth, comps., Who's Who in Scottish History (New York, 1974).

176. British Biography Index, 1975-. Reading, 1975-.

Quarterly index to biographical material; annual cumulation.

70

REFERENCE WORKS

Biographical Dictionaries, Lists and Directories

177. British Imperial Calendar and Civil Service List.
London, 1809-1973.

Irregular, with varied titles and contents; usually gives
royal households, holders of public office, with official
position, honours and salary; superseded by The Civil
Service Year Book, 1974- (London, 1974-.)

178. Burke, Sir John Bernard. Burke's Genealogical and
Heraldic History of the Peerage, Baronetage, and
Knightage. London, 1826-.

Annual, 1851-1940; quadrennial since 1949; arranged
alphabetically by title; gives full lineage.

179. Cokayne, George Edward. The Complete Peerage: Or, A
History of the House of Lords and all its Members from
the Earliest Times. 14 vols. London, 1910-59.

Vol. 13 entitled Peerage Creations and Promotions from 22
Jan. 1901 to 31 Dec. 1938; the most complete record of
the peerage.

180. Colonial Office List, 1862-1966. London, 1862-1966.

Annual to 1940: not published 1941-45; biennial 1946-66;
usually includes extensive historical and statistical
material, with maps and biographical section; superseded
by A Year Book of the Commonwealth, 1967- (London,
1967-).

181. Current Biography. Vol. 1-. New York, 1940-.

Monthly, with annual cumulation; international in scope;
see also Current Biography: Cumulated Index, 1940-1970
(New York, 1973).

182. Debrett's Peerage, Baronetage, Knightage and Companion-
age, with Her Majesty's Royal Warrant Holders. London,
1713-1973.

Biographical data, living children and collateral
branches; from 1976, Debrett's Peerage and Baronetage,
with Her Majesty's Royal Warrant Holders.

183. Dictionary of National Biography. Edited by Sir Leslie
Stephen and Sir Sidney Lee. 22 vols. London, 1908-09.

Biographical Dictionaries, Lists and Directories

With supplements: 1901-11 (1912), 1912-21 (1927),
1922-30 (1937), 1931-40 (1949), 1941-50 (1959), 1951-60
(1971), 1961-70 (1981); a most important reference work
for English biography; signed articles a source in
themselves; for example, Sir Orme Sargent wrote about Sir
Nevile Henderson and Sir Eric Phipps; errata notes
cumulated in Corrections and Addition to the Dictionary
of National Biography, 1923-1963 (Boston, MA, 1966); over
6000 short abstracts of original entries reproduced in
The Concise Dictionary of National Biography, Part II,
1901-1970 (London, 1982).

184. Dod's Parliamentary Companion, 1832-. London, 1832-.

Annual; includes biographies of royal family and members
of parliament, details of procedure, ministries and
government departments; see also Michael Stenton and
Stephen Lees, eds., Who's Who of British Members of
Parliament 1832-1979, 4 vols. (Brighton, 1976-81); vol. 3
for 1919-1945; based on Dod's Parliamentary Companion,
with additional information on subsequent career and date
of death.

185. Foreign Office List and Diplomatic and Consular Year
Book. Edited by members of the staff of the Foreign
Office. London, 1806-1965.

Vital annual information on organisation of the Foreign
Office and statement of service of members; includes
foreign embassies, legations and consulates in Great
Britain; superseded by The Diplomatic Service List,
1966- (London, 1966-); see also The Air Force List,
formerly The Monthly Air Force List (London, 1918-); The
Army List (London, 1814-); and The Navy List (London,
1814-).

186. International Who's Who, 1935-. London, 1935-.

Brief biographical data on internationally prominent
individuals.

187. Jones, Barry, and Dixon, J.V. The Macmillan Dictionary
of Biography. London, 1981.

Biographical entries on about 7,000 figures of historical
importance.

188. Kelly's Handbook to the Titled, Landed and Official
Classes, 1880-. London, 1880-.

REFERENCE WORKS

Biographical Dictionaries, Lists and Directories

Brief sketches of those with hereditary or honourary titles, members of parliament, government officials and public personalities.

189. Kirk-Greene, Anthony H.M. A Bibliographical Dictionary of the British Colonial Governor. London, 1981-.

Vol. 1 for Africa.

190. Obituaries from The Times, 1961-1970: Including an Index to all Obituaries Appearing in The Times during the Years, 1961-1970. Edited by Frank C. Roberts. Reading, 1975.

Continued as Obituaries from The Times, 1971-1975 (Reading, 1978); volume for 1951-1960 published in 1979.

191. Palmer, Alan. Who's Who in Modern History, 1860-1980. New York, 1981.

192. Pickrill, D.A. Ministers of the Crown. London, 1981.

Lists holders of public offices under the crown from the earliest records to 1981.

193. Thomson, Theodore Radford. A Catalogue of British Family Histories. 3rd ed. London, 1976.

194. Tunney, Christopher. A Biographical Dictionary of World War II. London, 1972.

Over 400 sketches of service personnel, statesmen, etc.; see also David Mason, Who's Who in World War II (London, 1978); and War Lords: Military Commanders of the Twentieth Century, edited by Michael Carver (London, 1976); and more generally John Keegan and Andrew Wheatcroft, Who's Who in Military History (London, 1976).

195. Vacher's Parliamentary Companion, 1831-. London, 1831-.

Subtitled: Lists of the House of Lords and House of Commons with Members Town Addresses and other Information Indispensable in Parliamentary Business; frequency of publication varies.

196. Who Was Who, 1897-1915, 1916-1928, 1929-1940, 1941-1950, 1951-1960, 1961-1970, 1971-1980: A Companion to Who's Who: Containing the Biographies of

Biographical Dictionaries, Lists and Directories

> those who Died during the Period. 7 vols. London,
> 1929-82.
>
> Essentially the original sketches; with corrections,
> additional information and date of death added; see also
> Who Was Who: A Cumulated Index, 1897-1980 (London,
> 1981).

197. Who's Who: An Annual Biographical Dictionary with which
     is Incorporated "Men and Women of the Time". London,
     1849-.

> Annual; the original who's who reference work; mainly
> focused on British biographies; fairly detailed
> information supplied by individuals themselves.

Annual Surveys and News Digests

198. Almanach de Gotha: Annuaire généalogique, diplomatique
     et statistique, 1763-. Gotha, 1763-1960.

> Annual, not published 1945-58; title varies; a standard
> work on European genealogy, and statistical and
> descriptive information about countries worldwide.

199. Annual Register of World Events: A Review of the Year,
     1758-. London, 1761-.

> Prior to 1954 known as Annual Register; includes survey
> articles on annual developments, international
> organisations and assessments of law, the arts,
> economics, etc.

200. British Broadcasting Corporation. Monitoring Service:
     Monitoring Report. Reading, 1940-.

> Daily concise summaries of major news items; Digest of
> World Broadcasts, 1939-1947 available on microfilm.

201. Europa Year Book: A World Survey. London, 1926-.

> Since 1960 it has appeared in annual two volume editions;
> an authoritative reference work covering all aspects of
> international organisation and individual countries; more
> than 100 pages usually devoted to the United Kingdom.

202. Facts on File: A Weekly World News Digest with Cumula-
     tive Index. Vol. 1-, Oct.-Nov. 1940-. New York,
     1940-.

REFERENCE WORKS

Annual Surveys and News Digests

Weekly, with annual bound volumes; classified digest of
news arranged by subject; five-year index, published
1957-.

203. International Year Book and Statesman's Who's Who, 1953.
     London, 1953-.

Annual; information on international organisations;
political and statistical data on individual countries;
and a biographical section.

204. Keesing's Contemporary Archives: Weekly Diary of World
     Events with Index Continually Kept Up-to-date.   Vol.
     1-, 1 July 1931-. London, 1931-.

Including public documents and source references; indexes
at intervals cumulated every two years; vol. 1 preceded
by a supplement, "Synopsis of Important Events,
1918-1931".

205. Milner, Anita Cheek. Newspaper Indexes: A Location and
     Subject Guide for Researchers. Metuchen, NJ, 1977.

Mainly surveys card files and unpublished indexes.

206. Royal Institute of International Affairs. The Bulletin
     of International News. 22 vols. London, 1925-45.

A daily digest of international news; see also Royal
Institute of International Affairs, Review of the Foreign
Press, 1939-1945 (London, 1939-45, repr. Munich, 1980);
ten different series, mainly geographical, in 27 vols.

207. Royal Institute of International Affairs. Survey of
     International Affairs, 1920/23-. London, 1925-73.

Pre-war series, 1920-38, 17 vols., edited by A.J. Toynbee
and others; wartime series, 1939-46, 11 vols., edited by
A.J. Toynbee; increasingly dated, but a useful starting
point for informed contemporary analysis; accompanied by
Documents on International Affairs, 1928-63, edited by
John W. Wheeler-Bennett and others (London, 1929-73); the
1963 volume in both series the last to be published by
Chatham House; see also Consolidated Index to the Survey
of International Affairs, 1920-1938, and Documents on
International Affairs, 1920-1938, edited by Edith M.R.
Ditmas (London, 1967); and D.C. Watt, "Contemporary
History and the Survey of International Affairs", in The
Study of International Affairs: Essays in Honour of
Kenneth Younger, edited by Roger Morgan (London, 1972).

Annual Surveys and News Digests

208. Statesman's Year-Book: Statistical and Historical Annual of the States of the World, 1864-. Vol. 1-. London, 1864-.

Compendium of ducuments, statistics and current information on politics, economics and society worldwide.

209. The Times, London. Index to The Times, 1906-. Vol. 1-. London, 1907-.

Title and frequency varies; detailed alphabetical index, giving date, page and columns; from 1973 renamed The Times Index; also indexes Sunday Times, Times Educational Supplement, Times Literary Supplement, and Times Higher Education Supplement.

210. Webber, Rosemary. World List of National Newspapers: A Union List of National Newspapers in Libraries in the British Isles. London, 1976.

Title listing with index by country; excluded are the holdings of the British Library's Newspaper Library at Colindale.

Encyclopedias and Dictionaries

211. Abraham, Louis Arnold, and Hawtrey, Stephen Charles. A Parliamentary Dictionary. 2nd rev. ed. London, 1964.

Definitions and some longer articles on British parliamentary practice and procedure; see also Norman W. Wilding and Philip Laundy, An Encyclopaedia of Parliament, 4th ed., rev. (New York, 1971).

212. Académie Diplomatique Internationale. Dictionnaire diplomatique. Edited by A.-F. Frangulis. 7 vols. Paris, 1933-68.

A standard reference work; vol. 5 for biographical details.

213. Diplomaticheskii slovar'. Edited by A.A. Gromyko, et al. 3 vols. Moscow, 1971-73.

Dictionary of modern diplomacy and international affairs, with Soviet emphasis; vol. 3 for index of subjects by country and register of current diplomatic officials.

REFERENCE WORKS

Encyclopedias and Dictionaries

214. Encyclopaedia Britannica: A New Survey of Universal
     Knowledge. 1st–14th eds. Chicago, 1768–.

     14th edition, 1929, contained signed articles, many by
     prominent diplomatic personalities, on current topics;
     vol. 1 contains a list of initials, names of contributors
     and their separate subjects.

215. Haensch, Günther, ed. Dictionary of International
     Relations and Politics: Systematic and Alphabetical in
     Four Languages – German, English/American, French,
     Spanish. 2nd ed. Munich, 1975.

     Grouped by subject; detailed table of contents and index.

216. Huggett, Frank E. A Dictionary of British History,
     1815–1973. Oxford, 1974.

217. Kenyon, J.P., ed. A Dictionary of British History.
     London, 1981.

218. Marwick, Arthur, ed. The Illustrated Dictionary of
     British History. London, 1980.

     Entire span of British history; 2000 short entries on
     topics and people.

219. Mourre, Michel. Dictionnaire d'histoire universelle.
     Paris, 1968.

     Includes events, institutions and persons.

220. Palmer, Alan. The Penguin Dictionary of Twentieth
     Century History, 1900–1982. London, 1983.

     See also his The Penguin Dictionary of Modern History
     (London, 1983).

221. Parrish, Thomas, and Marshall, S.L.A., eds. The Simon
     and Schuster Encyclopedia of World War II. New York,
     1978.

     See also The Historical Encyclopedia of World War II,
     edited by Marcel Baudot, et al. (London, 1980).

222. Plano, Jack C., and Olton, Roy, eds. The International
     Relations Dictionary. 3rd ed. Santa Barbara, CA,
     1982.

     Definitions of terms in twelve topical chapters.

Encyclopedias and Dictionaries

223. Seth, Ronald. <u>Encyclopaedia of Espionage</u>. London, 1972.

     Emphasis on Anglo-Soviet-American activities, especially
     in world war two; see also Vincent and Nan Buranelli,
     <u>Spy-Counterspy: An Encyclopedia of Espionage</u> (New York,
     1982).

224. Steinberg, Sigfrid H., and Evans, I.H., eds.
     <u>Steinberg's Dictionary of British History</u>. 2nd ed.
     London, 1970.

     No biographical entries; does not quite supersede J.A.
     Brendon, <u>A Dictionary of British History</u> (London, 1937),
     in which biographical entries take up more than half the
     book.

225. Vincent, Jack Ernest. <u>A Handbook of International
     Relations: A Guide to Terms, Theory and Practice</u>.
     Woodbury, NY, 1969.

Statistical and Factual

226. <u>An Almanack, 1869-</u>. Vol. 1-, 1869. London, 1869-.

     Also known as <u>Whitaker's Almanack</u>; sub-titled: <u>An
     Account of the Astronomical and other Phenomena and a
     Vast Amount of Information respecting the Government,
     Finances, Population, Commerce, and General Statistics of
     the Various Nations of the World with an Index</u>.

227. Butler, David E., and Sloman, Anne. <u>British Political
     Facts, 1900-1979</u>. London, 1980.

     Offers detailed charts, tables and information on
     ministries, party and election statistics, treaties,
     etc.

228. Central Statistical Office. <u>Annual Abstract of
     Statistics</u>. Vol. 1-, 1840/53-. London, 1854-.

     Annual; vols. 1-83 issued as <u>Statistical Abstract for the
     United Kingdom</u>, covering preceding fifteen years; vol. 83
     for 1924-38, published in 1940; vol. 84 appeared in 1948
     and covered 1935-46.

229. Cook, Chris, and Stevenson, John. <u>Longman Handbook of
     Modern British History, 1714-1980: Essential Facts and
     Figures</u>. London, 1983.

REFERENCE WORKS

Statistical and Factual

230. Feinstein, C.H. Statistical Tables of National Income,
     Expenditure and Output of the United Kingdom,
     1855-1965. London, 1976.

231. Kendall, Maurice G., ed. Sources and Nature of the
     Statistics of the United Kingdom. 2 vols. London,
     1952-57.

232. League of Nations. Statistical Yearbook of the League of
     Nations, 1926-1942/44. Geneva, 1927-45.

     Annual survey of worldwide business and commerce;
     continued by the Statistical Yearbook of the United
     Nations (1949-).

233. Mitchell, Brian R., and Deane, Phyllis, eds. Abstract of
     British Historical Statistics. London, 1962.

     Tables of economic historical statistics, with
     commentaries and sources, to 1938; continued and expanded
     to 1965 in Brian R. Mitchell and H.G. Jones, Second
     Abstract of British Historical Statistics (London, 1971).

234. Powicke, Sir F.M., and Fryde, E.B., eds. Handbook of
     British Chronology: Royal Historical Society Guides
     and Handbooks, no. 2. 2nd ed. London, 1961.

     Includes lists of rulers, officers of state and
     parliamentary tables; see also Christopher Robert Cheney,
     Handbook of Dates for Students of English History: Royal
     Historical Society Guides and Handbooks, no. 4 (London,
     1955).

Atlases and Gazetteers

235. American Geographical Society, Map Department. Index to
     Maps in Books and Periodicals. 10 vols. Boston, MA,
     1968.

     Useful guide to maps that were published in books; 1st
     supplement (1971).

236. Banks, Arthur. A World Atlas of Military History. New
     York, 1973-.

     Vol. 3 for 1861-1945 (1978).

237. Bartholomew Gazetteer of Britain. Compiled by Oliver
     Mason. Edinburgh, 1977.

Atlases and Gazetteers

Statistical section updated to 1971 census; see also The Times Index-Gazetteer of the World (London, 1965).

238. Bickmore, D.P., and Shaw, M.A. Atlas of Britain and Northern Ireland. London, 1963.

Intended as a genuinely national atlas; mainly physical and economic maps of Britain at mid-century.

239. Cook, Chris, and Stevenson, John, comps. Longman Atlas of Modern British History: A Visual Guide to British Society and Politics, 1700-1970. London, 1978.

Divided into economic, social and political history.

240. Darby, H.C., and Fullard, Harold, eds. The New Cambridge Modern History Atlas. London, 1970.

288 pages of maps, with subject index; vol. 14 of the New Cambridge Modern History, vol. 1- (London, 1957-).

241. Freeman-Grenville, G.S.P. An Atlas of British History. London, 1979.

From prehistoric times to 1978; likewise see also Malcolm Falkus and John Gillingham, eds., Historical Atlas of Britain (London, 1981).

242. Gilbert, Martin. British History Atlas. London, 1968.

About twenty of 118 maps deal with the twentieth century; all maps enhanced with additional historical information; among his other such atlases see also The Macmillan Atlas of the Holocaust (New York, 1982); First World War History Atlas (London, 1971); Recent History Atlas: 1870 to the Present Day (London, 1966).

243. Horrabin, James F. An Atlas-History of the Second Great War. 10 vols. London, 1942-46.

See also The Oxford War Atlas, 4 vols. (New York, 1941-46); and Peter Young, ed., Atlas of the Second World War (London, 1973).

244. The Times, London. The Times Atlas of the World: Mid-Century Edition. Edited by John Bartholomew and Times Publication Company. 5 vols. London, 1955-59.

Atlases and Gazetteers

Each volume covers a different section of the world, and each has its own index-gazetteer; see also The Times Atlas of the World: Comprehensive Edition, 2nd rev. ed. (London, 1971); and The Times Concise Atlas of World History, edited by Geoffrey Barraclough (London, 1978).

3. Scholarly Journals

Guides, Lists and Indexes

245. Boehm, Eric H., and Adolphus, Lalit. Historical Periodicals: An Annotated World List of Historical and Related Serial Publications. Santa Barbara, CA, 1961.

More than 4,500 current titles, arranged by country and area; an expanded version in Historical Periodicals Directory, vol. 1- (Santa Barbara, CA, 1981-); vol. 2 for western European periodicals, annuals and serial publications.

246. British Humanities Index, 1962-. London, 1963-.

Quarterly, with annual cumulation, containing separate subject and author sections; indexes about 400 British periodicals; formerly Subject Index to Periodicals, 1915-1961 (London, 1919-62); annual, 1915-22, 1926-53; quarterly, with annual cumulations, 1954-61.

247. British Union-Catalogue of Periodicals: A Record of the Periodicals of the World, from the Seventeenth Century to the Present Day, in British Libraries. Edited by J.D. Stewart, et al. 4 vols. London, 1955-58.

Supplement to 1960 (London, 1962); lists more than 140,000 titles filed in 441 libraries in the United Kingdom; then as British Union-Catalogue of Periodicals, Incorporating 'World List of Periodicals': New Periodical Titles, 1960-68, 1969-73; annual afterwards.

248. The Combined Retrospective Index Set to Journals in History, 1838-1974. Edited by Annadel N. Wile. 11 vols. Washington, DC, 1977.

Vols. 1-4 for world history; vols. 10-11, author index; English language journals.

249. Harrison, Royden John, et al. The Warwick Guide to British Labour Periodicals, 1790-1970: A Check List. Hassocks, 1977.

Guides, Lists and Indexes

Over 4,000 titles with library locations.

250. Historical Abstracts 1775-1945: Bibliography of the World's Periodical Literature. Vol. 1-, 1955-. Edited by Eric H. Boehm. Santa Barbara, CA, 1955-.

Signed abstract articles on all aspects of history from 1775 to 1945 published by 1964; beginning vol. 17, 1971, published in two parts: Part B for the twentieth century; indexes over 2,000 periodicals including articles in transactions, proceedings and Festschriften; five-year indexes, beginning vols. 17-20 (1970-74), for Part B; from vol. 31 (1980) includes books and theses; data base available for on-line computer search.

251. Index to Book Reviews in Historical Periodicals, 1972-. Metuchen, NJ, 1976-.

Annual index to reviews in about 100 English language periodicals; entry by author, with a title index; each volume includes approximately 5,000 reviews; see also Book Review Digest: Author/Title Index, 1905-1974, edited by Leslie Dunmore-Leiber, 4 vols. (New York, 1976).

252. Kirby, J.L. A Guide to Historical Periodicals in the English Language. London, 1970.

Historical Association, Helps for Students of History, no. 80; annotated list by period, area and specialization.

253. Kramm, Heinrich. Bibliographie Historischer Zeit-schriften, 1939-1951. 3 vols. Marburg, 1952-54.

Vol. 2 for Britain; list of historical periodicals, subdivided by subject.

254. Marconi, Joseph V. Indexed Periodicals: A Guide to 170 Years of Coverage in 33 Indexing Services. Ann Arbor, MI, 1976.

255. Readers' Guide to Periodical Literature, 1900-. Vol. 1-. New York, 1905-.

A cumulative index to 176 general interest periodicals.

256. Social Sciences Citation Index, 1972-. Philadelphia, PA, 1973-.

SCHOLARLY JOURNALS

Guides, Lists and Indexes

> International index to principal journals in the social
> sciences; data base for on-line computer searching for
> 1969 to the present.

257. Social Sciences and Humanities Index: Formerly Inter-
     national Index, 1907/15-74. New York, 1916-74.

> A cumulative index of scholarly journals from Britain and
> the United States; superseded by Humanities Index, vol.
> 1- (New York, 1974-), and Social Sciences Index, vol. 1-
> (New York, 1974-); both quarterly, with annual
> cumulation.

258. Steiner, Dale R. Historical Journals: A Handbook for
     Writers and Reviewers. Santa Barbara, CA, 1981.

> Information about the editorial policies and publishing
> requirements of more than 350 American and Canadian
> historical journals.

259. Ulrich's International Periodicals Directory: A
     Classified Guide to Current Periodicals, Foreign and
     Domestic. New York, 1932-.

> Standard and comprehensive work; see also the companion
> Irregular Serials and Annuals: An International
> Directory (New York, 1967-); and Ulrich's Quarterly,
> vol. 1-, Spring 1977- (New York, 1977-); records new
> serial titles, title changes and cessations; all Ulrich's
> publications available for computer search.

260. Woodward, David P. Guide to Current British Journals.
     2 vols. 2nd ed. London, 1973.

> Vol. 1 for information on more than 4,700 current
> periodicals, societies and their publications; vol. 2 is
> a directory of publishers.

Select British Titles

261. British Journal of International Studies. Edinburgh,
     1975-. Quarterly.

> Important contributions on foreign policy, especially the
> debate on appeasement.

262. Bulletin of the Institute of Historical Research.
     London, 1923-. Semiannual.

83

Select British Titles

Emphasis on bibliographical articles, 'notes and documents' and historical news; issues regular theses supplement, and corrections to Dictionary of National Biography; until 1953, vol. 26, included migrations of historical manuscripts.

263. Bulletin of the John Rylands Library. Manchester, 1903-. Biannual.

Miscellaneous contents; several other British libraries produce their own journals, with occasional historical articles; see for example The Bodleian Library Record (1914-); and The British Museum Quarterly (1926-).

264. English Historical Review. London, 1886-. Quarterly.

Among the leading British scholarly journals; numerous book reviews; longer articles sometimes published as Supplements.

265. Historical Journal. Cambridge, 1958-. Quarterly since 1969.

Formerly Cambridge Historical Journal, 1923-1957; few book reviews but significant articles on twentieth century foreign policy.

266. History: The Journal of the British Historical Association. London, 1912-. Triannual.

About 5-6 articles per issue; emphasis on British and European history; extensive review articles, editorial notes and book reviews.

267. History Today. London, 1951-. Monthly.

An illustrated magazine with short articles often written by professional historians.

268. International Affairs. London, 1922-. Quarterly.

Journal of the Royal Institute of International Affairs; by this title known from 1922-30; many government spokesmen contributed articles during 1918-1945 period; good book review section.

269. Journal of American Studies. Cambridge, 1967-. Tri-annual.

SCHOLARLY JOURNALS

Select British Titles

> For the British Association for American Studies;
> includes history, mainly by British historians; other
> area journals include Journal of African History (1960-);
> Slavonic and East European Review (1922-); Journal of
> Latin American Studies (1969-); Soviet Studies (1949-);
> European Studies Review (1971-); Journal of Imperial and
> Commonwealth History (1972-); Middle Eastern Studies
> (1964-); and Bulletin of the British Society for Middle
> Eastern Studies (1974-).

270. Journal of Contemporary History. London, 1966-.
     Quarterly.

     Specializes in twentieth century history; occasional
     thematic volumes; numerous contributions on foreign
     affairs.

271. Journal of the Royal United Service Institution. London,
     1857-. Quarterly.

     Minor variations in title; articles on current
     international relations and strategic studies; see also
     The Consolidated Author and Subject Index to the Journal
     of the Royal United Service Institution, 1857-1963,
     edited by Robin Higham (Ann Arbor, MI, 1964).

272. Millennium: Journal of International Studies. London,
     1972-. Quarterly.

     From the London School of Economics and Political
     Science; scholarly articles on international affairs.

273. Past and Present: A Journal of Historical Studies.
     Oxford, 1951-. Quarterly since 1969.

     Articles, debates and discussions; few reviews.

274. Political Quarterly. London, 1930-. Quarterly.

     Articles on British domestic and foreign policies.

275. Proceedings of the British Academy. London, 1903-.
     Annual.

     Usually publishes one historical lecture by fellows;
     includes obituary notices of historians who were fellows.

276. Round Table: The Commonwealth Journal of International
     Affairs. London, 1910-. Quarterly.

Select British Titles

> Founded in 1910 to promote imperial unity; inter-war articles reflect informed opinion on foreign and Commonwealth policies.

277. Times Literary Supplement, London, 1902-. Weekly.

> Currently publishes extensive review articles; Index, 1902-1939 (London, 1978).

278. Transactions of the Royal Historical Society. Fourth Series, vols. 1-32, London, 1918-50. Fifth Series, vol. 1-, London, 1951-. Annual.

> Contains eight papers read to the society in the previous year; see also A Centenary Guide to the Publications of the Royal Historical Society, 1868-1968, and of the Former Camden Society, 1838-1897, compiled by A.T. Milne (London, 1968).

279. Wiener Library Bulletin. London, 1947-. Quarterly.

> Largely reflects research interests of the Wiener Library and the Institute of Contemporary History; particularly totalitarianism and antisemitism; see also The Wiener Library Bulletin Index 1946/47-1968, compiled by Helen Kehr (Nendeln, 1979).

B. PARLIAMENT AND GOVERNMENT

1. Records, Guides and Indexes

280. Catalogue of Government Publications, 1922-.   London,
    1923-.

    Annual; continues the Quarterly List ... of Official
    Publications (London, 1897-1922); usefully amalgamated in
    Ruth Matteson Blackmore, comp., Cumulative Index to the
    Annual Catalogues of Her Majesty's Stationery Office
    Publications, 1922-1972, 2 vols. (Washington, DC, 1976).

281. Comfort, A.F., and Loveless, Christine. Guide to Govern-
    ment Data: A Survey of Unpublished Social Science
    Material in Libraries of Government Departments in
    London. London, 1974.

    Provides information on published and unpublished
    materials produced from 1940.

282. Craig, F.W.S. British Parliamentary Election Statistics,
    1918-1968. Glasgow, 1968.

    See also his British Parliamentary Election Results,
    1918-1949, rev. ed. (London, 1977); British General
    Election Manifestos, 1918-1966 (Chichester, 1970);
    Boundaries of Parliamentary Constituencies, 1885-1972
    (Chichester, 1972); and Minor Parties at British
    Parliamentary Elections, 1885-1974 (London, 1975).

283. Englefield, Dermot. Parliament and Information. London,
    1981.

284. Ford, Percy, and Ford, Grace. A Guide to Parliamentary
    Papers: What They Are; How to Find Them; How to Use
    Them. 3rd ed. Shannon, 1972.

    An introductory guide; with an appendix for lists of
    indexes, guides and catalogues to sources; see also the
    same authors' A Breviate of Parliamentary Papers,
    1917-1939 (Oxford, 1951); continued in A Breviate of
    Parliamentary Papers, 1940-1954: War and Reconstruction
    (Oxford, 1961).

285. Kinnear, Michael. The British Voter: An Atlas and
     Survey since 1885. London, 1981.

     Examines "the social, economic and organisation
     background of British politics" (Introduction); numerous
     tables and maps.

286. Ollé, James G. An Introduction to British Government
     Publications. 2nd ed. London, 1973.

     Including parliamentary and non-parliamentary
     publications; see also Frank Rodgers, A Guide to British
     Government Publications (New York, 1980); and David
     Butcher, Official Publications in Britain (London, 1983).

287. Parliament, House of Commons. General Alphabetical Index
     to the Bills, Reports, Estimates, Accounts and Papers
     Printed by Order of the House of Commons and to the
     Papers Presented by Command, 1801-1949. London,
     1853-1960.

     In progress; vol. 4 for general index, 1900-1949; a
     useful finding tool is Edward Di Roma and Joseph A.
     Rosenthal, comps., A Numerical Finding list of British
     Command Papers Published 1833-1962 (New York, 1967).

288. Parliament, House of Commons. General Index to the
     Bills, Reports and Papers, Printed by Order of the
     House of Commons and to the Reports and Papers
     Presented by Command, 1900-1948/49. London, 1960.

     Subject index to documents included in parliamentary
     papers of House of Commons.

289. Parliament. Parliamentary Debates: House of Commons;
     House of Lords. Fifth Series. vol. 1-. London,
     1909-.

     Official, complete and verbatim reports of debates and
     all division lists; sessional indexes.

290. Pemberton, John E. British Official Publications. 2nd
     rev. ed. London, 1973.

     Detailed description and explanation of various
     categories of government publications; useful table of
     command papers and royal commissions; see also Directory
     of British Official Publications: A Directory of
     Sources, compiled by Stephen Richard (London, 1981).

291. Richard, Stephen. <u>British Government Publications: An Index to Chairmen and Authors</u>. 3 vols. London, 1982.

For committees and commissions of inquiry; vol. 2 for 1900-40; vol. 3 for 1941-78; supersedes Annie Mary Morgan, ed., <u>British Government Publications: An Index to Chairmen and Authors, 1941-1966</u> (London, 1969).

292. Rodgers, Frank. <u>Serial Publications in the British Parliamentary Papers, 1900-1968: A Bibliography</u>. Chicago, IL, 1971.

About 130 serials in the House of Commons Sessional Papers; arranged by issuing agency.

293. Sims, John. <u>A List and Index of Parliamentary Papers Relating to India, 1908-1947</u>. London, 1981.

294. Staveley, Ronald, and Piggott, Mary. <u>Government Information and the Research Worker</u>. 2nd rev. ed. London, 1965.

Information on resources, facilities and services; separate chapter on the Foreign Office.

2. Treaties: Guides and Texts

295. Carnegie Endowment for International Peace. <u>The Treaties of Peace, 1919-1923</u>. 2 vols. New York, 1924.

296. Foreign Office. <u>British and Foreign State Papers, 1812-</u>. Vol. 1-. London, 1841-.

Annual with some delays; confidential papers not included; each volume contains country-subject index and chronological list of documents; beginning with vol. 116, 1922, incorporates <u>Hertslet's Commercial Treaties</u>, 31 vols. (London, 1827-1925).

297. Foreign Office. <u>Treaty Series, 1892-</u>. London, 1892-.

Issued as command papers, although numbered and indexed to be bound separately; periodic general indexes; for a complete consolidated index see Clive Parry and Charity Hopkins, <u>An Index of British Treaties, 1101-1968</u>, 3 vols. (London, 1970).

298. Grenville, J.A.S., ed. <u>The Major International Treaties 1914-1973: A History and Guide with Texts</u>. London, 1974.

299. Israel, Fred L., ed. Major Peace Treaties of Modern History, 1648-1967. 4 vols. New York, 1967.

300. League of Nations. Treaty Series: Publication of Treaties and International Engagements Registered with the Secretariat of the League. 205 vols. Geneva, 1920-46.

Index compiled every 500 treaties; for earlier period see The Consolidated Treaty Series, edited by Clive Parry, vol. 1- (New York, 1969-).

301. Mostecky, Vaclav, ed. Index to Multilateral Treaties: A Chronological List of Multi-Party International Agreements from the Sixteenth Century through 1963, with Citations to their Text. Cambridge, MA, 1965.

302. Rohn, Peter H. World Treaty Index. 5 vols. 2nd ed. Santa Barbara, CA, 1983.

Index and inventory to almost 45,000 treaties; vol. 1 for League of Nations treaty series; vol. 3 includes national treaty collections; vols. 4-5 contain index sections.

303. Toscano, Mario. The History of Treaties and International Politics, vol. 1, An Introduction to the History of Treaties and International Politics: The Documentary and Memoir Sources. Baltimore, MD, 1966.

Analysis of the variety of diplomatic documents with a chapter on treaty collections.

304. United Nations Secretariat. Systematic Survey of Treaties for the Pacific Settlement of International Disputes, 1928-1948. Lake Success, NY, 1949.

3. Official Diplomatic Series and Coloured Books

British

305. Cabinet Office, Cabinet History Series. Principal War Telegrams and Memoranda, 1940-1943. 7 vols. London, 1976.

Mainly telegrams exchanged between London and commanders in the field; arranged geographically for Middle East, Far East, India, Washington and miscellaneous.

DIPLOMATIC SERIES AND COLOURED BOOKS

British

306. Foreign Office. Documents on British Foreign Policy, 1919-1939. Edited by Sir Llewellyn Woodward, Rohan Butler, W.N. Medlicott, et al. London, 1946-.

In progress; Series 1, 1919-29, vols. 1-23, covers 1919-23 (1949-81); Series 1A, 1925-29, vols. 1-7, complete (1966-76); Series 2, 1929-38, vols. 1-19, covers 1930-38 (1946-82); Series 3, March 1938 - 3 September 1939, vols. 1-10, complete (1946-61); editors given "access to all papers in the Foreign Office Archives, and freedom in the selection and arrangement of documents" (Preface); chronological presentation of documents with reference given to original Foreign Office file numbers.

307. Foreign Office. Documents Concerning German-Polish Relations and the Outbreak of Hostilities Between Great Britain and Germany on September 3, 1939. Cmd. 6106. London, 1939.

Last of the inter-war foreign affairs command papers, or "Blue Books", presented to parliament; a convenient and thorough guide to all such material is Robert Vogel, A Breviate of British Diplomatic Blue Books, 1919-1939 (Montreal, Quebec, 1963); arranged chronologically with subject index.

Non-British

308. Australia, Department of Foreign Affairs. Documents on Australian Foreign Policy, 1937-1949. Edited by R.G. Neale. Vol. 1-. Canberra, 1975-.

309. Belgium, Académie Royale de Belgique. Documents diplomatiques belges, 1920-1940. Edited by Charles de Visscher and Fernand Vanlangenhove. 5 vols. Brussels, 1964-66.

310. Belgium, Ministry of Foreign Affairs. The Official Account of What Happened, 1939-1940. New York, 1940.

Foreign coloured books for the period 1918-45 are numerous and often difficult to locate; others on the immediate origins and early years of the war include France, Ministère des Affaires Etrangères, Le Livre Jaune Français: Documents diplomatiques, 1938-1939, Pièces relatives aux événements et aux négociations qui ont précédé l'ouverture des hostilités entre l'Allemagne d'une part, la Pologne, la Grande-Bretagne et la France d'autre part (Paris, 1939); (Eng. trans., London, 1940);

Non-British

Germany, Auswärtiges Amt, <u>Dokumente zur Vorgeschichte des</u>
<u>Krieges, Weissbuch 1940</u>, Nr. 3 (Berlin, 1939); one of
several such German publications; Greece, Ministry of
Foreign Affairs, <u>The Greek White Book: Diplomatic</u>
<u>Documents Relating to Italy's Aggression against Greece</u>
(London, 1942); Netherlands, Ministry of Foreign Affairs,
<u>Netherlands Orange Book: Summary of the Principal</u>
<u>Matters dealt with... in Connection with the State of</u>
<u>War....</u> (Leiden, 1940); Poland, Ministry of Foreign
Affairs, <u>The Polish White Book: Official Documents</u>
<u>Concerning Polish-German and Polish-Soviet Relations,</u>
<u>1933-1939</u> (London, 1940).

311. Canada, Department of External Affairs. <u>Documents on</u>
     <u>Canadian External Relations</u>. Vol. 1-. Ottawa,
     Ontario, 1967-.

     Vols. 1-9 cover period 1908-43.

312. France, Ministère des Affaires Etrangères. <u>Documents</u>
     <u>diplomatiques français, 1932-1939</u>. Paris, 1963-.

     Series 1 for July 1932-December 1935; series 2 for
     1936-39; no similar series for earlier or later period.

313. Germany, Auswärtiges Amt. <u>Documents on German Foreign</u>
     <u>Policy, 1918-1945</u>. Edited by an Anglo-French-American
     board of editors. Five series. Washington and London,
     1949-.

     English translation for Series C, to cover Jan.
     1933-Aug. 1937; Series D, complete in 13 vols., covers
     Sept. 1937-Dec. 1941; German only, <u>Akten zur deutschen</u>
     <u>auswärtigen Politik, 1918-1945</u> (Baden-Baden and
     Göttingen, 1950-), for Series A, to cover 1918-Nov. 1925;
     Series B, to cover Dec. 1925-Jan. 1933; Series E,
     complete in 8 vols., covers Dec. 1941-45.

314. Hungary, Ministry of Foreign Affairs. <u>Papers and</u>
     <u>Documents Relating to the Foreign Relations of</u>
     <u>Hungary</u>. Budapest, 1939-46.

     Only two volumes, covering 1919-Aug. 1921 published;
     continued in various other publications; see for example
     Institute of History of the Hungarian Academy of
     Sciences, <u>Diplomáciai iratok Magyarság</u>
     <u>külpolitikájahoz, 1936-1945</u>, edited by Lásló Zsigmond
     (Budapest, 1962-); 5 vols. to 1982; the last volume
     covering 1940-41.

Non-British

315. Italy, Ministero degli Affari Esteri, Commissione per la
     Pubblicazione dei Documenti Diplomatici Italiani. I
     documenti diplomatici italiani, 1861-1943. Nine
     Series. Rome, 1952-.

     Series 6 for 1918-22; Series 7, 1922-35, Series 8, 1935-
     39; Series 9, 1939-43.

316. New Zealand, Department of Internal Affairs. Documents
     Relating to New Zealand's Participation in the Second
     World War, 1939-1945. 3 vols. Wellington, 1949-63.

317. Portugal, Ministério dos Negócios Estrangeiros. Dez
     anos de politica externa, 1936-1947: A naçao
     portuguesa e a segunda guerra mundial. Lisbon, 1961-.

     Vol. 1 for relations with Britain, 1936-39.

318. Reparation Commission. Official Documents. 23 vols.
     London, 1922-30.

319. United States, Department of State. Foreign Relations
     of the United States: Diplomatic Papers. Washington,
     DC, 1861-.

     Until 1931 entitled Papers Relating to the Foreign
     Relations of the United States; complete for 1918-45.

320. USSR, Ministerstvo Inostrannikh Del SSSR. Dokumenti
     vneshnei politiki SSSR. Edited by A.A. Gromyko, et
     al. Vol. 1-. Moscow, 1957-.

     Documents from Soviet archives and foreign sources;
     vols. 1-21 for 1917-38; last vol. published 1977.

321. USSR and German Democratic Republic, Ministerstvo
     Inostrannikh Del SSSR i Ministerstvo Inostrannich Del
     GDR. Sovetsko-Germanskie otnosheniia ot peregovorov v
     Brest-Litovske do podpisaniia rapallskogo dogovora.
     Moscow, 1968-.

322. USSR and Poland, Academiia Nauk SSSR i Polskaia
     Academiia Nauk. Dokumenti i materiali po istorii
     sovetsko-polskikh otnoshenii. Edited by I.A. Khrenov,
     et al. Vol. 1-. Moscow, 1963-.

     Vols. 1-8 for 1917-45.

Non-British

323. Vatican, Secrétairerie d'Etat. <u>Actes et documents du
     Saint Siège relatifs à la seconde guerre mondiale</u>.
     Edited by Pierre Blet, et al. 11 vols. Rome, 1965-80.

4. British Official Histories

Historical works, sponsored by the British government and
published under its auspices, are known as official histories.
For the first world war the British government commissioned
mainly military histories. A series of economic and social
histories was sponsored and published by the Carnegie Endowment for International Peace. In 1942 the British war cabinet
decided that a series of civil histories should be commissioned, covering the economic, administrative and social experience of the war. Initially, these histories were intended
for confidential use, their purpose being "to fund experience
for Government use". A military series, including studies of
foreign policy and intelligence, and a medical series were
added after the war. At that time it was decided to release
all these volumes to the public. The original publication
dates, constrained by the then existing fifty year rule, included references only to publicly available documents.
Reprints of many of these volumes, however, are now available
with source references to confidential departmental files once
again a part of the text.

Guides and Historiography

324. Butler, J.R.M. "The British Official Military History of
     the Second World War." <u>Military Affairs</u>, 22(1958),
     149-51.

325. Connell, John. "Official History and the Unofficial
     Historian." <u>Journal of the Royal United Services
     Institution</u>, 110(1965), 329-34.

326. Edmonds, Sir James E., and "Pardon". "The British
     Official Histories of the Two World Wars." <u>Army
     Quarterly</u>, 64(1952), 196-205.

327. Higham, Robin, ed. <u>Official Histories: Essays and
     Bibliographies from around the World</u>. Manhattan, KS,
     1970.

     A useful survey by country of official histories
     world-wide; see also his "The History of the Second World
     War: British Official Series", <u>Library Quarterly</u>,
     34(1964), 240-48.

BRITISH OFFICIAL HISTORIES

Guides and Historiography

328. HMSO. <u>Histories of the First and Second World Wars:
Government Publications Sectional List, no. 60.</u>
London, 1982.

Complete annotated list of British official histories;
notes which are still in print, reprints and prices.

Official Histories

329. Foot, M.R.D. <u>S.O.E. in France: An Account of the Work
of the British Special Operations Executive in France,
1940-1941.</u> London, 1966.

An official history, though not part of the series edited
by Sir James Butler; commissioned by the Foreign Office.

330. Hinsley, F.H., et al. <u>British Intelligence in the
Second World War: Its Influence on Strategy and
Operations.</u> London, 1979-.

Not published by HMSO, but an official history; vol. 1
from Sept. 1939-June 1941; vol. 2, June 1941-1943 (1981);
vol. 3 will continue to the end of the war and contain a
full bibliography.

331. <u>History of the Second World War: United Kingdom Civil
Series.</u> Edited by Sir Keith Hancock. London, HMSO,
1949-62.

Relevant volumes include C.B.A. Behrens, <u>Merchant
Shipping and the Demands of War</u> (London, 1955, repr.
1978); Central Statistical Office, <u>Statistical Digest of
the War</u> (London, 1951, repr. 1975); H. Duncan Hall, <u>North
American Supply</u> (London, 1956, repr. 1982); H. Duncan
Hall, et al., <u>Studies of Overseas Supply</u> (London, 1956,
repr. 1982); W.K. Hancock and M.M. Gowing, <u>British War
Economy</u> (London, 1949, repr. 1975); William N. Medlicott,
<u>Economic Blockade,</u> 2 vols. (London, 1952-59, repr. 1978);
T.H. O'Brien, <u>Civil Defence</u> (London, 1955, repr. 1982);
D.J. Payton-Smith, <u>Oil: A Study in Wartime Policy and
Administration</u> (London, 1971); M.M. Postan, <u>British War
Production</u> (London, 1952, repr. 1975); M.M. Postan, et
al., <u>Design and Development of Weapons</u> (London, 1964,
repr. 1971); R.S. Sayers, <u>Financial Policy, 1939-1945</u>
(London, 1956, repr. 1982); and J.D. Scott and Richard
Hughes, <u>Administration of War Production</u> (London, 1955,
repr. 1982).

Official Histories

332. History of the Second World War: United Kingdom Military
     Histories. Edited by Sir James Butler. London, HMSO,
     London, 1952-.

     Relevant selected volumes include Basil Collier, The
     Defence of the United Kingdom (London, 1957); F.S.V.
     Donnison, Civil Affairs and Military Government: Central
     Organisation and Planning (London, 1966); his British
     Military Administration in the Far East (London, 1956);
     and Civil Affairs and Military Government in North-West
     Europe, 1944-1946 (London, 1961); Major L.F. Ellis, et
     al., Victory in the West, 1944-1945, 2 vols. (London,
     1962-69); and his The War in France and Flanders,
     1939-1940 (London, 1953); Norman H. Gibbs, et al., Grand
     Strategy, 1933-August 1945, 6 vols. (London, 1956-76,
     vols. 2, 6 repr. 1974); C.R.S. Harris, Allied Military
     Administration of Italy, 1943-1945 (London, 1957);
     Major-General S. Woodburn Kirby, et al., The War Against
     Japan, 5 vols. (London, 1962-69); Major-General I.S.O.
     Playfair, et al., The Mediterranean and the Middle East,
     6 vols. (London, 1954, vols. 1-3 repr. 1967-74); Captain
     Stephen W. Roskill, The War at Sea, 1939-1945, 3 vols.
     (London, 1954-61); and Sir Charles Webster and Noble
     Frankland, The Strategic Air Offensive Against Germany,
     1939-1945, 4 vols. (London, 1961).

333. Richards, Denis, and Saunders, Hilary St. G. History of
     the Royal Air Force, 1939-1945. 3 vols. London,
     1953-54, repr. 1975.

     Part of the HMSO series "Popular Military History".

334. Woodward, Sir Llewellyn. British Foreign Policy in the
     Second World War. 5 vols. London, 1971-76.

     The complete text with footnotes and references; single
     volume abridgement, with amendments but without
     references, published as British Foreign Policy in the
     Second World War (London, 1962, repr. 1972); both
     official histories, not part of the series edited by Sir
     James Butler, written under the auspices of the Cabinet
     Office.

C. MEMOIRS AND BIOGRAPHIES

Memoirs, diaries and collections of speeches and letters are a valuable source for the British diplomatic historian. Two aspects, however, pose immediate problems. Firstly, this literature is voluminous. Despite a propensity towards reticence and understatement in public life, former British officials seemingly cannot help putting pen to paper in retirement. A second problem relates to the quality of this memorialist output. As in all other branches of literature, it is naturally of uneven quality. But the researcher would be cautioned against treating this material lightly. In many cases, the reticence and understatement, carried into the written material, barely disguises revelations of the utmost value. In other words, British diplomatic memoirs must be read very carefully and between the lines. The rewards are often most gratifying.

The entries from this literature given below are necessarily selective. An attempt has been made to note only material having direct bearing on the foreign policy making process and its implementation. This is most widely interpreted in the case of British publications. There follows, in addition, a selection of non-British materials. Here the entries have been strictly limited to non-British diplomats and officials posted, at some point, to London.

It should be noted that career annotations are confined mainly to highlights between 1918 and 1945. Entries followed by an asterisk indicate that the writer has been the subject of a biography listed in the biographical section.

1. Memoirs, Diaries, Speeches and Letters

British

335. Addison, Christopher (1st Viscount Addison).* Politics from Within, 1911-1918. 2 vols. London, 1924.

Diary-based memoir of first minister of Health, 1919-21; minister without portfolio, 1921; minister of Agriculture and Fisheries, 1929-31; see also his Four and a Half Years: A Personal Diary from June 1914 to January 1919, 2 vols. (London, 1934).

British

336. Alexander, 1st Earl, of Tunis (Field Marshal Sir Harold
      R.L.G. Alexander).* The Alexander Memoirs, 1940-1945.
      Edited by John North. London, 1962.

    General officer commanding, Burma, 1942; commander-in-
    chief, Middle East, 1942-43; deputy commander-in-chief,
    North Africa, 1943; general officer commanding allied
    forces in Sicily, 1943-44; commander-in-chief, allied
    armies in Italy 1944.

337. Amery, Julian. Approach March: A Venture in Auto-
      biography. London, 1973.

    What he refers to as his "pre-political memoirs"
    (Preface); attaché British legation, Belgrade, 1939-40;
    with Albanian resistance, 1944; see also his Sons of the
    Eagle (London, 1948).

338. Amery, Leopold C.M.S. My Political Life. 3 vols.
      London, 1953-55.

    Memoirs by an independent Conservative; first lord of the
    Admiralty, 1922-24; secretary of state for the Colonies,
    1924-29; and for Dominion Affairs, 1925-29; see also his
    The German Colonial Claim (London, 1939); and John Barnes
    and David Nicholson, eds., The Leo Amery Diaries, vol. 1,
    1896-1929 (London, 1980-); includes diaries, and papers.

339. Angell, Sir Norman. After All. London, 1951.

    Memoirs by an author, lecturer, briefly an M.P., and
    Nobel peace prize winner for 1933; see also his widely
    translated The Great Illusion (London, 1910); and Peace
    with the Dictators (London, 1938).

340. Asquith, Herbert Henry (1st Earl of Oxford and
      Asquith).* Memories and Reflections, 1852-1927.
      2 vols. London, 1928.

    Wartime prime minister until 1916, and leader of the
    Liberal party until 1926; vol. 2 for post-war period; see
    also Speeches, 2 vols. (London, 1927); and H.H. Asquith:
    Letters to Venetia Stanley, edited by Michael and Eleanor
    Brock (London, 1982); of related interest is Margot
    Asquith, Autobiography, 2 vols. (London, 1920-22); More
    Memories (London, 1933); and Off the Record (London,
    1943).

341. Atholl, Duchess of (Katharine Marjory Stewart-Murray).
      Working Partnership. London, 1958.

British

Parliamentary secretary, Board of Education, 1924-29;
resigned parliamentary seat as protest against
appeasement, 1938.

342. Attlee, Clement Richard (1st Earl Attlee).* <u>As It
Happened</u>. London, 1954.

Member of both pre-world war two, Labour governments;
leader of the Labour party 1935-55; lord privy seal,
1940-42; deputy prime minister, 1942-45; prime minister,
1945-51; see also his <u>War Comes to Britain: Speeches of
the Rt. Hon. C.R. Attlee, M.P.</u>, edited by John Dugdale
(London, 1940); and <u>Purpose and Policy: Selected
Speeches, May 1945-November 1946</u> (London, 1947).

343. Avon, 1st Earl of (Robert Anthony Eden).* <u>The Eden
Memoirs</u>. 3 vols. London, 1960-65.

Carefully written memoirs, based on private papers and
government archives, of an M.P., 1923-57; various
positions in area of foreign affairs, 1926-35; secretary
of state for Foreign Affairs, 1935-38; for Dominion
Affairs, 1939-40; for War, 1940; for Foreign Affairs,
1940-45; later prime minister, 1955-57; memoirs written
in reverse order; hence vol. 2, <u>Facing the Dictators</u>,
examines the 1930s; vol. 3, <u>The Reckoning</u>, covers wartime
affairs; collected speeches and articles include <u>Places
in the Sun</u> (London, 1926); with preface by Stanley
Baldwin; <u>Foreign Affairs</u> (London, 1939); <u>Freedom and
Order: Selected Speeches 1939-1946</u> (London, 1947); for
an understanding of the personality, see his <u>Another
World, 1897-1917</u> (London, 1976).

344. Bailey, Frederick Marshman. <u>Mission to Tashkent</u>.
London, 1946.

Served world war one; political officer in Mesopotamia
and Persia, 1917-18; mission in central Asia, 1918-20;
political officer, Sikkim, 1921-28; minister to the court
of Nepal, 1935-38; see also his <u>No Passport to Tibet</u>
(London, 1957).

345. Baldwin, 1st Earl, of Bewdley (Stanley Baldwin)*. <u>This
Torch of Freedom: Speeches and Addresses</u>. London,
1935.

President of the Board of Trade, 1921-22; chancellor of
the Exchequer, 1922-23; prime minister, 1923-24, 1924-29,
1935-37; lord president of the Council, 1931-35; other

British

collections are On England (London, 1926); Our Inheritance (London, 1928); Service of Our Lives (London, 1937); and An Interpreter of England (London, 1939).

346. Balfour, Arthur James (1st Earl of Balfour).* Opinions and Argument from Speeches and Addresses of the Earl of Balfour, 1910-1927. London, 1927.

Prime minister, 1902-05; foreign secretary, 1916-19; lord president of the Council, 1919-22, 1925-29; see also his Chapters of Autobiography, edited by Blanche Dugdale (London, 1930).

347. Balfour, Harold (1st Baron Balfour of Inchrye). Wings Over Westminster. London, 1973.

M.P., 1929-45; parliamentary under-secretary of state for Air, 1938-44; minister resident in west Africa, 1944-45.

348. Barclay, Sir Roderick Edward. Ernest Bevin and the Foreign Office, 1932-1969. London, 1975.

A memoir despite the title; entered diplomatic service, 1932; served at embassies in Brussels, Paris, Washington, and in Foreign Office, 1932-46; counsellor in Foreign Office, 1946-49.

349. Barnes, George Nicoll. From Workshop to War Cabinet. London, 1924.

M.P., 1906-22; minister plenipotentiary, Paris peace conference, 1919; minister without portfolio, 1919.

350. Bartlett, Vernon. And Now, Tomorrow. London, 1960.

An autobiographical work from a very prolific writer, broadcaster, journalist and M.P.; London director of the League of Nations secretariat, 1922-32; see also his I Know What I Liked (London, 1975); This is My Life (London, 1937); and Behind the Scenes at the Paris Peace Conference, 1919 (London, 1919).

351. Beadon, Colonel Roger Hammet. Some Memories of the Peace Conference. London, 1933.

With British delegation to Paris peace conference, 1919; employed by Colonial Office in Iraq, 1925-28.

MEMOIRS

British

352. Bentwich, Norman and Helen. Mandate Memories, 1918-1948.
     London, 1964.

     Director of High Commission for Refugees from Germany,
     1933-35; attorney-general, government of Palestine,
     1920-31; among his numerous books see also My Seventy-
     Seven Years (London, 1962).

353. Bilainkin, George. Diary of a Diplomatic Correspondent.
     London, 1942.

     Excerpts for 1940; diplomatic correspondent for the
     Allied newspaper chain; see also his Second Diary of a
     Diplomatic Correspondent (London, 1947).

354. Birse, A.H. Memoirs of an Interpreter. London, 1967.

     Foreword by Lord Avon; joined intelligence department of
     War Office, 1940; subsequently, Russian language
     interpreter for Winston Churchill at major wartime
     conferences.

355. Boothby, Baron (Robert J.G. Boothby). Boothby:
     Recollections of a Rebel. London, 1978.

     Often in the public eye, but rarely in office; M.P.,
     1924-58; parliamentary private secretary to Winston S.
     Churchill, 1926-29; parliamentary secretary, ministry of
     Food, 1940-41; see also an earlier volume of memoirs, I
     Fight to Live (London, 1947); and the collection of
     articles, speeches and sketches in My Yesterday, Your
     Tomorrow (London, 1962).

356. Brabazon, 1st Baron, of Tara (John T.C. Moore
     Brabazon). The Brabazon Story. London, 1956.

     Parliamentary secretary, ministry of Transport, 1923-24,
     1924-27; minister of Transport, 1940-41; minister of
     Aircraft Production, 1941-42.

357. Brockway, Archibald Fenner. Inside the Left: Thirty
     Years of Platform, Press, Prison, and Parliament.
     London, 1942.

     Anti-war activist; prolific writer; and prominent
     I.L.P. and Labour party member; continued in Outside the
     Right (London, 1963); see also Towards Tomorrow (London,
     1977).

British

358. Brownrigg, Lieutenant-General Sir W. Douglas S.
   Unexpected: A Book of Memories. London, 1942.

   Served world war one; at War Office and in China,
   1919-31; commander various brigades, 1931-38; military
   secretary, secretary of state for War 1938-39;
   adjutant-general to BEF, 1939-40.

359. Bruce, Henry James. Silken Dalliance. 1946.

   Secretary-general, British delegation, interallied
   commission for Bulgaria, 1921; British delegate, 1924-26;
   adviser, National Bank of Hungary, 1931; see also his
   Thirty Dozen Moons (London, 1949).

360. Buchan, John (1st Baron Tweedsmuir).* Memory Hold-the-
   Door. London, 1940.

   Subordinate director, ministry of Information, 1917-18;
   M.P., 1927-35; governor-general, Canada, 1935-1940.

361. Buchanan, Sir George William. My Mission to Russia and
   Other Diplomatic Memories. 2 vols. London, 1923.

   Ambassador to Russia, 1910-18; Italy, 1919-21.

362. Bullard, Sir Reader William. The Camels Must Go: An
   Autobiography. London, 1961.

   Middle East department, Colonial Office, 1921; consul at
   Jedda, 1923-25; Athens, 1925-28; Addis Ababa, 1928;
   Moscow, 1930; Leningrad, 1931-34; Rabat, 1934; minister
   at Jedda, 1936-39; and Teheran, 1939-46.

363. Busk, Sir Douglas Laird. The Craft of Diplomacy.
   London, 1967.

   Joined diplomatic service, 1929; served in Foreign Office
   and Teheran, Budapest, Moscow, Tokyo, Ankara and Baghdad;
   later ambassador to Ethiopia, 1952-56.

364. Butler, Sir Harold Beresford. Confident Morning.
   London, 1950.

   Attended Paris peace conference, 1919; deputy-director
   and later director International Labour Office, 1920-38;
   minister in charge of British Information Services,
   Washington, 1942-46; see also his The Lost Peace: A
   Personal Impression (London, 1941).

MEMOIRS

Britist

365. Butler, R.A. "Rab" (1st Baron Butler).* The Art of the
     Possible. London, 1971.

     M.P., 1929-65; under-secretary of state for Foreign
     Affairs, 1938-41; minister of Education, 1941-45;
     additional reminiscences, including a sketch of Lord
     Halifax, in The Art of Memory: Friends in Perspective
     (London, 1982).

366. Cadogan, Sir Alexander. The Diaries of Sir Alexander
     Cadogan, O.M., 1938-1945. Edited by David Dilks.
     London, 1971.

     Indispensable diaries, well-edited, of the permanent
     under-secretary of state for Foreign Affairs, 1938-46.

367. Campbell, Sir Gerald. Of True Experience. London, 1949.

     Consul-general various cities in the United States,
     1920-38; high commissioner in Canada, 1938-41;
     director-general, British Information Services, New York,
     1941-42; minister at Washington, 1942-45.

368. Carton de Wiart, Sir Adrian. Happy Odyssey. London,
     1950.

     Served both world wars; head of British military mission
     in Poland, 1939.

369. Cecil, 1st Viscount, of Chelwood (E.A. Robert Cecil).* A
     Great Experiment. London, 1941.

     Mainly on the League; assistant secretary of state for
     Foreign Affairs, 1918; minister of Blockade, 1916-18;
     lord privy seal, 1923-24; chancellor of the Duchy of
     Lancaster, 1924-27; Nobel peace prize, 1937; see also his
     All the Way (London, 1949).

370. Chamberlain, Sir Austen.* Down the Years. London, 1935.

     M.P., 1892-1937; chancellor of the Exchequer, 1919-21;
     lord privy seal, 1921-22; foreign secretary, 1924-29;
     Nobel peace prize, 1925; first lord of the Admiralty,
     1931; see also his earlier Peace in Our Time: Addresses
     on Europe and the Empire (London, 1928).

371. Chamberlain, Neville.* In Search of Peace: Speeches,
     1937-1938. Edited by Arthur Bryant. London, 1939.

British

An essential collection by the minister of Health, 1923,
1924-29, 1931; chancellor of the Exchequer, 1923-24,
1931-37; prime minister, 1937-40; lord president of the
Council, 1940; see also the expanded version The Struggle
for Peace (London, 1939).

372. Chandos, 1st Viscount (Oliver Lyttleton). The Memoirs
of Lord Chandos. London, 1962.

M.P., 1940-54; president of the Board of Trade, 1940-41;
minister of state and member of the war cabinet, 1942-45.

373. Channon, Sir Henry. Chips: The Diaries of Sir Henry
Channon. Edited by Robert Rhodes James. London, 1967.

Parliamentary private secretary to under-secretary of
state for Foreign Affairs, 1938-41.

374. Chatfield, 1st Baron (Admiral of the Fleet Alfred E.M.
Chatfield). The Navy and Defence. London, 1942.

Supplemented by It Might Happen Again (London, 1947);
first sea lord and chief of naval staff, 1933-38;
minister for Co-ordination of Defence, 1939-40.

375. Churchill, Sir Winston Spencer.* Complete Speeches,
1897-1963. Edited by Robert Rhodes James. 8 vols.
London, 1974.

A nearly definitive collection of speeches by the
secretary for War and Air, 1919-21; secretary for Air and
Colonies, 1921; Colonial secretary, 1921-22; chancellor
of the Exchequer, 1924-29; first lord of the Admiralty,
1939-40; minister of Defence and prime minister, 1940-45;
prime minister, 1951-55; Churchill's own style of
memoir-histories, copiously documented, are The World
Crisis, 1914-1918, 4 vols. (London, 1923-29); and The
Second World War, 6 vols. (London, 1948-54).

376. Citrine, Walter M. (1st Baron Citrine). Men and Work:
An Autobiography. London, 1964.

Sequel in Two Careers (London, 1967);from the
general-secretary of the Trades Union Congress, 1926-46;
see also his I Search for Truth in Russia (London, 1938).

377. Clynes, John Robert. Memoirs: 1869-1937. 2 vols.
London, 1937.

MEMOIRS

British

Food controller, 1918-19; lord privy seal, 1924;
secretary of state for Home Affairs, 1929-31.

378. Cockburn, Claud. In Time of Trouble: An Autobiography.
London, 1956.

Continued in Crossing the Line (London, 1958); and View
from the West (London, 1961); controversial reminiscences
from the editor of The Week, 1933-46; and diplomatic
correspondent of the Daily Worker, 1935-46; see also
Patricia Cockburn, The Years of "The Week" (London,
1968).

379. Cockerill, Sir George Kynaston. What Fools We Were.
London, 1944.

Director of special intelligence, 1915-19; M.P., 1918-31.

380. Collier, Sir Laurence. Flight from Conflict. London,
1944.

Served in Foreign Office, 1913-41; minister to Norway,
1941; ambassador to Norwegian government, 1942-50.

381. Colville, Sir John Rupert. Footprints in Time:
Memories. London, 1976.

Assistant private secretary to Neville Chamberlain,
1939-40; to Winston Churchill, 1940-41, 1943-45; and to
Clement Attlee, 1945; based on extensive private diaries;
see also his The Churchillians (London, 1981).

382. Cooper, Alfred Duff (1st Viscount Norwich). Old Men
Forget. London, 1953.

With War Office and Treasury, 1928-35; secretary of state
for War, 1935-37; first lord of the Admiralty, 1937-38;
minister of Information, 1940-41; chancellor of the Duchy
of Lancaster, 1941-43; the Munich crisis' most famous
resignation; see also some of his collected press
writings in The Second World War: First Phase (London,
1939); and of related interest, Lady Diana Cooper, The
Light of Common Day (London, 1959); Philip Ziegler, Diana
Cooper (London, 1981); and A Durable Fire: The Letters
of Duff and Diana Cooper, edited by Artemis Cooper
(London, 1983).

383. Craigie, Sir Robert. Behind the Japanese Mask. London,
1946.

British

Entered Foreign Office, 1907; counsellor, then assistant
under-secretary of state, 1928-37; ambassador to Japan,
1937-41.

384. Croft, 1st Baron (Henry Page Croft). My Life of Strife.
London, 1948.

M.P., 1910-40; numerous parliamentary committees; joint
parliamentary under-secretary of state for War, 1940-45.

385. Crosby, Sir Josiah. Siam: The Crossroads. London,
1945.

Minister in Panama, 1931-34; Siam, 1934-41.

386. Crozier, Brigadier-General Frank Percy. A Brass Hat in
No Man's Land. London, 1930.

Served with the Lithuanian army against Germans in
Baltic, 1919; against Bolsheviks, 1919-20; and on Polish
front, 1919-20.

387. Crozier, William P. Off the Record: Political
Interviews, 1933-1943. Edited by A.J.P. Taylor.
London, 1973.

Transcripts of interview records by the editor of the
Manchester Guardian, 1932-44.

388. Cunningham, 1st Viscount, of Hyndhope (Admiral of the
Fleet Andrew Browne Cunningham). A Sailor's Odyssey.
London, 1951.

Deputy chief of naval staff, Admiralty, 1938-39;
commander-in chief, Mediterranean, 1939; chief of naval
staff, 1943-46.

389. D'Abernon, 1st Viscount (Edgar Vincent). An Ambassador
of Peace: Pages from the Diary of Viscount D'Abernon.
3 vols. London, 1929-30.

Began diplomatic career in 1880; ambassador at Berlin,
1920-26; see also his Portraits and Appreciations
(London, 1931); and Viscountess D'Abernon, Red Cross and
Berlin Embassy, 1915-1926 (London, 1946).

390. Dalton, Hugh. Memoirs. 3 vols. London, 1953-62.

British

Parliamentary under-secretary, Foreign Office, 1929-31;
minister of Economic Warfare, 1940-42; president of Board
of Trade, 1942-45; vols. 1 and 2 for 1887-1945; see also
his Hitler's War: Before and After (London, 1940); and
the Political Diaries of Hugh Dalton (London, 1982).

391. Davies, Sir Joseph. The Prime Minister's Secretariat,
     1916-1920. Newport, 1951.

     Secretary, prime minister's secretariat, 1917-20; M.P.,
     1918-22.

392. De Chair, Somerset. The Golden Carpet. London, 1944.

     M.P., 1935-45; parliamentary private secretary to Oliver
     Lyttelton, 1942-44.

393. Delmer, Sefton. Trail Sinister. London, 1961.

     Diplomatic and war correspondent of Daily Express,
     1927-40; at Foreign Office, 1941-45, engaged in "black
     propaganda"; sequel in Black Boomerang (London, 1962);
     see also his The Counterfeit Spy (London, 1973).

394. Domville, Admiral Sir Barry Edward. By and Large.
     London, 1936.

     Director of naval intelligence division, 1927-30;
     president, Royal Naval College, Greenwich, 1932-34;
     active in right-wing organisations; autobiography
     continued in Look to Your Moat (London, 1937); and From
     Admiral to Cabin Boy (London, 1947).

395. Douglas, Baron, of Kirtleside (Marshal of the Royal
     Air Force William Sholto Douglas). Years of Combat.
     London, 1963.

     Assistant chief of air staff, 1938-40; chief of air
     staff, 1940; air officer commanding-in-chief, various
     commands, 1940-45; sequel in Years of Command (London,
     1966).

396. Dreyer, Admiral Sir Frederic Charles. The Sea Heritage.
     London, 1955.

     Assistant chief of naval staff, 1924-27; deputy chief of
     naval staff, 1930-33; commander-in-chief, China station,
     1933-36; temporary chief of naval air services, 1942.

British

397. Driberg, Thomas E.N.* A Ruling Passion. London, 1977.

Journalist (Hickey columnist) with Daily Express; M.P.,
1942-55; author of books on Lord Beaverbrook and Guy
Burgess; see also his Colonnade, 1937-1947 (London,
1949).

398. Dugdale, Blanche. Baffy: The Diaries of Blanche
Dugdale, 1936-1947. Edited by Norman Rose. London,
1973.

A.J. Balfour's niece and biographer; active in League of
Nations Union; confidante of Chaim Weizmann.

399. Dukes, Sir Paul. The Unending Quest: Autobiographical
Sketches. London, 1950.

Intelligence service in Russia, 1918-20; Times
correspondent, 1921.

400. Eccles, 1st Viscount (David McAdam Eccles). Life and
Politics: A Moral Diagnosis. London, 1967.

M.P., 1943-62; economic adviser to ambassadors at Madrid
and Lisbon, 1940-42; ministry of Production, 1942-43; see
also Sybil and David Eccles, By Safe Hand (London, 1982).

401. Einzig, Paul. In the Centre of Things: An
Autobiography. London, 1960.

Correspondent with the Financial News, 1921, 1923,
1939-45; prolific author on finance, economic warfare,
appeasement, etc.

402. Ellis, Charles Howard. The Transcaspian Episode.
London, 1963.

Served European war and Afghan war, 1914-19; Foreign
Office and consular posts in Turkey, Berlin, Far East and
the United States, 1921-39; colonel on staff of missions
in the United States, Egypt and Far East, 1939-45.

403. Esher, 2nd Viscount (Reginald Baliol Brett).* Journals
and Letters of Reginald, Viscount Esher, 1870-1930. 4
vols. Edited by Maurice Brett and Oliver Brett.
London, 1934-38.

MEMOIRS

<u>British</u>

Member, Committee of Imperial Defence, 1905-18; head of a
British mission in Paris, 1914-18.

404. Foot, Sir Hugh. <u>A Start in Freedom</u>. London, 1964.

Colonial service, 1929-42; British military
administration, Cyrenaica, 1943; colonial secretary,
Cyprus, 1943-45.

405. Francis-Williams, Baron (Francis Williams). <u>Nothing So
Strange: An Autobiography</u>. London, 1970.

Journalist and author; editor of <u>Daily Herald</u>, 1936-40;
controller of news and censorship, ministry of
Information, 1941-45.

406. Fremantle, Admiral Sir Sydney R. <u>My Naval Career, 1880-
1928</u>. London, 1949.

Deputy-chief of naval staff, 1918-19; commander-in-chief,
Portsmouth station, 1923-25.

407. Fuller, Major-General John F.C. <u>Memoirs of an
Unconventional Soldier</u>. London, 1936.

Staff duties, directorate War Office, 1918-22; military
assistant to chief of the imperial general staff,
1926-27; prolific author on military affairs.

408. Gallacher, William. <u>Revolt on the Clyde: An
Autobiography</u>. London, 1936.

Continued in <u>The Last Memoirs of Willie Gallacher</u>
(London, 1966); "socialist agitator" (<u>Who's Who</u>);
Communist party M.P., 1935-50; see also his <u>The Chosen
Few: A Sketch of Men and Events in Parliament</u> (London,
1940); and <u>The Rolling of the Thunder</u> (London, 1947).

409. Geddes, 1st Baron (Auckland Campbell Geddes). <u>The
Forging of a Family</u>. London, 1952.

Minister of National Service, 1919; minister of
Reconstruction, 1919; president of the Board of Trade,
1919-20; ambassador at Washington, 1920-24.

410. Gibbs, Air Marshal Sir Gerald Ernest. <u>Survivor's Story</u>.
London, 1956.

109

British

> Served with RAF, 1918-41; director of overseas
> operations, Air ministry, 1942-43; senior air staff
> officer, 3rd tactical air force headquarters, south east
> Asia, 1943-44.

411. Gilchrist, Sir Andrew. <u>Bangkok Top Secret</u>. London,
     1970.

> Joined Siam branch of consular service, 1933; served in
> British legation, Bangkok, 1933-36, 1938-41; on active
> service in south east Asia, 1944-46.

412. Gladwyn, 1st Baron (H.M. Gladwyn Jebb). <u>Memoirs</u>.
     London, 1972.

> Diplomatic service at home and abroad, 1924-40; appointed
> to ministry of Economic Warfare, 1940; head of
> Reconstruction Department, 1942; counsellor in Foreign
> Office, attending wartime conferences, 1943-45.

413. Glubb, Sir John Bagot. <u>A Soldier with the Arabs</u>.
     London, 1957.

> Chief of general staff, the Arab Legion, Jordan, 1939-56.

414. Goddard, Air Marshal Sir Victor. <u>Epic Violet</u>. London,
     1982.

> Served first world war, 1914-18; deputy director of
> intelligence, Air ministry, 1938-39; chief of air staff,
> New Zealand, 1941-43; with air command, south east Asia,
> 1943-46.

415. Godley, General Sir Alexander. <u>Life of an Irish Soldier</u>.
     London, 1939.

> Began military service, 1886; military secretary to the
> secretary of state for War, 1920-22; commander-in-chief,
> British army on the Rhine, 1922-24; governor and
> commander-in-chief, Gibraltar, 1928-33.

416. Gollancz, Victor. <u>Reminiscences of Affection</u>. London,
     1968.

> Publisher and writer; founded the Left Book Club, 1936;
> see also his <u>Is Mr. Chamberlain Saving the Peace?</u>
> (London, 1939); and <u>Russia and Ourselves</u> (London, 1941).

417. Gore-Booth, Baron (Sir Paul Henry Gore-Booth). <u>With
     Great Truth and Respect</u>. London, 1974.

MEMOIRS

British

> Served Foreign Office, 1933-36; Vienna, 1936-37; Tokyo,
> 1938-42; and Washington, 1942-45; attended UNRRA
> conference, 1943.

418. Grafftey-Smith, Sir Laurence Baton. Bright Levant.
      London, 1970.

> Entered Levant consular service, 1914; served at Cairo,
> 1925-35; consul-general to Albania, 1939-40; minister to
> Saudi Arabia, 1945-47.

419. Grant Watson, Herbert Adolphus. An Account of a Mission
      to the Baltic States in 1919. London, 1958.

> Employed on special service in the Baltic provinces,
> 1919; transferred to Lisbon, 1920; counsellor of embassy,
> 1925; minister to Central America Republics, 1928-33;
> Cuba, 1933-35; Finland, 1935-37; and Cuba, 1937-40.

420. Greene, Sir Hugh Carleton. The Third Floor Front.
      London, 1969.

> Daily Telegraph correspondent, expelled from Berlin,
> 1939; joined BBC, 1940; later headed BBC from 1960-69.

421. Gregory, John Duncan. On the Edge of Diplomacy: Rambles
      and Reflections, 1902-1928. London, 1929.

> Assistant secretary, Foreign Office, 1920-25; assistant
> under-secretary of state, Foreign Office, 1925-28.

422. Grey, 1st Viscount, of Falloden (Sir Edward Grey).*
      Twenty-Five Years, 1892-1916. 2 vols. London, 1925.

> M.P., 1885-1916; foreign secretary, 1905-16; president,
> League of Nations Union, from 1918; temporary ambassador
> to the United States, 1919.

423. Griffith-Boscawan, Sir Arthur S.T. Memories. London,
      1925.

> Minister of Agriculture and Fisheries, 1921-22; minister
> of Health, 1922-23.

424. Grigg, P.J. Prejudice and Judgement. London, 1948.

> Principal private secretary to successive chancellors of
> the Exchequer, 1921-30; with Customs and Revenue, and
> Inland Revenue, 1930-34; finance member of government of

British

India, 1934-39; permanent under-secretary of state for
War, 1939-42; secretary of state for War, 1942-45.

425. Haig, Field Marshal Sir Douglas (1st Earl Haig).* The
Private Papers of Douglas Haig, 1914-1919. Edited by
Robert Blake. London, 1952.

Commander-in-chief, BEF, 1915-18; commander-in-chief,
home forces, 1919-21.

426. Hailsham, Baron, of Saint Marylebone (Quinton McGarel
Hogg). The Door Wherein I Went. London, 1975.

M.P., 1938-50; joint parliamentary under-secretary for
Air, 1945.

427. Haldane, Richard Burdon (1st Viscount Haldane of Cloan).*
An Autobiography. London, 1929.

Lord chancellor, 1912-15, 1924.

428. Halifax, 1st Earl of (Edward Frederick Lindley Wood, 1st
Baron Irwin).* Fulness of Days. London, 1957.

President of the Board of Education, 1922-24, 1932-35;
minister of Agriculture, 1924-25; viceroy of India,
1926-31; secretary of state for War, 1935; lord privy
seal, 1935-37; secretary of state for Foreign Affairs,
1938-40; ambassador at Washington, 1941-46; speeches in
Viscount Halifax: Speeches on Foreign Affairs, edited by
H.H.E. Craster (London, 1940); and The American Speeches
of the Earl of Halifax (London, 1947).

429. Hamilton, Mary Agnes. Remembering My Good Friends.
London, 1944.

Includes diplomats and politicians; by a biographer (of
J. Ramsay MacDonald and Arthur Henderson), novelist and
civil servant; M.P., 1929-31; see also Up-Hill All the
Way (London, 1953).

430. Hankey, 1st Baron (Maurice Pascal Alers Hankey).* The
Supreme Command, 1914-1918. 2 vols. London, 1961.

Secretary, Committee of Imperial Defence, 1912-18;
cabinet, 1919-38; minister without portfolio in war
cabinet, 1939-40; chancellor of the Duchy of Lancaster,
1940-41; paymaster-general, 1941-42; a director, Suez
Canal Company, 1938-39, 1945-62; British secretary,

MEMOIRS

British

numerous inter-war conferences, 1919-32; continued in The Supreme Control at the Paris Peace Conference, 1919: A Commentary (London, 1963); see also his Diplomacy by Conference: Studies in Public Affairs, 1920-1946 (London, 1946); Politics, Trials and Errors (Oxford, 1950); and Government Control in War (London, 1945).

431. Hardinge, 1st Baron, of Penshurst (Charles Hardinge).* Old Diplomacy: The Reminiscences of Lord Hardinge of Penshurst. London, 1947.

Permanent under-secretary of state for Foreign Affairs, 1916-20; ambassador at Paris, 1920-23.

432. Harington, General Sir Charles. Tim Harington Looks Back. London, 1940.

Deputy chief, imperial general staff, 1918-20; general officer commanding-in-chief, army of Black Sea, 1920-21; allied forces of occupation in Turkey, 1921-23; governor of Gibraltar, 1933-38.

433. Harris, Marshal of the Royal Air Force Sir Arthur. Bomber Offensive. London, 1947.

Joined RAF, 1919; deputy chief of air staff, 1940-41; commander-in-chief, Bomber Command, 1942-45.

434. Harris, Henry Wilson. Life So Far. London, 1954.

M.P., 1945-50; editor of the Spectator, 1932-53; author of numerous books on foreign policy, the League of Nations and disarmament.

435. Harris, Sir Percy Alfred. Forty Years in and out of Parliament. London, 1947.

M.P., 1922-45; chief whip, Liberal parliamentary party, 1935-45.

436. Harvey, 1st Baron, of Tasburgh (Oliver Charles Harvey). The Diplomatic Diaries of Oliver Harvey, 1937-1940. Edited by John Harvey. London, 1970.

Continued as The War Diaries of Oliver Harvey, 1941-1945 (London, 1978); entered Foreign Office, 1919; principal private secretary to secretary of state for Foreign

British

Affairs, 1936-39, 1941-43; minister at Paris, 1940; assistant under-secretary of state, Foreign Office, 1943-46.

437. Hastings, Sir Patrick. The Autobiography of Sir Patrick Hastings. London, 1948.

M.P., 1922-26; attorney-general, 1924; playwright.

438. Hayter, Sir William. A Double Life: The Memories of Sir William Hayter. London, 1974.

Served Foreign Office, 1930; Vienna, 1931; Moscow, 1934; Foreign Office, 1937; China, 1938; Washington, 1941; Foreign Office, 1944-48; see also his The Diplomacy of the Great Powers (London, 1960).

439. Headlam-Morley, Sir James Wycliffe. A Memoir of the Paris Peace Conference, 1919. Edited by Agnes Headlam-Morley, et al. London, 1972.

Historical adviser to Foreign Office, 1920-28; see also his Studies in Diplomatic History (London, 1930).

440. Henderson, Sir Nevile Meyrick. Failure of a Mission: Berlin, 1937-1939. London, 1940.

Entered diplomatic service, 1905; served at St. Petersburg, Tokyo, Rome, Nish, Paris, 1905-1921; counsellor, and then acting high commissioner, Constantinople, 1921-24; served at Cairo, 1924-28; Paris, 1928-29; minister at Belgrade, 1925-35; ambassador at Buenos Aires, 1935-37; and at Berlin, 1937-39; additional reminiscences, essential for an understanding of the man, in Water Under the Bridges (London, 1945).

441. Hewlett, Sir William Meyrick. Forty Years in China. London, 1943.

Acting consul-general at Chengtu, 1916-22; consul at Amoy, 1923-27; consul-general, Nanking, 1927-31; Hankow, 1932-35.

442. Hodgson, Sir Robert MacLeod. Spain Resurgent. London, 1953.

Commercial counsellor in Russia, 1919-21; agent, British commercial mission to Soviet government, 1921-24; chargé d'affaires at Moscow, 1924-27; minister to Albania,

MEMOIRS

British

1928-36; British agent in nationalist Spain, 1937-39;
chargé d'affaires in Burgos, 1939; diplomatic adviser to
the ministry of Information, 1944-45.

443. Hodson, Sir Arnhold Wienholt. Seven Years in Southern
        Abyssinia. London, 1927.

    Consular service, Abyssinia, 1914-26; governor of
    Falkland Islands, 1926-30; Sierra Leone, 1930-34; Gold
    Coast, 1934-1941; see also his Where Lions Reign (London,
    1929).

444. Hohler, Sir Thomas Beaumont. Diplomatic Petrel. London,
        1942.

    Minister at Budapest, 1920-24; Santiago, 1924-27;
    minister to Denmark, 1928-33; special emissary to
    Colombia, 1938.

445. Hollis, Sir Leslie Chasemore. One Marine's Tale.
        London, 1956.

    Admiralty, plans division, 1932-36; assistant secretary,
    Committee of Imperial Defence, 1936; senior assistant
    secretary in office of war cabinet, 1939-46; another
    volume in collaboration with James Leasor, War at the Top
    (London, 1959).

446. Home, 14th Earl of (Alexander Frederick Douglas-Home).*
        The Way the Wind Blows. London, 1976.

    Parliamentary private secretary to Neville Chamberlain,
    1937-39; joint parliamentary under-secretary, Foreign
    Office, 1945; prime minister, 1963-64; see also his
    Letters to a Grandson (London, 1983).

447. Howard, 1st Baron, of Penrith (Sir Esme William Howard).
        Theatre of Life, 1863-1936. 2 vols. London, 1935-36.

    Minister to Sweden, 1913-19; ambassador to Spain,
    1919-24; USA, 1924-30; member, British delegation to
    Paris peace conference, 1919; see also his The Prevention
    of War by Collective Action (London, 1933).

448. Hunt, Sir David. A Don at War. London, 1966.

British

> Served world war two, 1940-45; colonel general staff,
> allied force headquarters, 1945-46; see also his <u>On the
> Spot</u> (London, 1975).

449. Ironside, 1st Baron (Field Marshal William Edmund
     Ironside). <u>Archangel, 1918-1919</u>. London, 1953.

> Commander-in-chief British forces in Russia, 1918-19;
> quartermaster-general in India, 1933-36; governor,
> Gibraltar, 1938-39; inspector-general of overseas forces,
> 1939; chief of the imperial general staff, 1939-40;
> commander-in-chief, home forces, 1940; further diary
> extracts in <u>High Road to Command, 1920-1922</u>, edited by
> 2nd Baron Ironside (London, 1972); and <u>The Ironside
> Diaries, 1937-1940</u>, edited by Roderick Macleod and Denis
> Kelly (London, 1962).

450. Ismay, Baron (General Hastings Lionel Ismay).* <u>Memoirs</u>.
     London, 1960.

> Assistant secretary, Committee of Imperial Defence,
> 1925-30; deputy secretary, 1936-38; secretary, 1938;
> chief of staff to minister of Defence, 1940-46; deputy
> secretary, military, to war cabinet, 1940-45.

451. James, Admiral Sir William Miliburne. <u>The Sky Was Always
     Blue</u>. London, 1951.

> Prolific author on naval affairs; deputy chief of naval
> staff, 1935-38; commander-in-chief, Portsmouth, 1939-42;
> chief of naval information, 1943-44; M.P., 1943-45; see
> also his <u>The Portsmouth Letters</u> (London, 1946).

452. Jay, Douglas. <u>Change and Fortune</u>. London, 1980.

> Journalist with <u>The Times</u> and the <u>Economist</u>, 1930s;
> assistant secretary, ministry of Supply, 1941-43;
> principal assistant secretary, Board of Trade, 1943-45.

453. Johnston, Thomas. <u>Memories</u>. London, 1952.

> Parliamentary under-secretary for Scotland, 1929-31; lord
> privy seal, 1931; secretary of state for Scotland,
> 1941-45.

454. Jones, Thomas. <u>A Diary with Letters, 1931-1950</u>. London,
     1954.

British

Deputy secretary, cabinet, 1916-30; first secretary,
Pilgrim Trust, 1930-45; to be supplemented by Whitehall
Diary, 3 vols., edited by Keith Middlemas (London,
1969-71).

455. Kelly, Sir David Victor. The Ruling Few: Or, The Human
Background to Diplomacy. London, 1953.

Served at Buenos Aires, Foreign Office, Lisbon, Mexico,
Brussels, Stockholm and Cairo, 1919-37; counsellor in
Foreign Office, 1938-39; minister at Berne, 1940-42.

456. Kennedy, Major-General Sir John Noble. The Business of
War. London, 1957.

Deputy director of military operations, 1938; director of
plans, 1939; director of military operations, War Office,
1940-43; assistant chief of imperial general staff,
1943-45.

457. Keyes, 1st Baron (Roger Keyes).* The Naval Memoirs of
Admiral of the Fleet Sir Roger Keyes. 2 vols. London,
1934-35.

Entered navy, 1885; deputy chief of naval staff, 1921-25;
commander-in-chief, various stations, 1925-31; M.P.,
1934-43; director of combined operations, 1940-41; author
of several books on naval affairs; private papers in The
Keyes Papers: Selections from the Private and Official
Correspondence of Admiral of the Fleet Lord Keyes, 3
vols., edited by Paul G. Halpern (London, 1979-81).

458. Keynes, Baron (John Maynard Keynes).* The Collected
Writings of John Maynard Keynes. Edited by Sir Austen
Robinson and D.E. Moggridge. 29 vols. London,
1971-79.

Principal representative of the Treasury, Paris peace
conference, 1919; member, committee on finance and
industry, 1929-31; returned to Treasury, 1940; attended
Bretton Woods conference, 1944; engaged in negotiations
with United States on lend-lease, 1944-45; see
additionally Essays in Persuasion (London, 1931); and
Essays in Biography (London, 1933).

459. Killearn, 1st Baron (Miles Wedderburn Lampson).* The
Killearn Diaries, 1934-1946. Edited by Trefor Ellis
Evans. London, 1972.

British

Entered Foreign Office, 1903; minister to China, 1926-33; high commissioner for Egypt and the Sudan, 1934-36; ambassador to Egypt and high commissioner for the Sudan, 1936-46.

460. Kilmuir, 1st Viscount (David Patrick Maxwell Fyfe). Political Adventure. London, 1964.

M.P., 1935-54; solicitor-general, 1942-45; attorney-general, 1945; deputy chief prosecutor, trial of Nazi war criminals, Nuremberg, 1945-46.

461. King, Cecil. With Malice Toward None: A War Diary. Edited by William Armstrong. London, 1970.

Journalist and publisher; with Daily Mirror and Sunday Pictorial, 1929-63; see also his Strictly Personal (London, 1969).

462. King Hall, Sir Stephen. My Naval Life, 1906-1929. London, 1952.

Admiralty naval staff, 1919-20, 1928-29; intelligence officer, Mediterranean fleet, 1925-26; Atlantic fleet, 1927-28; founded K-H Newsletter Service, 1936.

463. Kirkbride, Sir Alec Seath. A Crackle of Thorns: Experiences in the Middle East. London, 1956.

Service in Transjordan and Palestine, 1921-45; British representative to Permanent Mandates Commission, Geneva, 1936, 1938, and 1939.

464. Kirkpatrick, Sir Ivone. The Inner Circle. London, 1959.

Foreign Office, 1920-30; 1st secretary, British embassy, Berlin, 1933-38; director of foreign division, ministry of Information, 1940; controller, European services, BBC, 1941-45; assistant, then permanent under-secretary of state, Foreign Office, 1945-50, 1953-57.

465. Knatchbull-Hugessen, Sir Hughe M. Diplomat in Peace and War. London, 1949.

Minister to the Baltic states, 1930-34; minister at Teheran, 1934-36; ambassador to China, 1936-38; Turkey, 1939-44; and Belgium, 1944-47.

466. Lansbury, George.* My Life. London, 1928.

MEMOIRS

<u>British</u>

M.P., 1922-40; editor of <u>Daily Herald</u>, 1919-23; first commissioner of works, 1929-31; leader of the Labour party, 1931-ɔᵥ, see also <u>My Quest for Peace</u> (London, 1938).

467. Lawford, Valentine. <u>Bound for Diplomacy</u>. London, 1963.

3rd secretary, Foreign Office, 1934; transferred to Paris, 1937; returned to Foreign Office, 1939-44; private secretary to Anthony Eden, 1940-45.

468. Lawrence, Thomas Edward [Thomas Edward Shaw].* <u>Seven Pillars of Wisdom: A Triumph</u>. London, 1926.

British delegation, Paris peace conference, 1919; adviser on Arab affairs, Colonial Office, 1921-22; see also <u>Revolt in the Desert</u> (London, 1927); and <u>The Letters of T.E. Lawrence</u>, edited by David Garnett (London, 1938).

469. Lawson, 1st Baron (John James Lawson). <u>A Man's Life</u>. London, 1932.

M.P., 1919-49; financial secretary to War Office, 1924; parliamentary secretary to ministry of Labour, 1929-31; secretary of state for War, 1945-56.

470. Lee, 1st Viscount, of Fareham (Arthur Hamilton Lee). <u>A Good Innings: The Private Papers of Viscount Lee of Fareham</u>. Edited by Alan Clark. London, 1974.

Director-general of food production, 1917-18; minister of Agriculture and Fisheries, 1919-21; first lord of the Admiralty, 1921-22; delegate to Washington conference, 1921-22.

471. Lee, Air Vice-Marshal Arthur S. Gould. <u>Special Duties: Reminiscences of a Royal Air Force Staff Officer in the Balkans, Turkey and the Middle East</u>. London, 1946.

Chief instructor, Turkish Air Force College, 1937-40; chief of air section, British armistice control commission, Rumania, 1944; chief of British military-air mission to Marshal Tito, 1945.

472. Lee, Jennie (Baroness Lee of Ashridge). <u>This Great Journey: A Volume of Autobiography, 1904-1945</u>. London, 1963.

British

M.P., 1929-31, 1945-70; married Aneurin Bevan, 1934; see also her My Life with Nye (London, 1980).

473. Leeper, Sir Reginald Wildig Allen. When Greek Meets Greek. London, 1950.

Foreign Office, 1918-23, 1929-43; 1st secretary, British legation, Warsaw, 1923-24, 1927-29; Riga, 1924; Constantinople, 1925; ambassador at the court of the king of the Hellenes, 1943-46.

474. Leith-Ross, Sir Frederick. Money Talks: Fifty Years of International Finance. London, 1968.

British representative on finance board of Reparation Commission, 1920-25; deputy controller, finance, the Treasury, 1925-32; chief economic adviser to the government, 1932-46; director-general, ministry of Economic Warfare, 1939-42; deputy director-general, European office, UNRRA, 1944-45.

475. Liddell Hart, Sir Basil Henry. Memoirs. 2 vols. London, 1965-66.

Military theorist, lecturer and author of over thirty books; military correspondent of the Daily Telegraph, 1925-35; of The Times, 1935-39; personal adviser to Leslie Hore-Belisha, 1937-38.

476. Lindley, Sir Francis Oswald. A Diplomat off Duty. London, 1928.

Foreign Office, 1897; high commissioner, Vienna, 1919-20; minister, 1920; Athens, 1922-23; Oslo, 1923-29; ambassador to Portugal, 1929-31; and Japan, 1931-34.

477. Lloyd George, David (1st Earl Lloyd-George of Dwyfor).* War Memoirs. 6 vols. London, 1933-36.

M.P., 1890-1945; prime minister, 1916-22; see also The Truth about Reparations and War-Debts (London, 1932); The Truth about the Peace Treaties, 2 vols. (London, 1938); and Lloyd George: Family Letters, 1885-1936, edited by Kenneth O. Morgan (London, 1973).

478. Lockhart, Sir Robert Bruce. The Diaries of Sir Robert Bruce Lockhart. 2 vols. Edited by Kenneth Young. London, 1973-81.

MEMOIRS

British

> Vol. 1 to 1938; vol. 2 to 1965; commercial secretary,
> Prague, 1919-22; with Evening Standard, 1929-37;
> political intelligence department, Foreign Office,
> 1939-40; deputy under-secretary of state, Foreign Office,
> 1941-45; author of numerous books, including Memoirs of a
> British Agent (London, 1932); Comes the Reckoning
> (London, 1947); and Friends, Foes and Foreigners (London,
> 1957).

479. Lomax, Sir John Garnett. The Diplomatic Smuggler.
London, 1965.

Consular service, 1920-38; commercial counsellor, Madrid,
1940; Berne, 1941; Angora, 1943; commercial minister,
Buenos Aires, 1946-49.

480. Londonderry, 7th Marquess of (Charles Stewart Henry Vane-
Tempest-Stewart). Ourselves and Germany. London,
1938.

Under-secretary for Air, 1920-21; secretary of state for
Air, 1931-35; see also Wings of Destiny (London, 1943).

481. Long, 1st Viscount (Walter Long).* Memories.
London, 1923.

Secretary of state for the Colonies, 1916-18; first lord
of the Admiralty, 1919-21.

482. Lothian, 11th Marquess of (Philip Henry Kerr).* The
American Speeches of Lord Lothian, July 1939 to
December 1940. London, 1940.

Private secretary to Lloyd George, 1916-21; secretary to
Rhodes trustees, 1925-39; chancellor of the Duchy of
Lancaster, 1931; under-secretary of state for India,
1931-32; ambassador to the United States, 1939-40.

483. Lytton, 2nd Earl of (Victor Alexander George Robert
Bulwer-Lytton). The Web of Life. London, 1938.

Junior appointments, 1916-22; governor of Bengal,
1922-27; chairman of League of Nations mission to
Manchuria, 1932; chairman, Council of Aliens, 1939-41.

484. McDonald, Iverach. A Man of the Times. London, 1976.

With Yorkshire Post, and then The Times; diplomatic
correspondent, 1937-48.

British

485. MacDonald, Malcolm John. People and Places: Random
     Reminiscences. London, 1969.

     Son of J. Ramsay MacDonald; M.P., 1929-45; parliamentary
     under-secretary, Dominions Office, 1931-35; secretary of
     state for Dominion Affairs, 1935-38, 1938-39; secretary
     of state for Colonies, 1935, 1938-40; minister of Health,
     1940-41; high commissioner to Canada, 1941-46; several
     books on ornithology; see also Titans and Others (London,
     1972).

486. McFadyean, Sir Andrew. Recollected in Tranquillity.
     London, 1964.

     Entered Treasury, 1910; Treasury representative, Paris,
     1919-20; secretary to British delegation, Reparation
     Commission, 1920-22; general secretary, Reparation
     Commission, 1922-24; and Dawes committee, 1924; see also
     his earlier Reparation Reviewed (London, 1930).

487. Maclean, Sir Fitzroy. Eastern Approaches. London, 1949.

     M.P., 1941-74; 3rd secretary, Foreign Office, 1933;
     transferred to Paris, 1934, and to Moscow, 1937; 2nd
     secretary, 1938; transferred to Foreign Office, 1939;
     resigned, 1939; brigadier commanding British military
     mission to Tito, 1943-45; see also his Disputed Barricade
     (London, 1957).

488. Macmillan, Baron (Hugh Pattison Macmillan). A Man of
     Law's Tale. London, 1952.

     Assistant director of intelligence, ministry of
     Information, 1918; lord advocate in Labour government,
     1924; minister of Information, 1939-40.

489. Macmillan, Harold. Memoirs. 6 vols. London, 1966-73.

     Vols. 1 and 2 for 1914-45; M.P., 1924-29, 1931-64;
     parliamentary secretary, ministry of Supply, 1940-42;
     parliamentary under-secretary of state, Colonies, 1942;
     minister resident at allied headquarters in north west
     Africa, 1942-45; secretary for Air, 1945; prime minister,
     1957-63; see also his The Price of Peace: Notes on the
     World Crisis (London, 1938, for private circulation); and
     The Past Masters: Politics and Politicians, 1906-1939
     (London, 1975).

MEMOIRS

<u>British</u>

490. Macready, Sir Gordon. <u>In the Wake of the Great</u>. London,
     1965.

     Assistant secretary, Committee of Imperial Defence,
     1926-32; assistant chief of the imperial general staff,
     1940-42; chief of British army staff, Washington, 1942.

491. Malcolm, Sir Ian. <u>Vacant Thrones: A Parliamentary
     Sketchbook, 1895-1931</u>. London, 1931.

     M.P., 1910-19; private secretary to A.J. Balfour at Paris
     peace conference, 1919.

492. Mallaby, Sir George Charles. <u>From My Level</u>. London,
     1965.

     Served in military secretariat of war cabinet, 1942-45;
     further recollections in <u>Each in His Office: Studies of
     Men in Power</u> (London, 1972).

493. Martel, Sir Giffard. <u>An Outspoken Soldier</u>. London,
     1949.

     Deputy director of mechanization, War Office, 1938-39;
     head of military mission at Moscow, 1943-44; of interest
     also is his <u>The Problem of Security</u> (London, 1941); and
     <u>The Russian Outlook</u> (London, 1947).

494. Martin, Kingsley.* <u>Father Figures: A First Volume of
     Autobiography, 1897-1931</u>. London, 1966.

     With the <u>Manchester Guardian</u>, 1927-31; then editor, <u>New
     Statesman</u>, 1931-60; prolific author; concluded as <u>Editor:
     A Second Volume of Autobiography, 1931-1945</u> (London,
     1968).

495. Masterman, Sir John C. <u>On the Chariot Wheel: An
     Autobiography</u>. London, 1975.

     Lieutenant, intelligence corps, 1940; employed with B1A
     section of MI5, 1941-45.

496. Maugham, 1st Viscount (Frederic Herbert Maugham). <u>At the
     End of the Day</u>. London, 1954.

     Lord chancellor, 1938-39; his <u>The Truth about the Munich
     Crisis</u> (London, 1944) is still important.

123

British

497. Meinertzhagen, Colonel Richard.* Middle East Diary,
     1917-1956. London, 1959.

     Member of Paris peace delegation, 1919; chief political
     officer in Palestine and Syria, 1919-20; military
     adviser, Middle East department, Colonial Office,
     1921-24; War Office, 1939-40; see additionally Army
     Diary, 1899-1926 (London, 1960); and Diary of a Black
     Sheep (London, 1964); recreations included "silence,
     solitude and space" (Who's Who).

498. Mersey, 2nd Viscount (Charles Bigham Mersey). A Picture
     of Life, 1872-1940. London 1941.

     Entered diplomatic service, 1896; attached to British
     delegation, Paris peace conference, 1919; deputy speaker,
     House of Lords, 1933-56; other publications include The
     Chief Ministers of England (London, 1923); and Journal
     and Memories (London, 1952).

499. Mitchell, Sir Harold Paton. Into Peace. London, 1945.

     Parliamentary private secretary, Department of Overseas
     Trade, 1931-35; ministry of Labour, 1939-41; ministry of
     Supply, 1941; liaison officer to Polish forces, 1944;
     vice-chairman of Conservative party, 1942-45; see also
     his In My Stride (London, 1951).

500. Montgomery, Field Marshal 1st Viscount, of Alamein,
     (Bernard Law Montgomery).* Memoirs. London, 1958.

     One in a series of military memoirs; served both world
     wars; commander, 8th army from July 1942; commander-in-
     chief, north France, 1945; commander, 21st army group,
     1944-45.

501. Moran, 1st Baron, of Manton, (Charles McMoran Wilson).
     Winston Churchill: The Struggle for Survival,
     1940-1965. London, 1966.

     Personal physician to Winston Churchill; based on the
     Moran diaries.

502. Morgan, General Sir Frederick Edgeworth. Peace and War:
     A Soldier's Life. London, 1961.

     Began military service, 1913; chief of staff to supreme
     allied commander, 1943-44; deputy chief of staff to

British

supreme commander, allied expeditionary force, 1944-45;
see also his Overture to Overlord (London, 1950).

503. Morgan, John Hartman. Assize of Arms: Being the Story
of the Disarmament of Germany and her Rearmament.
2 vols. London, 1945.

Memoir-history; with British military section, Paris
peace conference, 1919; member, Inter-Allied Military
Commission of Control in Germany, 1919-23.

504. Morrison, Baron, of Lambeth (Herbert Stanley Morrison).*
An Autobiography. London, 1960.

Minister of Transport, 1929-31; minister of Supply, 1940;
home secretary and minister of Home Security, 1940-45;
his Government and Parliament (London, 1954) is also
interesting.

505. Mosley, Sir Oswald Ernald.* My Life. London, 1968.

Married, 1st, Lady Cynthia Curzon; 2nd, Diana Mitford;
chancellor of the Duchy of Lancaster, 1929-30; leader of
the British Union of Fascists; of related interest is
Diana Mosley, A Life of Contrasts (London, 1977).

506. Mottistone, 1st Baron (John Edward Bernard Seely).
Adventure. London, 1930.

Parliamentary under-secretary and deputy minister,
ministry of Munitions, 1918-19; under-secretary of state
for Air, 1919; see also his Fear and be Slain:
Adventures by Land, Sea and Air (London, 1931).

507. Mott-Radclyffe, Sir Charles. Foreign Body in the Eye:
A Memoir of the Foreign Service. London, 1975.

Honourary attaché, diplomatic service, Athens and Rome,
1936-38; member, military mission to Greece, 1940-41;
liaison officer in Syria, 1941; M.P., 1942-70; parliamentary private secretary to secretary of state for
India, 1944-45; later member of Plowden Commission on
Overseas Representation Services, 1963-64.

508. Muggeridge, Malcolm. Chronicles of Wasted Time. 2 vols.
London, 1972-73.

Member, editorial staff, 1930-32, and Moscow
correspondent, 1932-33, Manchester Guardian; assistant

British

editor, Calcutta Statesman, 1934-45; served British
intelligence corps, 1939-45.

509. Myers, Brigadier Edmund C.W. Greek Entanglement.
London, 1955.

With SOE, Middle East, 1939-44; north west Europe,
1944-45.

510. Neame, Sir Philip. Playing with Strife. London, 1946.

Entered army, 1908; deputy chief of the general staff,
BEF, France, 1939-40; general officer commanding-in-
chief, Cyrenaica, 1941.

511. Nicolson, Sir Harold.* Harold Nicolson: Diaries and
Letters, 1930-1962. Edited by Nigel Nicolson. 3
vols. London, 1966-68.

Author, critic and M.P.; entered Foreign Office, 1909; on
British delegation to Paris peace conference, 1919; at
League of Nations, 1919-20; returned, and served at
Foreign Office and abroad, 1920-29; parliamentary
secretary to ministry of Information, 1940-41.

512. Oliphant, Sir Lancelot. An Ambassador in Bonds. London,
1946.

Entered Foreign Office, 1903; counsellor, 1923; assistant
under-secretary of state, 1929-36; deputy under-secretary
of state for Foreign Affairs, 1936-39; ambassador to
Belgium, 1939; captured and interned in Germany, 1940-41;
returned to Foreign Office, 1941-44.

513. O'Malley, Sir Owen St. Clair. The Phantom Caravan.
London, 1954.

Counsellor, Foreign Office, 1933-37; minister to Hungary,
1939-41; ambassador to Poland, 1942-45; and Portugal,
1945-47.

514. Parkinson, Sir Cosmo. The Colonial Office from Within,
1909-1945. London, 1947.

Joined Colonial Office, 1909; permanent under-secretary
of state for the Colonies, 1937-40, 1940-42; permanent
under-secretary of state for Dominion Affairs, 1940.

MEMOIRS

<u>British</u>

515. Parmoor, 1st Baron (Charles Alfred Cripps).
    <u>A Retrospect: Looking Back Over a Life of More than
    Eighty Years</u>. London, 1936.

    Lord president of the Council, 1924, 1929-31; British
    representative at League of Nations Council, 1924; leader
    of the House of Lords, 1929-31.

516. Parrott, Sir Cecil. <u>The Tightrope</u>. London, 1975.

    Post-1945 memoirs continued in <u>The Serpent and the
    Nightingale</u> (London, 1978); tutor to King Peter of
    Yugoslavia, at Belgrade, 1934-39; served with British
    legation, Oslo, 1939-40; Stockholm, 1940-45; later
    director of research, librarian and keeper of the papers
    at the Foreign Office, 1957-60.

517. Passfield, 1st Baron (Sidney James Webb). <u>The Letters of
    Sidney and Beatrice Webb</u>. 3 vols. Edited by Norman
    Mackenzie. London, 1978.

    Sidney Webb: M.P., 1922-29; president of the Board of
    Trade, 1924; secretary of state for Dominion Affairs,
    1929-30; and for Colonies, 1929-31; see also <u>The Diary of
    Beatrice Webb 1873-1943</u>, vol. 1-, edited by Norman and
    Jeanne MacKenzie (London, 1982-); in progress; entire
    typescript diaries available on microfiche since 1978;
    and Beatrice Webb, <u>Our Partnership</u> (London, 1948).

518. Percy, Eustace (Baron Percy of Newcastle). <u>Some
    Memories</u>. London, 1958.

    Diplomatic service, 1911-19; M.P., 1921-37; president,
    Board of Education, 1924-29; minister without portfolio,
    1935-36.

519. Peterson, Sir Maurice Drummond. <u>Both Sides of the
    Curtain</u>. London, 1950.

    Entered Foreign Office, 1913; served at Washington,
    Prague, Tokyo, Cairo and Madrid; minister to Bulgaria,
    1936-38; ambassador to Iraq, 1938-39; Spain, 1939-40; and
    Turkey, 1944-46.

520. Pethick-Lawrence, Baron (Frederick William Pethick-
    Lawrence).* <u>Fate Has Been Kind</u>. London, 1942.

127

British

> M.P., 1923-31, 1935-45; financial secretary to the
> Treasury, 1929-31; secretary of state for India and
> Burma, 1945-47.

521. Philby, Harry St. John Bridger. <u>Arabian Days</u>. London,
    1948.

> One of his numerous books on the Arab world; entered
> Indian civil service, 1907; adviser to ministry of the
> Interior, Mesopotamia, 1920-21; chief British
> representative, Transjordan, 1921-24; father of Kim
> Philby.

522. Philby, Kim.* <u>My Secret War</u>. London, 1968.

> Intelligence agent of USSR.

523. Piggott, Major-General Francis Stewart Gilderoy. <u>Broken</u>
    <u>Thread: An Autobiography</u>. London, 1950.

> Foreword by Lord Hankey; general staff, War Office,
> 1920-21; military attaché at Tokyo, 1921-26, 1936-39;
> deputy military secretary, War Office, 1931-35.

524. Ponsonby, Sir Charles Edward. <u>Ponsonby Remembers</u>.
    London, 1964.

> M.P., 1935-50; parliamentary private secretary to Anthony
> Eden, 1940-45.

525. Pownall, Lieutenant-General Sir Henry. <u>Chief of Staff:</u>
    <u>The Diaries of Lieutenant-General Sir Henry Pownall</u>.
    Edited by Brian Bond. 2 vols. London, 1973-74.

> Covers period, 1933-44; with Committee of Imperial
> Defence, 1933-36; director of military operations and
> intelligence, War Office, 1938-39; chief of general
> staff, BEF, 1939-40; vice-chief of imperial general
> staff, War Office, 1941; commander-in-chief, Far East,
> 1941-42; Persia-Iraq, 1943; chief of staff to Admiral
> Lord Louis Mountbatten, 1943-45.

526. Price, George Ward. <u>I Know These Dictators</u>. London,
    1938.

> Journalist and war correspondent, with <u>Daily Mail</u>; see
> also the same author's <u>Year of Reckoning</u> (London, 1939);
> and <u>Extra-Special Correspondent</u> (London, 1957).

MEMOIRS

British

527. Pritt, Denis Nowell. <u>The Autobiography of D.N. Pritt</u>.
3 vols. London, 1965-66.

Socialist M.P., 1935-50; prolific author of such books as
<u>Light on Moscow</u> (London, 1939); and <u>U.S.S.R., Our Ally</u>
(London, 1941); see also his <u>From Right to Left</u> (London,
1965).

528. Radcliffe, Baron (Cyril John Radcliffe). <u>Not in Feather
Beds</u>. London, 1968.

Director-general, ministry of Information, 1941-45.

529. Randall, Sir Alec Walter George. <u>Vatican Assignment</u>.
London, 1956.

Served British legation, Vatican, 1925-30; Bucharest,
1930-33; Foreign Office, 1933-35; Copenhagen, 1935-38;
Foreign Office counsellor, 1938-45.

530. Redcliffe-Maud, Baron (John Primatt Redcliffe-Maud).
<u>Experiences of an Optimist: The Memoirs of John
Redcliffe-Maud</u>. London, 1981.

Second secretary, ministry of Food, 1941-44; and office
of ministry of Reconstruction, 1944-45; delegate to UNRRA
conference, 1943.

531. Rees, Goronwy. <u>A Chapter of Accidents</u>. London, 1972.

Fellow of All Souls, 1931; leader writer, <u>Manchester
Guardian</u>, 1932; assistant editor, the <u>Spectator</u>, 1936;
see also <u>A Bundle of Sensations</u> (London, 1960).

532. Reith, 1st Baron (John C.W. Reith).* <u>Into the Wind</u>.
London, 1949.

Director-general, BBC, 1927-38; minister of Information,
1940; minister of Transport, 1940; minister of Works,
1940-42; with Admiralty, 1943-45; see also his <u>Wearing
Spurs</u> (London, 1966); and <u>The Reith Diaries</u>, edited by
Charles Stuart (London, 1976).

533. Rendel, Sir George Williams. <u>The Sword and the Olive:
Recollections of Diplomacy and the Foreign Service,
1913-1954</u>. London, 1957.

Head of the eastern department, Foreign Office, 1930-38;
minister to Bulgaria, 1938-41; ambassador to Yugoslav

British

government in London, 1941-43; British representative on
European committee of UNRRA, 1944-47.

534. Rennell, 1st Baron, of Rodd (James Rennell Rodd). Social
and Diplomatic Memoirs: Third Series, 1902-1919.
London, 1926.

Ambassador at Rome, 1908-19; British delegate to League
of Nations, 1921, 1923; president, court of conciliation
between Austria and Switzerland, 1925; M.P., 1928-32.

535. Richmond, Admiral Sir Herbert.* Statesmen and Sea Power.
London, 1946.

President of Royal Naval College, Greenwich, 1920-23;
commander-in-chief, East Indies, 1923-25; commandant,
Imperial Defence College, 1926-28; numerous publications
on naval strategy.

536. Riddell, Baron (George Allardice Riddell). Lord
Riddell's War Diary, 1914-1918. London, 1933.

Newspaper proprietor; chairman, News of the World,
1903-34; represented British press at peace conferences,
1919-22; continued in his Intimate Diary of the Peace
Conference and After, 1918-1923 (London, 1933).

537. Robertson, Field Marshal Sir William Robert.* Soldiers
and Statesmen, 1914-1918. 2 vols. London, 1926.

Chief of imperial general staff, 1915-18; general
officer, commander-in-chief, Britain, 1918-19; commander-
in-chief, British army on the Rhine, 1919-20; see also
his From Private to Field Marshal (London, 1921).

538. Rootham, Jasper St. John. Demi-Paradise. London, 1960.

Private secretary to Neville Chamberlain, 1938-39;
Treasury, 1939-40; later with Bank of England; see also
his Miss Fire: The Chronicle of a British Mission to
Mihailovic, 1943-1944 (London, 1946).

539. Rothermere, 1st Viscount (Harold Sidney Harmsworth).
My Campaign for Hungary. London, 1939.

Newspaper proprietor, Daily Mail, Daily Mirror, etc.;
controlled Associated Newspapers, 1922-32; see also My
Fight to Rearm Britain (London, 1939); and Warnings and
Predictions (London, 1939).

MEMOIRS

British

540. Russell, Sir Thomas Wentworth. Egyptian Service,
      1902-1946. London, 1949.

      Entered Egyptian civil service, 1902; served under
      twenty-nine different ministers of Interior, 1922-46.

541. Ryan, Sir Andrew. The Last of the Dragomans. London,
      1951.

      Entered Levant consular service, 1897; embassy dragoman,
      Constantinople, 1907-14, 1921-22; member, British
      delegation, Lausanne conference, 1922-23; consul-general
      at Rabat, 1924-30; minister at Jedda, 1930-36; and
      Albania, 1936-39.

542. Salter, Baron (Sir James Arthur Salter). Memoirs of
      a Public Servant. London, 1961.

      General secretary, Reparation Commission, 1920-22;
      director, economic and finance section, League of
      Nations, 1919-20, 1922-31; parliamentary secretary,
      ministry of Shipping, 1939-41; War Transport, 1941; head
      of British merchant shipping mission, Washington,
      1941-43; senior deputy director-general, UNRRA, 1944;
      chancellor of the Duchy of Lancaster, 1945; further
      recollections in Personality in Politics (London, 1947);
      and Slave of the Lamp: A Public Servant's Notebook
      (London, 1967).

543. Samuel, 1st Viscount, of Mount Carmel (Herbert Louis
      Samuel).* Memoirs. London, 1945.

      M.P., 1902-1918, 1929-35; high commissioner, Palestine,
      1920-25; secretary of state for Home Affairs, 1931-32;
      leader of Liberal parliamentary party, 1931-35.

544. Schuster, Sir George. Private Work and Public Causes: A
      Personal Record, 1881-1978. Cowbridge, 1979.

      Chief assistant to organiser of international credits,
      League of Nations, 1921; member, advisory committee to
      the Treasury, 1921-22; financial secretary, Sudan
      government, 1922-27; economic and financial adviser,
      Colonial Office, 1927-28; finance member of executive
      council of viceroy of India, 1928-34; M.P., 1938-45.

545. Scott, Charles Prestwich.* Political Diaries, 1911-
      1928. Edited by Trevor Wilson. London, 1970.

131

British

Editor of the Manchester Guardian, 1872-1929.

546. Scott, Sir Harold Richard. Your Obedient Servant.
London, 1959.

Entered Home Office, 1911; deputy secretary, later
secretary, ministry of Home Security, 1940-43; permanent
secretary, ministry of Aircraft Production, 1943-45.

547. Selby, Sir Walford H.M. Diplomatic Twilight, 1930-1940.
London, 1953.

Principal private secretary to secretary of state for
Foreign Affairs, 1924-32; minister at Vienna, 1933-37;
ambassador at Lisbon, 1937-40.

548. Selous, Gerald Holgate. Appointment to Fez. London,
1956.

Entered consular service, 1908; consul at Casablanca,
1924-28; Basra, 1929-32; commercial counsellor at Cairo,
1933-38; and Brussels, 1938-40; with Department of
Overseas Trade, 1940-42.

549. Shakespeare, Sir Geoffrey Hithersay. Let Candles be
Brought in. London, 1949.

Private secretary to David Lloyd George, 1921-23;
parliamentary secretary, ministry of Health, 1932-36;
Board of Education, 1936-37; Admiralty, 1937-40; and
Department of Overseas Trade, 1940; parliamentary
under-secretary of state, Dominions Office, 1940-42.

550. Shinwell, Baron (Emanuel Shinwell). Conflict Without
Malice: An Autobiography. London, 1955.

Financial secretary, War Office, 1929-30; parliamentary
secretary to Department of Mines, 1924, 1930-31; see also
I've Lived Through It All (London, 1973); and Lead with
the Left (London, 1981).

551. Sillitoe, Sir Percy. Cloak without Dagger. London,
1955.

Colonial service, 1920-23; director-general, security
service, 1946-53.

552. Simon, 1st Viscount, of Stackpole Elidor (John Allsebrook
Simon). Retrospect. London, 1952.

MEMOIRS

British

> M.P., 1906-18, 1922-40; secretary of state for Foreign
> Affairs, 1931-35; for Home Affairs, 1935-37; chancellor
> of the Exchequer, 1937-40; lord chancellor, 1940-45; see
> also his earlier Comments and Criticisms (London, 1930);
> and Portrait of My Mother (London, 1937).

553. Skrine, Sir Clarmont Percival. World War in Iran.
     London, 1962.

     Entered Indian civil service, 1912; served as political
     agent, consul-general various postings, 1921-39; resident
     for the Punjab states, 1939-41; consul-general at Meshed,
     1942-46.

554. Slessor, Marshal of the Royal Air Force Sir John. The
     Central Blue. London, 1956.

     Air staff, Air ministry, 1928-30; director of plans, Air
     ministry, 1937-41; assistant chief of air staff, 1942;
     see also his Air Power and Armies (London, 1936); and
     other publications on air power.

555. Slim, 1st Viscount (Field Marshal Sir William Slim).*
     Defeat into Victory. London, 1956.

     Various commands, Sudan, Syria-Persia-Iraq, Burma and
     India, 1939-45; commander-in-chief, allied land forces,
     south east Asia, 1945-46.

556. Snell, Baron (Henry Snell). Men, Movements and
     Myself. London, 1936.

     M.P., 1922-31; parliamentary under-secretary of state,
     India Office, 1931; deputy leader, House of Lords,
     1940-44.

557. Snowden, 1st Viscount (Philip Snowden).* An
     Autobiography. 2 vols. London, 1934.

     M.P., 1906-18, 1922-31; chancellor of the Exchequer,
     1924, 1929-31, 1931; lord privy seal, 1931-32.

558. Spears, Major-General Sir Edward. Assignment to
     Catastrophe. 2 vols. London, 1954.

     Head of British military mission, Paris, 1917-20; M.P.,
     1922-24, 1931-45; head of British mission to General de
     Gaulle, 1940; head of Spears mission to Syria and
     Lebanon, 1941; minister to Syria and Lebanon, 1942-44;

British

additional memoirs, Two Men Who Saved France (London,
1966); The Picnic Basket (London, 1967); and Fulfilment
of a Mission: Syria and Lebanon, 1941-1944 (London,
1977).

559. Spender, J.A. Life, Journalism and Politics. 2 vols.
London, 1927.

Editor of the Westminster Gazette, 1896-1922; prolific
author and biographer.

560. Steed, Henry Wickham. Through Thirty Years, 1892-1922:
A Personal Narrative. 2 vols. London, 1924.

Editor of The Times, 1919-22; historian and lecturer.

561. Stevenson, Frances (Countess Lloyd George of Dwyfor).
The Years that are Past. London, 1967.

Private secretary to Lloyd George, 1912-43; married to
him, 1943; more in her Lloyd George: A Diary, edited by
A.J.P. Taylor (London, 1971); and My Darling Pussy: The
Letters of Lloyd George and Frances Stevenson, 1913-1941,
edited by A.J.P. Taylor (London, 1975).

562. Storrs, Sir Ronald. Orientations. London, 1937.

Military governor of Jerusalem, 1917-20; governor,
Cyprus, 1926-32; and Northern Rhodesia, 1932-34; lecturer
and journalist, 1940-43.

563. Strang, 1st Baron (William Strang). Home and Abroad.
London, 1956.

Entered Foreign Office, 1919; counsellor at Moscow,
1930-32; assistant under-secretary of state in Foreign
Office, 1939-43; representative on European Advisory
Commission, 1943-45; later permanent under-secretary of
state, Foreign Office, 1949-53.

564. Strong, Major-General Sir Kenneth W.D. Intelligence at
the Top: The Recollections of an Intelligence
Officer. London, 1968.

Military attaché, Berlin, 1920-43; head of General
Eisenhower's intelligence staff, 1943-45; director-
general, political intelligence department, Foreign

MEMOIRS

<u>British</u>

Office, 1945-47; see also <u>Men of Intelligence: A Study of the Roles and Decisions of Chiefs of Intelligence from World War 1 to the Present Day</u> (London, 1970).

565. Stuart, 1st Viscount, of Findhorn (James Gray Stuart). <u>Within the Fringe: An Autobiography</u>. London, 1967.

M.P., 1923-59; a lord commissioner of the Treasury, 1935-41; joint parliamentary secretary to the Treasury, and government chief whip, 1941-45.

566. Stuart, Sir Campbell. <u>Opportunity Knocks Once</u>. London, 1952.

Deputy director of propaganda in enemy countries, 1918; representative of <u>The Times</u> at Imperial press conferences, 1920-30; with ministry of Information, 1939; director of propaganda in enemy countries, 1939-40; director of <u>The Times</u>, 1919-60.

567. Swinton, 1st Earl of (Philip Cunliffe-Lister, Baron Masham).* <u>I Remember</u>. London, 1948.

President of Board of Trade, 1922-23, 1924-29, 1931; secretary of state for Colonies, 1931-35; for Air, 1935-38; minister resident in west Africa, 1942-44; minister for Civil Aviation, 1944-45; further recollections in <u>Sixty Years of Power: Some Memories of the Men Who Wielded It</u> (London, 1966).

568. Swinton, Major-General Sir Ernest. <u>Over My Shoulder</u>. London, 1951.

Assistant secretary, Committee of Imperial Defence and war cabinet, 1913-14, 1915-18; controller of information, Air ministry, 1919-21; visited Hitler, 1936.

569. Sykes, Major-General Sir Frederick. <u>From Many Angles: An Autobiography</u>. London, 1942.

Chief of air staff, 1918-19; M.P., 1922-28, 1940-45; governor of Bombay, 1928-33; company director; member of numerous government committees.

570. Sylvester, Albert James. <u>Life with Lloyd George</u>. Edited by Colin Cross. London, 1975.

135

British

Diary extracts, 1931-45; private secretary to secretary
of war cabinet and cabinet, 1916-21; to successive prime
ministers, 1921-23; principal secretary to Lloyd George.

571. Tallents, Sir Stephen. Man and Boy. London, 1943.

Chief British delegate for relief and supply of Poland,
1919; commissioner for the Baltic provinces, 1919-20;
secretary, Empire Marketing Board, 1926-33; controller,
public relations and then overseas service, BBC, 1935-41.

572. Tedder, 1st Baron (Marshal of the Royal Air Force Arthur
William Tedder). With Prejudice: The War Memoirs.
London, 1966.

Director of training, Air ministry, 1934-36; air
commander-in-chief, Mediterranean air command, 1943;
deputy supreme commander, allied air forces in Europe,
1943-45; see also Air Power in War (London, 1948).

573. Teichman, Sir Eric. Affairs of China. London, 1938.

Chinese consular service, 1907; attached to legation at
Peking, 1907-19; Chinese secretary, then counsellor,
Peking, 1919-36; see also his Travels of a Consular
Officer in North-West China (London, 1921); and Travels
of a Consular Officer in Eastern Tibet (London, 1922).

574. Temperley, Arthur C. The Whispering Gallery of Europe.
London, 1938.

Foreword by Anthony Eden; military attaché, The Hague,
1920-24; deputy director, military operations and
intelligence, War Office, 1928-33; military
representative at the League of Nations, 1925-38.

575. Templewood, 1st Viscount (Sir Samuel John Gurney Hoare).*
Nine troubled Years. London, 1954.

M.P., 1910-44; secretary of state for Air, 1922-24,
1924-29; for India, 1931-35; for Foreign Affairs, 1935;
first lord of the Admiralty, 1936-37; secretary of state
for Home Affairs, 1937-39; lord privy seal, 1939-40;
ambassador to Spain on special mission, 1940-44; other
publications include The Fourth Seal (London, 1930);
Ambassador on Special Mission (London, 1946); and Empire
of the Air: The Advent of the Air Age, 1922-1929
(London, 1957).

MEMOIRS

British

576. Tennant, Ernest W.D. Account Settled. London, 1957.

    Businessman; frequent visitor to inter-war Germany;
member of the Anglo-German Fellowship.

577. Thomas, James Henry.* My Story. London, 1937.

    Secretary of state for Colonies, 1924, 1931, 1935-36;
lord privy seal, 1929-30; secretary of state for the
Dominions, 1930-35.

578. Thompson, Sir Geoffrey Harington. Front Line Diplomat.
    London, 1959.

    Entered diplomatic service, 1920; served at home and
abroad, including South America, Spain, United States,
Iraq and Turkey, 1920-45.

579. Thomson, Rear-Admiral George Pirie. Blue Pencil Admiral.
    London, 1947.

    Chief press censor, ministry of Information, 1941-45.

580. Thurtle, Ernest. Time's Winged Chariot: Memoirs and
    Comments. London, 1945.

    Parliamentary private secretary to the minister of
Pensions, 1924; secretary, ministry of Information,
1941-45.

581. Tilley, Sir John Anthony Cecil. London to Tokyo.
    London, 1942.

    Entered Foreign Office, 1893; assistant secretary,
1919-20; ambassador to Brazil, 1921-25; and Tokyo,
1926-31.

582. Tizard, Sir Henry.* A Scientist in and out of the Civil
    Service. London, 1955.

    Permanent secretary, Department of Scientific and
Industrial Research, 1927-29; chairman, Aeronautical
Research Committee, 1933-43; chairman, Air Defence
Committee, 1935-40, committee responsible for development
of radar; adviser, ministry of Aircraft Production,
1940-42.

583. Tree, Ronald. When the Moon was High: Memoirs of Peace
    and War, 1897-1942. London, 1975.

BRITISH FOREIGN POLICY, 1918-1945

British

M.P., 1933-45; parliamentary private secretary to R.S.
Hudson, 1936-38; and Sir John Reith, Alfred Duff-Cooper,
and Brendan Bracken, 1940-43.

584. Trevelyan, Baron (Humphrey Trevelyan). Public and
Private. London, 1980.

Indian political service, 1932-47; later deputy under-
secretary of state, Foreign Office, 1962; other publications include Worlds Apart (London, 1971); Diplomatic
Channels (London, 1973); and Public and Private (London,
1980).

585. Vansittart, Baron (Robert Gilbert Vansittart).*
Lessons of My Life: The Autobiography of Lord
Vansittart. London, 1943.

Entered Foreign Office, 1903; secretary to Lord Curzon,
1920-24; assistant under-secretary of state for Foreign
Affairs, 1928-30; permanent under-secretary of state for
Foreign Affairs, 1930-38; chief diplomatic adviser to
foreign secretary, 1938-41; further memoirs in The Mist
Procession (London, 1958); of related interest are Black
Record: Germans Past and Present (London, 1941); and
Bones of Contention (London, 1945); as well, plays and
film scripts.

586. Wavell, Archibald Percival (1st Earl Wavell).*
Speaking Generally: Broadcasts, Orders and Addresses
in Time of War, 1939-1943. London, 1946.

Military career, 1903-1941; commander-in-chief, India,
1941; supreme commander, south west Pacific, 1941-43;
viceroy of India, 1943-47; see also his The Viceroy's
Journal, edited by Penderel Moon (London, 1973); and
Soldiers and Soldiering (London, 1953).

587. Webster, Sir Charles Kingsley.* The Historian as
Diplomat: Charles Kingsley Webster and the United
Nations, 1939-1946. Edited by P.A. Reynolds and E.J.
Hughes. London, 1976.

With British delegation, Paris peace conference, 1918-19;
director of British Library of Information, New York,
1941-42; Foreign Office, 1943-46; numerous works on
diplomatic history.

588. Wedgwood, Josiah Clement (1st Baron Wedgwood).* Memoirs
of a Fighting Life. London, 1941.

138

MEMOIRS

British

M.P., 1906-42; chancellor of the Duchy of Lancaster,
1924.

589. Wellesley, Sir Victor. **Diplomacy in Fetters**. London,
1944.

Page of honour to Queen Victoria, 1887-92; counsellor,
far eastern department, Foreign Office, 1920-24;
assistant under-secretary, 1924-25; deputy under-
secretary, 1925-36; see also his **Recollections of a
Soldier-Diplomat** (London, 1947).

590. Wheeler-Bennett, Sir John W. **Knaves, Fools and Heroes:
In Europe Between the Wars**. London, 1974.

Diplomatic historian and biographer; assistant director,
British Press Service, New York, 1940-41; head of New
York office of Political Warfare Mission, 1942-44;
adviser to political intelligence department of Foreign
Office, 1944; assistant to British political adviser to
SHAEF, 1944-45; memoirs continued in **Special Relation-
ships: America in Peace and War** (London, 1975); and
Friends, Enemies and Sirens (London, 1978); see also his
**A Wreath to Clio: Studies in British, American and German
Affairs** (New York, 1967).

591. Willert, Sir Arthur. **Washington and Other Memories**.
Boston, 1972.

Journalist with **The Times**, 1906-20; Washington
representative of ministry of Information, 1917-18;
joined Foreign Office, 1921; resigned as head of news
department, 1935; with ministry of Information, 1939-45.

592. Wilson, 1st Baron (Field Marshal Sir Henry Maitland
Wilson). **Eight Years Overseas, 1939-1947**. London,
1950.

General officer commander-in-chief, Egypt, 1939;
Cyrenaica, 1941; Greece, 1941; and Persia-Iraq command,
1942-43; commander-in-chief, Middle East, 1943; supreme
allied commander, Mediterranean theatre, 1944; head of
British joint staff mission, Washington, 1944-45.

593. Wilson, Sir Arnold.* **Mesopotamia, 1917-1920: A Clash of
Loyalties**. London, 1931.

Civil commissioner in Persian Gulf, 1918-20; with
Anglo-Persian Oil Company, 1921-32; M.P., 1933-40;

British

diary extracts in Walks and Thoughts (London, 1934);
Thoughts and Talks (London, 1938); Walks and Talks Abroad
(London, 1936); and More Thoughts and Talks (London,
1939).

594. Windsor, Edward, Duke of.* A King's Story. London,
1951.

Prince of Wales, 1910-36; succeeded as king and
abdicated, 1936.

595. Wingate, Sir Ronald Evelyn Leslie. Not in the
Limelight. London, 1959.

Indian political service, 1919-39; with joint planning
staff, offices of the war cabinet, 1939-45.

596. Winterbotham, Frederick William. The Nazi Connection.
London, 1978.

Air staff and Foreign Office, 1929-45; served that time
with the Secret Intelligence Service; see also his
Secret and Personal (London, 1969).

597. Winterton, 6th Earl (Edward Turnour).* Orders of the
Day. London, 1953.

M.P., 1904-51; parliamentary under-secretary for India,
1922-24, 1924-29; chancellor of the Duchy of Lancaster,
1937-39; member of the cabinet, 1938-39; further random
recollections in Fifty Tumultuous Years (London, 1955).

598. Woolf, Leonard Sidney.* Downhill All the Way: An Autobiography of the Years 1919-1939. London, 1968.

Literary editor, The Nation, 1923-30; joint editor,
Political Quarterly, 1931-59.

599. Woolton, 1st Earl of (Frederick James Marquis). Memoirs.
London, 1959.

Minister of Food, 1940-43; minister of Reconstruction,
1943-45; lord president of the Council, 1945, 1951-52.

600. Young, Arthur Primrose. Across the Years. London, 1971.

In contact with anti-Hitler resistance; with ministry of
Labour, 1940-41.

MEMOI RS

Bri tish

601. Zetland, 2nd Marquess of (Lawrence John Lumley Dundas,
     Earl of Ronaldshay). 'Essayez': Memoirs. London,
     1956.

     Secretary of state for India, 1935-40; and for Burma,
     1937-40.

602. Zuckerman, Baron (Sir Solly Zuckerman). From Apes to
     Warlords, 1904-1946. London, 1978.

     Scientific advisory posts, RAF, 1939-46.

Non-British in London

603. Azcarate y Flores, Pablo. Mi Embajado en Londres Durante
     La Guerra Civil Espanola. Barcelona, 1976.

     Member of League of Nations secretariat, 1922-33; deputy
     secretary-general, 1933-36; Spanish ambassador at London,
     1936-39.

604. Bastianini, Giuseppe. Uomini, cose, fatti: Memorie di
     un ambasciatore. Milan, 1959.

     Italian ambassador at London, 1939-40.

605. Benes, Eduard. Pameti od Mnichova k nové válce a k
     novému vitežstvi. Prague, 1947. Eng. trans., Memoirs:
     From Munich to New War and New Victory. London, 1954.

     The first, and only, of three projected volumes by the
     Czech president, 1935-38; and president of the Czech
     National Committee in London, 1939-45.

606. Blondel, Jules-François. Ce que mes yeux ont vu de 1900
     à 1950: Récit d'un diplomate. 2 vols. Arras, n.d.

     Attached to London embassy, 1919-21; director of Comité
     National Français in London, 1942; see also Au fil de la
     carrière: Récit d'un diplomate, 1911-1938 (Paris, 1960).

607. Cambon, Pierre Paul. Correspondance, 1870-1924.
     3 vols. Paris, 1940-46.

     French ambassador at London, 1898-1920.

608. Casey, Baron (Richard Gardiner Casey). Personal
     Experience, 1939-1946. London, 1962.

Non-British in London

Minister of state resident in the Middle East, and member
of the British war cabinet, 1942-43; later Australian
foreign minister, 1951-60; see also his Friends and
Neighbours (Melbourne, 1954).

609. Dawes, Charles Gates.* Journal as Ambassador to Great
Britain. New York, 1939.

Recollections, based largely on diaries, of US ambassador
to London, 1929-32; equally important on the Dawes plan
is A Journal of Reparations (New York, 1939).

610. Dirksen, Herbert von. Moskau, Tokio, London:
Erinnerungen und Betrachtungen zu 20 Jahren deutscher
Aussenpolitik, 1919-1939. Stuttgart, 1949. Abr.
Eng. trans., Moscow, Tokyo, London: Twenty Years of
German Foreign Policy. London, 1951.

German ambassador at London, 1938-39.

611. Fitz-Randolph, Sigismond-Sizzo. Der Frühstücks-
Attaché aus London. Stuttgart, 1954.

Press attaché at German embassy in London, 1933-39.

612. Franckenstein, George. Facts and Features of My Life.
London, 1939.

Austrian minister at London, 1920-38.

613. Gaulle, Général Charles de. Mémoires de guerre.
3 vols. Paris, 1954-59. Eng. trans., The Complete War
Memoirs. London, 1964.

Commander-in-chief, Fighting French Forces, 1940-43;
president, French Committee for National Liberation,
1943-44; president, provisional government of the French
republic, 1944-46.

614. Grandi, Dino. Dino Grandi racconta. Venice, 1945.

Italy's ambassador at London, 1932-39.

615. Gripenberg, Georg Achates. Finland and the Great Powers:
Memoirs of a Diplomat. Lincoln, NE, 1965.

Finnish minister at London, 1933-41.

142

Non-British in London

616. Hägglöf, Gunnar. <u>Diplomat: Memoirs of a Swedish Envoy</u>
     <u>in London, Paris, Berlin, Moscow and Washington</u>.
     London, 1972.

     Attached to Swedish consulate-general in London, 1928-29;
     minister accredited to Belgian and Netherlands wartime
     governments in London, 1944.

617. Harriman, W. Averell. <u>Special Envoy to Churchill and</u>
     <u>Stalin, 1941-1946</u>. With the assistance of Elie Abel.
     New York, 1975.

     Roosevelt's special representative to London, with rank
     of minister, 1941; Combined Shipping Adjustment Board
     representative in London, 1941.

618. Henle, Günter. <u>Weggenosse des Jahrhunderts</u>. Stuttgart,
     1968.

     Served at German embassy in London from 1931-36.

619. Hesse, Fritz. <u>Das Spiel um Deutschland</u>. Munich, 1953.
     Eng. trans., <u>Hitler and the English</u>. London, 1954.

     <u>Deutsches Nachrichten Büro</u> representative and press
     attaché at German embassy, London, 1935-39.

620. Hymans, Paul. <u>Mémoires</u>. 2 vols. Brussels, 1958.

     Belgian minister at London, 1915-17; minister of Foreign
     Affairs, 1918-20, 1924-25, 1927-36; see also his
     <u>Fragments d'histoire: Impressions et souvenirs</u>
     (Brussels, 1940).

621. Kleffens, Eelco Nicolaas van. <u>The Rape of the</u>
     <u>Netherlands</u>. London, 1940.

     Dutch minister of Foreign Affairs, 1939-46; with
     government in exile, London, 1940-45.

622. Lee, Raymond E. <u>The London Observer: The Journal</u>
     <u>of General Raymond E. Lee, 1940-1941</u>. Edited by James
     R. Leutze. London, 1972.

     US military attaché, London, 1935-39, 1940-41.

623. Maisky, Ivan. <u>Vospominaniia sovetskogo posla</u>. 2 vols.
     Moscow, 1964.

Non-British in London

    Counsellor, Soviet embassy, London, 1925-27; then Soviet
    ambassador, 1932-43; translations from the Russian have
    appeared as Journey into the Past (London, 1962); Who
    Helped Hitler? (London, 1964); Spanish Notebooks (London,
    1966); and Memoirs of a Soviet Ambassador: The War,
    1939-1943 (London, 1967); of related interest is Before
    the Storm (London, 1944).

624. Massey, Vincent. What's Past is Prologue. London, 1963.

    Canadian high commissioner at London, 1935-46.

625. Monick, Emmanuel. Pour mémoire. Paris, 1970.

    French financial attaché, London, 1934-40.

626. Monnet, Jean. Mémoires. Paris, 1976. Eng. trans.,
    Memoirs. London, 1978.

    French representative on various inter-allied executive
    committees, London, 1917-18; chairman, Anglo-French
    economic co-ordination committee, 1939; member, British
    Supply Council, Washington, 1940-43.

627. Moravec, General Frantisek. Master of Spies: The
    Memoirs of General Moravec. London, 1975.

    Head of Czechoslovak military intelligence in Prague, and
    then with exiled organisation in London, 1937-45.

628. Palmstierna, Erik. Atskelliga Egenheter. Stockholm,
    1958.

    Swedish minister at London, 1920-37.

629. Passy, Colonel [A.E.V. Dewavrin]. Souvenirs. 3 vols.
    Monte Carlo, 1947.

    Head of counter-intelligence for Free French in London.

630. Pearson, Lester B. Mike: The Memoirs of the Right
    Honourable Lester B. Pearson. 3 vols. Toronto,
    Ontario, 1972-75.

    Canadian counsellor to high commission in London,
    1935-41; later prime minister, 1963-68.

MEMOIRS

Non-British in London

631. Putlitz, Wolfgang Gans Edler Herr zu. <u>Unterwegs nach</u>
     <u>Deutschland: Erinnerungen eines ehemaligen</u>
     <u>Diplomaten</u>. Berlin, 1956. Abr. Eng. trans., <u>The</u>
     <u>Putlitz Dossier</u>. London, 1957.

     Headed consular division, German embassy, London,
     1934-38.

632. Raczynski, Count Edward. <u>W Sojuszniczym Londynie:</u>
     <u>Dziennik Ambasadora Edwarda Raczynskiego, 1939-1945</u>.
     London, 1960. Eng. trans., <u>In Allied London</u>. London,
     1962.

     Polish ambassador at London, 1934-45; acting Polish
     minister for Foreign Affairs, 1941-43; see also his <u>The</u>
     <u>British-Polish Alliance: Its Origin and Meaning</u> (London,
     1948).

633. Ribbentrop, Joachim von. <u>Zwischen London und Moskau:</u>
     <u>Erinnerungen und letzte Aufzeichnungen</u>. Edited by
     Anneliese von Ribbentrop. Leoni am Starnberger See,
     1953. Eng. trans., <u>The Ribbentrop Memoirs</u>. London,
     1954.

     German ambassador at London, 1936-38.

634. Ritchie, Charles. <u>The Siren Years: A Canadian Diplomat</u>
     <u>Abroad, 1937-1945</u>. London, 1974.

     Second secretary, Canadian high commission, London, 1939;
     1st secretary, 1943-45; later high commissioner.

635. Rueff, Jacques. <u>Oeuvres complètes: I, De l'aube au</u>
     <u>crépuscule; Autobiographie de l'auteur</u>. Paris, 1977.

     Financial counsellor, French embassy in London, 1930-33;
     see also his <u>Combats pour l'ordre financier: Mémoires et</u>
     <u>documents pour servir à l'histoire du dernier demi-siècle</u>
     (Paris, 1972).

636. Saint-Aulaire, Comte Auguste de. <u>Confession d'un vieux</u>
     <u>diplomate</u>. Paris, 1953.

     Ambassador at London, 1920-24; see also his <u>Je suis</u>
     <u>diplomate</u> (Paris, 1954).

637. Schweppenburg, Leo Geyr von. <u>Erinnerungen eines</u>
     <u>Militärattachés: London, 1933-1937</u>. Stuttgart, 1949.
     Eng. trans., <u>The Critical Years</u>. London, 1952.

Non-British in London

German military attaché in London, 1933-37; foreword by
Leslie Hore-Belisha.

638. Shigemitsu, Marmoru. Japan and Her Destiny: My Struggle
     for Peace. London, 1958.

     Japanese ambassador at London, 1938-41.

639. Smuts, Jan Christiaan. Selections from the Smuts
     Papers. Edited by W.K. Hancock and Jean van der Poel.
     7 vols. London, 1966-73.

     Vols. 5-6 for 1919-45; South African representative,
     imperial war cabinet, 1917-18; prime minister, 1919-24;
     at Paris peace conference, 1919.

640. Soustelle, Jacques. Envers et contre tout. 2 vols.
     Paris, 1947-50.

     Joined de Gaulle in London, 1940; active in Free French
     information services; vice-chief of cabinet, 1944.

641. Stirling, Alfred. Lord Bruce: The London Years.
     Melbourne, 1974.

     Memoir-history-biography by counsellor in the Australian
     high commission; mainly dealing with period 1936-45.

642. Thayer, Charles W. Hands Across the Caviar. London,
     1953.

     US foreign service, 1933-53; in London, 1943-44.

643. Vogel, Georg. Diplomat unter Hitler und Adenauer.
     Düsseldorf, 1969.

     Various diplomatic postings, including consular division,
     London, 1937-39.

644. Wimmer, Lothar. Expériences et tribulations d'un
     diplomate autrichien entre deux guerres, 1929-1938.
     Neuchâtel, 1946.

     Austrian legation counsellor in London, 1930-34; and
     later ambassador, 1951-55; continued in Zwischen
     Ballhausplatz und Downing Street (Vienna, 1958).

645. Winant, John Gilbert. A Letter from Grosvenor Square:
     An Account of a Stewardship. London, 1947.

MEMOIRS

Non-British in London

US ambassador at London, 1941-46; only covers events of 1941.

646. Yoshida, Shigeru. The Yoshida Memoirs: The Story of Japan in Crisis. London, 1961.

Japanese ambassador at London, 1936-38.

2. British Biographies

647. Adam, Colin Forbes. Life of Lord Lloyd. London, 1948.

M.P., 1918-23, 1924-25; high commissioner for Egypt and the Sudan, 1925-29; chairman of the British Council, 1937-41; secretary of state for the Colonies, 1940-41; see also Lord Lloyd, The British Case (London, 1939); and his Egypt Since Cromer, 2 vols. (London, 1933-34).

648. Aldington, Richard. Lawrence of Arabia: A Biographical Enquiry. London, 1955.

Subsequent biographies include Suleiman Mousa, T.E. Lawrence: An Arab View (London, 1966); Philip Knightley and Colin Simpson, The Secret Lives of Lawrence of Arabia (London, 1969); H. Montgomery Hyde, Solitary in the Ranks: Lawrence of Arabia as Airman and Private Soldier (London, 1978); and Desmond Stewart, T.E. Lawrence (London, 1978).

649. Anderson, Mosa. Noel Buxton: A Life. London, 1952.

M.P., 1905-6, 1910-18, 1922-30; minister of Agriculture, 1924, 1929-30.

650. Aspinall-Oglander, Cecil. Roger Keyes. London, 1951.

651. Aster, Sidney. Anthony Eden. London, 1976.

Part of a "British Prime Ministers" series; the most complete is David Carlton, Anthony Eden (London, 1981); earlier efforts are Denis Bardens, Portrait of a Statesman (London, 1955); Lewis Broad, Sir Anthony Eden (London, 1955); Alan Campbell-Johnson, Sir Anthony Eden: A Biography (London, 1955); William Rees-Mogg, Sir Anthony Eden (London, 1956); Randolph S. Churchill, The Rise and Fall of Sir Anthony Eden (London, 1959); see also Anthony Nutting, "Lord Avon", in The Prime Ministers, edited by Herbert van Thal, vol. 2 (London, 1975); of interest is V.G. Trukhanovskii, Antoni Eden (Moscow, 1983).

652. Beesly, Patrick. <u>Very Special Admiral: The Life of
     Admiral J.H. Godfrey, CB</u>. London, 1980.

     Biography of the deputy director, plans division,
     Admiralty, 1933-35; director of naval intelligence,
     1939-42.

653. Bindoff, S.T., and Clark, G.N. <u>Charles Kingsley Webster,
     1886-1961</u>. London, 1963.

654. Birkenhead, Earl of. <u>Frederick Edwin, 1st Earl of
     Birkenhead</u>. 2 vols. London, 1933-35.

     Attorney-general, 1915-19; lord chancellor, 1920-22;
     secretary of state for India, 1924-28; see also William
     Camp, <u>The Glittering Prizes</u> (London, 1960); and John
     Campbell, <u>F.E. Smith: First Earl of Birkenhead</u> (London,
     1983).

655. Birkenhead, Earl of. <u>Halifax: The Life of Lord Halifax</u>.
     London, 1965.

     Based on Lord Halifax's private papers; supersedes
     previous biographies such as Alan Campbell Johnson,
     <u>Viscount Halifax</u> (London, 1941); and Stuart Hodgson, <u>Lord
     Halifax</u> (London, 1941).

656. Birkenhead, Earl of. <u>The Prof. in Two Worlds</u>. London,
     1961.

     Official life of Frederick Alexander Lindeman, 1st Baron
     Cherwell; Churchill's personal scientific adviser in
     wartime; another study is R.F. Harrod, <u>The Prof.: A
     Personal Memoir of Lord Cherwell</u> (London, 1959).

657. Birkenhead, Earl of. <u>Walter Monckton</u>. London, 1969.

     Biography of 1st Viscount Monckton; deputy director-
     general and then director-general of ministry of
     Information, 1940-41; solicitor-general, 1945.

658. Blake, Robert. <u>The Unknown Prime Minister: The Life and
     Times of Andrew Bonar Law, 1857-1923</u>. London, 1955.

     Chancellor of the Exchequer, 1916-18; prime minister,
     1922-23.

659. Blaxland, Gregory. <u>J.H. Thomas: A Life for Unity</u>.
     London, 1964.

660. Bolitho, Hector. <u>Alfred Mond: First Lord Melchett</u>.
     London, 1933.

M.P., 1906, 1910-23, 1924-28; minister of Health,
1921-22; see also Jean Goodman, The Mond Legacy (London,
1982); based on family papers.

661. Bonham-Carter, Victor. Soldier True: The life and Times
of Field-Marshal Sir William Robertson, 1860-1933.
London, 1963.

662. Bowle, John. Viscount Samuel: A Biography. London,
1957.

663. Boyle, Andrew. Montagu Norman: A Biography. London,
1967.

Governor of the Bank of England, 1920-44; equally useful
is Sir Henry Clay, Lord Norman (London, 1957).

664. Boyle, Andrew. Only the Wind Will Listen: Reith of the
B.B.C.. London, 1972.

665. Boyle, Andrew. Trenchard: Man of Vision. London, 1962.

Authorised biography of 1st Viscount Trenchard; chief of
air staff, 1918-29; see also Wing-Commander H.R. Allen,
The Legacy of Lord Trenchard (London, 1972).

666. Brittain, Vera. Pethick-Lawrence: A Portrait. London,
1963.

667. Broderick, Alan Houghton. Near to Greatness: A Life of
the Sixth Earl Winterton. London, 1965.

668. Buchan, William. John Buchan. London, 1982.

By his son; see also Janet Adam Smith, John Buchan: A
Biography (London, 1965).

669. Bullock, Alan. The Life and Times of Ernest Bevin.
3 vols. London, 1960-83.

Minister of Labour and National Service, 1940-45;
secretary of state for Foreign Affairs, 1945-51; see also
Francis Williams, Ernest Bevin (London, 1952).

670. Busch, Briton Cooper. Hardinge of Penshurst: A Study in
the Old Diplomacy. Hamden, CT, 1980.

671. Butler, Ewan. Mason-Mac: The Life of Lieutenant-General
Sir Noel Mason-MacFarlane. London, 1972.

Military attaché in Europe, including Berlin, 1937-39;
commander-in-chief, Gibraltar, 1942-44; chief
commissioner, allied control commission for Italy, 1944.

672. Butler, J.R.M. <u>Lord Lothian (Philip Kerr), 1882-1940.</u>
London, 1960.

673. Callwell, Sir Charles Edward. <u>Field Marshal Sir Henry
Wilson: His Life and Diaries.</u> 2 vols. London, 1927.

Authorised biography of chief of the imperial general
staff, 1918-22; see also Bernard Ash, <u>The Lost Dictator:
A Biography of Field Marshal Sir Henry Wilson</u> (London,
1968); and Basil Collier, <u>Brasshat: A Biography of
Field Marshal Sir Henry Wilson, 1864-1922</u> (London,
1961).

674. Cecil, David. <u>The Cecils of Hatfield House: An English
Ruling Family.</u> London, 1973.

Including 1st Viscount Cecil of Chelwood; see also
Kenneth Rose, <u>The Later Cecils</u> (London, 1975).

675. Chalmers, William Scott. <u>Full Cycle: The Biography of
Admiral Sir Bertram Home Ramsay.</u> London, 1959.

On staff of Imperial Defence College, 1931-33; allied
naval commander-in-chief, expeditionary force, 1944-45;
see also David Woodward, <u>Ramsay at War: The Fighting
Life of Admiral Sir Bertram Ramsay</u> (London, 1957).

676. Churchill, Randolph S. <u>Lord Derby, "King of Lancashire":
The Official Life of Edward, Seventeenth Earl of Derby,
1865-1948.</u> London, 1959.

Secretary of state for War, 1916-18, 1922-24; ambassador
to France, 1918-20.

677. Churchill, Randolph S., and Gilbert, Martin. <u>Winston S.
Churchill.</u> London, 1966-.

The official biography in progress; presently to 1941 in
six volumes; vols. 1-2 by Randolph S. Churchill;
accompanying each volume is a massive collection of
documents, Randolph S. Churchill and Martin Gilbert,
<u>Winston S. Churchill: Companion Volume</u> (London, 1967-);
in several parts, each companion volume publishes
material from the Churchill papers and numerous other
sources; supersedes all previous biographies; Henry
Pelling, <u>Churchill</u> (London, 1974) is an adequate interim
life; assessments include Robert Rhodes James, <u>Churchill,
A Study in Failure, 1900-1939</u> (London, 1970); and A.J.P.
Taylor, et al., <u>Churchill Revised: A Critical Assessment</u>
(London, 1968); see also Kenneth Young, <u>Churchill and
Beaverbrook: A Study in Friendship and Politics</u> (London,
1966).

678. Clark, Ronald W. Tizard. London, 1965.

679. Collier, Basil. Leader of the Few: The Authorized
     Biography of Air Chief Marshal the Lord Dowding of
     Bentley Priory. London, 1957.

     Director of training, Air ministry, 1926-29; air officer
     commanding-in-chief, fighter command, 1936-40; on special
     duty in Washington, 1940-41; see also Robert Wright,
     Dowding and the Battle of Britain (London, 1969).

680. Colville, John R. Man of Valour: The Life of Field-
     Marshal the Viscount Gort. London, 1972.

     Chief of imperial general staff, 1937-39; commander-in-
     chief, British field force, 1939-40, commander-in-chief,
     Gibraltar, 1941-42; Malta, 1942-44; and Palestine,
     1944-45.

681. Cooke, Colin. The Life of Richard Stafford Cripps.
     London, 1957.

     Solicitor-general, 1930-31; ambassador to Russia,
     1940-42; lord privy seal, 1942; minister of Aircraft
     Production, 1942-45; see also Eric Estorick, Stafford
     Cripps: A Biography (London, 1949); and Patricia
     Strauss, Cripps (London, 1943).

682. Coote, Colin. A Companion of Honour: The Story of
     Walter Elliot. London, 1965.

     Financial secretary to the Treasury, 1931-32; minister of
     Agriculture and Fisheries, 1932-36; secretary of state
     for Scotland, 1936-38; minister of Health, 1938-40;
     director of public relations, War Office, 1941-42.

683. Cosgrave, Patrick. R.A. Butler: An English Life.
     London, 1981.

     More a long essay than a biography; see also Gerald
     Sparrow, "R.A.B.": Study of a Statesman (London, 1965).

684. Cross, Colin. Philip Snowden. London, 1966.

685. Cross, J.A. Sir Samuel Hoare: A Political Biography.
     London, 1977.

686. Cross, J.A. Lord Swinton. London, 1983.

687. Dixon, Piers. Double Diploma: The Life of Sir Pierson
     Dixon, Don and Diplomat. London, 1968.

Served at British embassies in Madrid, 1932; Ankara, 1936; and Rome, 1938; principal private secretary to the secretary of state for Foreign Affairs, 1943-48.

688. Donaldson, Frances. Edward VIII. London, 1974.

See also Michael Bloch, The Duke of Windsor's War (London, 1983); based on the Windsors' private papers.

689. Donoghue, Bernard, and Jones, G.W. Herbert Morrison: Portrait of a Politician. London, 1973.

690. Evans, Trefor Ellis. Mission to Egypt, 1934-1946: Lord Killearn, High Commissioner and Ambassador. Cardiff, 1971.

Author in consular service, 1937-41; private secretary to Lord Killearn, 1941-45.

691. Feiling, Keith. The Life of Neville Chamberlain. London, 1946.

Based on Chamberlain's papers and still unsurpassed; see also Duncan Keith-Shaw, Prime Minister Neville Chamberlain (London, 1939); Derek Walker-Smith, Neville Chamberlain (London, 1940); Iain Macleod, Neville Chamberlain (London, 1961); William R. Rock, Neville Chamberlain (New York, 1969); H. Montgomery Hyde, Neville Chamberlain (London, 1976); and the family biographies by D.H. Elletson, The Chamberlains (London, 1966); and Sir Charles Petrie, The Chamberlain Tradition (London, 1952).

692. Fisher, Nigel. Harold Macmillan. London, 1982.

See also Anthony Sampson, Macmillan: A Study in Ambiguity (London, 1967); and Emrys Hughes, Macmillan: Portrait of a Politician (London, 1962).

693. Foot, Michael. Aneurin Bevan: A Biography. 2 vols. London, 1962-73.

M.P., 1929-60; editor, Tribune, 1942-45; minister of Health and Housing, 1945-51; vol. 1 for 1897-1945; see also Vincent Brome, Aneurin Bevan (London, 1953); and Mark M. Krug, Aneurin Bevan: Cautious Rebel (London, 1961).

694. Fraser, David. Alanbrooke. London, 1982.

Based on war diaries and letters of Field Marshal Sir Alan Brooke, 1st Viscount Alanbrooke; commander-in-chief, home forces, 1940-41; chief of the imperial general

staff, 1941-46; see also Sir Arthur Bryant, The Turn of
the Tide, 1939-1943 (London, 1957); and Triumph in the
West, 1943-1946 (London, 1959).

695. Fraser, Peter. Lord Esher: A Political Biography.
London. 1973.

696. Gardner, Brian. Allenby. London, 1965.

1st Viscount, Field Marshal Sir Edmund Allenby; military
career, 1884-1917; commander-in-chief, Egyptian
expeditionary force, 1917-19; high commissioner for
Egypt, 1919-25; see also Field Marshal Viscount Wavell,
Allenby: A Study in Greatness, 2 vols. (London,
1940-43).

697. Garvin, Katharine. J.L. Garvin: A Memoir. London,
1948.

Editor of the Observer, 1908-42; background in Alfred M.
Gollin, The Observer and J.L. Garvin, 1908-1914: A Study
in a Great Editorship (London, 1960).

698. Gilbert, Martin. Plough My Own Furrow: The Story of
Lord Allen of Hurtwood as Told Through his Writings and
Correspondence. London, 1965.

Chairman, Independent Labour party, 1922-26; director,
Daily Herald, 1925-30; advocate of Anglo-German
conciliation in 1930s; twice visited Hitler; see also
Arthur Marwick, Clifford Allen: The Open Conspirator
(London, 1964); W.H. Warwick, Clifford Allen (London,
1964); and of related interest, Lady Marjory Allen,
Memoirs of an Uneducated Lady (London, 1975).

699. Gilbert, Martin. Sir Horace Rumbold: Portrait of a
Diplomat, 1869-1941. London, 1973.

Minister at Berne, 1916-19; and Warsaw, 1919-20; high
commissioner, Constantinople, 1920-24; ambassador at
Madrid, 1924-28; and Berlin, 1928-33.

700. Gollin, Alfred M. Proconsul in Politics: A Study of
Lord Milner in Opposition and in Power. London, 1964.

Minister without portfolio, 1916-18; secretary of state
for War, 1918; secretary of state for Colonies, 1918-21;
other studies include Terence O'Brien, Milner (London,
1979); John Marlowe, Milner (London, 1976); Edward
Crankshaw, The Forsaken Idea: A Study of Viscount Milner
(London, 1952); and John Evelyn Wrench, Alfred, Lord
Milner, 1854-1925 (London, 1958).

701. Hamilton, Mary Agnes. <u>Arthur Henderson: A Biography</u>.
     London, 1938.

     Secretary of Labour party, 1911-34; home secretary, 1924;
     secretary of state for Foreign Affairs, 1929-31; Nobel
     peace prize, 1934; see also Edwin A. Jenkins, <u>From
     Foundry to Foreign Office: The Romantic Life Story</u> of
     <u>the Rt. Hon. Arthur Henderson, M.P.</u> (London, 1933).

702. Hamilton, Nigel. <u>Monty: The Making of a General</u>.
     London, 1981-.

     In progress; vol. 1 to 1942; vol. 2, 1942-44; earlier
     studies include Alun Chalfont, <u>Montgomery of Alamein</u>
     (London, 1976); Ronald W. Clark, <u>Montgomery of Alamein</u>
     (London, 1960); and Alan Moorehead, <u>Montgomery</u> (London,
     1946).

703. Hammond, John Lawrence. <u>C.P. Scott of the 'Manchester
     Guardian'</u>. London, 1934.

704. Harington, General Sir Charles. <u>Plumer of Messines</u>.
     London, 1935.

     1st Viscount Plumer; governor of Malta, 1919-24; high
     commissioner in Palestine, 1925-28.

705. Harris, Henry Wilson. <u>J.A. Spender</u>. London, 1946.

706. Harris, Kenneth. <u>Attlee</u>. London, 1982.

     Supersedes previous studies such as Francis Williams, <u>A
     Prime Minister Remembers</u> (London, 1961); and Roy
     Jenkins, <u>Mr. Attlee: An Interim Biography</u> (London,
     1948).

707. Harrod, R.F. <u>The Life of John Maynard Keynes</u>. London,
     1951.

     See also Robert Skidelsky, <u>John Maynard Keyes</u>, vol. 1,
     <u>Hopes Betrayed, 1883-1920</u> (London, 1983-); Milo Keynes,
     ed., <u>Essays on John Maynard Keynes</u> (London, 1980); and
     Seymour Harris, <u>John Maynard Keynes: Economist and
     Policy Maker</u> (London, 1955).

708. Hassall, Christopher. <u>Edward Marsh</u>. London, 1959.

     Private secretary to Winston Churchill, 1917-22, 1924-29;
     to J.H. Thomas, 1924, 1929-36; and to Malcolm MacDonald,
     1936-37.

BRITISH BIOGRAPHIES

709. Hill, Prudence. To Know the Sky: The Life of Air Chief Marshal Sir Roderic Hill. London, 1962.

Director, technical development, Air ministry, 1938-40; director-general, research and development, ministry of Aircraft Production, 1940-41; air marshal commanding air defence of Great Britain, 1943-44; fighter command, 1944-45.

710. Hoggart, Simon, and Leigh, David. Michael Foot: A Portrait. London, 1981.

Assistant editor, Tribune, 1937-38; acting editor, Evening Standard, 1942; later editor, Tribune, and leader of the Labour party, 1980-83.

711. Hore-Belisha, Leslie (Baron Hore-Belisha). The Private Papers of Hore-Belisha. Edited by R.J. Minney. London, 1960.

M.P., 1923-45; parliamentary secretary, Board of Trade, 1931-32; financial secretary to Treasury, 1932-34; minister of Transport, 1934-37; secretary of state for War, 1937-40; minister of National Insurance, 1945.

712. Hough, Richard. Mountbatten: Hero of Our Time. London, 1980.

1st Earl Mountbatten of Burma; entered navy, 1913; chief of combined operations, 1942-43; member of British chiefs of staff committee, 1942-43; supreme allied commander, south east Asia, 1943-46; see also Charles Smith, Fifty Years with Mountbatten (London, 1980); and John Terraine, The Life and Times of Lord Mountbatten (London, 1968).

713. Hunt, Barry D. Sailor-Scholar: Admiral Sir Herbert Richmond, 1871-1946. Waterloo, Ontario, 1982.

President, Royal Naval War College, Greenwich, 1920-23; commandant of the Imperial Defence College, 1927-28; see also Arthur J. Marder, Portrait of an Admiral: The Life and Papers of Sir Herbert Richmond (London, 1952).

714. Hyde, H. Montgomery. The Quiet Canadian: The Secret Service Story of Sir William Stephenson. London, 1962.

Director of British Security Co-ordination, part of MI6, in the western hemisphere, 1940-46; see also William Stevenson, A Man Called Intrepid (London, 1976).

715. Hyde, H. Montgomery. <u>Strong for Service: The Life of Lord Nathan of Churt</u>. London, 1968.

Lawyer and public servant; legal adviser to Zionist Organisation and Economic Board of Palestine; M.P., 1929-35, 1937-40; under-secretary of state, War Office, 1945.

716. James, Robert Rhodes. <u>Memoirs of a Conservative: J.C.C. Davidson's Memoirs and Papers, 1910-1937</u>. London, 1969.

Chancellor of the Duchy of Lancaster, 1923-24; parliamentary secretary, Admiralty, 1924-27; chancellor of the Duchy of Lancaster, 1931-37.

717. James, Admiral Sir William. <u>The Eyes of the Navy: A Biographical Study of Admiral Sir Reginald Hall</u>. London, 1955.

Director of intelligence division, Admiralty war staff, 1914-18; M.P., 1918-23, 1925-29; first set up, with Churchill's approval, Room 40 in the Admiralty Old Block, a team of codebreakers for both naval and diplomatic codes.

718. Jones, James Harry. <u>Josiah Stamp: The Life of the First Baron Stamp of Shortlands</u>. London, 1964.

British representative on the Dawes committee, 1924; and the Young committee, 1929; director, Bank of England, 1928-41; member, Economic Advisory Council, 1930-41.

719. Judd, Denis. <u>Lord Reading: A Life of Rufus Isaacs, First Marquess of Reading, 1860-1935</u>. London, 1982.

Lord chief justice of England, 1913-21; special ambassador to USA, 1918; viceroy of India, 1921-26; secretary of state for Foreign Affairs, 1931; supersedes previous studies by H. Montgomery Hyde, <u>Lord Reading: The Life of Rufus Isaacs, First Marquess of Reading</u> (London, 1967); and 2nd Marquess of Reading, <u>Rufus Isaacs: First Marquess of Reading</u> (London, 1945).

720. Judd, Denis. <u>King George VI</u>. London, 1982.

See also John W. Wheeler-Bennett, <u>King George VI: His Life and Reign</u> (London, 1958).

721. Koss, Stephen. <u>Asquith</u>. London, 1976.

See also Roy Jenkins, Asquith (London, 1964); and the
earlier J.A. Spender and Cyril Asquith, The Life of
Herbert Henry Asquith: Lord Oxford and Asquith, 2 vols.
(London, 1932).

722. Koss, Stephen. Lord Haldane: Scapegoat for Liberalism.
London, 1969.

See also E.M. Spiers, Haldane: An Army Reformer (London,
1980); Dudley Sommer, Haldane of Cloan: His Life and
Times, 1856-1928 (London, 1960); Sir Frederick Maurice,
The Life of Viscount Haldane, 2 vols. (London 1937-39);
and Sir Charles Harris, Lord Haldane (London, 1928).

723. Laffin, John. Swifter than Eagles: A Biography of Air
Chief Marshal Sir John Salmond. London, 1964.

Air officer commanding-in-chief, air defence of Great
Britain, 1925-29; chief of the air staff, 1930-33; with
ministry of Aircraft Production, 1939-41.

724. Lees-Milne, James. Harold Nicolson: A Biography. 2
vols. London, 1980-81.

725. Lewin, Ronald. The Chief: Field Marshal Lord Wavell,
Commander-in-Chief and Viceroy, 1939-1947. London,
1980.

Other studies by John Connell [J.H. Robertson], Wavell:
Scholar and Soldier (London, 1969); Sir Bernard
Fergusson, Wavell: Portrait of a Soldier (London, 1961);
Robert Woollcombe, The Campaigns of Wavell, 1939-1943
(London, 1959); and Robert J. Collins, Lord Wavell,
1883-1941: A Military Biography (London, 1947).

726. Lewin, Ronald. Slim the Standardbearer: A Biography of
Field-Marshal the Viscount Slim. London, 1976.

See also Sir Geoffrey Evans, Slim as Military Commander
(London, 1969).

727. Lord, John. Duty, Honour, Empire: The Life and Times of
Colonel Richard Meinertzhagen. London, 1970.

728. Lysaght, Charles Edward. Brendan Bracken. London, 1979.

The official biography, based on family papers, of 1st
Viscount Bracken; parliamentary private secretary to
Winston Churchill, 1940-41; minister of Information,
1941-45; first lord of the Admiralty, 1945; see also
Andrew Boyle, Poor, Dear Brendan (London, 1974); and

Anon., <u>Brendan Bracken, 1901-1958: Portraits and Appreciations</u> (London, 1958).

729. Macksey, Kenneth. <u>Armoured Crusader: A Biography of Major-General Sir Percy Hobart</u>. London, 1967.

Inspector, Royal Tank Corps, 1933-36; deputy director of staff duties, War Office, 1937; director of military training, War Office, 1937-38.

730. McLachlan, Donald. <u>In the Chair: Barrington-Ward of 'The Times', 1927-1948</u>. London, 1971.

Assistant editor, the <u>Observer</u>, 1919-27; and <u>The Times</u>, 1927-41; editor, <u>The Times</u>, 1941-48.

731. Mallet, Sir Charles. <u>Lord Cave: A Memoir</u>. London, 1931.

Minister, Home Office, 1916-19; lord chancellor, 1922-24, 1924-28.

732. Marlowe, John. <u>Late Victorian: The Life of Sir Arnold Talbot Wilson</u>. London, 1967.

733. Marquand, David. <u>Ramsay MacDonald</u>. London, 1977.

Supersedes previous studies such as Benjamin Sacks, <u>J. Ramsay MacDonald in Thought and Action</u> (Albuquerque, NM, 1952); Lord Elton, <u>The Life of James Ramsay MacDonald, 1866-1919</u> (London, 1939); Lauchlin MacNeill Weir, <u>The Tragedy of Ramsay MacDonald: A Political Biography</u> (London, 1938); H.H. Tiltman, <u>J. Ramsay MacDonald: Labour's Man of Destiny</u> (London, 1929); Mary Agnes Hamilton, <u>J. Ramsay MacDonald</u> (London, 1929).

734. Masters, Anthony. <u>Nancy Astor: A Life</u>. London, 1981.

Wife of 2nd Viscount Astor; first woman M.P., 1919-45; hostess for the "Cliveden Set"; other studies by John Grigg, <u>Nancy Astor: Portrait of a Pioneer</u> (London, 1980); Christopher Sykes, <u>Nancy: The Life of Lady Astor</u> (London, 1972); Lucy Kavaler, <u>The Astors</u> (London, 1966); and Maurice Collis, <u>Nancy Astor</u> (London, 1960).

735. Middlemas, Keith, and Barnes, John. <u>Baldwin: A Biography</u>. London, 1969.

Most thorough study; further biographies by Kenneth Young, <u>Stanley Baldwin</u> (London, 1976); H. Montgomery Hyde, <u>Baldwin: The Unexpected Prime Minister</u> (London,

1973); Arthur W. Baldwin, My Father: The True Story
(London, 1955); D.C. Somervell, Stanley Baldwin (London,
1953); G.M. Young, Stanley Baldwin (London, 1952); and
H. Wickham Steed, The Real Stanley Baldwin (London,
1930).

736. Morgan, Kenneth O., and Morgan, Jane. Portrait of a
Progressive: The Political Career of Christopher,
Viscount Addison. London, 1980.

Supersedes R.J. Minney, Viscount Addison: Leader of the
House (London, 1958).

737. Morris, A.J.A. C.P. Trevelyan, 1870-1958: Portrait of a
Radical. Belfast, 1977.

M.P., 1922-31; president, Board of Education, 1924,
1929-31.

738. Murray, Lady Mildred Octavia. The Making of a Civil
Servant: Sir Oswyn Murray, GCB, Secretary of the
Admiralty, 1917-1936. London, 1940.

Permanent secretary, Admiralty, 1917-36.

739. Newman, Aubrey. The Stanhopes of Chevening. London,
1969.

Includes study of 7th Earl Stanhope; parliamentary
under-secretary of state for Foreign Affairs, 1934-36;
first lord of the Admiralty, 1938-39; lord president of
the Council, 1939-40.

740. Nicol, Graham. Uncle George: Field Marshal Lord Milne
of Salonika and Rubislaw. London, 1976.

Entered army, 1885; general officer commanding-in-chief,
eastern command, 1923-26; chief of the imperial general
staff, 1926-33.

741. Nicolson, Nigel. Alex: The Life of Field Marshal Earl
Alexander of Tunis. London, 1973.

See also N. Hillson, Alexander of Tunis (London, 1952);
and W.G.F. Jackson, Alexander of Tunis (London, 1971).

742. Page, Bruce, et al. Philby: The Spy Who Betrayed a
Generation. London, 1968.

See also Patrick Seale and Maureen McCouville, Philby:
The Long Road to Moscow (New York, 1973); and E.H.

Cookridge, <u>The Third Man: The Full Story of Kim Philby</u>
(London, 1968).

743. Perham, Margery. <u>Lugard</u>. 2 vols. London, 1960.

1st Baron Lugard; soldier, administrator and author;
governor-general of Nigeria, 1914-19; member, Permanent
Mandates Commission of the League of Nations, 1922-36.

744. Petrie, Sir Charles. <u>The Life and Letters of the Rt.
Hon. Sir Austen Chamberlain</u>. 2 vols. London, 1939-40.

Vol. 2 for 1915-36.

745. Petrie, Sir Charles. <u>Walter Long and his Times</u>. London,
1936.

746. Pope-Hennessy, James. <u>Lord Crewe, 1858-1945: The
Likeness of a Liberal</u>. London, 1955.

Robert O.A. Crewe-Milnes; ambassador at Paris, 1922-28;
secretary of state for War, 1931.

747. Postgate, Raymond. <u>The Life of George Lansbury</u>. London,
1951.

748. Pound, Reginald, and Harmsworth, Geoffrey. <u>Northcliffe</u>.
London, 1959.

Alfred Charles William Harmsworth; journalist and
newspaper proprietor, founded Amalgamated Press, 1887;
founded <u>Daily Mail</u> and <u>Daily Mirror</u>; chief proprietor of
<u>The Times</u>, 1908; director of propaganda in enemy
countries, 1918; see also Paul Ferris, <u>The House of
Northcliffe</u> (London, 1971); and Hamilton Fyfe,
<u>Northcliffe</u> (London, 1930).

749. Reader, William J. <u>Architect of Air Power: The Life of
the first Viscount Weir of Eastwood, 1877-1959</u>.
London, 1968.

Government's leading civilian adviser on rearmament;
chairman of advisory committee on civil aviation, 1919;
adviser, Air ministry, 1935-39; director-general of
explosives, ministry of Supply, 1939-41; chairman of Tank
Board, 1942.

750. Reid, P.R. <u>Winged Diplomat: The Life Story of Air
Commodore Freddie West</u>. London, 1962.

Air attaché, British legations in Helsingfors, Riga,
Tallin, Kovno, 1936-38; Rome, 1940; Berne, 1940-45.

751. Richards, Denis. Portal of Hungerford: The Life of Marshal of the R.A.F. Viscount Portal of Hungerford. London, 1978.

Director of organisation, Air ministry, 1937-38; member of Air Council, 1939-40; air officer commander-in-chief, bomber command, 1940; chief of the air staff, 1940-45.

752. Robbins, Keith. Sir Edward Grey: A Biography of Lord Grey of Falloden. London, 1971.

See also G.M. Trevelyan, Grey of Falloden: Being the Life of Sir Edward Grey Afterwards Viscount Grey of Falloden (London, 1937).

753. Rolph, C.H. Kingsley: The Life, Letters and Diaries of Kingsley Martin. London, 1973.

754. Ronaldshay, Earl of (2nd Marquess of Zetland). The Life of Lord Curzon. 3 vols. London, 1928.

Official biography of the viceroy of India, 1898-1905; secretary of state for Foreign Affairs, 1919-24; lord privy seal, 1924-25; among subsequent studies see Harold Nicolson, Curzon: The Last Phase, 1919-1925 (London, 1934); Leonard Mosely, Curzon: The End of an Epoch (London, 1960); and Kenneth Rose, Superior Person (London, 1969); of related interest is Marchioness Curzon, Reminiscences (London, 1955).

755. Rose, Kenneth. King George V. London, 1983.

See also Harold Nicolson, King George the Fifth: His Life and Reign (London, 1952).

756. Rose, Norman. Vansittart: Study of a Diplomat. London, 1978.

See also Ian Colvin, Vansittart in Office: An Historical Survey of the Origins of the Second World War Based on the Papers of Sir Robert Vansittart (London, 1965).

757. Roskill, Stephen W. Hankey: Man of Secrets. 3 vols. London, 1970-74.

758. Roskill, Stephen W. Admiral of the Fleet Earl Beatty, The Last Naval Hero: An Intimate Biography. London, 1980.

Accepted surrender of German fleet, 1918; first sea lord, 1919-27; see also William Scott Chalmers, The Life and Letters of David, Earl Beatty (London, 1951).

759. Rowland, Peter. Lloyd George. London, 1975.

Other studies include W.R.P. George, Lloyd George
(Llandysul, 1983); Kenneth O. Morgan, Lloyd George
(London, 1974); the same author's David Lloyd George:
Welsh Radical as World Statesman (Cardiff, 1963); Donald
McCormick, The Mask of Merlin (London, 1963); Richard
Lloyd George, Lloyd George (London, 1960); William
George, My Brother and I (London, 1958); Frank Owen,
Tempestuous Journey: Lloyd George, His Life and Times
(London, 1954); Thomas Jones, Lloyd George (London,
1951); Malcolm Thompson, Lloyd George: The Official
Biography (London, 1948); and A.J. Sylvester, The Real
Lloyd George (London, 1947).

760. Sansom, Katharine. Sir George Sansom and Japan.
Tallahassee, FL, 1972.

Commercial counsellor, British embassy, Tokyo, 1923-40;
minister, adviser on far eastern affairs, Washington,
1942-47.

761. Skidelsky, Robert. Oswald Mosley. London, 1975.

See also Nicolas Mosley, Rules of the Game: Sir Oswald
and Lady Cynthia Mosley, 1896-1933 (London, 1982); and
the continuation in Beyond the Pale (London, 1983).

762. Stocks, Mary. Eleanor Rathbone: A Biography. London,
1949.

Independent M.P., 1929-46; active in League of Nations
Union and refugee problems; see also Eleanor Rathbone,
War Can be Averted (London, 1938).

763. Stocks, Mary. Ernest Simon of Manchester. Manchester,
1963.

1st Baron Simon of Wythenshawe; M.P., 1923-24, 1929-31;
parliamentary secretary, ministry of Health, 1931;
member, Economic Advisory Council, 1932-45.

764. Taylor, A.J.P. Beaverbrook. London, 1972.

Definitive life of William Maxwell Aitken, 1st Baron
Beaverbrook; minister of Information, 1918; minister for
Aircraft Production, 1940-41; minister of Supply,
1941-42; lord privy seal, 1943-45; of interest is Thomas
Driberg, Beaverbrook: A Study in Power and Frustration
(London, 1956); and David Farrer, G - For God Almighty:
A Personal Memoir of Lord Beaverbook (London, 1969).

765. Taylor, H.A. Jix - Viscount Brentford. London, 1933.

Biography of Sir William Joynson-Hicks; financial
secretary to the Treasury, 1923; minister of Health,
1923-24; home secretary, 1924-29.

766. Terraine, John. Haig: The Educated Soldier. London,
     1963.

     See also John Charteris, Field-Marshal Earl Haig (London,
     1929); and Alfred Duff Cooper, Haig, 2 vols. (London,
     1935-36).

767. Thomas, Hugh. John Strachey. London, 1973.

     M.P., 1929-31; parliamentary private secretary to Sir
     Oswald Mosley; helped found Left Book Club, 1936;
     under-secretary of state for Air, 1945.

768. Trythall, Anthony John. "Boney" Fuller: The
     Intellectual General. London, 1977.

769. Tulloch, Major-General Derek. Wingate in Peace and War.
     London, 1972.

     Major-General Orde Charles Wingate; military career,
     Sudan, Palestine, Transjordan and Ethiopia, 1928-41;
     commander of special force (Chindits), India and Burma,
     1942-44; see also Christopher Sykes, Orde Wingate
     (London, 1959).

770. Vernon, Betty D. Ellen Wilkinson, 1891-1947. London,
     1982.

     M.P., 1924-31, 1935-47; parliamentary private secretary
     to minister of Health, 1929-31; parliamentary secretary,
     ministry of Home Security, 1940-45.

771. Warner, Philip. Auchinleck: The Lonely Soldier.
     London, 1981.

     Commander-in-chief, Middle East, 1941-42; India, 1940-41,
     1943-47; still valuable is John Connell [J.H. Robertson],
     Auchinleck: A Biography of Field-Marshal Sir Claude
     Auchinleck (London, 1959); see also Roger Parkinson, The
     Auk: Auchinleck, Victor at Alamein (London, 1977).

772. Waterfield, Gordon. Professional Diplomat: Sir Percy
     Loraine of Kirkharle Bt., 1880-1961. London, 1973.

     On secretariat of Paris peace conference, 1919; minister
     to Persia, 1921-26; and Athens, 1926-29; high
     commissioner for Egypt and the Sudan, 1929-33; ambassador
     to Turkey, 1933-39; and Rome, 1939-40.

773. Wedgwood, C.V. The Last of the Radicals: Josiah
     Wedgwood, MP. London, 1951.

774. Wemyss, Lady Wester. The Life and Letters of Lord Wester
     Wemyss. London, 1935.

     First sea lord, 1917-19; at Paris peace conference, 1919.

775. Wheeler-Bennett, John W. John Anderson: Viscount
     Waverly. London, 1962.

     Permanent under-secretary of state, Home Office, 1922-32;
     governor of Bengal, 1932-37; lord privy seal, 1938-39;
     home secretary, 1939-40; lord president of the Council,
     1940-43; chancellor of the Exchequer, 1943-45.

776. Williams, Philip Maynard. Hugh Gaitskell: A Political
     Biography. London, 1979.

     Principal private secretary to minister of Economic
     Warfare, 1940-42; principal assistant secretary, Board of
     Trade, 1942-45; leader of the Labour party, 1955-63;
     supersedes Geoffrey McDermott, Leader Lost: A Biography
     of Hugh Gaitskell (London, 1972).

777. Wilson, Duncan. Leonard Woolf: A Political Biography.
     London, 1978.

778. Wingate, Sir Ronald. Lord Ismay: A Biography. London,
     1970.

779. Wrench, John Evelyn. Geoffrey Dawson and Our Times.
     London, 1955.

     Editor of The Times, 1912-19, 1923-41.

780. Young, Kenneth. Sir Alec Douglas-Home. London, 1970.

     See also John Dickie, The Uncommon Commoner: Sir Alec
     Douglas-Home (London, 1964); and Emrys Hughes, Sir Alec
     Douglas-Home (London, 1964).

781. Zebel, Sydney H. Balfour: A Political Biography.
     London, 1973.

     Supersedes Kenneth Young, Arthur James Balfour (London,
     1963); Blanche E.C. Dugdale, Arthur James Balfour: First
     Earl of Balfour, 2 vols. (London, 1936); and Sir Ian
     Malcolm, Lord Balfour: A Memoir (London, 1930), by
     Balfour's private secretary at the Paris peace
     conference.

D. SECONDARY LITERATURE

1. Histories of Britain, 1918-1945

782. Gilbert, Bentley B. Britain Since 1918. New York, 1967.

A brief survey of all aspects, including foreign policy;
in the same category can be included Arthur Marwick, The
Explosion of British Society, 1914-1970 (London, 1971);
Henry Pelling, Modern Britain, 1885-1955 (London, 1960);
E.E. Reynolds and N.E. Brasher, Britain in the Twentieth
Century, 1900-1964 (London, 1966); Peter Teed, The Move
to Europe: Britain 1880-1972 (London, 1976); David
Thomson, England in the Twentieth Century, 1914-1963
(London, 1965).

783. Havighurst, Alfred F. Britain in Transition: The
     Twentieth Century. London, 1979.

A comprehensive survey with good coverage of foreign
policy; similar surveys include T.O. Lloyd, Empire to
Welfare State: English History, 1906-1976 (London,
1979); Arthur Marwick, Britain in the Century of Total
War, 1900-1967 (London, 1968); L.C.B. Seaman,
Post-Victorian Britain, 1902-1951 (London, 1966); Anthony
Wood, Great Britain, 1900-1965 (London, 1978); and Keith
Robbins, Eclipse of a Great Power: Modern Britain, 1870-
1975 (London, 1983).

784. James, Robert Rhodes. The British Revolution: British
     Politics, 1880-1939. 2 vols. London, 1976-77.

Vol. 2 is subtitled: From Asquith to Chamberlain; see
also Martin Pugh, The Making of Modern British Politics,
1867-1939 (London, 1982).

785. McElwee, William. Britain's Locust Years, 1918-1940.
     London, 1962.

Argumentative on the inter-war years; should be
supplemented by the still useful and very detailed C.L.
Mowat, Britain between the Wars, 1918-1940 (London,
1955); and Ronald Blythe, The Age of Illusion: England
in the Twenties and Thirties, 1919-1940 (London, 1963).

786. Medlicott, W.N. Contemporary England, 1914-1964.
     London, 1967.

     Extensive coverage of foreign policy from a basically
     diplomatic historian.

787. Taylor, A.J.P. English History, 1914-1945. London,
     1965.

     Vol. 14 of the "Oxford History of England"; stimulating
     in its frequent analysis of foreign policy; extensive,
     annotated bibliography.

                    2. Foreign Policy Surveys

788. Altrincham, 1st Baron (Sir Edward Grigg). British
     Foreign Policy. London, 1944.

     A survey and contemporary analysis; parliamentary
     secretary to ministry of Information, 1939-40; financial
     secretary, War Office, 1940; joint parliamentary
     under-secretary of state for War, 1940-42; minister
     resident in the Middle East, 1944-45; see also his
     Britain Looks at Germany (London, 1938); and The Faith of
     an Englishman (London, 1936).

789. Barnett, Correlli. The Collapse of British Power.
     London, 1972.

     An analysis of "how the long-rotting and cumulatively
     over-strained structure of British power swiftly
     collapsed under the shock of the Second World War."
     (Preface).

790. Beloff, Max. Imperial Sunset. London, 1969-.

     Vol. 1 subtitled: Britain's Liberal Empire, 1897-1921.

791. Carr, E.H. Britain: A Study of Foreign Policy from the
     Versailles Treaty to the Outbreak of War. London,
     1939.

     Part of the "Ambassadors at Large" series; preface by
     Lord Halifax; for the wider European context see Carr's
     The Twenty Years' Crisis, 1919-1939 (London, 1946); and
     International Relations Between the Two World Wars,
     1919-1939 (London, 1947); also interesting is his Great
     Britain as a Mediterranean Power (Nottingham, 1937).

166

FOREIGN POLICY SURVEYS

792. Dilks, David, ed. Retreat from Power: Studies in
     Britain's Foreign Policy of the Twentieth Century.
     2 vols. London, 1981.

     A collection of fourteen essays, some previously
     published; subjects include the Foreign Office and the
     Dominions, the Hoare-Laval pact, appeasement and
     intelligence, and Operation Bracelet.

793. Foot, M.R.D. British Foreign Policy since 1898. London,
     1956.

     Other earlier studies include Maurice Bruce, British
     Foreign Policy (London, 1938); Ian Campbell Hannah, A
     History of British Foreign Policy (London, 1938); Sir
     Charles Petrie, Twenty Years' Armistice - and After:
     British Foreign Policy since 1918 (London, 1940); Michael
     Foot, Armistice, 1918-1939 (London, 1940); C.E. Sipple,
     British Foreign Policy since the World War (Iowa City,
     IA, 1932); and D.C. Somervell, Between the Wars (London,
     1948).

794. Gooch, G.P. British Foreign Policy since the War.
     London, 1935.

     See also his Studies in Diplomacy and Statecraft (London,
     1942).

795. Haig, Anthony. Congress of Vienna to Common Market: An
     Outline of British Foreign Policy, 1815-1972. London,
     1973.

796. Hayes, Paul. The Twentieth Century, 1880-1939. London,
     1978.

     The last in a "Modern British Foreign Policy" series;
     very critical.

797. Keith, Arthur B., ed. Speeches and Documents on Inter-
     national Affairs, 1918-1937. 2 vols. London, 1938.

     A standard collection of documentary material.

798. Kennedy, Aubrey Leo. Old Diplomacy and New, 1876-1922:
     From Salisbury to Lloyd George. London, 1922.

     Journalist and later assistant foreign editor of The
     Times, 1910-41; with European service of the BBC,
     1941-45.

799. Kennedy, Paul M. The Realities Behind Diplomacy:
     Background Influences on British External Policy,
     1865-1980. London, 1980.

     An interesting synthesis, including the results of recent
     research.

800. Lowe, C.J., and Dockrill, M.L. The Mirage of Power:
     British Foreign Policy, 1902-1922. 3 vols. London,
     1972.

     Vol. 2 for 1914-22; vol. 3 contains documents.

801. McDermott, Geoffrey. The Eden Legacy and the Decline of
     British Diplomacy. London, 1969.

     A survey which gives too much significance to one
     individual.

802. Medlicott, W.N. British Foreign Policy since Versailles,
     1919-1963. London, 1940.

803. Murray, Arthur Cecil (3rd Viscount Elibank). Reflections
     on Some Aspects of British Foreign Policy between the
     Two World Wars. London, 1946.

     Assistant military attaché, Washington, 1917-18; see also
     his Master and Brother (London, 1945); and At Close
     Quarters (London, 1946); both based on his wartime
     experiences.

804. Northedge, F.S. The Troubled Giant: Britain among the
     Great Powers, 1916-1939. London, 1966.

     His Descent from Power: British Foreign Policy,
     1945-1973 (London, 1974) is equally perceptive on the
     situation in 1945.

805. Porter, Bernard. Britain, Europe and the World, 1850
     1982: Delusions of Grandeur. London, 1983.

806. Reynolds, P.A. British Foreign Policy in the Inter-War
     Years. London, 1954.

     Intended for sixth form study, but still useful for
     introductory approach.

807. Rothstein, Andrew. British Foreign Policy and Its
     Critics, 1830-1950. London, 1969.

By a former member of the Information department, Soviet
trade delegation in London; intended to show the
imperialist motivations of British policy.

808. Seton-Watson, R.W. Britain and the Dictators: A Survey
of Post-War British Policy. London, 1938.

Concludes with the Anschluss; continued in From Munich to
Danzig (London, 1939); revised and enlarged edition of
Munich and the Dictators (London, 1939).

809. Strang, Lord. Britain in World Affairs: A Survey of the
Fluctuations in British Power and Influence, Henry VIII
to Elizabeth II. London, 1961.

810. Taylor, A.J.P. The Trouble Makers: Dissent over Foreign
Policy, 1792-1939. London, 1957.

Significantly concludes in 1939.

811. Trukhanovskii, V.G. Vneshniaia politika anglii na pervom
etape obshchego krizisa kapitalizma, 1918-1939.
Moscow, 1961.

812. Wiener, Joel H., ed. Great Britain: Foreign Policy and
the Span of Empire: A Documentary History, 1689-1971.
4 vols. New York, 1972.

3. Dimensions of Foreign Policy

For many years the study of British foreign policy was limited
to an analysis of multilateral relations. More recently,
historians have widened their search. The 'hidden dimensions'
of foreign policy are currently being examined in great
detail and are yielding interesting results. It is now
possible to understand and demonstrate both the limits and
choices facing the politicians, diplomats and the military in
the inter-war years. For intelligence, resistance and refugee
dimensions see pages 270-82.

The Military Dimension

813. Barclay, Cyril N. On Their Shoulders: British
Generalship in the Lean Years, 1939-1942. London,
1964.

Served world war one and two; prolific writer on military
subjects.

814. Barker, Rachel. Conscience, Government and War:
Conscientious Objection in Great Britain, 1939-1945.
London, 1982.

The Military Dimension

Well documented and detailed account of pacifism and
civil–military relations; other studies include Thomas
C. Kennedy, "Public Opinion and the Conscientious
Objector, 1915-1919", Journal of British Studies,
12(1973), 105-19; John Rae, Conscience and Politics: The
British Government and the Conscientious Objector to
Military Service, 1916-1919 (London, 1970); Denis Hayes,
Challenge of Conscience: The Story of the Conscientious
Objectors of 1939-1949 (London, 1949); and his
Conscription Conflict: The Conflict of Ideas in the
Struggle for and against Military Conscription in Britain
between 1901 and 1939 (London, 1949); and John W. Graham,
Conscription and Conscience: A History, 1916-1919
(London, 1922).

815. Barnett, Correlli. Britain and Her Army 1509-1970: A
       Military, Political and Social Survey. London, 1970.

   An introductory survey for the 1918-1945 period; see also
   Jock Haswell, The British Army: A Concise History
   (London, 1981).

816. Baylis, John. Anglo-American Defence Relations,
       1939-1980: The Special Relationship. New York, 1981.

817. Bialer, Uri. The Shadow of the Bomber: The Fear of Air
       Attack and British Politics, 1932-1939. London, 1980.

   Published by the Royal Historical Society, London; argues
   that policy was determined less by "a consistent set of
   strategic objectives, but according to idiosyncratic
   conceptions of national security" (Introduction); see
   also his "The Danger of Bombardment from the Air and the
   Making of British Air Disarmament Policy, 1932-1934", in
   War and Society: A Yearbook of Military History, vol. 1,
   edited by Brian Bond and Ian Roy (London, 1975); "The
   British Chiefs of Staff and the 'Limited Liability'
   Formula of 1938: A Note", Military Affairs, 42(1978),
   98-99; "'Humanization' of Air Warfare in British Foreign
   Policy on the Eve of the Second World War", Journal of
   Contemporary History, 13(1978), 79-96; and "Elite Opinion
   and Defence Policy: Air Power Advocacy and British
   Rearmament during the 1930s", British Journal of
   International Studies, 6(1980), 32-51.

818. Blair, P.E. "Air Power and Appeasement", in Essays
       Presented to Michael Roberts. Edited by John Bossy and
       Peter Jupp. Belfast, 1976.

DIMENSIONS OF FOREIGN POLICY

The Military Dimension

819. Bond, Brian. British Military Policy Between the Two
     World Wars. London, 1980.

     On the military constraints affecting foreign policy and
     vice versa; useful appendix with biographical notes.

820. Canning, Paul. "Yet Another Failure for Appeasement?
     The Case of the Irish Ports." International History
     Review, 4(1982), 371-92.

821. Coghlan, Francis A. "Armaments, Economic Policy and
     Appeasement: Background to British Foreign Policy,
     1931-1937." History, 57(1972), 205-16.

822. Collier, Basil. The Lion and the Eagle: British and
     Anglo-American Strategy, 1900-1950. London, 1972.

823. Dennis, Peter. Decision by Default: Peacetime Conscrip-
     tion and British Defence, 1919-1939. Durham, NC, 1972.

     A well documented study; see also his "The Reconstitution
     of the Territorial Force, 1918-1920", in Swords and
     Covenants, edited by Adrian Preston and Peter Dennis
     (London, 1976).

824. Dilks, David. "'The Unnecessary War'? Military Advice
     and Foreign Policy in Great Britain, 1931-1939", in
     General Staffs and Diplomacy Before the Second World
     War. Edited by Adrian Preston. London, 1978.

825. Dunbabin, J. "British Rearmament in the 1930s: A
     Chronology and Review." Historical Journal, 18(1975),
     581-609.

826. Ehrman, John. Cabinet Government and War, 1890-1940.
     London, 1967.

     The Lees Knowles lectures for 1957.

827. Fridenson, Patrick, and Lecuir, Jean. La France et la
     Grande-Bretagne face aux problèmes aériens, 1935 - mai
     1940. Paris, 1976.

     On French efforts to tighten co-operation in air defence
     matters; see also their "L'organisation de la coopération
     aérienne franco-britannique, 1935-mai 1940", Revue
     d'histoire de la deuxième guerre mondiale, 19(1969),
     43-74.

The Military Dimension

828. Gibbs, Norman H. "British Strategic Doctrine, 1918-
1939", in The Theory and Practice of War: Essays
Presented to Captain B.H. Liddell Hart on his
Seventieth Birthday. Edited by Michael Howard.
London, 1965.

   See also his The Origins of Imperial Defence (London,
   1955); and "Das britische Aufrüstungsprogramm 1933 bis
   1939 und das Ausmass seiner Abhängigkeit von der
   Entwicklung in Deutschland", in Wirtschaft und Rüstung am
   Vorabend des Zweiten Weltkrieges, edited by Friedrich
   Forstmeier and Hans-Erich Volkmann (Düsseldorf, 1975);
   and "The Naval Conferences of the Interwar Years: A
   Study in Anglo-American Relations", Naval War College
   Review, 30(1977), 50-63.

829. Gowing, Margaret. Britain and Atomic Energy, 1939-
1945. London, 1964.

   Commissioned by the British Atomic Energy Authority.

830. Higham, Robin. Armed Forces In Peacetime: Britain,
1918-1940, A Case Study. London, 1962.

   All aspects of the subject including disarmament,
   rearmament, and "politicans and defence"; valuable
   annotated bibliography; see also his The Military
   Intellectuals in Britain, 1918-1939 (New Brunswick, NJ,
   1966).

831. Holbrook, Francis. "Aeronautical Reciprocity and the
Anglo-American Island Race, 1936-1937." Journal of the
Royal Australian Historical Society, 57(1971), 321-35.

832. Howard, Michael. The Continental Commitment: The Dilemma
of British Defence Policy in the Era of the Two World
Wars. London, 1972.

   The Oxford University, Ford Lectures of 1971; "a starting
   point for further study of an inexhaustible subject"
   (Preface); see also his Studies in War and Peace (London,
   1970); War and the Liberal Conscience (London, 1978); and
   The Causes of Wars and other Essays (London, 1983).

833. Hyde, H. Montgomery. British Air Policy Between the
Wars, 1918-1939. London, 1976.

834. James, Peter V. "Britain and Airpower at Versailles,
1919-1920." International History Review, 5(1983),
39-58.

DIMENSIONS OF FOREIGN POLICY

The Military Dimension

835. Jeffrey, Keith. "Sir Henry Wilson and the Defence of the
     British Empire, 1918-1922." Journal of Imperial and
     Commonwealth History, 5(1977), 270-93.

836. Johnson, Franklyn Arthur. Defence by Committee: The
     British Committee of Imperial Defence, 1885-1959.
     London, 1960.

     Useful bibliography; foreword by Lord Ismay; see also
     Lord Hankey, "The Origin and Development of the Committee
     of Imperial Defence", Army Quarterly, 14(1927), 254-73;
     and Major-General H.L. Ismay, "The Machinery of the
     Committee of Imperial Defence", Journal of the Royal
     United Service Institution, 84(1939), 241-57.

837. Joubert de la Ferté, Sir Philip. The Third Service:
     The Story Behind the Royal Air Force. London, 1955.

     Air officer commanding-in-chief, various assignments,
     1934-39, 1941-43; assistant chief of air staff, 1941-43;
     deputy chief of staff, South East Asia Command, 1943-45;
     see also his Fun and Games (London, 1964).

838. Kemp, Peter. The Fleet Air Arm. London, 1954.

     Editorial staff, The Times, 1936-39, 1945-50; naval
     intelligence division, 1939-45; see also his Victory at
     Sea, 1939-1945 (London, 1957).

839. Kennedy, Paul M. The Rise and Fall of British Naval
     Mastery. London, 1976.

     See also his "Strategy versus Finance in Twentieth-
     Century Great Britain", International History Review,
     3(1981), 44-61; The Contradiction between British
     Strategic Planning and Economic Requirements in the Era
     of Two World Wars (Washington, DC, 1980), from the
     International Security Studies Program: The Wilson
     Center, Working Papers no. 11; "'Splendid Isolation'
     gegen 'Continental Commitment': Das Dilemma der
     britischen Deutschlandstrategie in der Zwischenkriegs-
     zeit, 1919-1939", in Tradition und Neubeginn: Inter-
     nationale Forschungen zur deutschen Geschichte im 20.
     Jahrhundert, edited by Joachim Hütter, et al. (Cologne,
     1975); and Strategy and Diplomacy, 1870-1945: Eight
     Studies (London, 1984).

840. Kyba, Patrick. Covenants Without the Sword: Public
     Opinion and British Defence Policy, 1931-1935.
     Waterloo, Ontario, 1983.

The Military Dimension

Based on a selection of cabinet papers and an extensive
study of newspapers and periodicals.

841. Leutze, James R. Bargaining for Supremacy: Anglo-
American Naval Collaboration, 1937-1941. Chapel Hill,
NC, 1977.

Based on a very wide array of British and American
archives, private papers and interviews; see also his
"Technology and Bargaining in Anglo-American Naval
Relations, 1938-1946", U.S. Naval Institute Proceedings,
103(1977), 51-61.

842. Liddell Hart, Basil H. The British Way in Warfare.
London, 1932.

See also the same author's When Britain Goes to War
(London, 1935); Europe in Arms (London, 1937); The
Defence of Britain (London, 1939); Thoughts on War
(London, 1944); and Brian Bond, Liddell Hart: A Study
of his Military Thought (London, 1977); Ronald Lewin,
"Sir Basil Liddell Hart: The Captain Who Taught
Generals", International Affairs, 47(1971), 79-86; and
Sir Frederick Pile, "Liddell Hart and the British Army,
1919-1939", in The Theory and Practice of War: Essays
Presented to Captain B.H. Liddell Hart, edited by Michael
Howard (London, 1965).

843. Louis, William Roger. British Strategy in the Far East,
1919-1939. London, 1971.

844. Luvaas, Jay. The Education of an Army: British Military
Thought, 1815-1940. Chicago, IL, 1964.

845. Marder Arthur J. From the Dreadnought to Scapa Flow:
The Royal Navy in the Fisher Era, 1904-1919. 5 vols.
London, 1961-70.

Vol. 5 for 1918-19; see also his "The Influence of
History on Sea Power: The Royal Navy and the Lessons of
1914-1918", Pacific Historical Review, 41(1972),
413-43; From the Dardanelles to Oran: Studies of the
Royal Navy in War and Peace, 1915-1940 (London, 1974);
Operation 'Menace': The Dakar Expedition and the Dudley
North Affair (London, 1976); and his last work, with
Japanese sources, Old Friends, New Enemies: The Royal
Navy and the Japanese Navy, Strategic Illusions 1936-1941
(London, 1981).

DIMENSIONS OF FOREIGN POLICY

The Military Dimension

846. Meyers, Reinhard. Britische Sicherheitspolitik,
     1934-1938. Düsseldorf, 1976.

     Based on a limited selection of cabinet material.

847. Murray, Williamson. "The Role of Italy in British
     Strategy, 1938-1939." Journal of the Royal United
     Services Institute for Defence Studies, 124(1979),
     43-49.

     See also his The Change in the European Balance of Power,
     1938-1939: The Path to Ruin (Princeton, NJ, 1984).

848. Parker, R.A.C. "Economic Rearmament and Foreign Policy:
     The United Kingdom before 1939 - A Preliminary Study."
     Journal of Contemporary History, 10(1975), 637-47.

     See also his "Ökonomie, Aufrüstung und Aussenpolitik
     Grossbritanniens vor 1939", in Wirtschaft und Rüstung am
     Vorabend des Zweiten Weltkrieges, edited by Friedrich
     Forstmeier and Hans-Erich Volkmann (Düsseldorf, 1975);
     and "British Rearmament, 1936-1939: Treasury, Trade
     Unions and Skilled Labour", English Historical Review,
     96(1981), 306-43.

849. Peden, G.C. British Rearmament and the Treasury, 1932-
     1939. Edinburgh, 1979.

     Based mainly on cabinet and Treasury files, and some
     personal interviews; see also his "Sir Warren Fisher and
     British Rearmament against Germany", English Historical
     Review, 94(1979), 29-47.

850. Powers, Barry D. Strategy Without Slide-Rule: British
     Air Strategy, 1914-1939. London, 1976.

     Besides the military aspects, includes public opinion,
     the press and political thought; thorough bibliography.

851. Pratt, Lawrence R. East of Malta, West of Suez:
     Britain's Mediterranean Crisis, 1936-1939. London,
     1975.

     See also the same author's "The Anglo-American Naval
     Conversations on the Far East of January 1938",
     International Affairs, 47(1971), 745-63.

852. Reussner, A. Les conversations franco-britanniques
     d'état-major, 1935-1939. Vincennes, 1969.

The Military Dimension

853. Roskill, Stephen W. <u>Naval Policy Between the Wars,</u>
     <u>1919-1939</u>. 2 vols. London, 1968-76.

     Very detailed analysis; vol. 1 to 1929; see also Sir
     Peter Gretton, "Naval Policy Between the Wars", <u>Journal</u>
     <u>of the Royal United Service Institution</u>, 113(1968),
     151-52.

854. Salewski, Michael. <u>Entwaffnung und Militärkontrolle in</u>
     <u>Deutschland, 1919-1927</u>. Munich, 1966.

     The most thorough study of the subject; see also John P.
     Fox, "Britain and the Inter-allied Military Commission of
     Control", <u>Journal of Contemporary History</u>, 4(1969),
     143-64.

855. Schofield, B.B. <u>British Sea Power: Naval Policy in the</u>
     <u>Twentieth Century</u>. London, 1967.

856. Shay, Robert Paul. <u>British Rearmament in the</u>
     <u>Thirties: Politics and Profits</u>. Princeton, NJ, 1977.

     Argues that "policy of appeasement was evolved in the
     belief that it might compensate for Britain's military
     weakness" (Introduction); includes Treasury papers and
     archives of business associations and private
     individuals.

857. Silverman, Peter. "The Ten Year Rule." <u>Journal of the</u>
     <u>Royal United Services Institute</u>, 116(1971), 42-45.

     And the responses by K. Booth, "The Ten Year Role: An
     Unfinished Debate", <u>ibid.</u>, 58-63; and Stephen W. Roskill,
     "The Ten Year Rule: The Historical Facts", <u>ibid.</u>,
     117(1972), 69-71.

858. Smith, Malcolm. "The RAF and Counter-Force Strategy
     before World War II." <u>Journal of the Royal United</u>
     <u>Services Institute for Defence Studies</u>, 121(1976),
     68-73.

     See also his "The Royal Air Force, Air Power and British
     Foreign Policy, 1932-1937", <u>Journal of Contemporary</u>
     <u>History</u>, 12(1977), 153-74.

859. Stanbridge, G.T. "The Chiefs of Staff Committee: 50
     Years of Joint Direction." <u>Journal of the Royal United</u>
     <u>Services Institute for Defence Studies</u>, 118(1973),
     25-32.

DIMENSIONS OF FOREIGN POLICY

The Military Dimension

860. Trotter, Ann. "The Dominions and Imperial Defence: Hankey's Tour in 1934." Journal of Imperial and Commonwealth History, 2(1974), 318-32.

861. Watt, D. C. Too Serious a Business: European Armed Forces and the Approach to the Second World War. London, 1975.

The origins of the second world war interpreted as "a civil war" (Chapter 1); useful bibliography; see also his "Anglo-German Naval Negotiations on the Eve of the Second World War", Journal of the Royal United Service Institution, 103(1958), 201-07, 384-91.

862. Wrench, David J. "The Influence of Neville Chamberlain on Foreign and Defence Policy, 1932-1935." Journal of the Royal United Services Institute for Defence Studies, 125(1980), 49-57.

Economic Foreign Policy

863. Bunselmeyer, Robert E. The Cost of the War, 1914-1919: British Economic War Aims and the Origins of Reparation. Hamden, CT, 1975.

Based on Public Record Office material, private papers and the press.

864. Clarke, Sir Richard. Anglo-American Economic Collaboration in War and Peace, 1942-1949. Edited by Sir Alec Cairncross. London, 1982.

Essentially four essays by a civil servant with the ministries of Information, Economic Warfare, Supply and Production, 1939-45.

865. Costigliola, Frank C. "Anglo-American Financial Rivalry in the 1920's." Journal of Economic History, 37(1977), 911-34.

866. Dayer, R.A. "The British War Debts to the United States and the Anglo-Japanese Alliance, 1920-1923." Pacific Historical Review, 45(1976), 569-95.

867. Dohrmann, Bernd. Die englische Europapolitik in der Wirtschaftskrise, 1921-1923: Zur Interdependenz von Wirtschaftsinteressen und Aussenpolitik. Munich, 1980.

Based on a wide selection of British archives, including the Board of Trade and the Treasury.

Economic Foreign Policy

868. Drummond, Ian M. British Economic Policy and the Empire, 1919-1939. London, 1972.

     Long introductory essay, with thirty-six related documents; see also his Imperial Economic Policy, 1917-1949: Studies in Expansion and Protection (London, 1974).

869. Dziambor, Godwin. Die deutsch-englischen Handelsbeziehungen unter dem Einfluss der englischen und deutschen Handelspolitik seit dem Weltkrieg. Hamburg, 1940.

     See also A. Bansa, Die deutsch-englische Wirtschaftrivalität (Berlin, 1935).

870. Eckes, Alfred E. A Search for Solvency: Bretton Woods and the International Monetary System, 1941-1971. Austin, TX, 1975.

871. Fung, Edmund S.K. "Britain, Japan and Chinese Tariff Autonomy, 1927-1928." Proceedings of the British Association for Japanese Studies, 6(1981), 23-36.

872. Garamvölgyi, Judit. Aus den Anfängen sowjetischer Aussenpolitik: Das britisch-sowjetische Handelsabkommen von 1921. Köln, 1967.

     See also M.W. Glenny, "The Anglo-Soviet Trade Agreement, March 1921", Journal of Contemporary History, 5(1970), 63-82.

873. Gull, E.M. British Economic Interests in the Far East. London, 1943.

874. Hilton, Stanley E. Brazil and the Great Powers, 1930-1939: The Politics of Trade Rivalry. Austin, TX, 1975.

     Specifically the United States, Germany and Great Britain; with the use of Brazilian archives.

875. Hoffman, Ross J.S. Great Britain and the Anglo-German Trade Rivalry. Philadelphia, PA, 1933.

876. Hogan, Michael J. Informal Entente: The Private Structure of Cooperation in Anglo-American Economic Diplomacy, 1918-1928. Columbia, MO, 1977.

     See also his "Informal Entente: Public Policy and Private Management in Anglo-American Petroleum Affairs, 1918-1924", Business History Review, 48(1974), 187-205.

Economic Foreign Policy

877. Kaiser, David E. Economic Diplomacy and the Origins of the Second World War: Germany, Britain, France and Eastern Europe, 1930-1939. Princeton, NJ, 1981.

   A useful study of pre-war economic diplomacy.

878. Kent, Marian. Oil and Empire: British Policy and Mesopotamian Oil, 1900-1920. London, 1976.

   Other aspects of oil diplomacy are analysed in William Stivers, Supremacy and Oil: Iraq, Turkey and Anglo-American World Order, 1918-1930 (Ithaca, NY, 1982); Helmut Mejcher, Imperial Quest for Oil: Iraq, 1910-1928 (London, 1976); and his "Oil and British Policy towards Mesopotamia, 1914-1918", Middle Eastern Studies, 8(1972), 377-91; Gareth G. Jones, "The British Government and the Oil Companies, 1912-1924: The Search for an Oil Policy", Historical Journal, 20(1977), 647-72; Stephen G. Rabe, "Anglo-American Rivalry for Venezuelan Oil, 1919-1929", Mid-America, 58(1976), 97-109; Peter J. Beck, "The Anglo-Peruvian Oil Dispute, 1932-1933", Journal of Contemporary History, 9(1974), 123-51; his "'A Tedious and Perilous Controversy': Britain and the Settlement of the Mosul Dispute, 1918-1926", Middle Eastern Studies, 17(1981), 256-76; and E.H. Davenport and Sidney R. Cooke, The Oil Trusts and Anglo-American Relations (London, 1923).

879. Kottman, Richard H. Reciprocity and the North Atlantic Triangle, 1932-1938. Ithaca, NY, 1968.

   An attempt to analyse the "neglected dimension" of the 1930s; based on American and Canadian sources; see also Arthur W. Schatz, "The Anglo-American Trade Agreement and Cordell Hull's Search for Peace, 1936-1938", Journal of American History, 57(1970), 85-103; Carl Kreider, The Anglo-American Trade Agreement: A Study of British and American Commercial Policies, 1934-1939 (Princeton, NJ, 1943); Henry J. Tasca, World Trading Systems: A Study of American and British Commercial Policies (Paris, 1939); and Percy W. Bidwell, Our Trade with Britain: Bases for a Reciprocal Tariff Agreement (New York, 1938).

880. Loveday, Alexander. Britain and World Trade and Other Essays. London, 1931.

   War Office, 1915-1919; joined League of Nations secretariat, 1919; director of its financial section and economic intelligence service, 1931-39; and of the economic, financial and transit department, 1939-46.

Economic Foreign Policy

881. MacDonald, C.A. "Economic Appeasement and the German 'Moderates'." Past and Present, 56(1972), 105-35.

882. McKercher, B.J.C. "A British View of American Foreign Policy: The Settlement of Blockade Claims, 1924-1927." International History Review, 3(1981), 358-84.

883. Meredith, David. "The British Government and Colonial Economic Policy, 1919-1939." Economic History Review, 28(1975), 484-99.

884. Murgescu, C. "Nicolae Titulescu, the Negotiator of the Financial Agreement with England in 1925." Revue roumaine d'études internationales, 2(1969), 161-97.

885. Nicholas, S.J. "British Multinational Investment before 1939." Journal of European Economc History, 11(1982), 605-30.

886. Offner, Arnold A. "Appeasement Revisited: The United States, Great Britain, and Germany, 1933-1940." Journal of American History, 64(1977), 373-93.

    Mainly on economic appeasement.

887. Parker, R.A.C. "The Pound Sterling, the American Treasury, and British Preparations for War, 1938-1939." English Historical Review, 98(1983), 261-79.

888. Perrot, M. La monnaie et l'opinion publique en France et en Angleterre de 1924 à 1936. Paris, 1955.

889. Platt, D.C.M., ed. Business Imperialism 1840-1930: An Inquiry based on British Experience in Latin America. London, 1977.

    See also J. Fred Rippy, British Investments in Latin America, 1822-1949 (Minneapolis, MN, 1959).

890. Pugach, Noel H. "Anglo-American Aircraft Competition and the China Arms Embargo, 1919-1921." Diplomatic History, 2(1978), 351-71.

891. Richardson, J. Henry. British Economic Foreign Policy. London, 1936.

892. Rowland, Benjamin M. "Preparing the American Ascendancy: The Transfer of Economic Power from

DIMENSIONS OF FOREIGN POLICY

Economic Foreign Policy

Britain to the United States, 1933-1944", in Balance of Power or Hegemony: The Interwar Monetary System. Edited by Benjamin M. Rowland. New York, 1976.

See also in the same collection, Robert J.A. Skidelsky, "The Retreat from Leadership: The Evolution of British Foreign Economic Policy, 1870-1939."

893. Schlote, W. British Overseas Trade from 1700 to the 1930s. London, 1952.

894. Trotter, Ann. "The Currency Weapon: Japan, Britain, and the United States in China, 1938-1941." Proceedings of the British Association for Japanese Studies, 5(1980), 57-67.

895. Wendt, Bernd Jürgen. Economic Appeasement: Handel und Finanz in der britischen Deutschland-Politik, 1933-1939. Düsseldorf, 1971.

See also his Appeasement 1938: Wirtschaftliche Rezession und Mitteleuropa (Frankfurt/M., 1966); "England und der deutsche 'Drang nach Südosten': Kapitalbeziehungen und Warenverkehr in Südosteuropa zwischen den Weltkriegen", in Deutschland in der Weltpolitik des 19. und 20. Jahrhunderts: Festschrift Fritz Fischer, edited by Imanuel Geiss and Bernd Jürgen Wendt (Düsseldorf, 1973); and "Strukturbedingungen der britischen Südosteuropa-politik am Vorabend des Zweiten Weltkrieges", in Wirtschaft und Rüstung am Vorabend des Zweiten Weltkrieges, edited by Friedrich Forstmeier and Hans-Erich Volkmann (Düsseldorf, 1975); Wilhelm Treue, "Das Dritte Reich und die Westmächte auf dem Balkan: Zur Struktur der Aussenhandelspolitik Deutschlands, Grossbritanniens und Frankreichs, 1933-1939", Vierteljahrshefte für Zeitgeschichte, 1(1953), 45-64; Alice Teichova, "Die deutsch-britischen Wirtschaftsinteressen in Mittel- und Südosteuropa am Vorabend des Zweiten Weltkriegs", in Wirtschaft und Rüstung am Vorabend des Zweiten Weltkrieges, edited by Friedrich Forstmeier and Hans-Erich Volkmann (Düsseldorf, 1975); and Ludmila Zhivkova, "British Economic Policy in the Balkans on the Eve of World War II", Studia Balcanica, 4(1971), 169-85.

Labour Foreign Policy

896. Attlee, C.R. War Comes to Britain. London, 1940.

See also C.R. Attlee, et al., Labour's Aims in War and Peace (London, 1940).

Labour Foreign Policy

897. Brand, C.F. The British Labour Party: A Short History.
     Stanford, CA, 1964.

     Other histories of the Labour party which have material
     on foreign policy include G.D.H. Cole, A History of the
     Labour Party from 1914 (London, 1948); Henry Pelling, A
     Short History of the Labour Party (London, 1961); Emanuel
     Shinwell, The Labour Story: Being a History of the
     Labour Party (London, 1963); Francis Williams, Fifty
     Years' March: The Rise of the Labour Party (London,
     1949).

898. Burridge, T.D. British Labour and Hitler's War. London,
     1976.

     See also the same author's "Barnacles and Trouble Makers:
     Labour's Left Wing and British Foreign Policy, 1939-
     1940", Canadian Journal of History, 16(1981), 1-25; and
     "Great Britain and the Dismemberment of Germany at the
     End of the Second World War", International History
     Review, 3(1981), 565-79.

899. Carlton, David. MacDonald Versus Henderson: The Foreign
     Policy of the Second Labour Government. London, 1970.

     From the first Hague conference of 1929 to the fall of
     the government in 1931.

900. Cline, Catherine A. Recruits to Labour: the British
     Labour Party, 1914-1931. Syracuse, NY, 1963.

901. Cowling, Maurice. The Impact of Labour, 1920-1924.
     London, 1974.

902. Dowse, Robert E. Left in Centre: The Independent Labour
     Party, 1893-1940. London, 1966.

     See also his "The Independent Labour Party and Foreign
     Politics, 1918-23", International Review of Social
     History, 7(1962), 33-46; and Arthur Marwick, "The
     Independent Labour Party in the Nineteen-Twenties",
     Bulletin of the Institute of Historical Research,
     35(1962), 62-74.

903. Glasgow, George. MacDonald as Diplomatist: The Foreign
     Policy of the First Labour Government in Great
     Britain. London, 1924.

904. Gordon, Michael R. Conflict and Consensus in Labour's
     Foreign Policy, 1914-1965. Stanford, CA, 1969.

Labour Foreign Policy

905. Grantham, John T. "Hugh Dalton and the International Post-War Settlement: Labour Foreign Policy Formulation, 1943-1944." Journal of Contemporary History, 14(1979), 713-27.

906. Graubard, Stephen. British Labour and the Russian Revolution, 1917-1924. Cambridge, MA, 1956.

907. Gupta, Partha Sarathi. Imperialism and the British Labour Movement, 1914-1964. London, 1975.

908. Henderson, Arthur. Labour and Foreign Affairs. London, 1922.

909. Jones, Bill. The Russia Complex: The British Labour Party and the Soviet Union. Manchester, 1977.

    Based on numerous interviews, the press, and Labour party sources.

910. Keserich, Charles. "The British Labour Press and Italian Fascism, 1922-1925." Journal of Contemporary History, 10(1975), 579-90.

911. Krieger, Wolfgang. Labour Party und Weimarer Republik: Ein Beitrag zur Aussenpolitik der britischen Arbeiterbewegung zwischen Programmatik und Parteitaktik, 1918-1924. Bonn, 1978.

    Based on a very wide array of British official archives, Labour party and TUC material, and private papers.

912. MacDonald, James Ramsay. The Foreign Policy of the Labour Party. London, 1923.

913. Maddox, William P. Foreign Relations in British Labour Politics, 1900-1924. Cambridge, MA, 1934.

914. Malmsten, Neal R. "The British Labour Party and the West Indies, 1918-1939." Journal of Imperial and Commonwealth History, 5(1977), 172-205.

915. Meehan, Eugene J. The British Left Wing and Foreign Policy: A Study of the Influence of Ideology. New Brunswick, NJ, 1960.

916. Miller, Kenneth E. Socialism and Foreign Policy: Theory and Practice in Britain to 1931. The Hague, 1967.

Labour Foreign Policy

A thorough discussion, both of theory and practice, of
the British "socialist alternative in international
relations" (Chapter 1); see also Henry R. Winkler, "The
Emergence of a Labour Foreign Policy in Great Britain,
1918-1929", Journal of Modern History, 28(1956), 247-58.

917. Naylor, John F. Labour's International Policy: The
     Labour Party in the 1930s. London, 1969.

918. Skop, Arthur L. "The British Labour Party and the German
     Revolution, November 1918-January 1919." European
     Studies Review, 5(1975), 277-97.

919. Tucker, William Rayburn. The Attitude of the British
     Labour Party Towards European and Collective Security
     Problems, 1920-1939. Geneva, 1950.

     See also his "British Labour and Revision of the Peace
     Settlement, 1920-1925", Southwestern Social Science
     Quarterly, 41(1960), 136-49.

920. Venkataramani, M.S. "Ramsay MacDonald and Britain's
     Domestic Politics and Foreign Relations, 1919-1931: A
     Study Based on MacDonald's Letters to an American
     Friend." Political Studies, 8(1960), 231-49.

921. Windrich, Elaine. British Labour's Foreign Policy.
     Stanford, CA, 1952.

Public Opinion, Propaganda and the Media

922. Adamthwaite, Anthony. "The British Government and the
     Media, 1937-1938." Journal of Contemporary History,
     18(1983), 281-97.

923. Addison, Paul. "Patriotism under Pressure: Lord
     Rothermere and British Foreign Policy", in The Politics
     of Reappraisal, 1918-1939. Edited by Gillian Peele
     and Chris Cook. London, 1975.

924. Aigner, Dietrich. Das Ringen um England: Das deutsch-
     britische Verhältnis, Die öffentliche Meinung,
     1933-1939, Tragödie zweier Völker. Munich, 1964.

     Massively researched but conspiratorial-minded account of
     British opinion toward Nazi Germany.

925. Aldgate, Anthony. Cinema and History: British Newsreels
     and the Spanish Civil War. London, 1979.

DIMENSIONS OF FOREIGN POLICY

Public Opinion, Propaganda and the Media

With a useful bibliography of a neglected aspect of the media; critical of what amounted to news management in favour of the government's policy of non-intervention; see also his "British Newsreels and the Spanish Civil War", History, 58(1973), 60-63.

926. Balfour, Michael. Propaganda in War, 1939-1945: Organisations, Policies and Publics in Britain and Germany. London, 1979.

Author was with ministry of Information from March 1939 to March 1942; assistant director of intelligence in the Political Warfare Executive; and thereafter in the Psychological Warfare Division of SHAEF from April 1942 until 1945; see also his "A War-Time Exercise in Empathy", in Studien zur Geschichte Englands und der deutsch-britischen Beziehungen: Festschrift für Paul Kluke, edited by Lothar Kettenacker, et al. (Munich, 1981); Ellic Howe, The Black Game (London, 1982); and Temple Willcox, "Projection or Publicity? Rival Concepts in the Pre-War Planning of the British Ministry of Information", Journal of Contemporary History, 18(1983), 97-116.

927. Barnes, James J., and Barnes, Patricia P. Hitler's "Mein Kampf" in Britain and America: A Publishing History. London, 1980.

See also James J. Barnes, "Mein Kampf in Britain", Wiener Library Bulletin, 27(1974), 2-10.

928. Berselli, Aldo. L'opinione pubblica inglese et l'avvento del fascismo, 1919-1925. Milan, 1971.

See also Richard Bosworth, "The British Press, the Conservatives and Mussolini, 1920-1934", Journal of Contemporary History, 5(1970), 163-82; and Elena Fasano Guarini, "Il 'Times' di fronte al fascismo, 1919-1932", Rivista storica del socialismo, 8(1965), 155-85.

929. Black, J.B. Organising the Propaganda Instrument: The British Experience. The Hague, 1975.

930. Briggs, Asa. The History of Broadcasting in the United Kingdom. 3 vols. London, 1961-70.

Public Opinion, Propaganda and the Media

See also Gerard Mansell, Let the Truth Be Told: Fifty Years of BBC External Broadcasting (London, 1982).

931. Camrose, 1st Viscount (William Ewart Berry). British Newspapers and their Controllers. London, 1947.

Founder of Allied Newspapers, 1924; and adviser to the ministry of Information, 1939-45; see also Carl J. Hambro, Newspaper Lords in British Politics (London, 1958); mainly on Lord Beaverbrook.

932. Cantril, Hadley, and Strunk, Mildred, eds. Public Opinion, 1935-1946. Princeton, NJ, 1951.

Opinion poll results from sixteen countries; including the British Institute of Public Opinion; results edited by subject; see also George H. Gallup, ed., The Gallup International Public Opinion Polls, Great Britain, 1937-1975, 2 vols. (New York, 1976).

933. Ceadel, Martin. Pacifism in Britain, 1914-1945: The Defining of a Faith. London, 1980.

Based on an extensive use of private papers, archives of peace societies, journals, and the literature of the peace movement; see also the same author's "The 'King and Country' Debate, 1933: Student Politics, Pacifism and the Dictators", Historical Journal, 22(1979), 397-422; Michael Pugh, "Pacifism and Politics in Britain, 1931-1935", Historical Journal, 23(1980), 641-56; Keith Robbins, The Abolition of War: The 'Peace Movement' in Britain, 1914-1919 (Cardiff, 1976); David C. Lukowitz, "British Pacifists and Appeasement: The Peace Pledge Union", Journal of Contemporary History, 9(1974), 115-27; and Donald Birn, "A Peace Movement Divided: Pacifism and Internationalism in Interwar Britain", Peace and Change, 1(1973), 20-24.

934. Ellwood, D.W. "'Showing the World What it Owed to Britain': Foreign Policy and Cultural Propaganda, 1935-1945", in Film, Politics and Propaganda, 1918-1945. Edited by D.W. Spring and Nicholas Pronay. London, 1981.

935. Foster, Alan. "'The Times' and Appeasement: The Second Phase." Journal of Contemporary History, 16(1981), 441-65.

DIMENSIONS OF FOREIGN POLICY

Public Opinion, Propaganda and the Media

936. Fromm, Hermann. "Das Dritte Reich im Urteil eines Engländers: Harold Nicolson und die Deutschen, 1933-1945", in Studien zur Geschichte Englands und der deutsch-britischen Beziehungen: Festschrift für Paul Kluke. Edited by Lothar Kettenacker, et al. Munich, 1981.

937. Gannon, Franklin Reid. The British Press and Germany, 1936-1939. London, 1971.

The 'psychology of appeasement' as illustrated in ten major British newspapers, and the archives of The Times and the Manchester Guardian; see also Brigitte Granzow, A Mirror of Nazism: British Opinion and the Emergence of Hitler, 1929-1933 (London, 1964); and G. Kloss, "The Image of Britain and the British in the German National Socialist Press", Wiener Library Bulletin, 24(1970), 21-29.

938. Goldman, Aaron. "The Link and the Anglo-German Review." South Atlantic Quarterly, 71(1972), 424-33.

939. Grenville, J.A.S. "British Propaganda, the Newsreels and Germany, 1933-1939", in Studien zur Geschichte Englands und der deutsch-britischen Beziehungen: Festschrift für Paul Kluke. Edited by Lothar Kettenacker, et al. Munich, 1981.

940. Griffiths, Richard. Fellow Travellers of the Right: British Enthusiasts for Nazi Germany, 1933-1939. London, 1980.

Well documented analysis of a previously unexplored area of foreign policy; see also Kenneth Lunn and Richard C. Thurlow, eds., British Fascism: Essays on the Radical Right in Inter-War Britain (London, 1980); and Robert Benewick, The Fascist Movement in Britain (London, 1972).

941. Heller, R. "East Fulham Revisited." The Journal of Contemporary History, 6(1971), 172-96.

On the rearmament issue see also T. Stannage, "The East Fulham By-Election, 25 October 1933", Historical Journal, 14(1971), 165-200; and Martin Ceadel, "Interpreting East Fulham", in By-Elections in British Politics, edited by Chris Cook and John Ramsden (London, 1973).

942. History of the Times, vol. 4, The 150th Anniversary and Beyond, 1912-1948. 2 parts. London, 1952.

Public Opinion, Propaganda and the Media

Single volume summary in Oliver Woods and James Bishop, The Story of The Times (London, 1983); among other press histories see David Ayerst, The Manchester Guardian: Biography of a Newspaper (London, 1971); Maurice Edelman, The Mirror: A Political History (London, 1966); Edward Hyams, The New Statesman: The History of the First Fifty Years, 1913-1963 (London, 1963); H.R.G. Whates, The Birmingham Post, 1857-1957 (Birmingham, 1957); Lord Burnham (Edward F. Lawson), Peterborough Court: The Story of the Daily Telegraph (London, 1955); M.A. Gibb and F. Beckwith, The Yorkshire Post: Two Centuries (Leeds, 1954); William Rust, The Story of the Daily Worker (London, 1949); The Economist, 1843-1943: A Centenary Volume (London, 1943); and Wilfrid H. Hindle, The Morning Post, 1772-1937: Portrait of a Newspaper (London, 1937).

943. Kieser, Rolf. Englands Appeasement-Politik und der Aufstieg des Dritten Reiches im Spiegel der britischen Presse, 1933-1939: Ein Beitrag zur Vorgeschichte des Zweiten Weltkrieges. Winterthur, 1964.

Based on a study of ten daily and two Sunday newspapers.

944. Lewis, John. The Left Book Club: A Historical Record. London, 1970.

See also Stuart Samuels, "The Left Book Club", Journal of Contemporary History, 1(1966), 65-86; and Sheila Hodges, Gollancz: The Story of a Publishing House, 1928-1978 (London, 1978).

945. Livingstone, Dame Adelaide. The Peace Ballot. London, 1935.

Organised by the League of Nations Union; the background with detailed results; see also Martin Ceadel, "The First British Referendum: The Peace Ballot, 1934-1935", English Historical Review, 95(1980), 810-39; and J.A. Thompson, "The 'Peace Ballot' and the 'Rainbow' Controversy", Journal of British Studies, 20(1981), 150-70.

946. McCallum, R.B. Public Opinion and the Last Peace. London, 1944.

947. MacDonald, Callum A. "Radio Bari: Italian Wireless Propaganda in the Middle East and British

Public Opinion, Propaganda and the Media

Countermeasures, 1934-1938." Middle Eastern Studies, 13(1977), 195-207.

948. McLaine, Ian. Ministry of Morale: Home Front Morale and the Ministry of Information in World War II. London, 1979.

A study of the ministry originally responsible for "the release of official news; security censorship of the press, films and the BBC; the maintenance of morale; the conduct of publicity campaigns for other departments; and the dissemination of propaganda to enemy, neutral, allied and empire countries." (Introduction).

949. Madge, Charles, and Harrison, Tom. Britain by Mass-Observation. London, 1939.

See also the Mass-Observation studies War Begins at Home (London, 1940); and Home Propaganda (London, 1941).

950. Margach, James. The Abuse of Power: The War Between Downing Street and the Media from Lloyd George to Callaghan. London, 1978.

951. Morris, A.J.A. "The 'Birmingham Post' and Anglo-German Relations, 1933-1935." University of Birmingham Historical Journal, 2(1968), 191-201.

952. Osgood, S.M. "Anglophobia and Other Vichy Press Obsessions." Wiener Library Bulletin, 22(1968), 13-18.

953. Postgate, Raymond, and Vallance, Aylmer. England Goes to Press: The English People's Opinion on Foreign Affairs as Reflected in Their Newspapers Since Waterloo, 1815-1937. London, 1937.

954. Pronay, Nicholas. "British Newsreels in the 1930s, Part I: Audiences and Producers." History, 56(1971), 63-72.

Continued in "British Newsreels in the 1930s, II: Their Policies and Impact", History, 57(1972), 63-72; see also Nicholas Pronay and F. Thorpe, British Official Films in the Second World War (Santa Barbara, CA, 1980).

955. Schadlich, Karlheinz. "'Appeaser' in Aktion: Hitlers britische Freunde in der Anglo-German Fellowship." Jahrbuch für Geschichte, 3(1969), 197-225.

Public Opinion, Propaganda and the Media

956. Sharf, Andrew. <u>The British Press and Jews Under Nazi Rule</u>. London, 1964.

Based on the Podro collection of press cuttings drawn from 150 British newspapers and periodicals.

957. Stannage, Tom. <u>Baldwin Thwarts the Opposition: The British General Election of 1935</u>. London, 1980.

Including public opinion as a factor in rearmament; see also James C. Robertson, "The British General Election of 1935", <u>Journal of Contemporary History</u>, 9(1974), 149-64; and Reginald Bassett, "Telling the Truth to the People: The Myth of the Baldwin 'Confession'", <u>Cambridge Journal</u>, 2(1948), 84-95.

958. Steed, H. Wickham. <u>The Press</u>. London, 1938.

959. Stubbs, John. "Appearance and Reality: A Case Study of 'The Observer' and J.L. Garvin, 1914-42", in <u>Newspaper History: From the Seventeenth Century to the Present</u>. Edited by George Boyce, et al. London, 1978.

960. Tallents, Sir Stephen. <u>The Projection of England</u>. London, 1932.

961. Taylor, Philip. <u>The Projection of Britain Overseas: British Overseas Publicity and Propaganda, 1919-1939</u>. London, 1981.

A well documented study, shedding valuable light on the news department of the Foreign Office; see also the same author's "Cultural Diplomacy and the British Council, 1934-1939", <u>British Journal of International Studies</u>, 4(1978), 244-65; "British Official Attitudes towards Propaganda Abroad, 1918-1939", in <u>Film, Politics and Propaganda</u>, edited by D.W. Spring and Nicholas Pronay (London, 1981); and "'If War Should Come': Preparing the Fifth Arm for Total War, 1935-1939", <u>Journal of Contemporary History</u>, 16(1981), 27-51.

962. Willert, Arthur. "British News Abroad." <u>Round Table</u>, 27 (1937), 533-46, 712-22.

Among his numerous articles see "Publicity and Propaganda in International Affairs", <u>International Affairs</u>, 17(1938), 809-26; and "British News Controls", <u>Foreign Affairs</u>, 17(1939), 712-22.

DIMENSIONS OF FOREIGN POLICY

Public Opinion, Propaganda and the Media

963. Woolf, Stuart. "British Attitudes towards Fascism, 1922-1940", in Inghilterra e Italia nel '900: Atti del convegno di Lucca, Ottobre 1972. Florence, 1973.

Also includes seven other essays on aspects of public opinion as a factor in Anglo-Italian relations from 1914-46.

The Foreign Office

964. Agbi, S. Olu. "The Foreign Office and Yoshida's Bid for Rapprochement with Britain in 1936-1937: A Critical Reconsideration of the Anglo-Japanese Conversations." Historical Journal, 21(1978), 173-79.

965. Anon. [R.L. Buell]. The British Foreign Office. New York, 1929.

For the United States Foreign Policy Association; a survey of organisation and contemporary problems.

966. Anon. "Changes in the Organisation of the Foreign and Diplomatic Service, 1921." The British Year Book of International Law, 1(1920-21), 97-108.

967. Ashton-Gwatkin, Frank T.A. The British Foreign Service. Syracuse, NY, 1950.

An insightful survey by a former diplomat and Foreign Office official, 1913-1947; and novelist with pen name of John Paris; see also his "Thoughts on the Foreign Office, 1918-1939", Contemporary Review, 188(1955), 374-78.

968. Beloff, Max. "The Whitehall Factor: The Role of the Higher Civil Service, 1919-1939", in The Politics of Reappraisal, 1918-1939. Edited by Gillian Peele and Chris Cook. London, 1975.

Includes the Foreign Office and the Treasury.

969. Bishop, Donald G. The Administration of British Foreign Relations. Syracuse, NY, 1961.

A thorough analysis of all aspects, including organisation, administration and overseas operations.

The Foreign Office

970. Boadle, Donald G. "The Formation of the Foreign Office
     Economic Relations Section, 1930-1937." Historical
     Journal, 20(1977), 919-36.

971. Boardman, Robert, and Groom, A.J.R., eds. The Management
     of Britain's External Relations. London, 1973.

     A collection of fourteen essays, mainly on the post-1945
     period, ranging from the organisation of the Foreign
     Office to the news media and foreign affairs; very useful
     bibliography.

972. Boyle, Peter G. "The British Foreign Office View of
     Soviet-American Relations, 1945-1946." Diplomatic
     History, 3(1979), 307-20.

973. Cecil, Algernon. "The Foreign Office", in The Cambridge
     History of British Foreign Policy, 1783-1919. Vol. 3.
     Edited by Sir A. Ward and G.P. Gooch. London, 1923.

974. Cline, Catherine Ann. "E.D. Morel and the Crusade
     against the Foreign Office." Journal of Modern
     History, 39(1967), 126-37.

     See also her E.D. Morel, 1873-1924 (Belfast, 1980).

975. Connell, John. [J.H. Robertson]. The 'Office': A
     Study of British Foreign Policy and Its Makers,
     1919-1951. London, 1958.

     By a former journalist, soldier, and chief military press
     censor, India, 1944.

976. Craig, Gordon A. "The British Foreign Office from Grey
     to Austen Chamberlain", in The Diplomats, 1919-1939.
     Edited by Gordon A. Craig and Felix Gilbert.
     Princeton, NJ, 1953.

     Other relevant studies in this collection include essays
     on Arthur Henderson, Lord Perth and Nevile Henderson.

977. Cromwell, Valerie. "The Foreign and Commonwealth
     Office", in 'The Times' Survey of Foreign Ministries of
     the World. Edited by Zara Steiner. London, 1982.

978. Edwards, Peter G. "The Foreign Office and Fascism,
     1924-1929." Journal of Contemporary History, 5(1970),
     153-61.

DIMENSIONS OF FOREIGN POLICY

The Foreign Office

979. Glenny, W.J. "The Trade Commissioner and Commercial
     Diplomatic Services." Journal of Public
     Administration, 2(1924), 276-87.

980. Hanak, Harry. "The Government, the Foreign Office, and
     Austria-Hungary, 1914-1918." Slavonic and East
     European Review, 47(1969) 161-97.

981. Kennedy, Aubrey L. Old Diplomacy and New, 1876-1922.
     London, 1923.

     See also his "Reorganisation of the Foreign Service",
     Quarterly Review, 283(1945), 397-412.

982. Lammers, Donald N. "From Whitehall after Munich: The
     Foreign Office and the Future Course of British
     Policy." Historical Journal, 16(1973), 831-56.

     See also his "Fascism, Communism and the Foreign Office,
     1937-1939", Journal of Contemporary History, 6(1971),
     66-86; and the Foreign Office documents in Bela Vago, The
     Shadow of the Swastika: The Rise of Fascism and Anti-
     Semitism in the Danube Basin, 1936-1939 (London, 1975).

983. Langford, Richard V. British Foreign Policy: Its
     Formulation in Recent Years. Washington, DC, 1942.

984. Larner, Christina. "The Amalgamation of the Diplomatic
     Service with the Foreign Office." Journal of
     Contemporary History, 7(1972), 107-26.

985. Manne, Robert. "The Foreign Office and the Failure of
     Anglo-Soviet Rapprochement." Journal of Contemporary
     History, 16(1981), 725-55.

986. Nicolson, Sir Harold. Diplomacy. London, 1939.

     Still stimulating despite its age; see also his The
     Evolution of Diplomatic Method (London, 1954).

987. Nightingale, Robert T. The Personnel of the British
     Foreign Office and Diplomatic Service, 1851-1929.
     London, 1930.

     Fabian Tract no. 232; argues that the diplomatic staff
     was too much drawn from the establishment.

988. Norton, Henry Kittredge. "Foreign Office Organization."
     Annals of the American Academy of Political and Social
     Science, 143, Supplement(1929), 1-83.

The Foreign Office

A comparative study of organisations in Britain, France, Germany, Italy and the United States.

989. O'Hara, Valentine J. "The Foreign Office and Lithuania." Contemporary Review, 125(1924), 745-52.

Member, political mission for the Baltic states, 1919; author and journalist.

990. Platt, D.C.M. The Cinderella Service: British Consuls since 1825. London, 1971.

991. Rooke, M.J. "The British Foreign Office and Anti-Semitism in Rumania, 1936-1939." Wiener Library Bulletin, Special Issue: Fifty Years of the Wiener Library, 46-51.

992. Ross, Graham. "Foreign Office Attitudes to the Soviet Union, 1941-1945." Journal of Contemporary History, 16(1981), 521-40.

993. Sallet, Richard. Der diplomatische Dienst: Seine Geschichte und Organisation in Frankreich, Grossbritannien und den Vereinigten Staaten. Stuttgart, 1953.

994. Selby, Sir Walford. "The Foreign Office." Nineteenth Century and After, 137(1945), 3-12.

995. Sharp, Alan J. "The Foreign Office in Eclipse, 1919-1922." History, 61(1976), 198-218.

996. Steiner, Zara, and Dockrill, M.L. "The Foreign Office Reforms, 1919-1921." Historical Journal, 17(1974), 131-56.

See also the same authors' "The Foreign Office at the Paris Peace Conference in 1919", International History Review, 2(1980), 55-86.

997. Strang, Lord. The Foreign Office. London, 1955.

Part of the New Whitehall Series by a Foreign Office career official; see also his "The Formulation and Control of Foreign Policy", Durham University Journal, 49(1957), 98-108; 2(1960), 3-21; and The Diplomatic Career (London, 1962).

998. Tilley, Sir John A.C., and Gaselee, Stephen. The Foreign Office. London, 1933.

DIMENSIONS OF FOREIGN POLICY

The Foreign Office

Written by the Chief Clerk (1913-1918) and Librarian
respectively of the Foreign Office; introduction by Sir
John Simon; part of the original Whitehall Series
published between 1925 and 1935.

999. Vansittart, Lord. "The Decline of Diplomacy." Foreign
   Affairs, 28(1950), 177-89.

1000. Warman, Roberta M. "The Erosion of Foreign Office
   Influence in the Making of Foreign Policy, 1916-1918."
   Historical Journal, 15(1972), 133-59.

1001. Watt, D.C. Personalities and Policies: Studies in the
   Formulation of British Foreign Policy in the Twentieth
   Century. London, 1965.

An indispensable and far-ranging collection of thirteen
essays; including a useful bibliographical essay on
research materials for the study of the British foreign
policy making élite.

1002. Willert, Sir Arthur. Aspects of British Foreign Policy.
   London, 1928.

See also the same author's "The Foreign Office from
Within", Strand Magazine, February 1936, 398-405; and The
Frontiers of England (London, 1935).

1003. Young, John Wilson. "The Foreign Office and the Depar-
   ture of General de Gaulle, June 1945-January 1946."
   Historical Journal, 25(1982), 209-16.

Britain and the League of Nations

British membership in the League of Nations spans the entire life of the organisation from 1919 to 1945. Considerable
research has been done on specific aspects of Britain's involvement with League related problems. However, our view of
the entire relationship remains unclear. Between 1919 and
1945 Britain's involvement with the League of Nations alter-
nated between two distinctive areas. On the one hand, several
foreign policy related problems, such as the application of
sanctions during the Italo-Ethiopian war, preoccupied policy
makers in London in 1935 and 1936. On the other hand, for almost twenty-six years Britain participated in the construc-
tive, less publicised, aspects of League activity. This
encompassed such matters as economic and financial reconstruction in Europe, intellectual co-operation, control of traffic
in drugs and human lives, mandates, refugee resettlement and

Britain and the League of Nations

disarmament. It is these latter areas which are largely
detailed in these entries below.

1004. Arnold-Forster, William. The Disarmament Conference.
      London, 1931.

      By a perceptive and well informed commentator; also
      useful is his "British Policy at the Disarmament
      Conference", Political Quarterly, 3(1932), 365-80.

1005. Atholl, Duchess of. "British Opinion and the League."
      Hungarian Quarterly, 2(1936), 26-36.

1006. Bachofen, Maja. Lord Cecil und der Völkerbund. Zürich,
      1959.

      See also Peter Raffo, "The League of Nations Philosophy
      of Lord Robert Cecil", Australian Journal of Politics and
      History, 20(1974), 186-96; J.A. Thompson, "Lord Cecil and
      the Pacifists in the League of Nations Union", Historical
      Journal, 20(1977), 949-59; David Carlton, "Disarmament
      with Guarantees: Lord Cecil, 1922-1927", Disarmament and
      Arms Control, 3(1965), 143-64.

1007. Barros, James. Office Without Power: Secretary-General
      Sir Eric Drummond, 1919-1933. London, 1979.

      16th Earl of Perth; private secretary to the foreign
      secretary, 1915-19; later British ambassador to Italy,
      1933-39; see also his The League of Nations and the Great
      Powers: The Greek-Bulgarian Incident (London, 1970).

1008. Beck, Peter. "From the Geneva Protocol to the Greco-
      Bulgarian Dispute: The Development of the Baldwin
      Government's Policy towards the Peacekeeping Role of
      the League of Nations, 1924-1925." British Journal of
      International Studies, 6(1980), 52-68.

1009. Bentwich, Norman. England in Palestine. London, 1932.

      See also his The Mandates System (London, 1930); other
      early accounts include A.M. Hyamson, Palestine Under the
      Mandate, 1920-1948 (London, 1950); Royal Institute of
      International Affairs, Information Department Paper, no.
      20, Great Britain and Palestine, 1915-1945 (London,
      1946); Paul L. Hanna, British Policy in Palestine
      (Washington, DC, 1942); and Paul Sidebotham, Great
      Britain and Palestine (London, 1937).

Britain and the League of Nations

1010. Bethell, Nicholas. The Palestine Triangle: The Struggle for the Holy Land, 1935-1948. London, 1979.

Essentially an analysis of relations between Britain and the Zionists; archival research strongly supplemented by numerous personal interviews.

1011. Birn, Donald. The League of Nations Union, 1918-1945. London, 1981.

See also his "The League of Nations Union and Collective Security", Journal of Contemporary History, 9(1974), 131-59; J.A. Thompson, "The League of Nations Union and Promotion of the League Idea in Great Britain", Australian Journal of Politics and History, 18(1972), 52-61; and Ernest Bramstead, "Apostles of Collective Security: The League of Nations Union and its Functions", Australian Journal of Politics and History, 13(1967), 347-64.

1012. Bridgeman, William Clive (1st Viscount Bridgeman of Leigh). "Naval Disarmament." Journal of the Royal Institute of International Affairs, 6(1927), 335-45.

M.P., 1906-29; parliamentary secretary, Board of Trade, 1919-20; secretary of Mines, 1920-22; home secretary, 1922-24; first lord of the Admiralty, 1924-29.

1013. Carlton, David. "The Anglo-French Compromise on Arms Limitation, 1928." Journal of British Studies, 8(1969), 141-62.

See also his "Great Britain and the League Council Crisis of 1926", Historical Journal, 11(1968), 354-64; and "The Problem of Civil Aviation in British Disarmament Policy, 1919-1934", Journal of the Royal United Services Institute, 111(1966), 307-16.

1014. Carter, Gwendolen M. The British Commonwealth and International Security: The Role of the Dominions, 1919-1939. Toronto, Ontario, 1947.

Largely on policies and attitudes toward the League; see also C.A.W. Manning, The Policies of the British Dominions in the League of Nations (London, 1932); and H. Duncan Hall, "The British Commonwealth and the Founding of the League Mandate System", in Studies in International History: Essays Presented to W. Norton

Britain and the League of Nations

Medlicott, edited by K. Bourne and D.C. Watt (London, 1967).

1015. Cataluccio, F. "La questione arabo dopo la prima guerra mondiale: I mandati britannici in Iraq e Palestine." Archivio storico italiano, 125(1967), 291-351.

1016. Chamberlain, Sir Austen. The League. London, 1926.

League of Nations Union, Pamphlet, no. 203.

1017. Chaput, Rolland A. Disarmament in British Foreign Policy. London, 1935.

1018. Charvet, Félix. L'influence britannique dans la S.D.N.: Des origines de la S.D.N. jusqu'à nos jours. Paris, 1938.

See also Jean Schwoebel, L'Angleterre et la sécurité collective (Paris, 1938).

1019. Cohen, Gavriel. Churchill and Palestine, 1939-1942. Jerusalem, 1976.

Hebrew commentary with British documents in English; see also his The British Cabinet and the Question of Palestine, April-July, 1943 (Tel Aviv, 1976); and Nathaniel Katzburg, From Partition to White Paper: British Policy in Palestine, 1936-1940 (Jerusalem, 1974); with a selection of relevant British documents.

1020. Cohen, Michael. Palestine, Retreat from the Mandate: The Making of British Policy, 1936-1945. London, 1978.

Based on British and Zionist archives; see also his "American Influence on British Policy in the Middle East during World War II: First Attempts at Coordinating Allied Policy on Palestine", American Jewish Historical Quarterly, 67(1977), 50-70; "Direction of Policy in Palestine, 1936-1945", Middle Eastern Studies, 11(1975), 237-61; "British Strategy and the Palestine Question, 1936-1939", Journal of Contemporary History, 7(1972), 157-83; and "Appeasement in the Middle East: The British White Paper on Palestine, May 1939", Historical Journal, 16(1973), 571-96; continued in "The Testing of a Policy, 1942-1945", Historical Journal, 19(1976), 727-58.

1021. Crozier, Andrew J. "The Establishment of the Mandates System, 1919-1925: Some Problems Created by the Paris

Britain and the League of Nations

       Peace Conference." Journal of Contemporary History, 14(1979), 483-513.

1022. Cushendun, Lord. "Disarmament." Journal of the Royal Institute of International Affairs, 7(1928), 77-93.

       1st Baron Cushendun (Ronald John McNeill); parliamentary under-secretary of state for Foreign Affairs, 1922-24, 1924-25; financial secretary to the Treasury, 1925-27; chancellor of the Duchy of Lancaster, 1927-29.

1023. Egerton, George W. Great Britain and the Creation of the League of Nations: Strategy, Politics and International Organization, 1914-1919. Chapel Hill, NC, 1978.

       See also the same author's "The Lloyd George Government and the Creation of the League of Nations", American Historical Review, 79(1974), 419-44; Peter Raffo, "The Anglo-American Negotiations for a League of Nations", Journal of Contemporary History, 9(1974), 153-76; and Roland N. Stromberg, "Uncertainties and Obscurities about the League of Nations", Journal of the History of Ideas, 32(1972), 139-54.

1024. Ekoko, Edho. "The British Attitude Towards Germany's Colonial Irredentism in Africa in the Inter-War Years." Journal of Contemporary History, 14(1979), 287-308.

1025. Gifford, Prosser, and Louis, William Roger, eds. France and Britain in Africa: Imperial Rivalry and Colonial Rule. New Haven, CT, 1971.

       Includes essays on British mandates, 1919-39; see also by the same editors Imperial Rivalry and Colonial Rule: Britain and Germany in Africa (New Haven, CT, 1967).

1026. Hailey, 1st Baron (Malcolm Hailey). Britain and Her Dependencies. London, 1943.

       Governor in India, 1924-34; member, Permanent Mandates Commission, League of Nations, 1935-39.

1027. Henderson, Arthur. Conference for the Reduction and Limitation of Armaments: Preliminary Report on the Work of the Conference. Geneva, 1936.

       Report from the conference president, 1932-34.

Britain and the League of Nations

1028. Hill, C.J. "Great Britain and the Saar Plebiscite of 13
      January 1935." Journal of Contemporary History,
      9(1974), 121-42.

      For earlier views see Margaret Lambert, The Saar (London,
      1934); Royal Institute of International Affairs,
      Information Department Paper, no. 11, The Saar Problem
      (London, 1934); Sarah Wambaugh, The Saar Plebiscite
      (London, 1940); and her Plebiscites Since the World War,
      With a Collection of Official Documents (Washington, DC,
      1933).

1029. Jenks, Clarence Wilfred. Britain and the I.L.O. London,
      1969.

      David Davies Memorial Lecture for 1969; by the legal
      adviser to the ILO, 1931-48; later director-general; see
      also Antony Alcock, The History of the International
      Labour Organisation (London, 1971); George Alexander
      Johnston, The International Labour Organisation: Its
      Work for Social and Economic Progress (London, 1970); by
      the assistant director of the ILO, 1945-48; and the
      official history by M. Stewart, Britain and the I.L.O.:
      The Story of Fifty Years (London, 1969).

1030. Klieman, Aaron S. "The Divisiveness of Palestine:
      Foreign Office Versus Colonial Office on the Issue of
      Partition, 1937." Historical Journal, 22(1979),
      423-41.

1031. Louis, William Roger. Great Britain and Germany's Lost
      Colonies. London, 1967.

      See also his "The United Kingdom and the Beginning of the
      Mandates System, 1919-1922", International Organization,
      23(1969), 73-96; which analyses the origins of the
      mandates in light of British archives; "Colonial
      Appeasement, 1936-1938", Revue belge de philologie et
      d'histoire, 4(1971), 1175-91; and Kenneth Robinson, The
      Dilemmas of Trusteeship: Aspects of British Colonial
      Policy between the Wars (London, 1965).

1032. Marshall-Cornwall, General Sir James Handyside.
      Geographic Disarmament. London, 1935.

      Attended Paris peace conference, 1919; military attaché,
      Berlin, Stockholm, Oslo and Copenhagen, 1928-32; chief of
      British military mission to Egypt, 1937-38; general
      officer commanding-in-chief, western command, 1941-42.

DIMENSIONS OF FOREIGN POLICY

Britain and the League of Nations

1033. Mossek, M. Palestine Immigration Policy under Sir
      Herbert Samuel: British, Zionist and Arab Attitudes.
      London, 1978.

      See also Elie Kedourie, "Sir Herbert Samuel and the
      Government of Palestine", Middle Eastern Studies,
      5(1969), 44-68.

1034. Most, Eckhard. Grossbritannien und der Völkerbund:
      Studien zur Politik der Friedenssicherung 1925 bis
      1934. Frankfurt/M., 1981.

      Based on British, German but not League of Nations
      archives.

1035. Murray, Gilbert. "The British People and the League of
      Nations", in Pierre Munch, ed., Les origines et
      l'oeuvre de la Société des Nations. Vol. I.
      Copenhagen, 1923.

      See also his The League of Nations Movement: Some
      Recollections of the Early Days (London, 1955).

1036. Noel-Baker, Philip J. (Baron Noel-Baker). The First
      World Disarmament Conference, 1932-1933, and Why It
      Failed. London, 1979.

      M.P., 1929-31, 1936-70; member, League of Nations
      secretariat, 1919-22; parliamentary private secretary to
      secretary of state for Foreign Affairs, 1929-31; to
      ministry of War Transport, 1942-45; Nobel peace prize,
      1959; see also his "The League of Nations", in The
      Baldwin Age, edited by John Ramsden (London, 1960);
      Disarmament (London, 1926); The League of Nations at Work
      (London, 1926); The Geneva Protocol for the Pacific
      Settlement of International Disputes (London, 1925); and
      "The Making of the Covenant from the British Point of
      View", in Pierre Munch, ed., Les origines et l'oeuvre de
      la Société des Nations, vol. 2 (Copenhagen, 1924).

1037. Rose, Norman. "The Debate on Partition, 1937-1938: The
      Anglo-Zionist Aspect, Part I, The Proposal." Middle
      Eastern Studies, 6(1970), 297-318.

      Continued in "The Withdrawal", Middle Eastern Studies,
      7(1971), 3-24; see also his "Palestine's Role in
      Britain's Imperial Defence: An Aspect of Zionist
      Diplomacy, 1938-1939", Wiener Library Bulletin, 22(1968),

Britain and the League of Nations

32-35; and the wider background in Gentile Zionists: A
Study in Anglo-Zionist Diplomacy, 1929-1939 (London,
1973).

1038. Sharma, Shiva Kumar. Der Völkerbund und die Grossmächte:
Ein Beitrag zur Geschichte der Völkerbundspolitik
Grossbritanniens, Frankreichs und Deutschlands,
1929-1933. Frankfurt/M., 1978.

A thorough study with a useful bibliography.

1039. Sheffer, G. "British Colonial Policy-Making Towards
Palestine, 1929-1939." Middle Eastern Studies,
14(1978), 307-22.

See also his "Intentions and Results of British Policy in
Palestine: Passfield's White Paper", Middle Eastern
Studies, 9(1973), 43-60.

1040. Sluglett, Peter. Britain in Iraq, 1914-1932. London,
1976.

Largely based on British archival materials.

1041. Upthegrove, Campbell L. Empire by Mandate: A History of
the Relations of Great Britain with the Permanent
Mandates Commission of the League of Nations. New
York, 1954.

1042. Walters, Francis Paul. A History of the League of
Nations. 2 vols. London, 1952.

Joined secretariat of League of Nations, 1919; deputy
director-general, 1939-40; other less successful studies
of the League include James Avery Joyce, Broken Star:
The Story of the League of Nations, 1919-1939 (Swansea,
1978); Elmer Bendiner, A Time for Angels: The Tragicomic
History of the League of Nations (New York, 1975); the
Historical Association pamphlet by Peter Raffo, The
League of Nations (London, 1974); George Scott, The Rise
and Fall of the League of Nations (London, 1973); a
collection of various documents with commentary in Ruth
B. Henig, The League of Nations (Edinburgh, 1973); Byron
Dexter, The Years of Opportunity: The League of Nations,
1920-1926 (New York, 1967); the still interesting Alfred
Zimmern, The League of Nations and the Rule of Law,
1918-1935 (London, 1936); and P.A. Reynolds, "The League
of Nations", in The New Cambridge Modern History, vol.
12, rev. ed. (London, 1968).

202

Britain and the League of Nations

1043. Wasserstein, Bernard. The British in Palestine: The Mandatory Government and the Arab-Jewish Conflict, 1917-1929. London, 1978.

1044. Wheeler-Bennett, John W. Disarmament and Security since Locarno, 1925-1931: Being the Political and Technical Background of the General Disarmament Conference, 1932. London, 1932.

   See also his The Disarmament Deadlock (London, 1934).

1045. Williams, Sir John Fischer. Some Aspects of the Covenant of the League of Nations. London, 1934.

   British member, Permanent Court of Arbitration, The Hague, 1936-47; assistant legal adviser, Home Office, 1918-20; British legal representative, Reparation Commission, 1920-30; among his numerous articles and books see "Great Britain and the League", International Affairs, 17(1938), 187-210; and The Geneva Protocol of 1924 (London, 1925).

1046. Winkler, Henry R. The League of Nations Movement in Great Britain, 1914-1919. New Brunswick, NJ, 1952.

   See also the author's "The Development of the League of Nations Idea in Great Britain, 1914-1919", Journal of Modern History, 20(1948), 95-112.

1047. Zimmern, Alfred. "L'Angleterre, les Dominions et la Société des Nations." Revue des études coopératives, 9(1930), 258-87.

   Political intelligence department, Foreign Office, 1918-19; deputy director, League of Nations Institute of Intellectual Co-operation, Paris, 1926-30; deputy director, research department, Foreign Office, 1943-45.

4. Bilateral and Area Studies

North and South Atlantic

1048. Allen, Harry Cranbrook. Great Britain and the United States: A History of Anglo-American Relations, 1783-1952. London, 1959.

   Among numerous general surveys see also Arthur Campbell Turner, The Unique Partnership: Britain and the United States (New York, 1971); Herbert George Nicholas, Britain

Nor th and South Atlantic

and the U.S.A. (Baltimore, MD, 1963); Bruce M. Russet,
Community and Contention: Britain and America in the
Twentieth Century (Cambridge, MA, 1963); Henry L. Roberts
and Paul A. Wilson, eds., Britain and the United States
(London, 1953); Sir Arthur Willert, The Road to Safety:
A Study in Anglo-American Relations (London, 1952); and
Clarence Crane Brinton, The United States and Britain
(London, 1945).

1049. Beloff, Max. "The Special Relationship: An Anglo-
American Myth", in A Century of Conflict, 1850-1950:
Essays for A.J.P. Taylor. Edited by Martin Gilbert.
London, 1966.

1050. Fry, Michael G. Illusions of Security: North Atlantic
Diplomacy, 1918-1922. Toronto, Ontario, 1972.

On the efforts of the 'Atlanticists' to foster permanent
Anglo-American co-operation after the first world war;
for the general historical background see John Bartlett
Brebner, North Atlantic Triangle: The Interplay of
Canada, the United States and Great Britain (London,
1945).

1051. Reynolds, David. The Creation of the Anglo-American
Alliance, 1937-1941: A Study in Competitive
Co-operation. London, 1982.

A multi-faceted approach to the complex Anglo-American
relationship; concentrates on the post-Munich period;
useful bibliography.

1052. Shearman, Hugh. Anglo-Irish Relations. London, 1948.

A survey with five chapters on the 1918-45 period; see
also G. Boyce, "From War to Neutrality: Anglo-Irish
Relations, 1921-1950", British Journal of International
Studies, 5(1978), 15-36; and D.W. Harkness, "Mr. de
Valera's Dominion: Irish Relations with Britain and the
Commonwealth, 1932-1938", Journal of Commonwealth
Political Studies, 8(1970), 206-28.

1053. Wigley, Philip G. Canada and the Transition to Commonwealth: British-Canadian Relations, 1917-1926.
London, 1977.

1054. Willson, Beckles. America's Ambassadors to England,
1785-1929: A Narrative of Anglo-American Diplomatic
Relations. New York, 1929.

Western Europe

1055. Albrecht-Carrié, René. Britain and France: Adaptations
      to a Changing Context of Power. New York, 1970.

      A survey since 1815; see also Jean Albert-Sorel, Histoire
      de France et d'Angleterre: La rivalité, l'entente,
      l'alliance (Paris, 1950); R.B. McCallum, England and
      France 1939-1943 (London, 1944); Catherine Gavin, Britain
      and France, The Entente Cordiale: A Study of Twentieth
      Century Relations (London, 1941); Douglas Johnson, et
      al., eds., Britain and France: Ten Centuries (London,
      1980); S.M. Osgood, "Le mythe de 'la perfide Albion' en
      France, 1919-1940", Cahiers d'histoire, 20(1975), 5-20;
      and John C. Cairns, "A Nation of Shopkeepers in Search of
      a Suitable France: 1919-1940", American Historical
      Review, 79(1974), 710-43.

1056. Centre National de la Recherche Scientifique. Les
      relations franco-britanniques de 1935 à 1939. Paris,
      1975.

      Twenty-three papers on all aspects of the subject;
      presented at conferences in London, 1971 and Paris, 1972.

1057. Furnia, Arthur H. The Diplomacy of Appeasement: Anglo-
      French Relations and the Prelude to World War II,
      1931-1938. Washington, DC, 1960.

1058. Gardiner, Rolf, and Rocholl, Heinz. Britain and
      Germany. London, 1928.

      Proceedings of a symposium; British contributors included
      G.P. Gooch and Kingsley Martin.

1059. Gilbert, Martin. Britain and Germany Between the Wars.
      London, 1964.

      A valuable collection of documents with commentary.

1060. Hachey, Thomas E., ed. Anglo-Vatican Relations, 1914-
      1939: Confidential Annual Reports of the British
      Ministers to the Holy See. Boston, MA, 1972.

      From Public Record Office files FO371.

1061. Joll, James, ed. Britain and Europe: Pitt to Churchill,
      1793-1940. London, 1961.

      Includes nineteen documents on the 1918-1940 period; see
      also R.C. Birch, Britain and Europe, 1871-1939 (London,

Western Europe

1966); G.P. Gooch, "England and Europe: A Retrospect", Hungarian Quarterly, 4(1938), 577-85; and Hugh Dalton, "England and Europe", Contemporary Review, 148(1935), 129-37.

1062. Jordan, William M. Great Britain, France, and the German Problem, 1918-1939. London, 1943.

See also Arnold Wolfers, Britain and France between Two Wars: Conflicting Strategies of Peace since Versailles (New York, 1940).

1063. Kaarsted, Tage. Great Britain and Denmark, 1914-1920. Odense, 1979.

See also Susan Seymour, Anglo-Danish Relations and Germany, 1933-1945 (Odense, 1983).

1064. Koliopoulos, John S. Greece and the British Connection, 1935-1941. London, 1977.

Based on British and Greek archives; see also Dimitri Kitsikis, "La Grèce entre l'Angleterre et l'Allemagnè de 1936 à 1941", Revue historique, 238(1967), 85-116; written with access to Greek archives.

1065. Lefèvre, Joseph. L'Angleterre et la Belgique à travers les cinq derniers siècles. Brussels, 1946.

Also useful is The History of Anglo-Belgian Relations, edited by H.W. Howes (London, 1943).

1066. Mander, John. Our German Cousins: Anglo-German Relations in the 19th and 20th Centuries. London, 1974.

A cultural and historical analysis; see also Paul M. Kennedy, "Idealists and Realists: British Views of Germany, 1864-1939", Transactions of the Royal Historical Society, 25(1975), 137-56.

1067. Quartararo, Rosaria. Roma tra Londra e Berlino: La politica estera fascista dal 1930 al 1940. Rome, 1980.

A well documented study, based on both British and Italian archives, including the papers of Dino Grandi; no bibliography but with 200 pages of footnotes, not always accurate; see also the earlier Virginio Gayda, Italia e Inghilterra (Rome, 1941); and Amadeo Giannini, I rapporti italo-inglese (Milan, 1940).

BILATERAL AND AREA STUDIES

Western Europe

1068. Waites, Neville, ed. Troubled Neighbours: Franco-British Relations in the Twentieth Century. London, 1971.

A collection of very useful essays; topics include Locarno, the Rhineland crisis, Munich and wartime diplomacy.

Eastern Europe and the USSR

1069. British Documents on Foreign Affairs: Reports and Papers from the Foreign Office Confidential Print, The Soviet Union, 1917-1939. Edited by D.C. Watt. 15 vols. Frederick, MD, 1984.

Part 2, subtitled From the First to the Second World War, of a forthcoming, multi-volume series; further volumes subdivided by area, such as North America, Asia, etc., and subject, for example, the Paris peace conference of 1919 and the League of Nations.

1070. Carmi, Ozer. La Grande-Bretagne et la Petite Entente. Geneva, 1972.

From Versailles to its disintegration in 1937; based on a wide variety of sources; see also Günter Reichert, Das Scheitern der kleinen Entente: Internationale Beziehungen im Donauraum von 1933 bis 1938 (Munich, 1971).

1071. Cienciala, Anna M. Poland and the Western Powers, 1938-1939: A Study in the Interdependence of Eastern and Western Europe. London, 1968.

A well documented study, including Polish language materials; useful bibliographical essay.

1072. Coates, William P., and Coates, Zelda K. A History of Anglo-Soviet Relations. 2 vols. London, 1943-58.

See also the same authors' Armed Intervention in Russia 1918-1922 (London, 1935).

1073. Crankshaw, Edward. Britain and Russia. London, 1944.

Similar early studies include F.D. Klingender, Russia - Britain's Ally, 1812-1942 (London, 1942); J.A.R. Marriott, Anglo-Russian Relations, 1689-1943 (London 1944); K.W.B. Middleton, Britain and Russia: An

Eastern Europe and the USSR

Historical Essay (London, 1947); and B.H. Sumner,
Anglo-Soviet Relations (Leeds, 1948).

1074. Franke, Reiner. "Die Tschechoslowakei in der politischen
Meinung Englands, 1918-1938", in Die demokratisch-
parlamentarische Struktur der ersten Tschechoslowak-
ischen Republik. Edited by Karl Bosl. Munich, 1975.

See also Harry Hanak, "Great Britain and Czechoslovakia,
1918-1948: An Outline of their Relations", in
Czechoslovakia Past and Present, edited by Miloslav
Rechcigl (The Hague, 1968); and J.V. Polisensky, Britain
and Czechoslovakia: A Study in Contacts (Prague, 1966).

1075. Gorodetsky, Gabriel. The Precarious Truce: Anglo-Soviet
Relations, 1924-1927. London, 1977.

Based on British archives and Soviet published sources.

1076. Kettle, Michael. Russia and the Allies, 1917-1920.
London, 1981-.

In progress; vol. 1 for 1917-18; mainly on Anglo-Soviet
relations; similarly see also John Silverlight, The
Victors' Dilemma: Allied Intervention in the Russian
Civil War (London, 1970); and John Bradley, Allied
Intervention in Russia, 1917-1920 (New York, 1968).

1077. Krasilnikov, Aleksei N. SSSR i Angliia: Sovetsko-
Angliiskie otnosheniia v 1917-1967gg. Moscow, 1967.

See also his Politika anglii v otnoshenii SSSR, 1929-1932
gg. (Moscow, 1959); Viktor Ivanovich Popov,
Diplomaticheskie otnosheniia mezhdu SSSR i Angliei,
1929-1939gg. (Moscow, 1965); his Anglo-Sovetskie
otnosheniia, 1927-1929 (Moscow, 1958); Svetlana Nikonova,
Antisovietskaia vneshnaia politika angliiskikh
konservatorov, 1924-1927 (Moscow, 1963); Fedor D. Volkov,
Tainy uaitkholla i Dauning-strit (Moscow, 1980); his
SSSR-Angliia, 1929-1945gg. (Moscow, 1964); and Anglo-
Sovietskie Otnosheniia, 1929-1945gg. (Moscow, 1958).

1078. Niedhart, Gottfried. Grossbritannien und die Sowjetunion
1934-1939: Studien zur britischen Politik der
Friedenssicherung zwischen den beiden Weltkriegen.
Munich, 1972.

See also his "Der Bündniswert der Sowjetunion im Urteil
Grossbritanniens, 1936-1939", Militärgeschichtliche
Mitteilungen, 5(1971), 55-67.

BILATERAL AND AREA STUDIES

Eastern Europe and the USSR

1079. Northedge, F.S., and Wells, Audrey. Britain and Soviet Communism: The Impact of a Revolution. London, 1982.

A comprehensive account of Anglo-Soviet relations.

1080. Piszczkowski, Tadeusz. Anglia a Polska, 1914-1939: W Swietle Dokumentow Brytyjskich. London, 1975.

Based on Polish secondary sources and Foreign Office materials; see also Maria Nowak-Kielbikowa, "British Policy towards Poland in the 1930's", Acta Poloniae Historica, 40(1979), 97-122.

1081. Recker, Marie-Luise. England und der Donauraum, 1919-1929: Problem einer europäischen Nachkriegsordnung. Stuttgart, 1976.

Widely based on British archives, including Treasury and Board of Trade files; see also Marie Sz-Ormos, "Sur les causes de l'échec du pacte danubien, 1934-1935", Acta Historica, 14(1968), 21-81; and Thomas L. Sakmyster, Hungary, the Great Powers and the Danubian Crisis, 1936-1939 (Athens, GA, 1980).

1082. Senn, Alfred E. The Great Powers, Lithuania and the Vilna Question, 1920-1928. Leiden, 1966.

1083. Ullman, Richard H. Anglo-Soviet Relations, 1917-1921. 3 vols. Princeton, NJ, 1961-72.

1084. White, Stephen. Britain and the Bolshevik Revolution: A Study in the Politics of Diplomacy, 1920-1924. London, 1979.

Widely researched in British, Dutch, Soviet and American archives.

Middle East

1085. Bullard, Sir Reader William. Britain and the Middle East from Earliest Times to 1963. London, 1964.

Other general surveys include Matthew A. Fitzsimons, Empire by Treaty: Britain and the Middle East in the Twentieth Century (London, 1965); John Bagot Glubb, Britain and the Arabs: A Study of Fifty Years, 1908-1958 (London, 1959); M.V. Seton-Williams, Britain and the Arab States: A Survey of Anglo-Arab Relations, 1920-1948 (London, 1948) and A.H. Hourani, Great Britain and the Arab World (London, 1945).

Middle East

1086. Busch, Briton Cooper. <u>Britain, India and the Arabs,</u>
<u>1914-1921.</u> Berkeley, CA, 1971.

1087. Darwin, John. <u>Britain, Egypt and the Middle East:</u>
<u>Imperial Policy in the Aftermath of War, 1918-1922.</u>
London, 1981.

Concentrates on coalition government policy in Egypt,
Turkey, Persia and Iraq; see also Jukka Nevakivi,
<u>Britain, France and the Arab Middle East, 1914-1920</u>
(London, 1969); and Elie Kedourie, <u>England and the Middle</u>
<u>East: The Destruction of the Ottoman Empire, 1914-1921</u>
(London, 1956); with European and Arabic language
sources.

1088. DeLuca, Anthony R. <u>Great Power Rivalry at the Turkish</u>
<u>Straits: The Montreux Conference and Convention of</u>
<u>1936.</u> New York, 1981.

Analysis with background and developments to 1946.

1089. Friedman, Isaiah. <u>The Question of Palestine, 1914-1918:</u>
<u>British-Jewish-Arab Relations.</u> London, 1973.

See also Abdul Latif Tibawi, <u>Anglo-Arab Relations and the</u>
<u>Question of Palestine, 1914-1921</u> (London, 1977); based on
British archives and Arabic sources; Neil Caplan,
"Britain, Zionism and the Arabs, 1917-1925", <u>Wiener</u>
<u>Library Bulletin</u>, 31(1978), 4-17; and Joseph Heller,
"Anglo-Zionist Relations, 1939-1947", <u>Wiener Library</u>
<u>Bulletin</u>, 31(1978), 63-73.

1090. Leatherdale, Clive. <u>Britain and Saudi Arabia,</u>
<u>1925-1939.</u> London, 1983.

1091. Marlowe, John. <u>A History of Modern Egypt and Anglo-</u>
<u>Egyptian Relations, 1800-1956.</u> Hamden, CT, 1965.

See also Keith M. Wilson, <u>Imperialism and Nationalism in</u>
<u>the Middle East: The Anglo-Egyptian Experience,</u>
<u>1882-1982</u> (New York, 1983); R.O. Collins, <u>Shadows in the</u>
<u>Grass: Britain in the Southern Sudan, 1918-1956</u> (New
Haven, CT); Peter Mansfield, <u>The British in Egypt</u> (New
York, 1972); L.A. Fabunmi, <u>The Sudan in Anglo-Egyptian</u>
<u>Relations: A Case Study in Power Politics, 1800-1956</u>
(London, 1960); and Royal Institute of International
Affairs, <u>Great Britain and Egypt, 1914-1951</u> (London,
1952).

Middle East

1092. Monroe, Elizabeth. <u>Britain's Moment in the Middle East, 1914-1956</u>. London, 1963.

On staff of the Royal Institute of International Affairs, 1933; director, Middle East division, ministry of Information, 1940-44; see also the same author's <u>The Mediterranean in Politics</u> (London, 1938).

1093. Williams, Ann. <u>Britain and France in the Middle East and North Africa, 1914-1967</u>. London, 1968.

See also Henry H. Cumming, <u>Franco-British Rivalry in the Post-War Near East: The Decline of French Influence</u> (London, 1938).

1094. Wright, Sir Denis. <u>The English Amongst the Persians during the Qajar Period, 1787-1921</u>. London, 1977.

Based on British and Persian sources; useful bibliography; author was vice-consul at Constantza, 1939-41; Trebizond, 1941-43; acting consul, Mersin, 1943-45; ambassador to Iran, 1963-71.

1095. Zhivkova, Ludmila. <u>Anglo-Turkish Relations, 1933-1939</u>. London, 1976.

With material from Bulgarian archives; see also the same author's "Anglo-Turkish Relations, 1934-1935", <u>Etudes balkaniques</u>, 7(1971), 82-98; Stephen F. Evans, <u>The Slow Rapprochement: Britain and Turkey in the Age of Kemal Atatürk, 1919-1938</u> (Beverley, 1982); and Philip P. Graves, <u>Briton and Turk</u> (London, 1941).

1096. Zürrer, Werner. <u>Persien zwischen England und Russland, 1918-1925: Grossmachteinflüsse und nationaler Wiederaufstieg am Beispiel des Iran</u>. Bern, 1978.

Wide use of archival material, including Soviet studies; see also Ishtiaq Ahmad, <u>Anglo-Iranian Relations, 1905-1919</u> (Bombay, 1974); and N.S. Fatemi, <u>Diplomatic History of Persia, 1917-1923: Anglo-Russian Power Politics in Iran</u> (New York, 1952).

Asia and the Far East

See also below, From Manchuria to the Pacific War, 1931-1941, pages 241-44.

Asia and the Far East

1097. Adamec, Ludwig. Afghanistan's Foreign Affairs to the Mid-Twentieth century: Relations with the USSR, Germany and Britain. Tucson, AZ, 1974.

1098. Clifford, Nicholas R. Retreat from China: British Policy in the Far East, 1937-1941. Seattle, WA, 1967.

Relies essentially on American archives; see also his "Britain, America and the Far East, 1937-1940: A Failure in Cooperation", Journal of British Studies, 3(1963), 137-54; and "Sir Frederick Maze and the Chinese Maritime Customs, 1937-1941", Journal of Modern History, 37(1965), 18-34.

1099. Endicott, Stephen Lyon. Diplomacy and Enterprise: British China Policy, 1933-1937. Vancouver, BC, 1975.

Based on British public and private archives.

1100. Fitzhardinge, L.F. "Australia, Japan and Great Britain, 1914-1918: A Study in Triangular diplomacy." Historical Studies, 14(1970), 250-59.

See also D.K. Dignan, "Australia and British Relations with Japan, 1914-1921", Australian Outlook, 21(1967), 135-50.

1101. Hassnain, F.M. British Policy towards Kashmir, 1846-1921: Kashmir in Anglo-Russian Politics. New Delhi, 1974.

1102. Kennedy, Malcolm D. The Estrangement of Great Britain and Japan, 1917-1935. Manchester, 1969.

See also his "The Future of Anglo-Japanese Relations", Asiatic Review, 35(1939), 777-85.

1103. Kiernan, E. Victor Gordon. British Diplomacy in China, 1885-1970. London, 1970.

1104. Lowe, Peter. Britain in the Far East: A Survey from 1918 to the Present. London, 1981.

Concentrates particularly on China; earlier accounts include Guy Wint, The British in Asia (New York, 1954); Gilbert E. Hubbard, British Far Eastern Policy (New York, 1943); Chin-Lin Hsia, British Far Eastern Policy, 1937-1940 (Chungking, 1940); and Royal Institute of

212

BILATERAL AND AREA STUDIES

Asia and the Far East

International Affairs, British Far Eastern Policy
(London, 1939).

1105. Nish, Ian. Alliance in Decline: A Study in Anglo-
Japanese Relations, 1908-1923. London, 1972.

Still useful is Chung-Fu Chang, The Anglo-Japanese
Alliance (London, 1931).

1106. Nish, Ian, ed. Anglo-Japanese Alienation 1919-1952:
Papers of the Anglo-Japanese Conference on the History
of the Second World War. London, 1982.

Paired chapters, one by a British scholar, one by a
Japanese, are used to illustrate differing perspectives.

1107. Pratt, Sir John T. China and Britain. London, 1944.

Chinese consular service, 1909-25; with Foreign Office,
1925-38; head of far eastern section, ministry of
Information, 1939-41; see also his War and Politics in
China (London, 1943); and "America, Britain and China",
Contemporary Review, 158(1940), 47-55.

1108. Rose, Saul. Britain and South-East Asia. Baltimore,
MD, 1962.

1109. Samra, Chattar Singh. India and Anglo-Soviet Relations,
1917-1947. New York, 1959.

1110. Stremski, Richard. The Shaping of British Policy during
the Nationalist Revolution in China. Taipei, 1979.

A publication of Soochow University; based on British and
American archives.

1111. Wesley-Smith, Peter. Unequal Treaty, 1897-1997: China,
Great Britain and Hong Kong's New Territories. London,
1980.

Both the legal and historical relationship.

5. Appeasement: The Debate

1112. Beloff, Max. "Appeasement: For and Against."
Government and Opposition, 7(1972), 112-19.

1113. Brügel, Johann W. "Die Appeasement-Politik im
      Kreuzfeuer der Kritik." Neue Politische Literatur,
      8(1963), 803-22.

1114. "Cato." [Michael Foot, Frank Owen and Peter Howard].
      Guilty Men. London, 1940.

      From the Left Book Club; the original and very dramatic
      statement of the "guilty men" thesis; on the origin of
      this book see Michael Foot, Debts of Honour (London,
      1980).

1115. Dent, Philip. "The D'Abernon Papers: Origins of
      'Appeasement'." British Museum Quarterly, 37(1973),
      103-7.

1116. Dilks, David. "Appeasement Revisited." University of
      Leeds Review, 15(1972), 28-56.

      An inaugural lecture, with material from the Neville
      Chamberlain papers.

1117. Einzig, Paul. Appeasement Before, During and After the
      War. London, 1941.

1118. Gilbert, Martin. The Roots of Appeasement. London,
      1966.

      A pioneering study of appeasement and its historical
      antecedents.

1119. Gilbert, Martin, and Gott, Richard. The Appeasers.
      London, 1963.

      The aims and methods of the "appeasers"; based on
      considerable private information.

1120. Grenville, J.A.S. "Contemporary Trends in the Study of
      the British 'Appeasement' Policies of the 1930s."
      Internationales Jahrbuch für Geschichts- und
      Geographie-Unterricht, 17(1976), 236-47.

1121. Gruner, W.D. "'British Interest' in der
      Zwischenkriegszeit: Aspekte britischer Europa-Politik
      1918-1938", in Gleichgewicht, Revision, Restauration:
      Die Aussenpolitik der Ersten Tschechoslowakischen
      Republik im Europasystem der Pariser Vorverträge.
      Edited by Karl Bosl. Munich, 1976.

      An attempt to examine the various structural determinants
      of external policy, as well as the domestic context; for

his further contributions to this debate see also
"'British Interest' und Friedenssicherung: Zur
Interaktion von britischer Innen- und Aussenpolitik im
frühen 19. Jahrhundert", Historische Zeitschrift,
224(1977), 92-104; and "The British Political, Social and
Economic System and the Decision for Peace and War:
Reflections on Anglo-German Relations, 1800-1939",
British Journal of International Studies, 6(1980),
189-218.

1122. Haigh, R.H., and Turner, P.W. British Policies and
     Society, 1918-1938: The Effect on Appeasement.
     Manhattan, KS, 1980.

     For Military Affairs/Aerospace Historian; a short essay
     based essentially on secondary sources; likewise see also
     the same authors' Defense Policy between the Wars,
     1918-1938, Culminating in the Munich Agreement of
     September 1938 (Manhattan, KS, 1979).

1123. Herz, John H. "The Relevancy and Irrelevancy of
     Appeasement." Social Research, 31(1964), 296-320.

     See also his "Sinn und Sinnlosigkeit der
     Beschwichtigungspolitik: Zur Problematik des
     Appeasement-Begriffes", Politische Viertel-
     jahresschrift, 5(1964), 370-89.

1124. Herzfeld, Hans. "Zur Problematik der Appeasement-
     Politik", in Geschichte und Gegenwartsbewusstsein,
     historische Betrachtungen und Untersuchungen:
     Festschrift für Hans Rothfels zum 70. Geburtstag.
     Edited by Waldemar Besson and Friedrich von
     Gaertringen. Göttingen, 1963.

1125. Jones, R.J. Barry. "The Study of 'Appeasement' and the
     Study of International Relations." British Journal of
     International Studies, 1(1975), 68-76.

1126. Kennedy, Paul M. "The Tradition of Appeasement in
     British Foreign Policy, 1865-1939." British Journal of
     International Studies, 2(1976), 195-215.

     Analyses appeasement's roots in moral, economic,
     strategic and domestic motives; see also his "'Appease-
     ment' and British Defence Policy in the Inter-War Years",
     British Journal of International Studies, 4(1978),
     161-77; and "The Study of Appeasement: Methodological
     Crossroads or Meeting-Place?" British Journal of
     International Studies, 6(1980), 181-88.

1127. Lanyi, George A. "The Problem of Appeasement." World Politics, 15(1963), 316-28.

1128. Lundgreen, Peter. Die englische Appeasement-Politik bis zum Münchener Abkommen: Voraussetzungen, Konzeption, Durchführung. Berlin, 1969.

Based on a thorough study of politics, opinion and pressure groups in the 1930s.

1129. Mann, G. "Von der Tyrannei historischer Erfahrungen: Die Politik des 'Appeasement' und des 'No Appeasement'." Aussenpolitik, 3(1952), 81-88.

1130. Mommsen, W.J., and Kettenacker, L., eds. The Fascist Challenge and the Policy of Appeasement. London, 1983.

Proceedings of a conference in May 1980, held under the auspices of the German Historical Institute, London; twenty-eight essays designed "to throw new light on the 1930s" (Foreword).

1131. Niedhart, Gottfried. "Appeasement: Die britische Antwort auf die Krise des Weltreichs und des internationalen Systems vor dem Zweiten Weltkrieg." Historische Zeitschrift, 226(1978), 67-88.

A useful survey and analysis of the literature; among his contributions to the discussion see also "Weltherrschaft versus World Appeasement", Neue Politische Literatur, 23(1978), 281-91; "Britische Deutschlandpolitik vor dem Zweiten Weltkrieg: Friedensbedürfnis und gescheiterte Friedenssicherung", in Aus Politik und Zeitgeschichte, supplement to Das Parlament, 13(1977), 26-39; "Europa in der britischen Weltpolitik vor dem Zweiten Weltkrieg", Francia, 5(1977), 789-97; "Friede als nationales Interesse: Grossbritannien in der Vorgeschichte des Zweiten Weltkriegs", Neue Politische Literatur, 17(1972), 451-70; and "Weltmacht-Anspruch und Wirklichkeit: Zur britischen Aussenpolitik im 20. Jahrhundert", Neue Politische Literatur, 13(1968), 233-41.

1132. Presseisen, Ernst L. Amiens and Munich: Comparisons in Appeasement. The Hague, 1978.

An attempt at a comparative model of appeasement.

1133. Rock, William R. British Appeasement in the 1930s. London, 1977.

An analysis of the meaning, origins, motives and proponents of appeasement; good bibliographical essay;

see also his "British Appeasement (1930's): A Need for Revision?" South Atlantic Quarterly, 78(1979), 290-301.

1134. Rowse, A.L. All Souls and Appeasement: A Contribution to Contemporary History. London, 1961.

Of interest is his less well-known The End of an Epoch: Reflections on Contemporary History (London, 1948); and Memories of Men and Women (London, 1980).

1135. Schlenke, Manfred. "Die Westmächte und das national-sozialistische Deutschland: Motive, Ziele und Illusionen der Appeasement-Politik." Mitteilungen der Gesellschaft der Freunde der Wirtschaftshochschule Mannheim, 16(1967), 35-43.

1136. Schmidt, Gustav. England in der Krise: Grundzüge und Grundlagen der britischen Appeasement-Politik, 1930-1937. Opladen, 1981.

A thorough thematic study based on an intensive examination of primary and secondary material; see also his "Politisches System und Appeasement-Politik, 1930-1937: Zur Scharnierfunktion der Rüstungspolitik für die britische Innen- und Aussenpolitik", Militär-geschichtliche Mitteilungen, 13(1979), 37-53; "Strategie und Aussenpolitik des 'Troubled Giant'", Militär-geschichtliche Mitteilungen, 7(1973), 208-18; and "Britische Strategie und Aussenpolitik: Wahlchancen und Determinanten britischer Sicherheitspolitik im Zeitalter der neuen Weltmächte, 1897-1929", Militärgeschichtliche Mitteilungen", 5(1971), 197-218.

1137. Schroeder, Paul W. "Munich and the British Tradition." Historical Journal, 19(1976), 223-43.

Argues that appeasement was another approach to the traditional policy of maintaining the European balance of power.

1138. Seeland, Rolf. Appeasement: Eine Methode zur Lösung internationaler Konflikte. Hamburg, 1968.

1139. Skidelsky, Robert. "Going to War with Germany: Between Revisionism and Orthodoxy." Encounter, 39(1972), 56-65.

1140. Walker, Stephen G. "Solving the Appeasement Puzzle: Contending Historical Interpretations of British Diplomacy during the 1930s." British Journal of International Studies, 6(1980), 219-46.

1141. Watt, D.C. "Appeasement: The Rise of a Revisionist School?" <u>Political Quarterly,</u> 36(1965), 191-213.

An early summary of the 'orthodox view' and the 'new criticism'; see also his "Appeasement Reconsidered: Some Neglected Factors", <u>Round Table,</u> 53(1963), 358-71; "Christian Essay in Appeasement: Lord Lothian and His Quaker Friends", <u>Wiener Library Bulletin,</u> 14(1960), 30-31; and "The Historiography of Appeasement", in <u>Crisis and Controversy: Essays in Honour of A.J.P. Taylor,</u> edited by Alan Sked and Chris Cook (London, 1976).

1142. Wendt, Bernd Jürgen. "Grossbritannien - Demokratie auf dem Prüfstand: Appeasement als Strategie des Status Quo", in <u>Innen- und Aussenpolitik unter national-sozialistischer Bedrohung: Determinanten internationaler Beziehungen in historischen Fallstudien.</u> Edited by Erhard Forndran, et al. Opladen, 1977.

See also his "Aspekte der deutschen Appeasement-Forschung", <u>Internationales Jahrbuch für Geschichts- und Geographie-Unterricht,</u> 17(1976), 248-75.

E. PEACEMAKING AND DETENTE, 1918-1933

1. 1920s General

1143. Artaud, Denise. La question des dettes interalliées et
    la reconstruction de l'Europe, 1917-1929. 2 vols.
    Paris, 1978.

    And the same author's "La question des dettes
    interalliées et la reconstruction de l'Europe", Revue
    historique, 261(1979), 363-82; and La reconstruction de
    l'Europe, 1919-1929 (Paris, 1973).

1144. Bergmann, Carl. Der Weg der Reparationen: Von
    Versailles über den Dawesplan zum Ziel. Frankfurt/M.,
    1926. Eng. trans., The History of Reparation. London,
    1927.

    By a German expert, closely in contact with the British.

1145. Frasure, Carl. British Policy on War Debts and
    Reparations. Philadelphia, PA, 1940.

1146. Kölling, Mirjam. "Aspekte britischer Aussenpolitik in
    den zwanziger Jahren." Zeitschrift für Geschichts-
    wissenschaft, 21(1973), 1423-42.

1147. Leffler, Melvyn P. The Elusive Quest: America's Pursuit
    of European Stability and French Security, 1919-1933.
    Chapel Hill, NC, 1979.

    Thoroughly based on American archives and numerous
    collections of private papers; useful bibliography.

1148. MacKinder, Sir Halford John. Democratic Ideals and
    Reality: A Study in the Politics of Reconstruction.
    London, 1919.

    M.P., 1910-20; British high commissioner for south
    Russia, 1919-20.

1149. Maier, Charles S. Recasting Bourgeois Europe: Stabiliz-
    ation in France, Germany, and Italy in the Decade after
    World War I. Princeton, NJ, 1975.

An interesting and widely documented study of postwar
society, politics and economics.

1150. Marks, Sally. The Illusion of Peace: International
Relations 1918-1933. New York, 1976.

See also the same author's "Reparations Reconsidered: A
Reminder", Central European History, 2(1969), 356-65;
David Felix, "Reparations Reconsidered with a Vengeance",
Central European History, 4(1971), 171-79; and Sally
Marks, "Reparations Reconsidered: A Rejoinder", Central
European History, 5(1972), 358-61.

1151. Orde, Anne. Great Britain and International Security,
1920-1926. London, 1977.

A well documented and brief synthesis.

1152. Pink, Gerhard P. The Conference of Ambassadors: Paris,
1920-1931. Geneva, 1942.

Vol. 12 of Geneva Studies, 1942.

1153. Seydoux, Jacques. De Versailles au Plan Young:
Réparations, dettes interalliées, reconstruction
européenne. Paris, 1932.

1154. Stern-Rubarth, Edgar. Three Men Tried: Austen
Chamberlain, Stresemann, Briand and their Fight for a
New Europe: A Personal Memoir. London, 1939.

By a Weimar spokesman of the 1920s.

1155. Toynbee, Arnold J. The Conduct of British Empire Foreign
Relations since the Peace Settlement. London, 1928.

See also Oswald Hauser, "Das britische Commonwealth
zwischen nationaler Souveränität und imperialer
Integration, 1917-1931", Vierteljahrshefte für
Zeitgeschichte, 16(1968), 230-46.

1156. Trachtenberg, Marc. Reparation in World Politics:
France and European Economic Diplomacy, 1916-1923. New
York, 1980.

A revisionist analysis portraying hardline Englishmen
against moderate Frenchmen; see also his "Reparation at
the Paris Peace Conference", Journal of Modern History,
51(1979), 24-55; and "Versailles after Sixty Years",
Journal of Contemporary History, 17(1982), 487-506.

1920s GENERAL

1157. Weill-Raynal, Etienne. Les réparations allemandes et
     la France. 3 vols. Paris, 1947-49.

     By a member of the Reparation Commission.

1158. Wheeler-Bennett, John W., and Langermann, F.E.
     Information on the Problem of Security, 1917-1926.
     London, 1927.

1159. Williams, Roland E.J. Voughan, ed. The Hungarian
     Question in the British Parliament, 1919-1930. London,
     1933.

     Extracts from speeches in the House of Lords and House of
     Commons.

        2. Armistice and Peacemaking, 1918-1919

1160. Anderson, Edgar. "British Policy Toward the Baltic
     States, 1918-1920." Journal of Central European
     Affairs, 19(1959), 276-89.

     See also the same author's "An Undeclared Naval War: The
     British-Soviet Naval Struggle in the Baltic, 1918-1920",
     Journal of Central European Affairs, 22(1962), 43-78;
     John Bradley, "L'Intervention alliée dans les états
     baltes, 1919", Revue d'histoire moderne et contemporaine,
     23(1976), 236-57; Wilhelm Lenz, "Zur britischen Politik
     gegenüber den baltischen Deutschen, 1918-1919", in Das
     Vergangene und die Geschichte: Festschrift für Reinhard
     Wittram, edited by Rudolf von Thadden, et al. (Göttingen,
     1973); Edward William Polson Newman, Britain and the
     Baltic (London, 1930); and the more general study based
     on German and American archives by Hugh I. Rodgers,
     Search for Security: A Study in Baltic Diplomacy,
     1920-1934 (Hamden, CT, 1975).

1161. Arslanian, Artin H. "British Wartime Pledges, 1917-1918:
     The Armenian Case." Journal of Contemporary History,
     13(1978), 517-30.

     See also his "Britain and the Question of Mountainous
     Karabagh", Middle Eastern Studies, 16(1980), 92-104.

1162. Barraclough, Geoffrey. "Das Britische Reich und der
     Frieden", in Ideologie und Machtpolitik, 1919: Plan
     und Werk der Pariser Friedenskonferenzen, 1919. Edited
     by Hellmuth Rössler. Göttingen, 1966.

1163. Boothe, L.E. "A Fettered Envoy: Lord Grey's Mission to
     the United States, 1919-1920." Review of Politics,
     33(1971), 78-94.

1164. Bosworth, Richard. "Sir Rennell Rodd e l'Italia." Nuova rivista storica, 54(1970), 420-36.

1165. Burnett, Philip Mason, ed. Reparation at the Paris Peace Conference: From the Standpoint of the American Delegation. 2 vols. New York, 1940.

   More than 500 documents, many dealing with Britain.

1166. Calder, Kenneth J. Britain and the Origins of the New Europe, 1914-1918. London, 1976.

   On the wartime problem of national self-determination as determined by strategic necessities; well documented.

1167. Crosby, Gerda Richards. Disarmament and Peace in British Politics, 1914-1919. Cambridge, MA, 1957.

1168. Czernin, Ferdinand, ed. Versailles, 1919: The Forces, Events and Personalities that Shaped the Treaty. New York, 1964.

   A useful collection of documents, concentrating on five main clauses of the treaty; other general accounts include Charles L. Mee, The End of Order: Versailles, 1919 (New York, 1980); George Goldberg, The Peace to End Peace: The Paris Peace Conference of 1919 (London, 1969); Pierre Renouvin, Le traité de Versailles (Paris, 1969); and Paul Birdsall, Versailles: Twenty Years After (London, 1941).

1169. Davis, Rodney O. "Lloyd George: Leader or Led in British War Aims, 1916-1918", in Power, Public Opinion and Diplomacy: Essays in Honor of Eber Malcolm Carroll. Edited by Lillian Parker Wallace and William C. Askew. Durham, NC, 1959.

1170. Debo, Richard K. "Mésentente Glaciale: Great Britain, France, and the Question of Intervention in the Baltic, 1918." Canadian Journal of History, 12(1977), 65-86.

   See also his "Prelude to Negotiations: The Problem of British Prisoners in Soviet Russia, November 1918-July 1919", Slavonic and East European Review, 58(1980), 58-75.

1171. Dimitrov, Theodore D., ed. Harold Nicolson and the Balkans: Confidential Documents. Geneva, 1979.

Prepared for "International Documentation on Macedonia";
deals with 1919.

1172. Dockrill, Michael L., and Goold, J. Douglas. Peace
Without Promise: Britain and the Peace Conferences,
1919-1923. London, 1981.

Based on Foreign Office and cabinet documents, and the
private papers of Balfour, Curzon, Hardinge, Lloyd George
and Philip Kerr.

1173. Egerton, George W. "Britain and the 'Great Betrayal':
Anglo-American Relations and the Struggle for United
States Ratification of the Treaty of Versailles,
1919-1920." Historical Journal, 21(1978), 885-911.

1174. Elcock, Howard. Portrait of a Decision: The Council of
Four and the Treaty of Versailles. London, 1972.

Mainly based on British sources; see also his "Britain
and the Russo-Polish Frontier, 1919-1921", Historical
Journal, 12(1969), 137-54.

1175. Fest, W.B. Peace or Partition: The Habsburg Monarchy
and British Policy, 1914-1918. London, 1978.

See also Harry Hanak, Great Britain and Austria-Hungary
During the First World War: A Study in the Formation of
Public Opinion (London, 1962); and Hugh Seton-Watson and
Christopher Seton-Watson, The Making of a New Europe:
R.W. Seton-Watson and the Last Years of Austria-Hungary
(London, 1981).

1176. Floto, Inga. Colonel House in Paris: A Study of
American Policy at the Paris Peace Conference, 1919.
Aarhus, 1973.

Other studies for relevant powers include Francis Deak,
Hungary at the Paris Peace Conference (New York, 1942);
Sally Marks, Innocent Abroad: Belgium at the Paris Peace
Conference of 1919 (Chapel Hill, NC, 1981); Alma Luckau,
The German Delegation at the Paris Peace Conference (New
York, 1941); René Albrecht-Carrié, Italy at the Paris
Peace Conference (New York, 1938); C.A. Macartney,
Hungary and her Successors: The Treaty of Trianon and
its Consequences (London, 1937); John M. Thompson,
Russia, Bolshevism and the Versailles Peace (Princeton,
NJ, 1966); Andrej Mitrovic, "The 1919-1920 Peace Con-
ference in Paris and the Yugoslav State: An Historical
Education", in The Creation of Yugoslavia, 1914-1918,

edited by Dimitrije Djordjevic (Santa Barbara, CA, 1980);
Sherman David Spector, Rumania at the Paris Peace
Conference (New York, 1962); and Kay Lundgreen-Nielson,
The Polish Problem at the Paris Peace Conference: A
Study of the Policies of the Great Powers and the Poles,
1918-1919 (Odense, 1979).

1177. Fowler, Wilton B. British-American Relations, 1917-
      1918: The Role of Sir William Wiseman. Princeton, NJ,
      1969.

      Chief adviser on American affairs to British delegation,
      Paris, 1918-19; well documented with useful annotated
      bibliography.

1178. Fry, Michael G. Lloyd George and Foreign Policy.
      Montreal, 1977-.

      In progress; vol. 1 for 1890-1916; see also his "Britain,
      the Allies, and the Problem of Russia, 1918-1919",
      Canadian Journal of History, 2(1967), 62-84.

1179. Gruner, W.D. "Friedenssicherung und politisch-
      soziales System: Grossbritannien auf den Pariser
      Friedenskonferenzen, 1919", in L'Europe de Versailles,
      1918-1923: Bilan, perspectives et controverses.
      Geneva, 1979.

1180. Guinn, Paul. British Strategy and Politics, 1914-
      1918. London, 1965.

      On the relation between military considerations and
      domestic politics.

1181. Haupts, Leo. "Zur deutschen und britischen Friedens-
      politik in der Krise der Pariser Friedenskonferenz:
      Britisch-deutsche Separatverhandlungen im April-Mai
      1919?" Historische Zeitschrift, 217(1973), 54-98.

      On the Anglo-German negotiations at The Hague which, it
      is argued, neither took seriously.

1182. Helmreich, Paul. From Paris to Sèvres: The Partition of
      the Ottoman Empire at the Peace Conference of
      1919-1920. Columbus, OH, 1974.

      A analysis of allied diplomacy, including much on
      Britain; based on wide research; see also M. Llewellyn
      Smith, Ionian Vision: Greece in Asia Minor, 1919-1922
      (London, 1973); A.E. Montgomery, "The Making of the

Treaty of Sèvres of 10 August 1920", Historical Journal, 15(1972), 775-87; and George F. Abbott, Greece and the Allies, 1914-1922 (London, 1922).

1183. Hérisson, Charles D. Les nations anglo-saxonnes et la paix. Paris, 1936.

1184. House, Edward Mandell, and Seymour, Charles, eds. What Really Happened at Paris: The Story of the Peace Conference, 1918-1919, by American Delegates. New York, 1921.

1185. Huston, James A. "The Allied Blockade of Germany 1918-1919." Journal of Central European Affairs, 10(1950), 145-66.

1186. Kernek, Sterling J. "Distractions of Peace during War: The Lloyd George Government's Reactions to Woodrow Wilson, December, 1916-November 1918." Transactions of the American Philosophical Society, 65(1975), 1-117.

1187. Keynes, John Maynard. The Economic Consequences of the Peace. London, 1919.

Continued in A Revision of the Treaty (London, 1922); see also Helmut Lippelt, "J.M. Keynes und das finanz-politische Ordnungsproblem auf der Pariser Friedens-konferenz", in Das Vergangene und die Geschichte: Festschrift für Reinhard Wittram, edited by Rudolf von Thadden, et al. (Göttingen, 1973).

1188. Louis, William Roger. "Great Britain and the African Peace Settlement of 1919." American Historical Review, 71(1966), 875-92.

1189. Mantoux, Etienne. The Carthaginian Peace or the Economic Consequences of Mr. Keynes. London, 1946.

1190. Mantoux, Paul. Les délibérations du conseil des quatre, 24 mars-28 juin 1919. 2 vols. Paris, 1955.

Interpreter for the supreme war council, 1919; director of the political section, League of Nations, 1920-27; the English translation, Paris Peace Conference, 1919: Proceedings of the Council of Four, March 24-April 18 (Geneva, 1964) is incomplete.

1191. Marston, F.S. The Peace Conference of 1919: Organiza-tion and Procedure. London, 1944.

Good bibliography, with useful list of original sources
and secondary works.

1192. Martin, Laurence W. Peace without Victory: Woodrow
      Wilson and the British Liberals. New Haven, CT, 1958.

1193. Maurice, Sir Frederick. The Armistices of 1918-1943.
      London, 1943.

      Entered army, 1892; director of military operations,
      imperial general staff, 1915-18.

1194. Mayer, Arno J. Politics and Diplomacy of Peacemaking:
      Containment and Counterrevolution at Versailles,
      1918-1919. New York, 1967.

1195. Mejcher, Helmut. "British Middle East Policy, 1917-21:
      The Inter-Departmental Level." Journal of Contemporary
      History, 8(1973), 81-101.

1196. Nelson, Harold I. Land and Power: British and Allied
      Policy on Germany's Frontiers, 1916-1919. London,
      1963.

1197. Nicolson, Harold. Peacemaking, 1919. London, 1933.

      With extensive extracts from the author's 1919 diary; see
      also his "Peacemaking at Paris: Success, Failure, or
      Farce?" Foreign Affairs, 25(1947), 190-203.

1198. Northedge, F.S. "1917-1919: The Implications for
      Britain." Journal of Contemporary History, 3(1968),
      191-209.

1199. Paasdivirta, Juhani. The Victors in World War I and
      Finland: Finland's Relations with the British, French
      and the United States Governments in 1918-1919.
      Helsinki, 1965.

1200. Renouvin, Pierre. L'armistice de Rethondes: 11 novembre
      1918. Paris, 1968.

      Very useful bibliography; see also John Terraine, To Win
      a War: 1918, The Year of Victory (London, 1978); Cyril
      N. Barclay, Armistice, 1918 (London, 1968); and Harry R.
      Rudin, Armistice, 1918 (New Haven, CT, 1944).

1201. Riddell, Lord, et al. The Treaty of Versailles and
      After. London, 1935.

1202. Rodman, Barbee-Sue. "Britain Debates Justice: An
      Analysis of the Reparations Issue of 1918." Journal of
      British Studies, 7(1968), 140-54.

1203. Rothwell, Victor. British War Aims and Peace Diplomacy,
      1914-1918. London, 1971.

      See also his "Mesopotamia in British War Aims,
      1914-1918", Historical Journal, 13(1970), 273-94.

1204. Schmidt, Alex P. Churchills privater Krieg: Inter-
      vention und Konterrevolution im russischen Bürgerkrieg,
      November 1918-März 1920. Zurich, 1974.

      Based on British sources; useful bibliography.

1205. Schmidt, Gustav. "Effizienz und Flexibilität politisch-
      sozialer Systeme: Die deutsche und englische Politik,
      1918-1919." Vierteljahrshefte für Zeitgeschichte,
      25(1977), 137-87.

1206. Schuster, Peter. Henry Wickham Steed und die Hapsburger-
      monarchie. Vienna, 1970.

      With a brief discussion of Wickham Steed and the
      Versailles treaty.

1207. Temperley, Harold W.V., ed. A History of the Peace
      Conference of Paris. 6 vols. London, 1920-24.

1208. Tillman, Seth P. Anglo-American Relations at the Paris
      Peace Conference of 1919. Princeton, NJ, 1961.

1209. Zsuppan, Ferenc Tibor. "The Hungarian Soviet Republic
      and British Military Representatives, April-June 1919."
      Slavonic and East European Review, 47(1969), 198-218.

3. The Search for Security, 1920-1924

1210. Bardoux, Jacques. Lloyd George et la France. Paris,
      1923.

      See also the same author's Le socialisme au pouvoir,
      l'expérience de 1924: Le dialogue J. Ramsay MacDonald-
      Edouard Herriot (Paris, 1930).

1211. Beaverbrook, Lord. The Decline and Fall of Lloyd George.
      London, 1963.

1212. Bertram-Libal, Gisela. Aspekte der britischen
      Deutschlandpolitik, 1919-1922. Göppingen, 1972.

Argues that Lloyd George pursued a logical policy aimed
at the economic rehabilitation of Europe; see also the
same author's "Die britische Politik in der
Oberschlesienfrage 1919-1922", in Vierteljahrshefte für
Zeitgeschichte, 20(1972), 105-32; and F. Gregory
Campbell, "The Struggle for Upper Silesia, 1919-1922", in
Journal of Modern History, 42(1970), 361-85.

1213. Boadle, Donald Graeme. Winston Churchill and the German
Question in British Foreign Policy, 1918-1922. The
Hague, 1973.

Based on published sources and a very limited selection
of cabinet archives.

1214. Busch, Briton Cooper. Mudros to Lausanne: Britain's
Frontier in West Asia, 1918-1923. Albany, NY, 1976.

See also A.L. Macfie, "The Straits Question: The
Conference of Lausanne, November 1922-July 1923", Middle
Eastern Studies, 15(1979), 211-38.

1215. Cassels, Alan. "Repairing the Entente Cordiale and the
New Diplomacy." Historical Journal, 23(1980), 133-53.

1216. Chester, Lewis, et al. The Zinoviev Letter. London,
1967.

On the subject see also E.H. Carr, "The Zinoviev Letter",
Historical Journal, 22(1979), 209-10; Christopher Andrew,
"More on the Zinoviev Letter", Historical Journal,
22(1979), 211-14; Sibyl Crowe, "The Zinoviev Letter: A
Reappraisal", Journal of Contemporary History, 10(1975),
407-32; Natalie Grant, "The 'Zinoviev Letter' Case",
Soviet Studies, 19(1967), 264-77; and Robert D. Warth,
"The Mystery of the Zinoviev Letter", South Atlantic
Quarterly, 49(1950), 441-53.

1217. Cienciala, Anna M. "The Secret Anglo-French Agreement on
Danzig and the Saar, and its Consequences, 1919-1926."
Zeitschrift für Ostforschung, 27(1978), 434-55.

1218. Conte, Francis. "Lloyd George et le traité de Rapallo."
Revue d'histoire moderne et contemporaine, 23(1976),
44-67.

1219. Davies, Norman. "Lloyd George and Poland, 1919-1920."
Journal of Contemporary History, 6(1971), 132-54.

See also his "Sir Maurice Hankey and the Inter-Allied Mission to Poland, July-August 1920", Historical Journal, 15(1972), 553-61.

1220. Debo, Richard K. "Lloyd George and the Copenhagen Conference of 1919-1920: The Initiation of Anglo-Soviet Negotiations." Historical Journal, 24(1981), 429-41.

For an earlier analysis see Jean Haton, "Une phase décisive de l'histoire des relations anglo-soviétiques après la première guerre mondiale: Les négociations de Copenhague, novembre 1919-février 1920", Revue d'histoire diplomatique, 73(1959), 67-81.

1221. Fabre-Luce, Alfred. La crise des alliances: Essai sur les relations franco-britanniques depuis la signature de la paix. Paris, 1922.

1222. Fritz, Stephen E. "La Politique de la Ruhr and Lloyd Georgian Conference Diplomacy: The Tragedy of Anglo-French Relations, 1919-1923." Proceedings of the Annual Meeting of the Western Society for French History, 3(1975), 566-82.

1223. Gajda, Patricia A. Postscript to Victory: British Policy and the German-Polish Borderland, 1919-1925. Washington, DC, 1982.

Argues that British policy turned from orthodoxy to revisionism on the question.

1224. Georges-Gaulis, Berthe. Angora, Constantinople, Londres: Moustafa Kémal et la politique anglaise en Orient. Paris, 1922.

1225. Goold, J. Douglas. "Lord Hardinge as Ambassador to France, and the Anglo-French Dilemma over Germany and the Near East, 1920-1922." Historical Journal, 21(1978), 913-37.

1226. Hall, Hines H. "Lloyd George, Briand, and the Failure of the Anglo-French Entente." Journal of Modern History, 50(1978), offprint.

1227. Hooker, James R. "Lord Curzon and the 'Curzon Line'." Journal of Modern History, 30(1958), 137-38.

1228. Klieman, Aaron S. Foundations of British Policy in the Arab World: The Cairo Conference of 1921. London, 1970.

1229. Larew, Karl G. "Great Britain and the Greco-Turkish
      War, 1921-1922." Historian, 35(1973), 256-70.

1230. Loyrette, J.E.L. The Foreign Policy of Poincaré: France
      and Great Britain in Relation to the German Problem,
      1918-1923. London, 1956.

1231. McDougall, Walter A. France's Rhineland Diplomacy,
      1914-1924: The Last Bid for a Balance of Power in
      Europe. Princeton, NJ, 1978.

      Based on French, German, Belgian and British archives and
      private papers; useful bibliography.

1232. Macfarlane, L.F. "Hands Off Russia: British Labour and
      the Russo-Polish War, 1920." Past and Present,
      38(1967), 126-52.

      See also Siegfried Bunger, "Die 'Hands off Russia'
      Bewegung in England", Zeitschrift für Geschichts-
      wissenschaft, 6(1958), 1249-83.

1233. Manning, A.F. "Reports of the British Embassy in Rome
      on the Rise of Fascism." Risorgimento, 1(1980), 33-45.

1234. Marcovitch, Lazare. "Lord Curzon and Pashitch: Light on
      Jugoslavia, Turkey and Greece in 1922." Journal of
      Central European Affairs, 13(1953), 329-37.

1235. Marks, Sally. "Ménage à Trois: The Negotiations for an
      Anglo-French-Belgian Alliance in 1922." International
      History Review, 4(1982), 524-52.

1236. Martin, Thomas S. "The Urquhart Concession and Anglo-
      Soviet Relations, 1921-1922." Jahrbücher für
      Geschichte Osteuropas, 20(1972), 551-70.

1237. Mills, John S. The Genoa Conference. London, 1922.

1238. Montgomery, A.E. "Lloyd George and the Greek Question,
      1918-1922", in Lloyd George: Twelve Essays. Edited by
      A.J.P. Taylor. London, 1971.

1239. Nelson, Keith L. Victors Divided: America and the
      Allies in Germany, 1918-1923. Berkeley, CA, 1975.

      Based on American, German, French and British archives.

1240. Nish, Ian. "Britain and the Ending of the Anglo-
      Japanese Alliance." Bulletin of the Japan Society of
      London, 53(1967), 2-5.

On this subject see also the same author's "Japan and the
Ending of the Anglo-Japanese Alliance", in Studies in
International History: Essays presented to W. Norton
Medlicott, edited by K. Bourne and D.C. Watt (London,
1967); Dennis Smith, "The Royal Navy and Japan: In the
Aftermath of the Washington Conference, 1922-1926",
Proceedings of the British Association for Japanese
Studies, 3(1978), 69-86; Ira Klein, "Whitehall,
Washington and the Anglo-Japanese Alliance, 1919-1921",
Pacific Historical Review, 41(1972), 460-83; Michael G.
Fry, "The North Atlantic Triangle and the Abrogation of
the Anglo-Japanese Alliance", Journal of Modern History,
39(1967), 46-64; Merze Tate and Fidele Foy, "More Light
on the Abrogation of the Anglo-Japanese Alliance",
Political Science Quarterly, 74(1959) 532-54; John
Chalmers Vinson, "The Drafting of the Four Power Treaty
of the Washington Conference", Journal of Modern History,
25(1953), 40-47; the same author's "The Imperial
Conference of 1921 and the Anglo-Japanese Alliance",
Pacific Historical Review, 21(1962), 257-67; Donald
Birn, "Open Diplomacy at the Washington Conference of
1921-1922: The British and French Experience",
Comparative Studies in Society and History, 12(1970),
297-319; S. Asada, "Japan's 'Special Interests' and the
Washington Conference, 1921-1922", American Historical
Review, 66(1962), 62-70; Burton F. Beers, Vain Endeavor:
Robert Lansing's Attempts to End the Anglo-Japanese
Rivalry (Durham, NC, 1962); and Thomas Buckley, The
United States and the Washington Conference, 1921-1922
(Knoxville, TN, 1970).

1241. Noel-Baker, Philip J.   The Geneva Protocol.   London,
      1925.

      See also Djoura Djourovitch, Le protocole de Genève
      devant l'opinion anglaise (Paris, 1928); David Miller,
      The Geneva Protocol (London, 1925); and Arthur Henderson,
      Labour and the Geneva Protocol (London, 1925).

1242. Pinon, René.   L'Avenir de l'entente franco-anglaise.
      Paris, 1924.

1243. Schuker, Stephen A.   The End of French Predominance in
      Europe: The Financial crisis of 1924 and the Adoption
      of the Dawes Plan.   Chapel Hill, NC, 1976.

      Very well documented; thorough bibliography.

1244. Selsam, J. Paul. The Attempts to Form an Anglo-French Alliance, 1919-1924. Philadelphia, PA, 1936.

1245. Soutou, Georges. "Die deutschen Reparationen und das Seydoux-Projekt, 1920-1921." Vierteljahrshefte für Zeitgeschichte, 23(1975), 237-70.

1246. Stamm, Christoph. Lloyd George zwischen Innen- und Aussenpolitik: Die britische Deutschlandpolitik, 1921-1922. Köln, 1977.

    Useful bibliography for German sources on the subject.

1247. Steinbach, Lothar. "Britische Aussenpolitik in der Ära Lloyd George." Neue Politische Literatur, 14(1969), 534-46.

1248. Walder, David. The Chanak Affair. London, 1969.

    Based on British archives, interviews and numerous military sources; no footnotes; see also J.G. Darwin, "The Chanak Crisis and the British Cabinet", History, 65(1980), 32-48.

1249. Weidenfeld, Werner. Die Englandpolitik Gustav Stresemanns: Theoretische und praktische Aspekte der Aussenpolitik. Mainz, 1972.

    Heavily based on German archives and private papers; very useful bibliography.

1250. Weikardt, Charles R. Das Rheinland in den deutsch-britischen Beziehungen, 1918-1923: Eine Untersuchung zum Wesen der britischen Gleichgewichtspolitik. Bonn, 1967.

1251. Williams, Aneurin. "Armenia, British Pledges and the Near East." Contemporary Review, 121(1922), 418-25.

    A thorough analysis, with Armenian sources, is Akaby Nassibian, Britain and the Armenian Question, 1915-1923 (London, 1984).

1252. Williamson, David G. "Great Britain and the Ruhr Crisis, 1923-1924." British Journal of International Studies, 3(1977), 70-91.

1253. Zwehl, Konrad von. Die Deutschlandpolitik Englands von 1922 bis 1924 unter besonderer Berücksichtigung der Reparationen und Sanktionen. Augsburg, 1974.

    Mainly based on British archives.

4. Detente and Disintegration, 1925-1933

1254. Bardoux, Jacques. L'Île et l'Europe: La politique
anglaise, 1930-1932. Paris, 1933.

1255. Bennett, Edward W. German Rearmament and the West,
1932-1933. Princeton, NJ, 1979.

By a former member of the Central Intelligence Agency; an
extensively documented study; with much of interest on
British policy; see also his Germany and the Diplomacy of
the Financial Crisis, 1931 (Cambridge, MA, 1962).

1256. Bickert, Hans G. "Die Vermittlerrolle Grossbritanniens
während der Reparationskonferenz von Lausanne 1932."
Aus Politik und Zeitgeschichte, supplement to Das
Parlament, 23(1973), 13-22.

1257. Carlton, David. "Great Britain and the Coolidge Naval
Disarmament Conference of 1927." Political Science
Quarterly, 83(1968), 573-98.

See also Robert W. Dubay, "The Geneva Naval Conference of
1927: A Study of Battleship Diplomacy", Southern
Quarterly, 8(1970), 177-99.

1258. Edwards, Peter G. "The Austen Chamberlain-Mussolini
Meetings." Historical Journal, 14(1971), 153-64.

Five meetings, 1924-29; see also his "Britain, Mussolini
and the 'Locarno-Geneva System'", European Studies
Review, 10(1980), 1-16.

1259. Ferrell, Robert H. Peace in their Time: The Origins of
the Kellogg-Briand Pact. New Haven, CT, 1952.

1260. Flory, Harriette. "The Arcos Raid and the Rupture of
Anglo-Soviet Relations, 1927." Journal of Contemporary
History, 12(1977), 707-23.

See also Harvey L. Dyck, "German-Soviet Relations and the
Anglo-Soviet Break, 1927", Slavic Review, 25(1966),
67-83; and Robert D. Warth, "The Arcos Raid and the
Anglo-Soviet Cold War of the 1920s", World Affairs
Quarterly, 29(1958), 115-51.

1261. Glasgow, George. From Dawes to Locarno: Being a
Critical Record of an Important Achievement in European
Diplomacy, 1924-1925. London, 1926.

Foreword by J. Ramsay MacDonald.

1262. Jacobson, Jon. Locarno Diplomacy: Germany and the West, 1925-1929. Princeton, NJ, 1972.

A thorough analysis based mainly on German archives; see also his "The Conduct of Locarno Diplomacy", Review of Politics, 34(1972), 67-81.

1263. Jarausch, Konrad Hugo. The Four Power Pact, 1933. Madison, WI, 1965.

See also Lothar Krecker, "Die diplomatischen Verhandlungen über den Viererpakt vom 15. Juli 1933", Welt als Geschichte, 21(1961), 227-37.

1264. Karoly, Laszlo. Velikobritaniia i Lokarno. Moscow, 1961.

1265. Lammers, Donald N. "The Engineers' Trial (Moscow, 1933) and Anglo-Soviet Relations." South Atlantic Quarterly, 62(1963), 256-67.

See also his "Britain, Russia and the Revival of Entente Diplomacy, 1934", Journal of British Studies, 6(1967), 99-123; and "The Second Labour Government and the Restoration of Relations with Soviet Russia (1929)", Bulletin of the Institute of Historical Research, 37(1964), 60-72.

1266. MacDonald, J. Ramsay. "The London Naval Conference, 1930." Journal of the Royal Institute of International Affairs, 9(1930), 429-51.

On the same subject see also Wolf-Heinrich Bickel, Die Anglo-Amerikanischen Beziehungen, 1927-1930, im Licht der Flottenfrage (Zürich, 1970); Raymond G. O'Connor, Perilous Equilibrium: The United States and the London Naval Conference of 1930 (Lawrence, KS, 1962); J.L. Godfrey, "Anglo-American Naval Conversations Preliminary to the London Naval Conference of 1930", South Atlantic Quarterly, 49(1950), 303-16; Raymond Bouy, Le désarmement naval: La conférence de Londres (Paris, 1931); Laura P. Morgan, The Background of the London Naval Conference (Washington, DC, 1931); and Conyers Read, "More Light on the London Naval Treaty of 1930", Proceedings of the American Philosophical Society, 93(1949), 290-308; subsequent events are analysed in Stephen E. Pelz, Race to Pearl Harbor: The Failure of the Second London Naval Conference and the Onset of World War II (Cambridge, MA, 1974); particularly valuable for its use of Japanese foreign ministry archives and private papers.

1267. Ministerium für Auswärtige Angelegenheiten der DDR.
Locarno-Konferenz 1925: Eine Dokumentensammlung. East
Berlin, 1962.

1268. Newman, Michael. "Britain and the German-Austrian
Customs Union Proposal of 1931." European Studies
Review, 6(1976), 449-72.

See also F.G. Stambrook, "A British Proposal for the
Danubian States: The Customs Union Project of 1932",
Slavonic and East European Review, 42(1963), 64-88.

1269. Owen, G.L. "The Metro-Vickers Crisis: Anglo-Soviet
Relations between Trade Agreements, 1932-1934."
Slavonic and East European Review, 49(1971), 92-112.

1270. Rass, Hans Heinrich. Britische Aussenpolitik, 1929-1931:
Ebenen und Faktoren der Entscheidung. Frankfurt/M.,
1975.

1271. Rolo, P.J.V. Britain and the Briand Plan: The Common
Market that Never Was. Keele, 1972.

An inaugural lecture at the University of Keele; see also
R.W. Boyce, "Britain's First 'No' to Europe: Britain and
the Briand Plan, 1929-1930", European Studies Review,
4(1980), 17-46; Karl Dietrich Erdmann, "Der Europa-Plan
Briands im Lichte der englischen Akten", Geschichte in
Wissenschaft und Unterricht, 1(1950), 16-32; Walter
Lipgens, "Europäische Einigungsidee 1923-1930 und Briands
Europa-Plan im Urteil der deutschen Akten", Historische
Zeitschrift, 203(1966), 46-89, 316-63.

1272. Rössler, Hellmuth, ed. Locarno und die Weltpolitik,
1924-1932. Göttingen, 1969.

A collection of seven essays; with one on the
Commonwealth, 1917-31.

1273. Stambrook, F.G. "The Foreign Secretary and Foreign
Policy: The Experiences of Austen Chamberlain in 1925
and 1927." International Review of History and
Political Science, 6(1969), 109-27.

1274. Urbanitsch, Peter. Grossbritannien und die Verträge
von Locarno. Vienna, 1968.

Based on German archives and the papers of Austen
Chamberlain, Lord Cecil and Lord D'Abernon; see also
Sibyl Crowe, "Sir Eyre Crowe and the Locarno Pact",
English Historical Review, 87(1972), 49-74; Jean Baptiste

Duroselle, "The Spirit of Locarno: Illusions of
Pactomania", Foreign Affairs, 50(1972) 752-64; F.G.
Stambrook, "'Das Kind': Lord D'Abernon and the Origins
of the Locarno Pact", Central European History, 1(1968),
233-63; Douglas Johnson, "Austen Chamberlain and the
Locarno Agreements", University of Birmingham Historical
Journal, 8(1961), 60-91; George A. Grün, "Locarno: Idea
and Reality", International Affairs, 31(1955), 477-85;
Felix Hirsch, "Locarno: Twenty-Five Years After",
Contemporary Review, 178(1950), 279-85; Sir Edward Grigg,
"The Merits and Defects of the Locarno Treaty as a
Guarantee of World Peace", International Affairs,
14(1935), 176-97; and Henry Wickham Steed, "Locarno and
British Interests", Journal of the British Institute of
International Affairs, 4(1925), 286-99.

1275. USSR, Ministervo Inostrannikh Del. Lokarnskaia
      Konferentsiia 1925g. Edited by A.F. Dobrov. Moscow,
      1959.

1276. Wheeler-Bennett, John W., and Latimer, Hugh. Information
      on the Reparation Settlement: Being the Background and
      History of the Young Plan and the Hague Agreements,
      1929-1930. London, 1930.

F. DIPLOMACY IN CRISIS

1. 1930s General

1277. Bell, Philip M.H. "Great Britain and the Rise of
      Germany, 1932-1934." International Relations, 2(1964),
      609-18.

1278. Conwell-Evans, T.P. None So Blind: A Study of the
      Crisis Years, 1930-1939, Based on the Papers of M.G.
      Christie. London, 1947.

      Group Captain Malcolm Grahame Christie, air attaché at
      Berlin from 1927-30, thereafter, part of Sir Robert
      Vansittart's own intelligence network; only 100 copies of
      this book were printed.

1279. Cowling, Maurice. The Impact of Hitler: British
      Politics and British Policy, 1933-1940. London, 1975.

      On the relation between foreign and domestic policy.

1280. Dilks, David. "Baldwin and Chamberlain", in The
      Conservatives: A History from their Origins to 1965.
      Edited by Lord Butler. London, 1977.

1281. Duroselle, Jean Baptiste. La décadence, 1932-1939.
      Paris, 1979.

      Principally on France but with material relevant to
      Britain; likewise see also Robert J. Young, In Command
      of France: French Foreign Policy and Military
      Planning, 1933-1940 (Cambridge, MA, 1978); Anthony P.
      Adamthwaite, France and the Coming of the Second World
      War (London, 1977); and Jacques Néré, The Foreign
      Policy of France from 1914 to 1945 (London, 1975).

1282. George, Margaret. The Warped Vision: British Foreign
      Policy, 1933-1939. Pittsburgh, PA, 1965.

      Argues that appeasement was the foreign policy of
      decadent British conservatism.

1283. Goldman, Aaron. "Sir Robert Vansittart's Search for
Italian Co-operation Against Hitler, 1933-1936."
Journal of Contemporary History, 9(1974), 93-130.

See also his "Two Views of Germany: Nevile Henderson
vs. Vansittart and the Foreign Office, 1937-1939",
British Journal of International Studies, 6(1980),
247-77; and Giuliano Cora, "Lord Vansittart e la
diplomazia di ieri", Nuova antologia, 484(1962), 19-24.

1284. Hanak, Harry. "The Visit of Czechoslovak Foreign
Minister Dr. Eduard Benes to Moscow in 1935 as seen by
the British Minister in Prague, Sir Joseph Addison."
Slavonic and East European Review, 54(1976), 586-92.

1285. Hauser, Oswald. England und das Dritte Reich: Eine
dokumentierte Geschichte der englisch-deutschen
Beziehungen von 1933 bis 1939 auf Grund
unveröffentlicher Akten aus dem britischen
Staatsarchiv. 2 vols. Stuttgart, 1972-82.

Vol. 2 ends in August 1938; an extensive analysis with
reprinted documents, many from the Public Record Office;
see also his "England und Hitler", in Was weiter wirkt:
Beiträge zur Geschichte des 20. Jahrhunderts, edited by
Otmar Franz (Stuttgart, 1971).

1286. Henke, Josef. England in Hitlers politischem Kalkül,
1935-1939. Boppard/R., 1973.

See also the same author's "Hitlers England-Konzeption:
Formulierung und Realisierungsversuche", in Hitler,
Deutschland und die Mächte: Materialien zur
Aussenpolitik des Dritten Reiches, edited by Manfred
Funke (Düsseldorf, 1977); Andreas Hillgruber, "England in
Hitlers aussenpolitischer Konzeption", Historische
Zeitschrift, 218(1974), 65-84; also published as
"England's Place in Hitler's Plans for World Dominion",
Journal of Contemporary History, 9(1974), 5-22; Axel
Kuhn, Hitlers aussenpolitisches Programm: Entstehung
und Entwicklung, 1919-1939 (Stuttgart, 1970), which
includes an examination of Britain's place in Hitler's
foreign policy programme after 1933; and A.V.N. van
Woerden, "Hitler Faces England: Theories, Images and
Policies", Acta Historiae Neerlandica, 3(1968), 141-59.

1287. Holland, R.F. Britain and the Commonwealth Alliance,
1918-1939. London, 1981.

1288. Kennedy, Aubrey Leo. Britain Faces Germany. London,
1937.

1289. Kennedy, Thomas C. "'Peace in Our Time': The Personal
Diplomacy of Lord Allen of Hurtwood, 1933-1938", in
Doves and Diplomats: Foreign Offices and Peace
Movements in Europe and America in the Twentieth
Century. Edited by Solomon Wank. Westport, CT, 1978.

1290. Kettenacker, Lothar. "Die englische Illusionspolitik vor
dem 2. Weltkrieg, 1932-1937." Wehrwissenschaftliche
Rundschau, 15(1965), 100-11.

1291. Medlicott, W.N. Britain and Germany: The Search for
Agreement, 1930-1937. London, 1969.

1292. Meyers, Reinhard. "Die Dominions und die britische
Europapolitik der dreissiger Jahre", in Tradition und
Neubeginn: Internationale Forschungen zur deutschen
Geschichte im 20. Jahrhundert. Edited by Joachim
Hütter, et al. Köln, 1975.

See also his "Britain, Europe and the Dominions in the
1930s: Some Aspects of British, European and
Commonwealth Policies", Australian Journal of Politics
and History, 22(1976), 36-50; Nicholas Mansergh, Survey
of British Commonwealth Affairs: Problems of External
Policy, 1931-1939 (London, 1952); and Rudolf von
Albertini, "England als Weltmacht und der Strukturwandel
des Commonwealth", Historische Zeitschrift, 208(1969),
52-80.

1293. Nish, Ian. "Yoshida as a Diplomat." Proceedings of the
British Association for Japanese Studies, 3(1978),
87-96.

Japanese ambassador at London, 1936-38.

1294. Pozdeeva, Lidiia V. Angliia i remilitarizatsiia
Germanii, 1933-1936gg. Moscow, 1956

1295. Rhodes, Benjamin D. "Sir Ronald Lindsay and the British
View from Washington", in Essays in Twentieth-Century
American Diplomatic History: Dedicated to Professor
Daniel M. Smith. Edited by Clifford L. Egan and
Alexander W. Knott. Lanham, MD, 1982.

1296. Robertson, Esmonde M. Hitler's Pre-War Policy and
Military Plans, 1933-1939. London, 1963.

1297. Spier, Eugen. Focus: A Footnote to the History of the
Thirties. London, 1963.

On the role Spier played in the inception and financing
of Churchill's "Focus in Defence of Freedom and Peace";
see also his The Protecting Power (London, 1951).

1298. Tamchina, Rainer. "Commonwealth und Appeasement: Die
Politik der britischen Dominions." Neue Politische
Literatur, 17(1972), 471-89.

See also the same author's "In Search of Common Causes:
The Imperial Conference of 1937", Journal of Imperial and
Commonwealth History, 1(1972), 79-105.

1299. Thompson, Neville. The Anti-Appeasers: Conservative
Opposition to Appeasement in the 1930s. London, 1971.

See also his "The Failure of Conservative Opposition to
Appeasement in the 1930s", Canadian Journal of History,
3(1968), 27-52.

1300. Waterlow, Sir Sydney P. "The Decline and Fall of Greek
Democracy, 1933-1936." Political Quarterly, 18(1947),
95-106, 205-19.

British minister at Bangkok, 1926-28; Addis Ababa,
1928-29; and Athens, 1933-39.

1301. Weinberg, Gerhard L. The Foreign Policy of Hitler's
Germany, 1933-1939. 2 vols. Chicago, IL, 1970-80.

Vol. 1 to 1936; widely based on primary and secondary
sources; very useful bibliographies; see also Hans-Adolf
Jacobsen, Nationalsozialistische Aussenpolitik, 1933-1938
(Frankfurt/M., 1968); on the nature of Hitler's
objectives in foreign policy, including Anglo-German
relations, see Klaus Hildebrand, Deutsche Aussenpolitik,
1933-1945: Kalkül oder Dogma? (Stuttgart, 1976); the
essays by various scholars on foreign policy methods and
relations in Hitler, Deutschland und die Mächte:
Materialien zur Aussenpolitik des Dritten Reiches, edited
by Manfred Funke (Düsseldorf, 1977); reprinted essays,
mostly on the 1930s, in Nationalsozialistische
Aussenpolitik, edited by Wolfgang Michalka (Darmstadt,
1978); and Wolfgang Michalka, Ribbentrop und die deutsche
Weltpolitik, 1933-1940 (Munich, 1980).

2. From Manchuria to the Pacific War, 1931-1941

1302. Acland, Sir Francis Dyke. Japan Must Be Stopped.
London, 1937.

Under-secretary of state for Foreign Affairs, 1911-15.

1303. Bassett, Reginald. Democracy and Foreign Policy: A Case
      History, the Sino-Japanese Dispute, 1931-1933. London,
      1952.

      On the evolution of public opinion during the crisis.

1304. Borg, Dorothy. The United States and the Far Eastern
      Crisis of 1933-1938. Cambridge, MA, 1964.

      Interesting for its revelation regarding British policy
      by American observers; see also the twenty-six essays in
      Dorothy Borg and Shumpei Okamoto, eds., Pearl Harbour as
      History: Japanese-American Relations, 1931-1941 (New
      York, 1973); on other major power involvement see Gary
      B. Ostrower, Collective Insecurity: The United States
      and the League of Nations during the Early Thirties
      (Cranbury, NJ, 1979); George A. Lensen, The Damned
      Inheritance: The Soviet Union and the Manchurian Crises,
      1924-1935 (Tallahassee, FL, 1974); and John P. Fox,
      Germany and the Far Eastern Crisis, 1931-1938: A Study
      in Diplomacy and Ideology (London, 1982).

1305. Casella, Alessandro. Le conflit sino-japonais de 1937
      et la Société des Nations. Paris, 1968.

      See also the earlier study by Westel W. Willoughby, The
      Sino-Japanese Controversy and the League of Nations
      (Baltimore, MD, 1935).

1306. Clive, Sir Robert. Reshaping the Far East. London,
      1943.

      Lecture to the Royal Central Asian Society; British
      ambassador to Japan, 1934-37; and Belgium, 1937-39.

1307. Esthus, R.A. "President Roosevelt's Commitment to
      Britain to Intervene in a Pacific War." Mississippi
      Valley Historical Review, 50(1963), 28-38.

      On the background to Pearl Harbour in 1941.

1308. Haggie, Paul. Britannia at Bay: The Defence of the
      British Empire against Japan, 1931-1941. London, 1981.

      Explores the "third dimension" of the threat to Britain
      (Preface); based on a wide array of Public Record Office
      documents and various private papers; see also his
      "Admiral Sir Howard Kelly and the Shanghai Crisis, 1932",
      Naval Review, 64(1976), 195-202.

1309. Hecht, Robert A. "Great Britain and the Stimson Note of
      January 7, 1932." Pacific Historical Review, 38(1969),
      177-91.

1310. Holcomb, Michael. "Sir John Simon's War with Henry L.
      Stimson", in Essays in Twentieth-Century American
      Diplomatic History: Dedicated to Professor Daniel M.
      Smith. Edited by Clifford L. Egan and Alexander W.
      Knott. Lanham, MD, 1982.

1311. League of Nations. Appeal of the Chinese Government:
      Report of the Commission of Enquiry (Lytton Report).
      Geneva, 1932.

      See also Lord Lytton's analysis in his "The Problem of
      Manchuria", International Affairs, 11(1932), 737-56; and
      The League, the Far East and Ourselves (London, 1934);
      League of Nations Union, Pamphlet, no. 369.

1312. Lee, Bradford A. Britain and the Sino-Japanese War,
      1937-1939: A Study in the Dilemmas of British
      Decline. Stanford, CA, 1973.

      "Appeasement in an East Asian context" (Preface);
      thoroughly based on British archival sources; useful
      bibliographical essay.

1313. Lowe, Peter. Great Britain and the Origins of the
      Pacific War: A Study of British Policy in East Asia,
      1937-1941. London, 1977.

      Principally based on British archives and relevant
      private papers; see also his "Great Britain and the
      Coming of the Pacific War, 1939-1941", Transactions of
      the Royal Historical Society, 14(1974), 43-62; "Great
      Britain and the Outbreak of War with Japan, 1941", in War
      and Society: Essays in Honour and Memory of J.R.
      Western, 1928-1971, edited by M.R.D. Foot (London, 1973);
      and "The Dilemmas of an Ambassador: Sir Robert Craigie
      in Tokyo, 1937-1941", Proceedings of the British
      Association for Japanese Studies, 2(1977), 34-56.

1314. Megaw, M. Ruth. "The Scramble for the Pacific: Anglo-
      United States Rivalry in the 1930s." Historical
      Studies, 17(1977), 458-73.

1315. Neidpath, James. The Singapore Naval Base and the
      Defence of Britain's Eastern Empire, 1919-1941.
      London, 1981.

Origins, development and collapse of the "Singapore strategy"; based on a wide array of Public Record Office archives, and various private papers; of the numerous other studies on this subject, see also David W. McIntyre, The Rise and Fall of the Singapore Naval Base (London, 1979); Louis Allen, Singapore, 1941-1942 (London, 1977); Raymond Callahan, "The Illusion of Security: Singapore, 1919-1942", Journal of Contemporary History, 9(1974), 69-92; and Noel Barber, Sinister Twilight: The Fall of Singapore (London, 1971).

1316. Pritchard, R. John. "The Far East as an Influence on the Chamberlain Government's Pre-War European Policies." Millennium, 2(1973), 7-23.

1317. Rothwell, Victor. "The Mission of Sir Frederick Leith-Ross to the Far East, 1935-1936." Historical Journal, 18(1975), 147-69.

1318. Shai, Aron. Origins of the War in the East: Britain, China and Japan, 1937-1939. London, 1976.

Examines "the Asian context" of appeasement (Preface); based essentially on British archives; see also his "Was There a Far Eastern Munich?" Journal of Contemporary History, 9(1974), 161-69; and "Le conflit anglo-japonais de Tientsin, 1939", Revue d'histoire moderne et contemporaine, 22(1975), 293-302.

1319. Taboulet, Georges. "La France et l'Angleterre face au conflit sino-japonais, 1937-1939." Revue d'histoire diplomatique, 88(1974), 112-44.

1320. Thorne, Christopher. The Limits of Foreign Policy: The West, the League and the Far Eastern Crisis of 1931-1933. London, 1972.

A thoroughly documented study; see also the same author's "Viscount Cecil, the Government and the Far Eastern Crisis of 1931", Historical Journal, 14(1971), 805-26; "The Shanghai Crisis of 1932: The Basis of British Policy", American Historical Review, 75(1970), 1616-39; and "The Quest for Arms Embargoes: Failure in 1933", Journal of Contemporary History, 5(1970), 129-49.

1321. Trotter, Ann. Britain and East Asia, 1933-1937. London, 1975.

Based on a variety of British archival material and private papers; as well as Japanese language sources; see also the same author's "Tentative Steps for an

Anglo-Japanese Rapprochement in 1934", <u>Modern Asian Studies</u>, 8(1974), 59-83; and "Backstage Diplomacy: Britain and Japan in the 1930s", <u>Journal of Oriental Studies</u>, 15(1977), 37-45.

1322. Wheeler, Gerald E. "Isolated Japan: Anglo-American Diplomatic Cooperation, 1927-1936." <u>Pacific Historical Review</u>, 30(1961), 163-78.

1323. Whyte, Sir Alexander Frederick. <u>The Future of East and West</u>. London, 1932.

M.P., 1910-18; political adviser to national government of China, 1929-32; head of American division, ministry of Information, 1939-40; see also his "China, Japan and Manchuria", <u>Nineteenth Century</u>, 111(1932), 281-92.

1324. Woodhead, Henry George Wandesforde. <u>A Journalist in China</u>. London, 1934.

One of several books on the Far Eastern crisis by the editor of the <u>Peking and Tientsin Times</u>, 1914-30; with ministry of Information, 1942-45.

3. The Italo-Ethiopian War, 1935-1936

1325. Asante, S.K.B. <u>Pan-African Protest: West Africa and the Italo-Ethiopian Crisis, 1934-1941</u>. London, 1977.

Based on British and west African sources; see also his "The Catholic Missions, British West African Nationalists, and the Italian Invasion of Ethiopia, 1935-1936", <u>African Affairs</u>, 73(1974), 204-16; and Robert G. Weisbord, "British West Indian Reaction to the Italian-Ethiopian War: An Episode in Pan-Africanism", <u>Caribbean Studies</u>, 10(1970), 34-41.

1326. Baer, George W. <u>The Coming of the Italian-Ethiopian War</u>. Cambridge, MA, 1967.

From the Wal Wal incident to the start of the war; see also his <u>Test Case: Italy, Ethiopia and the League of Nations</u> (Stanford, CA, 1976).

1327. Barker, A.J. <u>The Civilizing Mission: The Italo-Ethiopian War, 1935-1936</u>. London, 1968.

For another essentially military account, see Angelo Del Boca, <u>The Ethiopian War, 1935-1941</u> (Chicago, IL, 1969).

ITALO-ETHIOPIAN WAR, 1935-1936

1328. Barros, James. Britain, Greece and the Politics of Sanctions: Ethiopia, 1935-1936. London, 1982.

1329. Carlton, David. "The Dominions and British Foreign Policy in the Abyssinian Crisis." Journal of Imperial and Commonwealth History, 1(1972), 59-77.

1330. Chukumba, Stephen U. The Big Powers Against Ethiopia: Anglo-French-American Maneuvers during the Italo-Ethiopian Dispute, 1934-1938. Washington, DC, 1977.

An attempt at a comparative study; based solely on published accounts and the press; major power involvement is also analysed extensively in Franklin D. Laurens, France and the Italo-Ethiopian Crisis, 1935-1936 (The Hague, 1967); and Brice Harris, The United States and the Italo-Ethiopian Crisis (Stanford, CA, 1964).

1331. Friedlander, Robert A. "New Light on the Anglo-American Reaction to the Ethiopian War, 1935-1936." Mid-America, 45(1963), 115-25.

1332. Hardie, Frank M. The Abyssinian Crisis. London, 1974.

Argues that the crisis was "the first great act of appeasement" (Introduction); essentially based on British sources.

1333. Marder, Arthur J. "The Royal Navy and the Ethiopian Crisis of 1935-1936." American Historical Review, 75(1970), 1327-56.

Further assessed in Francesco Lefebvre D'Ovidio, "Politica e strategia britannica nel Mediterraneo, 1936-1939", Storia e politica, 17(1978), 509-17; Rosaria Quartararo, "Imperial Defence in the Mediterranean on the Eve of the Ethiopian Crisis", Historical Journal, 20(1977), 185-220; based on both British and Italian archives; and the same author's "La crisi mediterranea nel 1935-1936", Storia contemporanea, 6(1975), 801-46.

1334. Mori, Renato. Mussolini e la conquista dell'Etiopia. Florence, 1978.

A thoroughly documented study; other major studies of relevance include Esmonde M. Robertson, Mussolini as Empire-Builder: Europe and Africa, 1932-1936 (London, 1977); Denis Mack Smith, Mussolini's Roman Empire (London, 1976); Manfred Funke, Sanktionen und Kanonen: Hitler, Mussolini und der internationale Abessinienkonflikt, 1934-1936 (Düsseldorf, 1970); and

an earlier work which used some foreign ministry
archives, Luigi Villari, Storia diplomatica del conflitto
italo-etiopico (Bologna, 1943).

1335. Olla, Paola Brundu. "Il tentativo di 'detente' italo-
britannica dell'autunno 1935." Il politico, 43(1978),
422-46.

1336. Parker, R.A.C. "Great Britain, France and the Ethiopian
Crisis, 1935-1936." English Historical Review,
89(1974), 293-332.

With some extracts from the Royal archives.

1337. Post, Gaines, Jr. "The Machinery of British Policy in
the Ethiopian Crisis." International History Review,
1(1979), 522-41.

1338. Pugh, M. "Peace with Italy: BUF Reactions to the
Abyssinian War, 1935-1936." Wiener Library Bulletin,
27(1974), 11-18.

1339. Quartararo, Rosaria. "Le origini del piano Hoare-Laval."
Storia contemporanea, 8(1977), 749-90.

Other analyses of this incident include James C.
Robertson, "The Hoare-Laval Plan", Journal of
Contemporary History, 10(1975), 433-64; Henderson B.
Braddick, "The Hoare-Laval Plan: A Study in
International Politics", Review of Politics, 24(1962),
342-64; and Ernst L. Presseisen, "Foreign Policy and
British Public Opinion: The Hoare-Laval Pact of 1935",
World Affairs Quarterly, 29(1958), 256-77.

1340. Robertson, James C. "The Origins of British Opposition
to Mussolini over Ethiopia." Journal of British
Studies, 9(1969), 122-42.

Further background material in his "British Policy in
East Africa, March 1891 to May 1935", English Historical
Review, 93(1978), 835-44; P.G. Edwards, "Britain, Fascist
Italy and Ethiopia, 1925-1928", European Studies Review,
4(1974), 359-74; Giuseppe Vedovato, "Gli accordi
italo-etiopico dell'agosto 1928", Rivista di studi
politici internazionali, 22(1955), 560-634; and
Giovanni Buccianti, L'egemonia sull'Etiopia, 1918-1923:
Lo scontro diplomatico tra Italia, Francia e Inghilterra
(Milan, 1977).

1341. Toscano, Mario. "Eden's Mission to Rome on the Eve of the Italo-Ethiopian Conflict", in Studies in Diplomatic History and Historiography in Honour of G.P. Gooch. Edited by A.O. Sarkissan. London, 1961.

1342. "Vigilantes" [Konni Zilliacus]. Abyssinia: The Essential Facts in the Dispute and an Answer to the Question "Ought We to Support Sanctions?" London, 1935.

A New Statesman and Nation publication; other contemporary studies include Alfred Zimmern, "The League's Handling of the Italo-Abyssinian Dispute", International Affairs, 14(1935), 751-68; his "The Testing of the League", Foreign Affairs, 14(1936), 373-86; Lord Davies, Nearing the Abyss: The Lesson of Ethiopia (London, 1936); Henry Rowan-Robinson, England, Italy, Abyssinia (London, 1935); and Royal Institute of International Affairs, Information Department Papers, no. 16, Abyssinia and Italy (London, 1935).

1343. Waley, Daniel Philip. British Public Opinion and the Abyssinian War, 1935-1936. London, 1976.

See also Paul Vaucher and Paul-Henri Siriex, L'Opinion britannique, la Société des Nations, et la guerre italo-éthiopienne (Paris, 1936).

4. The Anglo-German Naval Agreement, 1935

1344. Bloch, Charles. "La Grande-Bretagne face au réarmement allemand et l'accord naval de 1935." Revue d'histoire de la deuxième guerre mondiale, 16(1966), 41-68.

1345. Dülffer, Jost. "Das deutsch-englische Flottenabkommen vom 18. Juni 1935." Marine-Rundschau, 69(1972), 641-59.

For the wider historical context, see his Weimar, Hitler und die Marine: Reichspolitik und Flottenbau, 1920-1939 (Düsseldorf, 1973); and Rolf Bensel, Die deutsche Flottenpolitik von 1933-1939: Eine Studie über die Rolle des Flottenbaus in Hitlers Aussenpolitik (Frankfurt/M., 1958).

1346. Hall, Hines H. "The Foreign Policy-Making Process in Britain, 1934-1935, and the Origins of the Anglo-German Naval Agreement." Historical Journal, 19(1976), 477-99.

1347. Haraszti, Eva. Treaty-Breakers or "Realpolitiker"? The
      Anglo-German Naval Agreement of June 1935. Boppard/R.,
      1974.

      Based on a wide array of European language sources; with
      an appendix of fourteen documents, most from the Public
      Record Office.

1348. Ingrim, Robert. Hitlers glücklichster Tag: London, am
      18. Juni 1935. Stuttgart, 1962.

1349. Malanowski, Wolfgang. "Das deutsch-englische Flotten-
      abkommen vom 18. Juni 1935 als Ausgangspunkt für
      Hitlers doktrinäre Bündnispolitik." Wehrwissen-
      schaftliche Rundschau, 5(1955), 408-20.

1350. Olla, Paola Brundu. Le origini diplomatiche dell'accordo
      navale anglo-tedesco del giugno 1935. Milan, 1974.

      Based essentially on British sources; with an appendix of
      twenty-six relevant documents; no bibliography.

1351. Watt, D.C. "The Anglo-German Naval Agreement of
      1935: An Interim Judgement." Journal of Modern
      History, 28(1956), 155-75.

           5.   The Reoccupation of the Rhineland, 1936

1352. Bishop, Larry V. "England, France and the Rhineland
      Crisis of 1936." Research Studies, 34(1966), 219-29.

      See also George Sakwa, "The Franco-Polish Alliance and
      the Remilitarization of the Rhineland", Historical
      Journal, 16(1973), 125-46; R. Debicki, "The
      Remilitarization of the Rhineland and its Impact on the
      Franco-Polish Alliance", Polish Review, 14(1969), 45-55;
      Charles Keserich, "The Popular Front and the Rhineland
      Crisis of March 1936", International Review of History
      and Political Science, 7(1970), 87-102; R.A.C. Parker,
      "The First Capitulation: France and the Rhineland Crisis
      of 1936", World Politics, 8(1955), 355-73; and for the
      consequences, David Owen Kieft, Belgium's Return to
      Neutrality: An Essay in the Frustrations of Small Power
      Diplomacy (London, 1972).

1353. Bolen, C. Waldron. "Hitler Remilitarizes the Rhineland",
      in Power, Public Opinion, and Diplomacy: Essays in
      Honor of Eber Malcolm Carroll. Edited by Lillian
      Parker Wallace and William C. Askew. Durham, NC, 1959.

1354. Braubach, Max. Der Einmarsch deutscher Truppen in die
      entmilitarisierte Zone am Rhein im März 1936: Ein
      Beitrag zur Vorgeschichte des zweiten Weltkrieges.
      Opladen, 1956.

1355. Bussmann, Walter. "Masstäbe diplomatischer
      Urteilsbildung im Foreign Office während der
      Rheinlandkrise, 1936", in Studien zur Geschichte
      Englands und der deutsch-britischen Beziehungen:
      Festschrift für Paul Kluke. Edited by Lothar
      Kettenacker, et al. Munich, 1981.

1356. Emmerson, James Thomas. The Rhineland Crisis, 7 March
      1936: A Study in Multilateral Diplomacy. Ames, IA,
      1977.

      The most thorough study; based on British and German
      archives; likewise see also Eva Haraszti, The Invaders:
      Hitler Occupies the Rhineland (Budapest, 1983); with over
      100 pages of documents, mainly British.

1357. Fiedler, R. "Hitlers 'aufregendste' Stunden: Vor 25
      Jahren, Einmarsch in die entmilitarisierte Zone."
      Politische Studien, 12(1961), 168-74.

1358. Funke, Manfred. "7. März 1936: Fallstudie zum
      aussenpolitischen Führungsstil Hitlers." Aus Politik
      und Zeitgeschichte, supplement to Das Parlament,
      6(1970), 3-34.

1359. Knapp, W.F. "The Rhineland Crisis of March 1936", in
      The Decline of the Third Republic. St. Antony's
      Papers, No. 5. Edited by James Joll. London, 1959.

1360. Meyers, Reinhard. "Das Ende des Systems von Locarno:
      Die Remilitarisierung des Rheinlandes in britischer
      Sicht", in Centre National de la Recherche
      Scientifique, Les relations franco-allemandes,
      1933-1939. Paris, 1976.

      See also his "Sicherheit und Gleichgewicht: Das
      britische Kabinett und die Remilitarisierung des
      Rheinlandes 1936", Rheinische Vierteljahresblätter,
      38(1974), 406-49.

1361. Robertson, Esmonde M. "Zur Wiederbesetzung des Rhein-
      landes, 1936." Vierteljahrshefte für Zeitgeschicte,
      10(1962), 178-205.

See also his "Hitler and Sanctions: Mussolini and the Rhineland", European Studies Review, 7(1977), 409-35.

1362. Royal Institute of International Affairs. Germany and the Rhineland: A Record of the Proceedings of Three Meetings held at Chatham House on March 18, 25 and April 2, 1936. London, 1936.

Special supplement to International Affairs, April, 1936; contributors included Harold Nicolson, Norman Angell, and Lord Lothian.

1363. Ruby, Edmond. "Hitler réoccupe la Rhénanie, 7 mars 1936." Ecrits de Paris, 249(1966), 29-43.

1364. Watt, D.C. "German Plans for the Reoccupation of the Rhineland: A Note." Journal of Contemporary History, 1(1966), 193-99.

See also his "The Reoccupation of the Rhineland", History Today, 6(1956), 244-51.

1365. Yeuell, Donovan P. "The German Occupation of the Rhineland." U.S. Naval Institute Proceedings, 81(1955), 1205-15.

6. The Spanish Civil War, 1936-1939

1366. Abendroth, Hans-Henning. Hitler in der spanischen Arena: Die deutsch-spanischen Beziehungen im Spannungsfeld der europäischen Interessenpolitik vom Ausbruch des Bürgerkrieges bis zum Ausbruch des Weltkrieges, 1936-1939. Paderhorn, 1973.

Specific studies of other major power involvement in the Spanish civil war include Manfred Merkes, Die deutsche Politik gegenüber dem spanischen Bürgerkrieg, 1936-1939 (Bonn, 1969); John F. Coverdale, Italian Intervention in the Spanish Civil War (Princeton, NJ, 1975); David Cattell, Soviet Diplomacy and the Spanish Civil War (Berkeley, CA, 1957); and Richard P. Traina, American Diplomacy and the Spanish Civil War (Bloomington, IN, 1968).

1367. Atholl, Duchess of. Searchlight on Spain. London, 1938.

1368. Bartholdt, Johannes. "Crisis 1936: The Dilemmas of British Foreign Policy." Millennium, 2(1973), 3-16.

1369. Beevor, Anthony. The Spanish Civil War. London, 1982.

SPANISH CIVIL WAR, 1936-1939

A revisionist view of the roles of Britain and the USSR.

1370. Blythe, Henry. Spain over Britain: A Study of the
      Strategical Effects of Italian Intervention on the
      Defense of the British Empire. London, 1937.

1371. Brome, Vincent. The International Brigades: Spain,
      1936-1939. London, 1965.

1372. Carlton, David. "Eden, Blum and the Origins of Non-
      Intervention." Journal of Contemporary History,
      6(1971), 40-55.

      See also Geoffrey Warner, "France and Non-Intervention in
      Spain, July-August, 1936", International Affairs,
      38(1962), 203-20; M.D. Gallagher, "Léon Blum and the
      Spanish Civil War", Journal of Contemporary History,
      6(1971), 56-64.

1373. Edwards, Jill. The British Government and the Spanish
      Civil War, 1936-1939. London, 1979.

      A thorough study based on a wide variety of British and
      some Spanish sources; supersedes William Kleine-
      Ahlbrandt, The Policy of Simmering: A Study of British
      Policy during the Spanish Civil War, 1936-1939 (The
      Hague, 1962).

1374. Foreman, John. "L'Attitude de la Grande Bretagne envers
      l'Italie et l'Espagne, 1936-1938." Relations
      internationales, 2(1974), 147-63.

1375. Gretton, Sir Peter. "The Nyon Conference - the Naval
      Aspect." English Historical Review, 90(1975), 103-12.

      See also James W. Cortada. "Ships, Diplomacy and the
      Spanish Civil War: Nyon Conference, September 1937", Il
      politico, 37(1972), 673-89.

1376. Potter, Marguerite. "What Sealed Baldwin's Lips?"
      Historian, 27(1964), 21-36.

      On the Hoare-Laval plan.

1377. Schieder, Wolfgang, and Dipper, Christof, eds. Der
      spanische Bürgerkrieg in der internationalen Politik,
      1936-1939. Munich, 1976.

      The international implications are also examined in
      Robert H. Whealey, "Foreign Intervention in the Spanish
      Civil War", in The Republic and the Civil War in Spain,

edited by Raymond Carr (London, 1971); Robert A.
Friedlander, "Great Power Politics and Spain's Civil War:
The First Phase", Historian, 28(1965), 72-95; Dante A.
Puzzo, Spain and the Great Powers, 1936-1941 (New York,
1962); and Patricia van der Esch, Prelude to War: The
International Repercussions of the Spanish Civil War,
1936-1939 (The Hague, 1951).

1378. Thomas, Hugh. The Spanish Civil War. Rev. ed. London,
1976.

A very comprehensive military, diplomatic and political
analysis; see also Gabriel Jackson, The Spanish Republic
and the Civil War, 1931-1939 (Princeton, NJ, 1965); and
Hellmuth Günther Dahms, Der spanische Bürgerkrieg,
1936-1939 (Tübingen, 1962).

1379. Watkins, K.W. Britain Divided: The Effect of the
Spanish Civil War on British Public Opinion. London,
1963.

Opinion as reflected in a very wide array of newspapers,
weeklies and journals.

G. THE APPROACH TO WAR, 1937-1939

1. General

1380. Aster, Sidney. "Ivan Maisky and Parliamentary Anti-
      appeasement, 1938-1939", in Lloyd George: Twelve
      Essays. Edited by A.J.P. Taylor. London, 1971.

1381. Chadwick, William Owen. Britain, the Pope and
      Appeasement. Oxford, 1982.

      The 1981 Ford lecture; a discussion of papal diplomacy
      from 1938-44; see also John S. Conway, "The Vatican,
      Great Britain, and Relations with Germany, 1938-1940",
      Historical Journal, 16(1973), 147-67.

1382. Colvin, Ian. The Chamberlain Cabinet: How the Meetings
      in 10 Downing Street, 1937-1939, Led to the Second World
      War. London, 1971.

1383. Fuchser, Larry William. Neville Chamberlain and Appease-
      ment: A Study in the Politics of History. New York,
      1982.

      Extensive use of Neville Chamberlain's letters to his
      family, although without direct quotation.

1384. Hoggan, David L. Der erzwungene Krieg: Die Ursachen und
      Urheber des 2. Weltkriegs. Tübingen, 1966.

      A revisionist view, never published in English; likewise
      see Otto Werner, England's Kriegspolitik gegen
      Deutschland (Munich, 1971); and Peter H. Nicoll, Englands
      Krieg gegen Deutschland: Die Ursachen, Methoden und
      Folgen des Zweiten Weltkriegs (Tübingen, 1963); an
      expanded version of his Britain's Blunder (London, 1953).

1385. Lukowitz, David C. "George Lansbury's Peace Missions to
      Hitler and Mussolini in 1937." Canadian Journal of
      History, 15(1980), 67-82.

1386. MacDonald, C.A. The United States, Britain and Appease-
      ment, 1936-1939. London, 1981.

253

An "examination of the American impact on British foreign relations in the classic era of appeasement." (Introduction).

1387. Middlemas, Keith. Diplomacy of Illusion: The British Government and Germany, 1937-1939. London, 1972.

1388. Namier, Lewis B. Diplomatic Prelude, 1938-1939. London, 1948.

With Foreign Office, 1915-20; political secretary to the Jewish Agency for Palestine, 1929-31; see also his Europe in Decay: A Study in Disintegration (London, 1952); and In the Nazi Era (London, 1952); his material contains documents obtained from Czech and Polish diplomats.

1389. Orvik, Nils. "From Collective Security to Neutrality: The Nordic Powers, the League of Nations, Britain and the Approach of War, 1935-1939", in Studies in International History: Essays Presented to W. Norton Medlicott. Edited by K. Bourne and D.C. Watt. London, 1967.

1390. Ovendale, Ritchie. Appeasement and the English Speaking World: Britain, the United States, the Dominions and the Policy of 'Appeasement', 1937-1939. Cardiff, 1975.

Based on British, American and Dominion sources.

1391. Parker, R.A.C. "Grossbritannien und Deutschland, 1936-1937", in Weltpolitik, 1933-1939. Edited by Oswald Hauser. Göttingen, 1973.

1392. Powers, Richard Howard. "Winston Churchill's Parliamentary Commentary on British Foreign Policy, 1935-1938." Journal of Modern History, 26(1954), 179-82.

1393. Rock, William R. Appeasement on Trial: British Foreign Policy and its Critics, 1938-1939. Hamden, CT, 1966.

On parliamentary and press opposition to appeasement.

1394. Rose, Norman. "The Resignation of Anthony Eden." Historical Journal, 25(1982), 911-31.

1395. Sencourt, Robert. "The Foreign Policy of Neville Chamberlain." Quarterly Review, 292(1954), 141-55.

See also his "How Neville Chamberlain Fought Hitler", Quarterly Review, 292(1954), 413-25.

GENERAL

1396. Stadelmann, Rudolf. "Deutschland und England am Vorabend des Zweiten Weltkriegs", in Festschrift für Gerhard Ritter zu seinem 60. Geburtstag. Edited by Richard Nürnberger. Tübingen, 1950.

1397. Strauch, Rudi. Sir Nevile Henderson, britischer Botschafter in Berlin von 1937 bis 1939: Ein Beitrag zur diplomatischen Vorgeschichte des Zweiten Weltkrieges. Bonn, 1959.

See also Vaughan B. Baker, "Nevile Henderson in Berlin: A Re-evaluation", Red River Historical Journal of World History, 2(1977), 341-57; and John D. Marble, "The Henderson-Weizsäcker Relationship Prior to the Munich Conference", ibid., 134-40.

1398. Thorne, Christopher. The Approach of War, 1938-1939. London, 1967.

1399. Vieth, Jane Karoline. "Joseph P. Kennedy and British Appeasement: The Diplomacy of a Boston Irishman", in U.S. Diplomats in Europe, 1919-1941. Edited by Kenneth Paul Jones. Santa Barbara, CA, 1981.

American ambassador at London, 1938-40.

1400. Watt, D.C. "Roosevelt and Neville Chamberlain: Two Appeasers." International Journal, 28(1973), 185-204.

See also his "Misinformation, Misconception, Mistrust: Episodes in British Policy and the Approach of War, 1938-1939", in High and Low Politics in Modern Britain: Ten Studies, edited by Michael Bentley and John Stevenson (London, 1983).

2. Anschluss and Munich, 1938

1401. Ashton-Gwatkin, Frank T.A. "The Personal Story of the Runciman Mission." Listener, 40(1948), 595-97.

By a Foreign Office member of the mission; part of an anniversary series published between 21 October and 9 December 1948; other participants were Robert Bruce Lockhart, Lord Vansittart, Harold Nicolson, Lewis B. Namier, Cyril Falls and Lord Templewood.

1402. Black, Naomi. "Decision-Making and the Munich Crisis." British Journal of International Studies, 6(1980), 278-309.

255

1403. Bolech Cecchi, Donatella. L'accordo di due imperi: L'accordo italo-inglese del 16 aprile 1938. Milan, 1977.

See also the same author's "I rapporti italo-britannici durante la crisi dei Sudeti e la conferenza di Monaco", Il politico, 41(1976), 277-314; "'L'accordo di due imperi', L'accordo italo-inglese del 16 aprile 1938: Le relazioni italo-inglesi dal luglio 1937 alle dimissioni di Anthony Eden", Il politico, 38(1973), 737-69; "L'entrata in vigore dell'accordo anglo-italiano del 16 aprile 1938", Il politico, 41(1976), 449-91; and D.C. Watt, "Gli accordi mediterranei anglo-italiani del 16 aprile 1938", Rivista di studi politici internazionali, 26(1959), 59-76.

1404. Braddick, Henderson B. Germany, Czechoslovakia, and the "Grand Alliance" in the May Crisis, 1938. Denver, CO, 1969.

On this subject see also William V. Wallace, "The Making of the May Crisis of 1938", Slavonic and East European Review, 41(1963), 368-90; D.C. Watt, "The May Crisis of 1938: A Rejoinder to Mr. Wallace", Slavonic and East European Review, 44(1966), 475-80; William V. Wallace, "A Reply to Mr. Watt", Slavonic and East European Review, 44(1966), 480-86; Gerhard L. Weinberg, "The May Crisis, 1938", Journal of Modern History, 29(1957), 213-25; D.C. Watt, "Hitler's Visit to Rome and the May Weekend Crisis: A Study in Hitler's Response to External Stimuli", Journal of Contemporary History, 9(1974), 23-32; Heinz Königer, Der Weg nach München: Über die Mai- und Septemberkrise im Jahre 1938 und ihre Vorgeschichte (Berlin, 1958); and the same author's "Über die Maikrise von 1938 und ihre Behandlung in der westdeutschen Geschichtsschreibung", Zeitschrift für Geschichtswissenschaft, 7(1959), 60-79.

1405. Brügel, Johann W. Tschechen und Deutsche, 1918-1938. Munich, 1967.

Czechoslovakia before Munich: The German Minority Problem and British Appeasement Policy (London, 1973) is his adaptation with new British archival material; see also the same author's "Der Runciman Bericht", Vierteljahrshefte für Zeitgeschichte, 26(1978), 652-59.

1406. Butler, R.A. "The Issues in British Foreign Policy." International Affairs, 17(1938), 386-94.

1407. Calvet, Henri. "Aux origines de Munich: Le rôle du 'Times'." Revue d'histoire de la deuxième guerre mondiale, 3(1953), 25-32.

See also R.J. Mokken, "The Times and Munich", Gazette, 4(1958), 145-63.

1408. Crozier, Andrew. "Prelude to Munich: British Foreign Policy and Germany, 1935-1938." European Studies Review, 6(1976), 357-81.

1409. Douglas, Roy. In the Year of Munich. London, 1977.

Written exclusively on the basis of Public Record Office material and some private papers; continued in The Advent of War, 1939-1940 (London, 1978); and New Alliances, 1940-1941 (London, 1982); see also his "Chamberlain and Eden, 1937-1938", Journal of Contemporary History, 13(1978), 97-116.

1410. Dreifort, John. "France, Britain and Munich: An Interim Assessment." Proceeedings of the Annual Meeting of the Western Society for French History, 1(1973), 356-75.

See also Gilbert Fergusson, "Munich: The French and British Roles", International Affairs, 44(1968), 649-65.

1411. Eatwell, Roger. "Munich, Public Opinion and Popular Front." Journal of Contemporary History, 6(1971), 122-39.

1412. Fitzsimons, M.A. "The Masque of Uncertainty: Britain and Munich." Review of Politics, 12(1950), 489-505.

1413. Gedye, G.E.R. Fallen Bastions. London, 1939.

Well informed study by author expelled from Austria by Gestapo, 1938; previously on staff of Inter-allied Rhineland High Commission, Cologne, 1919-22; journalist with The Times, Daily Express, and New York Times, 1922-41; special military duties in Middle East, 1941-45.

1414. Gehl, Jürgen. Austria, Germany and the Anschluss, 1931-1938. London, 1963.

On the subject of the Anschluss, see also Norbert Schausberger, Der Griff nach Österreich; Der Anschluss (Vienna, 1978); Lajos Kerekes, Anschluss 1938 (Budapest, 1963); Gordon Brook-Shepherd, Anschluss: The Rape of

Austria (London, 1963); and Ulrich Eichstädt, Von
Dollfuss zu Hitler: Geschichte des Anschlusses
Österreichs, 1933-1938 (Wiesbaden, 1955).

1415. Hadley, William Waite. Munich: Before and After.
London, 1944.

By the editor of the Sunday Times, 1932-50; for another
informed contemporary account see Hubert Ripka, Munich:
Before and After (London, 1939).

1416. Hauser, Oswald. "Lord Halifax und Hitler, November
1937", in Staat und Gesellschaft im politischen Wandel:
Beiträge zur Geschichte der modernen Welt. Edited by
W. Pöls. Stuttgart, 1979.

See also Lois G. Schwoerer, "Lord Halifax's Visit to
Germany, November 1937", Historian, 32(1970), 353-75.

1417. Henson, E.L. "Britain, America, and the Month of
Munich." International Relations, 2(1962), 291-301.

1418. Hill, Leonidas. "Three Crises, 1938-1939." Journal of
Contemporary History, 3(1968), 113-44.

Based on the Weizsäcker papers; analyses the Munich,
Prague and Polish crises.

1419. Institut d'Etudes Slaves. Munich, 1938: Mythes et
réalités. Paris, 1979.

A collection of papers; vol. 52 of Revue des études
slaves.

1420. Kennedy, Aubrey Leo. "Munich: The Disintegration of
British Statesmanship." Quarterly Review, 286(1948),
425-44.

1421. Kenny, Marion L. "The Role of the House of Commons in
British Foreign Policy during the 1937-1938 Session",
in Essays in Honour of Conyers Read. Edited by Norton
Downs. Chicago, IL, 1953.

1422. Lammers, Donald N. Explaining Munich: The Search for
Motive in British Policy. Stanford, CA, 1966.

With particular emphasis on policy and attitudes towards
the USSR; takes into consideration Soviet published
sources.

258

1423. Lee, Dwight Erwin, ed. Munich: Blunder, Plot or Tragic Necessity? Lexington, MA, 1970.

See also Francis L. Loewenheim, ed., Peace or Appeasement? Hitler, Chamberlain, and the Munich Crisis (Boston, MA, 1965); another selection of contemporary documents and subsequent historical assessments.

1424. Murray, Williamson. "German Air Power and the Munich Crisis", in War and Society: A Yearbook of Military History. Vol. 2. Edited by Brian Bond and Ian Roy. London, 1977.

See also his "Munich 1938: The Military Confrontation", Journal of Strategic Studies, 2(1979), 282-302.

1425. Newman, Michael. "The Origins of Munich: British Policy in Danubian Europe, 1933-1937." Historical Journal, 21(1978), 371-86.

1426. Parker, R.A.C. "Anglo-French Conversations, April and September 1938", in Centre National de la Recherche Scientifique, Les relations franco-allemandes, 1933-1939. Paris, 1976.

1427. Poliakov, V.G. Angliia i Munchenskii sgovor, mart-sentyabr 1938g. Moscow, 1960.

1428. Pyper, C.B. Chamberlain and his Critics: A Statesman Vindicated. London, 1962.

1429. Quartararo, Rosaria. "Inghilterra e Italia: Dal patto di Pasqua a Monaco, Con un'appendice sul 'canale segreto' italo-inglese." Storia contemporanea, 7(1976), 607-716.

1430. Robbins, Keith. "Konrad Henlein, the Sudeten Question and British Foreign Policy." Historical Journal, 12(1969), 674-97.

See also Harindar Aulach, "Britain and the Sudeten Issue, 1938: The Evolution of a Policy", Journal of Contemporary History, 18(1983), 233-59.

1431. Schieche, E. "Prags Annahme des englisch-französischen Plans vom 21. September 1938." Stifter-Jahrbuch, 3(1953), 7-25.

1432. Scott, William. "Neville Chamberlain and Munich: Two Aspects of Power", in The Responsibility of Power: Historical Essays in Honor of Hajo Holborn. Edited by Leonard Krieger and Fritz Stern. New York, 1967.

1433. Sontag, Raymond J. "Appeasement, 1937." Catholic
      Historical Review, 38(1952), 385-96.

1434. Stronge, Brigadier H.C.T. "The Czechoslovak Army and the
      Munich Crisis: A Personal Memorandum", in War and
      Society: A Yearbook of Military History. Vol. 1.
      Edited by Brian Bond and Ian Roy. London, 1975.

      British military attaché, Belgrade and Prague, 1936-39.

1435. Taylor, Telford. Munich: The Price of Peace. New York,
      1979.

      Over a thousand pages; massively documented with both
      published and archival sources; similarly well documented
      studies include Boris Celovsky, Das Münchener Abkommen,
      1938 (Stuttgart, 1958); and Helmut K.G. Rönnefarth, Die
      Sudetenkrise in der internationalen Politik: Entstehung,
      Verlauf, Auswirkung, 2 vols. (Wiesbaden, 1961); other
      analyses are by Roger Massip and Jean Descola, Il y a 40
      ans: Munich (Paris, 1978); Keith Robbins, Munich, 1938
      (London, 1968); Laurence Thompson, The Greatest Treason:
      The Untold Story of Munich (London, 1968); Keith Eubank,
      Munich (Norman, OK, 1963); John W. Wheeler-Bennett,
      Munich: Prologue to Tragedy (London, 1948); Henri
      Noguères, Munich ou la drôle de paix (Paris, 1963);
      Geneviève Vallette and Jacques Bouillon, Munich, 1938
      (Paris, 1964); and for a Soviet oriented view see Andrew
      Rothstein, The Munich Conspiracy (London, 1958).

1436. Teichova, Alice. An Economic Background to Munich:
      International Business and Czechoslovakia, 1918-1938.
      London, 1974.

      With much on British interests and investments in central
      Europe.

1437. Vital, David. "Czechoslovakia and the Powers, September
      1938." Journal of Contemporary History, 1(1966),
      37-67.

1438. Wallace, William V. "Roosevelt and British Appeasement,
      1938." Bulletin of the British Association of American
      Studies, 5(1962), 4-30.

1439. Watt, D.C. "Der Einfluss der Dominions auf die
      britische Aussenpolitik vor München 1938."
      Vierteljahrshefte für Zeitgeschichte, 8(1960), 64-74.

      For an earlier analysis see H.V. Hodson, "British Foreign
      Policy and the Dominions", Foreign Affairs, 17(1939),
      753-63.

1440. Webster, Charles. "Munich Reconsidered: A Survey of
British Policy." International Affairs, 37(1961),
137-53.

1441. Zorach, Jonathan. "Czechoslovakia's Fortifications:
Their Development and Role in the 1938 Munich Crisis."
Militärgeschichtliche Mitteilungen, 20(1976), 81-94.

See also his "The British View of the Czechs in the Era
before the Munich Crisis", Slavonic and East European
Review, 57(1979), 56-70; and Milan Hauner,
"Czechoslovakia as a Military Factor in British
Considerations of 1938", Journal of Strategic Studies,
1(1978), 194-222.

3. From Munich to Danzig, 1938-1939

1442. Alexandroff, Alan, and Rosecrance, Richard. "Deterrence
in 1939." World Politics, 29(1977), 404-24.

See also Robert Jervis, "Deterrence and Perception",
International Security, 7(1983), 3-30.

1443. Aster, Sidney. 1939: The Making of the Second World
War. London, 1973.

An analysis from the post-Munich period to the outbreak
of war; based on a wide array of private papers,
interviews, and Public Record Office materials.

1444. Ball, Adrian. The Last Day of the Old World: 3rd
September, 1939. London, 1963.

Largely based on personal interviews; see also Ronald
Seth, The Day War Broke Out: The Story of the 3rd
September, 1939 (London, 1963).

1445. Batowski, Henryk. "The Polish-British and Polish-
French Treaties of 1939." Polish Western Affairs,
14(1973), 78-98.

See also his "August 31st, 1939 in Berlin", Polish
Western Affairs, 4(1963), 20-50; and Kryzys Dyplomatyczny
w Europie: Jesien 1938 - Wiosna 1939 (Warsaw, 1962).

1446. Bloch, Charles. "Les relations anglo-allemandes de
l'accord de Munich à la dénonciation du traité naval de
1935." Revue d'histoire de la deuxième guerre
mondiale, 5(1955), 33-49, 41-65.

1447. Broszat, Martin. "Die Reaktion der Mächte auf den 15. März 1939." Bohemia: Jahrbuch des Collegium Carolinum, 8(1967), 253-80.

1448. Chanady, A., and Jensen, J. "Germany, Rumania and the British Guarantees of March-April, 1939." Australian Journal of Politics and History, 16(1970), 201-17.

1449. Chikvaidze, A.D. Angliiskii kabinet nakanune vtoroi mirovoi voini. Tbilisi, 1976.

1450. Cienciala, Anna M. "O Polityce Angielskiej w 1939r." Bellona, 3(1959), 297-301.

1451. Crowe, David M. "Great Britain and the Baltic States, 1938-1939", in The Baltic States in Peace and War, 1917-1945. Edited by V. Stanley Vardys and Romuald J. Misiunas. London, 1978.

    See also Georg Vigrabs, "Die Stellungnahme der Westmächte und Deutschlands zu den baltischen Staaten im Frühling und Sommer 1939", Vierteljahrshefte für Zeitgeschichte, 7(1959), 261-79; and August Rei, "The Baltic Question at the Moscow Negotiations in 1939", East and West, 4(1955), 20-29.

1452. Dell'Omodarme, Marcello. "La missione Wohlthat." Rivista di studi politici internationali, 26(1959), 235-42.

1453. Doherty, Julian Campbell. Das Ende des Appeasement: Die britische Aussenpolitik, die Achsenmächte, und Osteuropa nach dem Münchener Abkommen. Berlin, 1973.

    From Munich to the outbreak of war; based on a variety of British and German archives, private papers and interviews; see also his "Die Dominions und die britische Aussenpolitik von München bis zum Kriegsausbruch 1939", Vierteljahrshefte für Zeitgeschichte, 20(1972), 209-34.

1454. Douglas, Roy, ed. 1939: A Retrospect of Forty Years After. London, 1983.

    Proceedings of a conference at Surrey University; a multi-national approach.

1455. Douglas-Hamilton, James. "Ribbentrop and War." Journal of Contemporary History, 5(1970), 45-63.

    On unofficial Anglo-German contacts in the summer of 1939.

1456. Fleming, Nicholas. <u>August 1939: The Last Days of Peace</u>. London, 1979.

   On the same period see also Walther Hofer, <u>War Premeditated</u> (London, 1959).

1457. Haraszti, Eva. "Three Documents Concerning Great Britain's Policy in East-Central Europe in the Period after the Munich Agreement." <u>Acta Historica</u>, 22(1976), 139-75.

1458. Henke, Josef. "Hitler und England Mitte August 1939: Ein Dokument zur Rolle Fritz Hesses in den deutsch-britischen Beziehungen am Vorabend des Zweiten Weltkrieges." <u>Vierteljahrshefte für Zeitgeschichte</u>, 21(1973), 231-42.

1459. Kettenacker, Lothar. "Die Diplomatie der Ohnmacht: Die gescheiterte Friedensstrategie der britischen Regierung vor Ausbruch des Zweiten Weltkrieges", in <u>Sommer 1939: Die Grossmächte und der Europäische Krieg</u>. Edited by Wolfgang Benz and Hermann Graml. Stuttgart, 1979.

1460. Kulski, Wladyslaw W. "The Anglo-Polish Agreement of August 25th, 1939: Highlight of my Diplomatic Career." <u>Polish Review</u>, 21(1976), 23-40.

1461. Lenz, Wilhelm, and Kettenacker, Lothar. "Lord Kemsleys Gespräch mit Hitler Ende Juli 1939." <u>Vierteljahrshefte für Zeitgeschichte</u>, 19(1971), 305-21.

1462. Levine, H.S. "The Mediator: Carl J. Burckhardt's Efforts to Avert a Second World War." <u>Journal of Modern History</u>, 45(1973), 439-55.

1463. MacDonald, C.A. "Britain, France and the April Crisis of 1939." <u>European Studies Review</u>, 2(1972), 151-69.

1464. Manne, Robert. "The British Decision for Alliance with Russia, May 1939." <u>Journal of Contemporary History</u>, 9(1974), 3-26.

1465. Metzmacher, Helmut. "Deutsch-englische Ausgleichsbemühungen im Sommer 1939." <u>Vierteljahrshefte für Zeitgeschichte</u>, 14(1966), 369-412.

1466. Meyer-Hermann, E. "Göring und die englische Kriegserklärung am 3. September 1939." <u>Geschichte in Wissenschaft und Unterricht</u>, 9(1958), 375-86.

1467. Mosley, Leonard. On Borrowed Time: How World War Two Began. London, 1969.

A popular account, but solidly based on archival material and numerous interviews.

1468. Nekrich, A.M. Politika angliiskogo imperialisma v Evrope, oktiabr 1938-sentiabr 1939. Moscow, 1955.

1469. Newman, Simon. The British Guarantee to Poland: A Study in the Continuity of British Foreign Policy. London, 1976.

See also Gottfried Niedhart, "Die britisch-französische Garantieerklärung für Polen vom 31. März 1939: Aussen-politischer Kurswechsel der Westmächte?", Francia, 2(1974), 597-618; William R. Rock, "The British Guarantee to Poland, March 1939: A Problem in Diplomatic Decision Making", South Atlantic Quarterly, 65(1966), 229-40; Keith Eubank, "The British Pledge to Poland: Prelude to War", Southwestern Social Science Quarterly, 45(1965), 340-48; Karel Lapter, "Angielskie Gwarancje dla Polski w 1939r", Sprawy Miedzynarodowe, 6(1959), 3-31; and T. Desmond Williams, "Negotiations Leading to the Anglo-Polish Agreement of 31 March 1939", Irish Historical Studies, 10(1957), 59-93, 156-92.

1470. Nikonov, A.D. The Origins of World War II and the Prewar European Political Crisis of 1939. Moscow, 1955.

1471. Pankrashova, M., and Sipols, V.Y. Why War Was Not Prevented: A Documentary Review of the Soviet-British-French Talks in Moscow, 1939. Moscow, 1970.

With numerous extracts from Soviet archives; see also G. Deborine, "Les négotiations anglo-franco-soviétiques de 1939 et le traité de non-agression germano-soviétique", Recherches internationales à la lumière du marxisme, 5(1961), 139-66; Ernst Deuerlein, "Die gescheiterte Anti-Hitler-Koalition: Die politischen und militärischen Verhandlungen zwischen Grossbritannien, Frankreich und der Sowjetunion im Frühjahr und Sommer 1939", Wehrwissenschaftliche Rundschau, 9(1959), 634-50; Horst Schützler, "Die politischen Verhandlungen der Sowjetunion mit Grossbritannien und Frankreich im Frühjahr und Sommer 1939", Zeitschrift für Geschichts-wissenschaft, 7(1959), 1716-42; and Werner Basler, "Die britisch-französisch-sowjetischen Militärbesprechungen im August 1939", Zeitschrift für Geschichtswissenschaft, 5(1957), 18-56.

1472. Parker, R.A.C. "The British Government and the Coming of War with Germany, 1939", in War and Society: Historical Essays in Honour and Memory of J.R. Western, 1928-1971. Edited by M.R.D. Foot. London, 1973.

1473. Prazmowska, A.J. "War over Danzig? The Dilemma of Anglo-Polish Relations in the Months Preceding the Outbreak of the Second World War." Historical Journal, 26(1983), 177-83.

1474. Rhodes, Benjamin D. "The British Royal Visit of 1939 and the 'Psychological Approach' to the United States." Diplomatic History, 2(1978), 197-211.

1475. Rock, William R. "Grand Alliance or Daisy Chain: British Opinion and Policy Toward Russia, April-August, 1939", in Power, Public Opinion, and Diplomacy: Essays in Honor of Eber Malcolm Carroll. Edited by L.P. Wallace and W.C. Askew. Durham, NC, 1959.

1476. Salter, Sir Arthur. Security: Can We Retrieve It? London, 1939.

1477. Shamir, Haim. "Die Kristallnacht, die Notlage der deutschen Juden und die Haltung Englands?" Jahrbuch des Instituts für deutsche Geschichte, 1(1972), 171-214.

1478. Stafford, Paul. "The Chamberlain-Halifax Visit to Rome: A Reappraisal." English Historical Review, 98(1983), 61-100.

1479. Strang, Lord. The Moscow Negotiations. Leeds, 1968.

An important analysis by a British participant; other relevant reminiscences are by Admiral Sir Reginald Plunkett-Ernle-Erle-Drax, "Mission to Moscow", Naval Review, 40-1(1952-53), 339-413, 51-63; N.G. Kuznetsov, Pered voina (Moscow, 1968); and André Beaufre, Le Drame de 1940 (Paris, 1965).

1480. Teichova, Alice. "Die geheimen britisch-deutschen Ausgleichsversuche am Vorabend des Zweiten Weltkrieges." Zeitschrift für Geschichtswissenschaft, 7(1959), 755-96.

See also the same author's "Great Britain in European Affairs, March 15 to August 21, 1939", Historica, 3(1961), 239-336.

1481. USSR, Ministerstvo Inostrannikh Del. <u>SSSR v borbe za mir</u>
<u>nakanune vtoroi mirovoi voini, sentiabr 1938g. - avgust</u>
<u>1939g.: Dokumenti i materiali.</u> Edited by A.A.
Gromyko, et al. Moscow, 1971.

Almost 450 documents from Soviet archives and foreign
sources.

1482. Watt, D.C. "Pirow's Berlin Mission in November 1938:
'Free Hand' for Hitler and Relief for the Jews."
<u>Wiener Library Bulletin</u>, 12(1958), 53.

The wider background is in his "South African Attempts to
Mediate between Britain and Germany, 1935-1938", in
<u>Studies in International History: Essays Presented to</u>
<u>W. Norton Medlicott</u>, edited by K. Bourne and D.C. Watt
(London, 1967).

H.   THE SECOND WORLD WAR, 1939-1945

1.   Origins and Conduct of the War

1483. Adamthwaite, Anthony P.   The Making of the Second World
      War.   London, 1977.

      Introductory essay with eighty-one documents; similar in
      format is his The Lost Peace: International Relations in
      Europe, 1918-1939 (London, 1980).

1484. André, Gianluca, and Pastorelli, Pietro.   La seconda
      guerra mondiale.   2 vols.   Milan, 1964-67.

1485. Baumont, Maurice.   The Origins of the Second World War.
      New Haven, CT, 1978.

      Abr. Eng. trans. of La faillite de la paix, 1918-1939, 2
      vols. (Paris, 1946).

1486. Bullock, Alan.   Hitler and the Origins of the Second
      World War.   London, 1967.

      A useful synthesis of the evidence to that date.

1487. Calvocoressi, Peter, and Wint, Guy.   Total War: Causes
      and Courses of the Second World War.   London, 1972.

      See also the essays in The Second World War as a National
      Experience, edited by Sidney Aster (Ottawa, Ontario,
      1981).

1488. Eubank, Keith.   The Origins of World War II.   New York,
      1969.

      A companion volume is his The Road to World War II: A
      Documentary History (New York, 1973).

1489. Hillgruber, Andreas.   Zur Entstehung des Zweiten
      Weltkrieges: Forschungsstand und Literatur.
      Düsseldorf, 1980.

1490. Israelian, Victor L.   The Anti-Hitler Coalition:
      Diplomatic Co-operation Between the U.S.S.R., U.S.A.
      and Britain during the Second World War, 1941-1945.
      Moscow, 1971.

267

See also V.G. Trukhanovskii, British Foreign Policy
during World War II (Moscow, 1970).

1491. Jacob, Sir Ian. "The High Level Conduct and Direction of
World War II." The Journal of the Royal United Service
Institution, 101(1956), 364-72.

See also his "The Turning Point: Grand Strategy,
1942-1943", Round Table, 62(1972), 529-35.

1492. Jacobsen, Hans-Adolf, and Smith, Arthur L. World War II,
Policy and Strategy: Selected Documents with
Commentary. Santa Barbara, CA, 1979.

A collection of 214 documents from numerous sources; see
also Hans-Adolf Jacobsen, 1939-1945: Der zweite
Weltkrieg in Chronik und Dokumenten (Darmstadt, 1959).

1493. Lafore, Lawrence. The End of Glory: An Interpretation
of the Origins of World War II. New York, 1970.

1494. Liddell Hart, Sir Basil H. History of the Second World
War. London, 1971.

Other essentially military accounts by British historians
include Michael Howard, History of the Second World War
(London, 1971); Basil Collier, A Short History of the
Second World War (London, 1967); Peter Young, World War,
1939-1945: A Short History (London, 1966); Cyril Falls,
The Second World War: A Short History (London, 1950);
and John F.C. Fuller, The Second World War, 1939-1945: A
Strategical and Tactical History (London, 1948).

1495. Medlicott, W.N. The Coming of War in 1939. London,
1963.

1496. Michel, Henri. The Second World War. London, 1975.

A comprehensive analysis; extensive bibliography.

1497. Niedhart, Gottfried, ed. Kriegsbeginn 1939:
Entfesselung oder Ausbruch des Zweiten Weltkriegs?
Darmstadt, 1976.

Eighteen previously published studies by historians on
the subject; mainly on Anglo-German relations.

1498. Parkinson, Roger. Peace for Our Time: Munich to
Dunkirk, the Inside Story. London, 1972.

Continued in Blood, Toil, Tears, and Sweat: The War History from Dunkirk to Alamein; Based on the War Cabinet Papers of 1940 to 1942 (London, 1973); and A Day's March Nearer Home: The War History from Alamein to VE Day; Based on the War Cabinet Papers of 1942 to 1945 (London, 1974).

1499. Remak, Joachim. The Origins of the Second World War. Englewood Cliffs, NJ, 1976.

An introductory essay; with selected documents, 1915-41.

1500. Robertson, Esmonde M., ed. The Origins of the Second World War: Historical Interpretations. London, 1971.

A collection of thirteen previously published essays; none specifically on Britain, yet all are relevant.

1501. Royal Institute of International Affairs. Chronology of the Second World War. London, 1947.

See also Andreas Hillgruber and Gerhard Hümmelchen, Chronik des Zweiten Weltkrieges: Kalendarium militärischer und politischer Ereignisse, 1939-1945 (Düsseldorf, 1978).

1502. Snell, John, ed. The Outbreak of the Second World War: Design or Blunder? Boston, MA, 1962.

A collection of readings and documents; see also his Illusion and Necessity: The Diplomacy of Global War, 1939-1945 (Boston, 1963).

1503. Sontag, Raymond J. "The Origins of the Second World War." Review of Politics, 25(1963), 497-508.

1504. Steinert, Marlis G. Les origines de la seconde guerre mondiale. Paris, 1974.

Introductory essay with supporting documents and extracts by various historians.

1505. Taylor, A.J.P. The Origins of the Second World War. London, 1961.

To be read in conjunction with William Roger Louis, ed., The Origins of the Second World War: A.J.P. Taylor and his Critics (New York, 1972); and A.J.P. Taylor, A Personal History (London, 1983).

1506. Vidalenc, J. Le second conflit mondial, mai 1939-mai 1945. Paris, 1970.

1507. Woodward, Sir Llewellyn. "Diplomatic history of the Second World War", in New Cambridge Modern History, vol. 12, rev. ed. London, 1968.

See also his "Some Reflections on British Policy, 1939-1945", International Affairs, 31(1955), 273-90.

2. Refugees, Resistance and Peace Moves

1508. Auty, Phyllis, and Clogg, Richard, eds. British Policy Towards Wartime Resistance in Yugoslavia and Greece. London, 1975.

Proceedings of a conference at the School of Slavonic and East European Studies held in July 1973; ten papers, many by former SOE officials, focus largely on events in 1943.

1509. Bennett, Jeremy. British Broadcasting and the Danish Resistance Movement 1940-1945: A Study of the Wartime Broadcasts of the BBC Danish Services. London, 1966.

Based on both British and Danish sources.

1510. Bentwich, Norman. I Understand the Risks: The Story of the Refugees from Nazi Oppression Who Fought in the British Forces in the World War. London, 1950.

See also his The Refugees from Germany, April 1933 to December 1935 (London, 1936).

1511. Best, S. Payne. The Venlo Incident. London, 1950.

1512. Clogg, Richard. "The Greek Government-in-Exile, 1941-1944." International History Review, 1(1979), 376-98.

1513. Cookridge, E.H. [Edward Spiro]. Inside SOE: The Story of Special Operations in Western Europe, 1940-1945. London, 1966.

The Special Operations Executive entrusted with executing plans for resistance, sabotage and subversion in Europe; see also M.R.D. Foot, "L'Aide à la résistance en Europe", Revue d'histoire de la deuxième guerre mondiale, 23(1973), 39-52; his "Special Operations, Parts 1 and 2", in The Fourth Dimension of Warfare, vol. 1, edited by Michael Elliott-Bateman (Manchester, 1970); and "Reflections on SOE", Manchester Literary and Philosophical

Society: Memoirs and Proceedings, 111(1968), 87-96;
Josef Garlinski, Poland, SOE and the Allies (London,
1969); and Special Operations, edited by Patrick Howarth
(London, 1955).

1514. Cremieux-Brilhac, Jean-Louis, ed. Les voix de la
      liberté: Ici Londres, 1940-1944. 5 vols. Paris,
      1975.

      Transcripts from the BBC archives of the wartime French
      section; see also André Gillois, Histoire secrète des
      français à Londres de 1940 à 1944 (Paris, 1973).

1515. Cruickshank, Charles. The Fourth Arm: Psychological
      Warfare, 1938-1945. London, 1977.

      An analysis of the Political Warfare Executive; based
      extensively on Public Record Office materials; see also
      his The German Occupation of the Channel Islands (London,
      1975); and SOE in the Far East (London, 1983).

1516. Deakin, F.W.D. The Embattled Mountain. London, 1971.

      Seconded to SOE, 1941; led first British military mission
      to Tito, May 1943; first secretary, British embassy,
      Belgrade, 1945-46.

1517. Douglas-Hamilton, James. Motive for a Mission: The
      Story behind Hess's Flight to Britain. London, 1971.

      By the son of the Duke of Hamilton on whose estate Hess
      landed; see also James Leasor, Rudolf Hess: The
      Uninvited Envoy (London, 1962).

1518. Fieldhouse, H. Noel. "The Anglo-German War of 1939-1942:
      Some Movements to End it by a Negotiated Peace."
      Transactions of the Royal Society of Canada, 9(1971),
      285-312.

1519. Fox, John P. "The Jewish Factor in British War Crimes
      Policy in 1942." English Historical Review, 92(1977),
      82-106.

      See also his "Great Britain and the German Jews, 1933",
      Wiener Library Bulletin, 26(1972), 40-6.

1520. Gilbert, Martin. Auschwitz and the Allies. London,
      1981.

      Including British attitudes and policy; documented with
      new material from numerous archives worldwide.

1521. Glees, Anthony. Exile Politics during the Second World
      War: The German Social Democrats in Britain. London,
      1982.

      See also Werner Röder, Die deutschen sozialistischen
      Exilgruppen in Grossbritannien, 1940-1945 (Hanover,
      1969).

1522. Goldman, Aaron. "Defence Regulation 18B: Emergency
      Internment of Aliens and Political Dissenters in Great
      Britain during World War II." Journal of British
      Studies, 12(1973), 120-36.

1523. Graham-Murray, James. The Sword and the Umbrella. Isle
      of Man, 1964.

      On the peace moves by the German opposition to Hitler.

1524. Gubbins, Major-General Sir Colin. "SOE and the Co-
      ordination of Regular and Irregular War", in The Fourth
      Dimension of Warfare. Vol. 1. Edited by Michael
      Elliott-Bateman. Manchester, 1970.

      See also his "Resistance Movements in the War", Journal
      of the Royal United Service Institution, 93(1948),
      210-23.

1525. Hearst, Ernest. "The British and the Slaughter of the
      Jews, Parts 1 and 2." Wiener Library Bulletin,
      21(1967), 32-28, 30-40.

1526. Hirszowicz, Lukasz. "The Soviet Union and the Jews
      during World War II: British Foreign Office
      Documents." Soviet Jewish Affairs, 3(1973), 104-19,
      73-90.

1527. Hoffmann, Peter. The History of the German Resistance,
      1933-1945. Cambridge, MA, 1977.

      Primarily concerned with those attempts to overthrow the
      regime or assassinate its leaders; a massively documented
      book; supersedes previous studies such as Walter
      Schmitthener and Hans Buchheim, eds., Der deutsche
      Widerstand gegen Hitler (Berlin, 1966); Hans Rothfels,
      The German Opposition to Hitler: An Assessment (London,
      1961); and Hermann Graml, et al., eds., The German
      Resistance to Hitler (London, 1970).

1528. Kacewicz, George V. Great Britain, the Soviet Union and
      the Polish Government in Exile, 1939-1945. The Hague,
      1979.

272

REFUGEES, RESISTANCE AND PEACE MOVES

With Polish language sources.

1529. Kettenacker, Lothar. "Die britische Haltung zum
deutschen Widerstand während des Zweiten Weltkriegs",
in Das "Andere Deutschland" im Zweiten Weltkrieg:
Emigration und Widerstand in internationaler
Perspektive. Edited by Lothar Kettenacker. Stuttgart,
1977.

1530. King, Frank P. "British Policy and the Warsaw Rising."
Journal of European Studies, 4(1974), 1-18.

1531. Knight, Jonathan. "Churchill and the Approach to
Mussolini and Hitler in May 1940: A Note." British
Journal of International Studies, 3(1977), 92-96.

1532. Lampe, David. The Last Ditch: The Secrets of the
Nationwide British Resistance Organization and the Nazi
Plans for the Occupation of Britain, 1940-1944.
London, 1968.

1533. Lonsdale Bryans, James. Blind Victory: Secret Communic-
ations, Halifax-Hassell. London, 1951.

See also his "Zur britischen amtlichen Haltung gegenüber
der deutschen Widerstandsbewegung", Vierteljahrshefte für
Zeitgeschichte, 1(1953), 347-56.

1534. Ludlow, Peter W. "The Unwinding of Appeasement", in
Das "Andere Deutschland" im Zweiten Weltkrieg:
Emigration und Widerstand in internationaler
Perspektive. Edited by Lothar Kettenacker. Stuttgart,
1977.

Concentrates on British reaction to peace feelers in the
"phoney war" period; including relevant documents; see
also his "Papst Pius XII, die britische Regierung und die
deutsche Opposition im Winter 1939-1940", Vierteljahrshefte für Zeitgeschichte, 22(1974), 299-341; and
"The Refugee Problem in the 1930s: The Failures and
Successes of Protestant Relief Programmes", English
Historical Review, 90(1975), 564-603.

1535. Martin, Bernd. Friedensinitiativen und Machtpolitik im
Zweiten Weltkrieg, 1939-1942. Düsseldorf, 1974.

An enormously detailed account based on German, American
and British archives and private papers; mainly on Anglo-
German contacts; see also his "Britisch-deutsche
Friedenskontakte in den ersten Monaten des Zweiten

273

Weltkrieges: Ein Dokumentation über die
Vermittlungsversuche von Birger Dahlerus", <u>Zeitschrift</u>
<u>für Politik</u>, 19(1972), 206-21; Walter Lipgens,
<u>Europa-Föderationspläne der Widerstandsbewegungen,</u>
<u>1940-1945</u> (Munich, 1968); and Maxime Mourin, <u>Les</u>
<u>tentatives de paix dans la seconde guerre mondiale,</u>
<u>1939-1945</u> (Paris, 1959).

1536. Pavlowitch, Stevan K. "Out of Context: The Yugoslav
Government in London, 1941-1945." <u>Journal of</u>
<u>Contemporary History</u>, 16(1981), 89-118.

1537. Rings, Werner. <u>Life with the Enemy: Collaboration and</u>
<u>Resistance in Hitler's Europe, 1939-1945</u>. London,
1982.

A good general introduction; still valuable are Jorgen
Haestrup, <u>European Resistance Movements, 1939-1945: A</u>
<u>Complete History</u> (London, 1981); his <u>Kontakt med England,</u>
<u>1940-1943</u> (Copenhagen, 1954); M.R.D. Foot, <u>Resistance:</u>
<u>An Analysis of European Resistance to Nazism, 1940-1945</u>
(London, 1976); Henri Michel, <u>The Shadow War: Resistance</u>
<u>in Europe, 1939-1945</u> (London, 1972); the ten essays by
British academics in <u>Resistance in Europe, 1939-1945:</u>
<u>Based on the Proceedings of a Symposium at the University</u>
<u>of Salford, March, 1973</u>, edited by Stephen Hawes and
Ralph White (London, 1975); the essays of two
international conferences held at Liège, 1958 and Milan,
1961 in <u>European Resistance Movements, 1939-1945</u> (London,
1960 and New York, 1964); and those in mimeographed form
in <u>Great Britain and European Resistance: Proceedings of</u>
<u>a Conference Held at St. Antony's College</u> (Oxford, 1962).

1538. Sherman, A.J. <u>Island Refuge: Britain and Refugees from</u>
<u>the Third Reich, 1933-1939</u>. London, 1973.

Widely researched, with useful bibliography.

1539. Simpson, Sir John Hope. <u>The Refugee Problem: Report of</u>
<u>a Survey</u>. London, 1939.

M.P., 1922-24; vice-president, Refugee Settlement
Commission, Athens, 1926-30; mission to Palestine, 1930;
director-general, National Food Relief Commission, China,
1931-33.

1540. Stafford, David. <u>Britain and European Resistance, 1940-</u>
<u>1945: A Survey of the Special Operations Executive,</u>
<u>with Documents</u>. London, 1980.

"Concerned primarily with demonstrating how SOE and its
activities related to the strategic and diplomatic
objectives of the British government" (Preface); see also
the same author's "SOE and British Involvement in the
Belgrade Coup d'État of March 1941", Slavic Review,
36(1977), 399-419; "The Detonator Concept: British
Strategy, SOE and European Resistance after the Fall of
France", Journal of Contemporary History, 10(1975),
185-217; "Britain Looks at Europe, 1940: Some Origins of
SOE", Canadian Journal of History, 10(1975), 231-48; and
Jean Overton Fuller, The German Penetration of SOE:
France, 1941-1944 (London, 1975).

1541. Stein, Joshua B. "Britain and the Jews of Danzig,
      1938-1939." Wiener Library Bulletin, 32(1979) 29-33.

      See also his "Great Britain and the Evian Conference,
      1938", Wiener Library Bulletin, 29(1976), 40-52.

1542. Stevens, Austin. The Dispossessed: German Refugees in
      Britain. London, 1975.

      German Jewish refugees, before and during the second
      world war.

1543. Sykes, Christopher. Troubled Loyalty. London, 1968.

      Study of the German resistance figure Adam von Trott zu
      Solz; with much on his British contacts; see also David
      Astor, "Why the Revolt against Hitler was Ignored: On
      the British Reluctance to Deal with German Anti-Nazis",
      Encounter, 32(1969), 3-13; and Hans Rothfels, "Trott und
      die Aussenpolitik des Widerstandes", Vierteljahrshefte
      für Zeitgeschichte, 12(1964), 300-23.

1544. Tolstoy, Nikolai. Victims of Yalta. London, 1978.

      On the forced repatriation of over three million Russians
      during 1944-47; see also Nicholas Bethell, The Last
      Secret (London, 1974).

1545. Varsori, Antonio. "Italy, Britain and the Problem of a
      Separate Peace during the Second World War, 1940-1943."
      Journal of Italian History, 1(1978), 455-91.

      See also his "L'antifascismo e gli alleati: Le missioni
      di Lussu e Gentili a Londra e Washington nel 1941-1942",
      Storia e politica, 19(1980), 457-507; and "La politica
      inglese e il Conte Sforza, 1941-1943", Rivista di studi
      politici internazionali, 43(1976), 31-57.

1546. Viault, Birdsall S. "Les démarches pour le rétablissement de la paix, septembre 1939-août 1940." Revue d'histoire de la deuxième guerre mondiale, 17(1967) 13-30.

See also his "Mussolini et la recherche d'une paix négociée, 1939-1940." Revue d'histoire de la deuxième guerre mondiale, 27(1977), 1-18.

1547. Wasserstein, Bernard. Britain and the Jews of Europe, 1939-1945. London, 1979.

Based on British, Israeli and Zionist archives.

1548. Watt, D.C. "Les alliés et la résistance allemande, 1939-1944." Revue d'histoire de la deuxième guerre mondiale, 9(1959), 65-86.

1549. Wendt, Bernd Jürgen. München 1938: England zwischen Hitler und Preussen. Frankfurt/M., 1965.

On the German resistance of the time.

1550. Woodhouse, C.M. "Early British Contacts with the Greek Resistance in 1942." Balkan Studies, 12(1971), 347-63.

1551. Young, A.P. The 'X' Documents: The Secret History of Foreign Office Contacts with the German Resistance, 1937-1939. Edited by Sidney Aster. London, 1974.

On the A.P. Young-Carl Goerdeler contacts; with an appendix analysing Foreign Office reaction; on Goerdeler's further contacts with the British, see Gerhard Ritter, The German Resistance (London, 1958).

1552. Zayas, Alfred M. de. Nemesis at Potsdam: The Anglo-Americans and the Expulsion of the Germans, Background, Execution, Consequences. London, 1977.

On the transfer of fifteen million Germans at the end of the second world war; with multilingual documentation.

3. Intelligence: Prewar and Wartime

1553. Andrew, Christopher. "The Mobilization of British Intelligence for the Two World Wars", in Mobilization for Total War: The Canadian, American and British Experience, 1914-1918, 1939-1945. Edited by N.F. Dreisziger. Waterloo, Ontario, 1981.

INTELLIGENCE: PREWAR AND WARTIME

See also his "Governments and Secret Services: A Historical Perspective", *International Journal*, 24(1979), 167-86; "Whitehall, Washington and the Intelligence Services", *International Affairs*, 53(1977), 390-404; "The British Secret Service and Anglo-Soviet Relations in the 1920s: Part I, From the Trade Negotiations to the Zinoviev Letter", *Historical Journal*, 20(1977), 673-706; and the sequel "British Intelligence and the Breach with Russia in 1927", *Historical Journal*, 25(1982), 957-64.

1554. Ball, Desmond J. "Allied Intelligence Cooperation Involving Australia during World War II." *Australian Outlook*, 32(1978), 299-309.

1555. Bazna, Elyesa. *I was Cicero*. London, 1962.

Autobiography of the spy for Germany in the British wartime embassy in Ankara; see also Ludwig C. Moyzisch, *Operation Cicero* (London, 1950).

1556. Beesly, Patrick. *Very Special Intelligence: History of the Admiralty's Operational Intelligence Centre, 1939-1945*. London, 1977.

See also Donald McLachlan, *Room 39: Naval Intelligence in Action 1939-45* (London, 1968); the same author's "Naval Intelligence in the Second World War", *Journal of the Royal United Service Institution*, 112(1967), 221-28; and "Intelligence: The Common Denominator, Parts 1 and 2", in *The Fourth Dimension of Warfare*, vol. 1, edited by Michael Elliott-Bateman (Manchester, 1970).

1557. Bennett, Ralph. *Ultra in the West: The Normandy Campaign of 1944-1945*. London, 1979.

See also his "Ultra and Some Command Decisions", *Journal of Contemporary History*, 16(1981), 131-51; and Jock Haswell, *The Intelligence and Deception of the D-Day Landings* (London, 1979).

1558. Bertrand, Gustave. *Enigma ou la plus grande énigme de la guerre, 1939-1945*. Paris, 1973.

By a member of French intelligence and a cipher expert.

1559. Boyle, Andrew. *The Climate of Treason*. London, 1979.

Revelations about British spies Guy Burgess, Donald MacLean, Kim Philby and Anthony Blunt; for more on the subject see also Chapman Pincher, *Their Trade is Treachery* (London, 1981).

277

1560. Calvocoressi, Peter. Top Secret Ultra. London, 1980.

Memoir-history by a former RAF intelligence officer, stationed at Bletchley Park, which housed the Code and Cypher School, and where Enigma messages were decyphered; see also Gordon Welchman, The Hut Six Story: Breaking the Enigma Codes (London, 1982).

1561. Clayton, Aileen. The Enemy is Listening. London, 1981.

On the Y Service, the RAF intelligence branch responsible for interception of enemy communication.

1562. Collier, Basil. Hidden Weapons: Allied Secret or Undercover Services in World War II. London, 1982.

A critical assessment of the use made of intelligence from all sources.

1563. Cruickshank, Charles. Deception in World War II. London, 1979.

On British attempts at tactical deception of the Germans in Europe and the Middle East.

1564. Ellis, Kenneth L. "British Communication and Diplomacy since 1844." Journal of the Society of Archivists, 4(1973), 592-95.

1565. Evans, N.E. "Air Intelligence and the Coventry Raid." Journal of the Royal United Services Institute for Defence Studies, 121(1976), 66-74.

1566. Farago, Ladislas. The Game of the Foxes: The Untold Story of German Espionage in the United States and Great Britain During World War II. London, 1971.

1567. Fisher, John. Burgess and Maclean: A New Look at the Foreign Office Spies. London, 1977.

1568. Foot, M.R.D., and Langley, J.M. MI9: Escape and Evasion, 1939-1945. London, 1979.

The intelligence section dealing with training in cases of capture and escape techniques; see also Airey Neave, Saturday at MI9: A History of Underground Escape Lines in Northwest Europe, 1940-1945 (London, 1969).

1569. Garlinski, Josef. Intercept: The Enigma War. London, 1979.

Widely researched, with Polish sources and interviews.

1570. Hilton, Stanley E. Hitler's Secret War in South America: German Military Espionage and Allied Counter-Espionage in Brazil, 1939-1945. London, 1981.

With sources in Portuguese, German and English.

1571. Horner, D.M. "Special Intelligence in the South-West Pacific Area in World War II." Australian Outlook, 32(1978), 310-27.

1572. Hyde, H. Montgomery. Secret Intelligence Agent. London, 1982.

Another similar contribution is Richard Deacon, With My Little Eye: Memoirs of a Spy Hunter (London, 1982).

1573. Irving, David, ed. Breach of Security: The German Secret Intelligence File on Events Leading to the Second World War. London, 1968.

Analyses and reproduces intelligence reports of the Forschungsamt from October 1938 to September 1939; with some related subsequent material.

1574. Jones, Reginald Victor. Most Secret War: British Scientific Intelligence, 1939-1945. London, 1978.

Memoir-history by assistant director of scientific intelligence, Air ministry, 1941-46; based on his wartime reports; see also his "Science, Intelligence and Policy", Journal of the Royal United Services Institute for Defence Studies, 124(1979), 9-17; and Brian Johnson, The Secret War (London, 1978).

1575. Kahn, David. Hitler's Spies: German Military Intelligence in World War II. London, 1978.

See also his "Codebreaking in World Wars I and II: The Major Successes and Failures, their Causes and their Effects", Historical Journal, 23(1980), 617-39.

1576. Kramer, Paul. "Nelson Rockefeller and British Security Coordination." Journal of Contemporary History, 16(1981), 73-88.

1577. Lewin, Ronald. Ultra Goes to War: The Secret Story. London, 1978.

A major study based on the limited Ultra signals
declassified in 1977; see also his complementary study
dealing with the war against Japan, The Other Ultra
(London, 1982).

1578. Masterman, Sir John C. The Double-Cross System in the
      War of 1939-1945. London, 1972.

      Report, originally written in 1945, based on his work in
      section B1A of MI5, which dealt with double or "turned
      round" agents.

1579. Montagu, Ewen. Beyond Top Secret U. London, 1977.

      'Top Secret U' being the highest designation of
      classified documents derived from deciphered enemy
      messages from the Enigma machine or other sources; headed
      section 17M of the Naval Intelligence Department, and its
      representative on the XX Committee, which controlled the
      traffic transmitted by double agents; see also his The
      Man Who Never Was: The Story of Operation Mincemeat
      (London, 1953); and David Mure, Practise to Deceive
      (London, 1978).

1580. Morris, L.P. "British Secret Missions in Turkestan,
      1918-1919." Journal of Contemporary History, 12(1977),
      363-79.

1581. Peis, Gunther. The Mirror of Deception. London, 1976.

      An assessment of the double-cross system; largely based
      on interviews with former agents.

1582. Rohwer, Jürgen, and Jäckel, Eberhard, eds. Die
      Funkauflärung und ihre Rolle im Zweiten Weltkrieg.
      Stuttgart, 1979.

      Papers and discussion of conference in 1978 on the role
      of signals intelligence in world war two.

1583. Salmon, Patrick. "British plans for Economic Warfare
      Against Germany, 1937-1939: The Problem of Swedish
      Iron Ore." Journal of Contemporary History, 16(1981),
      53-71.

1584. Spiller, Roger J. "Some Implications of Ultra."
      Military Affairs, 40(1976), 49-53.

1585. Stafford, David. "'Ultra' and the British Official
      Histories: A Documentary Note." Military Affairs,
      42(1978), 29-31.

1586. Toscano, Mario. "Specific Problems in the History of World War II", in his Designs in Diplomacy: Pages from European Diplomatic History in the Twentieth Century. Baltimore, MD, 1970.

Specifically on several intelligence aspects.

1587. Wark, Wesley K. "Baltic Myths and Submarine Bogeys: British Naval Intelligence and Nazi Germany, 1933-1939." Journal of Strategic Studies, 6(1983), 60-81.

See also his "British Intelligence on the German Air Force and Aircraft Industry, 1933-1939", Historical Journal, 25(1982), 627-48; and "British Intelligence and Nazi Germany before the War", in The Missing Dimension: Governments and Intelligence Communities in the Twentieth Century, edited by Christopher Andrew and David Dilks (London, 1984).

1588. Wells, Anthony. "Naval Intelligence and Decision-Making in an Era of Technical Change", in Technical Change and British Naval Policy 1860-1939. Edited by Bryan Ranft. London, 1977.

1589. West, Nigel. MI5: British Security Service Operations, 1909-1945. London, 1981.

See also his A Matter of Trust: MI5, 1945-1972 (London, 1982); and MI6: British Secret Service Operations, 1909-1945 (London, 1983); John Bulloch, MI5: The Origin and History of the British Counter-Espionage Service (London, 1963); Richard Deacon, A History of the British Secret Service (London, 1969); Jock Haswell, British Military Intelligence (London, 1973); and E.H. Cookridge [Edward Spiro], Secrets of the British Secret Service: Behind the Scenes of the Work of British Counter-Espionage during the War (London, 1948).

1590. Winterbotham, Frederick William. The Ultra Secret. London, 1974.

First details from the British side on Ultra.

1591. Woytak, Richard A. On the Border of War and Peace: Polish Intelligence and Diplomacy in 1937-1939 and the Origins of the Ultra Secret. Boulder, CO, 1979.

Important for its use of Polish language sources; see also his "The Origins of the Ultra-Secret Code in Poland, 1937-1938", Polish Review, 23(1978), 79-85; and Wladyslaw

Kozaczuk, Enigma: How the German Machine Cipher was Broken, and How it was Read by the Allies in World War II, edited by Christopher Kasparek (Frederick, MD, 1983).

1592. Young, Robert J. "Spokesman for Economic Warfare: The Industrial Intelligence Centre in the 1930s." European Studies Review, 6(1976), 473-89.

4. Diplomacy at War

General Wartime

1593. Barker, Elisabeth. Churchill and Eden at War. London, 1978.

Principally based on the Eden papers, Public Record Office material, and some Macedonian sources; see also her British Policy in South-East Europe in the Second World War (London, 1976).

1594. Bartlett, C.J. "Inter-Allied Relations in the Second World War." History, 63(1978), 390-95.

1595. Bemis, Samuel F. "Roosevelt's Internationalism - and Churchill's." Yale Review, 40(1950), 149-52.

1596. Boehm, Hermann. Norwegen zwischen England und Deutschland: Die Zeit vor und während des Zweiten Weltkrieges. Lippoldsberg, 1956.

1597. Cosgrave, Patrick. Churchill at War. London, 1974-.

Vol. 1 for 1939-40; in progress; other studies of Churchill's wartime leadership include Raymond Callahan, Churchill: Retreat from Empire (Wilmington, DE, 1984); J.M. Lee, The Churchill Coalition, 1940-1945 (London, 1980); David Dilks, "Allied Leadership in the Second World War: Churchill", Survey, 21(1975), 19-29; Ronald Lewin, Churchill as Warlord (London, 1973); Reginald W. Thompson, Generalissimo Churchill (London, 1973); Maxwell Philip Schoenfeld, The War Ministry of Winston Churchill (London, 1972); Brian Gardner, Churchill in his Time: A Study in a Reputation, 1939-1945 (London, 1968); Lewis Broad, The War that Churchill Waged (London, 1960); and the recollections of high level colleagues in Sir John W. Wheeler-Bennett, ed., Action This Day: Working with Churchill (London, 1968).

1598. Feis, Herbert. Churchill, Roosevelt, Stalin: The War they Waged and the Peace they Sought. Princeton, NJ, 1957.

282

DIPLOMACY AT WAR

General Wartime

1599. Fisk, Robert. In Time of War: Ireland, Ulster and the
Price of Neutrality, 1939-1945. London, 1983.

1600. Goldman, Aaron. "Germans and Nazis: The Controversy
over 'Vansittartism' in Britain during the Second World
War." Journal of Contemporary History, 14(1979),
155-91.

1601. Hachey, Thomas E., ed. Confidential Dispatches:
Analyses of America by the British Ambassador,
1939-1945. Evanston, IL, 1974.

Reproduces fourteen "Political Reviews" prepared under
Lord Lothian and Lord Halifax; authors of individual
reviews identified in principal persons' glossary;
see also H.G. Nicholas, ed., Washington Despatches,
1941-1945: Weekly Political Reports from the British
Embassy (London, 1981); with an introduction by Sir
Isaiah Berlin, describing his role in the drafting of the
reports.

1602. Howard, Michael. The Mediterranean Strategy in the
Second World War. London, 1968.

The Lees-Knowles lectures for 1966; see also his "La
pensée stratégique", Revue d'histoire de la deuxième
guerre mondiale, 23(1973), 1-9; Centre National de la
Recherche Scientifique, La guerre en Méditerranée,
1939-1945 (Paris, 1971); Trumbull Higgins, "The
Anglo-American Historians' War in the Mediterranean,
1942-1945", Military Affairs, 34(1970), 84-88; and his
Soft Underbelly: The Anglo-American Controversy over the
Italian Campaign, 1939-1945 (London, 1968).

1603. Jedrzejewicz, Waclaw, ed. Poland in the British
Parliament, 1939-1945. 3 vols. London, 1946-62.

1604. Kersaudy, François. Churchill and de Gaulle. London,
1981.

A thoroughly documented study of the relationship; see
also Douglas Johnson, "Le général de Gaulle et M. Winston
Churchill", Etudes gaulliennes, 3(1975), 87-93; and
Patrick Keatinge, "De Gaulle and Britain, 1940-1946",
International Relations, 12(1965), 754-69.

1605. Kettenacker, Lothar. "Preussen in der alliierten
Kriegszielplanung, 1939-1947", in Studien zur

General Wartime

Geschichte Englands und der deutsch-britischen
Beziehungen: Festschrift für Paul Kluke. Edited by
Lothar Kettenacker, et al. Munich, 1981.

1606. Kimball, Warren F. "Churchill and Roosevelt: The
Personal Equation." Prologue: Journal of the National
Archives, 6(1974), 169-82.

1607. King, F.P. The New Internationalism: Allied Policy and
the European Peace, 1939-1945. Newton Abbot, 1973.

Based on British and American documents.

1608. Loewenheim, Francis L., et al., eds. Roosevelt and
Churchill: Their Secret Wartime Correspondence. New
York, 1975.

Extracts from more than 1700 messages; with introduction
and extensive editorial notes; see also Warren F.
Kimball, ed., Churchill and Roosevelt: The Complete
Correspondence, 3 vols. (Princeton, NJ, 1984).

1609. Louis, William Roger. Imperialism at Bay: The United
States and the Decolonization of the British Empire,
1941-1945. London, 1978.

As well as "a history of the origins of the trusteeship
system of the United Nations" (Preface).

1610. Pawle, Gerald. The War and Colonel Warden. London,
1963.

Based on the recollections of Commander C.R. Thompson,
personal assistant to Winston Churchill, 1940-45.

1611. Quinlan, Paul D. Clash Over Romania: British and
American Policies toward Romania, 1938-1947. Los
Angeles, CA, 1977.

1612. Roskill, Stephen W. Churchill and the Admirals. London,
1977.

Critical of Churchill's wartime naval policy; see also
Arthur J. Marder, Winston is Back: Churchill at the
Admiralty, 1939-1940 (London, 1975); an English
Historical Review Supplement, number 5; the reply in
Stephen W. Roskill, "Marder, Churchill and the Admiralty,
1939-1942", Journal of the Royal United Services
Institute, 117(1972), 49-53; and the general study from

DIPLOMACY AT WAR

General Wartime

1911 to 1955 by Sir Peter Gretton, Former Naval Person: Winston Churchill and the Royal Navy (London, 1968).

1613. Ross, Graham, ed. The Foreign Office and the Kremlin: British Documents on Anglo-Soviet Relations, 1941-1945. London, 1984.

See also his "Allied Diplomacy in the Second World War", British Journal of International Studies, 1(1975), 283-92.

1614. Thompson, R.W. Churchill and Morton. London, 1976.

Record of correspondence, from 1960-1962, between R.W. Thompson and Desmond Morton.

1615. USSR, Ministry of Foreign Affairs. Correspondence between the Chairman of the Council of Ministers of the U.S.S.R. and the Presidents of the U.S.A. and the Prime Ministers of Great Britain during the Great Patriotic War of 1941-1945. 2 vols. Moscow, 1957.

See also Dokumenty ob ostnosheniiakh SSSR i Velikobritanii v gody velikoi otechestvennoi voiny, 1941-1945gg., 2 vols. (Moscow, 1983).

1616. Voigt, Johannes H. Indien im Zweiten Weltkrieg. Stuttgart, 1978.

A widely documented study; see also Milan Hauner, India in Axis Strategy: Germany, Japan and Indian Nationalists in the Second World War (Stuttgart, 1980).

1617. Weber, Frank G. The Evasive Neutral: Germany, Britain and the Quest for a Turkish Alliance in the Second World War. Columbia, MO, 1979.

The role of Turkish neutrality based on non-Turkish archives; see also Johannes Glasneck and Inge Kircheisen, Türkei und Afghanistan: Brennpunkte der Orientpolitik im Zweiten Weltkrieg (Berlin, 1968); Edward Weisband, Turkish Foreign Policy, 1943-1945: Small State Diplomacy and Great Power Politics (Princeton, NJ, 1973), with Turkish language sources; and Nihat Erim Kocaeli, "The Development of the Anglo-Turkish Alliance", Asiatic Review, 42(1946), 347-51.

General Wartime

1618. Weinberg, Gerhard L. World in the Balance: Behind the
      Scenes of World War II. London, 1981.

      Six essays, some previously published; useful
      bibliographical essay.

The Sole Belligerent

1619. Baer, Barbara. "British Views of the Importance of
      French Africa to the Allied War Effort, 1940-1941."
      Proceedings of the French Colonial Historical Society,
      2(1977), 16-23.

1620. Barclay, Glen St. J. Their Finest Hour. London, 1977.

      A diplomatic and military analysis of the period June
      1940 to June 1941; based on British, Australian and New
      Zealand archives; see also his "Singapore Strategy: The
      Role of the United States in Imperial Defense", Military
      Affairs, 49(1975), 54-58.

1621. Batowski, Henryk. "Polish-British Relations in September
      1939: On the Basis of Foreign Office Archives."
      Polish Western Affairs, 13(1972), 108-16.

1622. Bédarida, François. La stratégie secrète de la drôle
      de guerre: Le conseil suprême interallié, septembre
      1939-avril 1940. Paris, 1979.

      The French records of the Supreme War Council, with an
      introduction and commentary; see also his "France,
      Britain and the Nordic Countries", Scandinavian Journal
      of History, 2(1977), 7-27.

1623. Bell, Philip M.H. A Certain Eventuality: Britain and
      the Fall of France. Farnborough, 1974.

      See also Eleanor M. Gates, End of the Affair: The
      Collapse of the Anglo-French Alliance, 1939-1940
      (Berkeley, CA, 1981); Douglas Johnson, "Britain and
      France in 1940", Transactions of the Royal Historical
      Society, 22(1972), 141-57; John C. Cairns, "De Gaulle
      Confronts the British: The Legacy of 1940",
      International Journal, 23(1968), 187-210; and his "Great
      Britain and the Fall of France: A Study in Allied
      Disunity", Journal of Modern History, 27(1955), 365-409.

DIPLOMACY AT WAR

The Sole Belligerent

1624. Berlin, Isaiah. Mr. Churchill in 1940. London, n.d.

See also his Against the Current (London, 1980).

1625. Bond, Brian. "Leslie Hore-Belisha at the War Office", in
Politicians and Defence: Studies in the Formulation of
British Defence Policy, 1845-1970. Edited by Ian
Beckett and John Gooch. Manchester, 1981.

His France and Belgium (London, 1975) is also useful on
Anglo-French strategy, 1939-40; see also A.J. Trythall,
"The Downfall of Leslie Hore-Belisha", Journal of
Contemporary History, 16(1981), 391-411.

1626. Centre National de la Recherche Scientifique. Français
et Britanniques dans la drôle de guerre. Paris, 1979.

Proceedings of an Anglo-French conference, 1975, under
the auspices of the Comité d'Histoire de la Deuxième
Guerre Mondiale; relevant essays on military problems,
public opinion and diplomacy.

1627. Creveld, Martin van. "Prelude to Disaster: The British
Decision to Aid Greece, 1940-1941." Journal of
Contemporary History, 9(1974), 65-92.

See also Sheila Lawlor, "Greece, March 1941: The
Politics of British Military Intervention", Historical
Journal, 25(1982), 933-46.

1628. Davidson, Major-General F.H.N. "My Mission to Belgium,
1940." Journal of the Royal United Service
Institution, 94(1969), 80-82.

Director of military intelligence, War Office, 1940-44.

1629. Dilks, David. "The Twilight War and the Fall of France:
Chamberlain and Churchill in 1940." Transactions of
the Royal Historical Society, 28(1978), 61-86.

1630. Grace, Richard J. "Whitehall and the Ghost of Appeasement: November 1941." Diplomatic History, 3(1979),
173-91.

1631. Haglund, David G. "George C. Marshall and the Question
of Military Aid to England, May-June 1940." Journal of
Contemporary History, 15(1980), 745-60.

The Sole Belligerent

1632. Häikiö, Martti. Maaliskuusta maaliskuuhun: Suomi
Englannin politiikassa, 1939-1940. Helsinki, 1976.

1633. Hanak, Harry. "Sir Stafford Cripps as British Ambassador
in Moscow, May 1940 to June 1941." English Historical
Review, 94(1979), 48-70.

1634. Kedourie, Elie. "Wavell and Iraq, April-May, 1941."
Middle Eastern Studies, 2(1966), 373-86.

1635. Kent, George O. "Britain in the Winter of 1940-1941 as
Seen from the Wilhelmstrasse." Historical Journal,
6(1963), 120-30.

1636. Kimball, Warren F. The Most Unsordid Act: Lend-Lease,
1939-1941. Baltimore, MD, 1969.

See also his "Lend-Lease and the Open Door: The
Temptation of British Opulence, 1937-1942", Political
Science Quarterly, 86(1971), 232-59; and "'Beggar My
Neighbour': America and the British Interim Finance
Crisis, 1940-1941", Journal of Economic History,
29(1969), 758-72; Philip Goodhart, Fifty Ships that Saved
the World: The Foundation of the Anglo-American Alliance
(New York, 1965); Edward R. Stettinius, Lend-Lease:
Weapon for Victory (New York, 1944); Daniel S. Greenberg,
"U.S. Destroyers for British Bases: Fifty Old Ships Go
to War", U.S. Naval Institute Proceedings, 88(1962),
70-83; and Charles Smith, "Lend-Lease to Great Britain,
1941-1942", Southern Quarterly, 10(1972), 195-208.

1637. Kimche, Jon. The Unfought Battle. London, 1968.

On events in September 1939; see also Nicholas Bethell,
The War Hitler Won: September 1939 (London, 1972).

1638. Lash, Joseph P. Roosevelt and Churchill, 1939-1941: The
Partnership that Saved the West. New York, 1976.

On this subject see also James Leutze, "The Secret of the
Churchill-Roosevelt Correspondence: September 1939-May
1940", Journal of Contemporary History, 10(1975), 465-91.

1639. Lowe, Peter. "Winston Churchill and Japan, 1914-1942."
Proceedings of the British Association for Japanese
Studies, 6(1981), 39-48.

Mainly on events in 1940-41.

DIPLOMACY AT WAR

The Sole Belligerent

1640. Lukacs, John. The Last European War, September 1939-
      December 1941. New York, 1976.

      See also Hanson W. Baldwin, The Crucial Years, 1939-1941:
      The World at War (New York, 1976).

1641. Marzari, Frank. "Western-Soviet Rivalry in Turkey,
      1939." Middle Eastern Studies, 7(1971), 63-77,
      201-20.

      See also Henryk Batowski, "Pour une alliance
      balkanique en 1941", Revue d'histoire de la deuxième
      guerre mondiale, 19(1969), 1-16.

1642. Mickelson, Martin L. "Another Fashoda: The Anglo-Free
      French Conflict over the Levant, May-September, 1941."
      Revue français d'histoire d'outre-mer, 63(1976),
      75-100.

1643. Nekrich, A.M. Vneshniaia politika anglii, 1939-1941gg.
      Moscow, 1963.

      See also V.N. Yegorov, Politika anglii na dalnem vostoke,
      sentiabr 1939-dekabr 1941gg. (Moscow, 1960).

1644. Nevakivi, Jukka. The Appeal that was Never Made: The
      Allies, Scandinavia and the Finnish 'Winter War',
      1939-1940. London, 1976.

      By a member of the Finnish foreign service and historian;
      based mainly on Finnish language and British sources;
      see also R.A.C. Parker, "Britain, France and Scandinavia,
      1939-40", History, 61(1976), 369-87; A.F. Upton, Finland,
      1939-1940 (London, 1974); and Max Jakobson, The Diplomacy
      of the Winter War (Cambridge, MA, 1961).

1645. Pankhurst, Richard. "The Ethiopian National Anthem in
      1941: A Chapter in Anglo-Ethiopian Wartime Relations."
      Ethiopia Observer, 15(1972), 63-66.

1646. Parkinson, Roger. Dawn on our Darkness: The Summer of
      1940. London, 1977.

      Combines eye-witness accounts with official documents;
      among the other numerous accounts of this period see
      Peter Fleming, Invasion 1940 (London, 1975); Laurence
      Thompson, 1940: Year of Legend, Year of History (London,
      1966); and Basil Collier, The Battle of Britain (London,
      1962); and the sequel 1941: Armageddon (London, 1982).

289

The Sole Belligerent

1647. Reynolds, David. "Roosevelt, the British Left, and the
Appointment of John G. Winant as United States
Ambassador to Britain in 1941." International History
Review, 4(1982), 393-413.

See also his "Lord Lothian and Anglo-American Relations,
1939-1940", Transactions of the American Philosophical
Society, 63(1983), 1-65; and Bert R. Whittemore, "A Quiet
Triumph: The Mission of John Gilbert Winant to London,
1941", Historical New Hampshire, 30(1975), 1-11.

1648. Rougier, Louis. Mission secrète à Londres: Les accords
Pétain-Churchill. Montreal, 1945.

Vichy government emissary to London, 1940; see also his
Les accords secrets franco-britanniques de l'automne
1940: Histoire et imposture (Paris, 1954); Prince Xavier
de Bourbon, Les accords secrets franco-anglais de
décembre 1940 (Paris, 1949); and General Gaston Schmitt,
Les accords secrets franco-britanniques de novembre-
décembre 1940: Histoire ou mystification (Paris, 1957).

1649. Shlaim, Avi. "Prelude to Downfall: The British Offer
of Union to France, June 1940." Journal of
Contemporary History, 9(1974), 27-63.

On the same subject see also David Thomson, The Proposal
for Anglo-French Union in 1940 (London, 1966); Max
Beloff, "The Anglo-French Union Project of June 1940", in
Mélanges Pierre Renouvin: Etudes d'histoire des
relations internationales (Paris, 1966); and Léon Noël,
"Le project d'union franco-britannique de juin 1940",
Revue d'histoire de la deuxième guerre mondiale, 6(1956),
22-37.

1650. Thomas, R.T. Britain and Vichy: The Dilemma of Anglo-
French Relations (London, 1979).

1651. Wanty, Emile. "Improvisations de la liaison belgo-
britannique du 10 au 18 mai 1940." Revue d'histoire de
la deuxième guerre mondiale, 14(1964), 29-50.

1652. Wilson, Theodore A. The First Summit: Roosevelt and
Churchill at Placentia Bay, 1941. Boston, MA, 1969.

1653. Woolf, Stuart. "Inghilterra, Francia e Italia:
settembre 1939-giugno 1940." Rivista di storia
contemporanea, 1(1972), 477-95.

Coalition Warfare and Diplomacy

1654. Allen, R.G.D. "Mutual Aid between the U.S. and the British Empire, 1941-1945." Journal of the Royal Statistical Society, 109(1946), 243-77.

1655. Armstrong, Anne. Unconditional Surrender: The Impact of the Casablanca Policy upon World War II. New Brunswick, NJ, 1961.

   Of related interest is Raymond G. O'Connor, Diplomacy for Victory: FDR and Unconditional Surrender (New York, 1971); John L. Chase, "Unconditional Surrender Reconsidered", Political Science Quarterly, 70(1955), 258-79; and Lord Hankey, "Unconditional Surrender", Contemporary Review, 176(1949), 193-98.

1656. Beaumont, Joan. Comrades in Arms: British Aid to Russia, 1941-1945. London, 1980.

   Based mainly on Public Record Office materials and private papers; see also her "A Question of Diplomacy: British Military Mission, 1941-1945", Journal of the Royal United Services Institute for Defence Studies, 118(1973), 74-77; and "Great Britain and the Rights of Neutral Countries: The Case of Iran, 1941", Journal of Contemporary History, 16(1981), 213-28.

1657. Beitzell, Robert. The Uneasy Alliance: America, Britain and Russia, 1941-1943. New York, 1968.

   For an earlier account see David J. Dallin, The Big Three: The United States, Britain, Russia (New Haven, CT, 1945); no footnotes or bibliography.

1658. Chan Lau Kit-Ching. "The Hong Kong Question During the Pacific War, 1941-1945." Journal of Imperial and Commonwealth History, 2(1973), 56-78.

   See also his "Britain's Reaction to Chiang Kai-Shek's Visit to India, February, 1942", Australian Journal of Politics and History, 21(1975), 52-61.

1659. Charmley, John. "Harold Macmillan and the Making of the French Committee of Liberation." International History Review, 4(1982), 553-67.

1660. DeNovo, John A. "The Culbertson Economic Mission and Anglo-American Tensions in the Middle East, 1944-1945." Journal of American History, 63(1977), 913-36.

Coalition Warfare and Diplomacy

1661. Dunn, Walter Scott. Second Front Now - 1943.
University, AL, 1980.

On the same subject see also John Grigg, 1943: The
Victory that Never Was (London, 1980); George Bruce,
Second Front Now: The Road to D-Day (London, 1979);
Keith Sainsbury, "'Second Front in 1942': Anglo-American
Differences over Strategy", British Journal of
International Studies, 4(1978), 47-58; Mark A. Stoler,
The Politics of the Second Front: American Planning in
Coalition Warfare, 1941-1943 (Westport, CT, 1977);
Trumbull Higgins, Winston Churchill and the Second Front,
1940-1943 (New York, 1957); Igor N. Zemskov,
Diplomaticheskaia istoriia otkritiia vtorogo fronta v
Evrope, 1941-1944gg. (Moscow, 1980); and his earlier
"Diplomatic History of the Second Front", International
Affairs (Moscow), 7(1961), 49-57.

1662. Duroselle, Jean Baptiste. "Le conflit stratégique anglo-
américain de juin 1940 à juin 1944." Revue d'histoire
moderne et contemporaire, 10(1963), 161-84.

1663. Ellwood, David W. L'alleato nemico: La politica
dell'occupazione anglo-americana in Italia, 1943-1946.
Milan, 1977.

See also his "Al tramonto dell'impero britannico: Italia
e Balcani nella strategia inglese, 1942-1946", Italia
contemporanea, 31(1979), 73-91.

1664. Filippone-Thaulero, Giustino. La Gran Bretagna e
l'Italia dalla conferenza di Mosca a Potsdam,
1943-1945. Rome, 1979.

With an appendix of ten related documents from the Public
Record Office.

1665. Funk, Arthur Layton. The Politics of Torch: The Allied
Landings and the Algiers Putsch, 1942. Lawrence, KS,
1974.

See also his "Negotiating the 'Deal with Darlan'",
Journal of Contemporary History, 8(1973), 81-117; and
Robert L. Melko, "Darlan between Britain and Germany,
1940-1941", Journal of Contemporary History, 8(1973),
57-80.

1666. Gandin, Robert. Darlan, Weygard, Cunningham: Artisans
de la victoire, 1939-1944. Paris, 1977.

DIPLOMACY AT WAR

Coalition Warfare and Diplomacy

1667. Herring, George C. "The United States and British
       Bankruptcy, 1944-1945: Responsibilities Deferred."
       Political Science Quarterly, 86(1971), 260-80.

1668. Hughes, E.J. "Winston Churchill and the Formation of the
       United Nations Organization." Journal of Contemporary
       History, 9(1974), 177-94.

1669. Kettenacker, Lothar. "The Anglo-Soviet Alliance and the
       Problem of Germany, 1941-1945." Journal of
       Contemporary History, 17(1982), 435-58.

1670. Kirby, David. "Morality or Expediency? The Baltic
       Question in British-Soviet Relations, 1941-1942", in
       The Baltic States in Peace and War, 1917-1945. Edited
       by V. Stanley Vardys and Romuald J. Misiunas. London,
       1978.

1671. Kuklick, Bruce. "The Genesis of the European Advisory
       Commission." Journal of Contemporary History, 4(1969),
       189-201.

1672. LaFeber, Walter. "Roosevelt, Churchill and Indochina,
       1942-1945." American Historical Review, 80(1975),
       1277-94.

       See also Christopher Thorne, "Indochina and
       Anglo-American Relations, 1942-1945", Pacific Historical
       Review, 45(1976), 73-96.

1673. Langer, John Daniel. "The Harriman-Beaverbrook Mission
       and the Debate over Unconditional Aid to the Soviet
       Union, 1941." Journal of Contemporary History,
       14(1979), 463-82.

1674. Langer, William L. "Political Problems of a Coalition."
       Foreign Affairs, 26(1947), 73-89.

1675. McNeill, William H. America, Britain and Russia: Their
       Co-operation and Conflict, 1941-1946. New York, 1970.

       A reprint of a volume in the Royal Institute of
       International Affairs wartime survey.

1676. Nelson, Daniel J. Wartime Origins of the Berlin Dilemma.
       University, AL, 1978.

       With special emphasis on the role of the European
       Advisory Commission; documentary annexes.

293

Coalition Warfare and Diplomacy

1677. Néré, Jacques. "Logistique et stratégie de l'alliance
anglo-américaine: Les temps difficiles, 1939-mars
1943." Revue d'histoire de la deuxième guerre
mondiale, 27(1957), 1-18.

1678. Neumann, William L. Making the Peace, 1941-1945: The
Diplomacy of the Wartime Conferences. Washington, DC,
1950.

See also his After Victory: Churchill, Roosevelt, Stalin
and the Making of the Peace (New York, 1967).

1679. Roberts, Walter R. Tito, Mihailovic and the Allies,
1941-1945. New Brunswick, NJ, 1973.

Includes published Yugoslav sources.

1680. Sharp, Tony. The Wartime Alliance and the Zonal Division
of Germany. London, 1975.

Specifically on the relation between the negotiations and
overall military strategy; based on British and American
archives and interviews; see also his "The Origins of the
'Teheran Formula' on Polish Frontiers", Journal of
Contemporary History, 12(1977), 381-93.

1681. Siracusa, Joseph M. "The Meaning of Tolstoy: Churchill,
Stalin and the Balkans, Moscow, October 1944."
Diplomatic History, 3(1979), 443-63.

On the same subject see also Albert Resis, "The
Churchill-Stalin Secret 'Percentages' Agreement on the
Balkans, Moscow, October 1944", American Historical
Review, 83(1979), 368-87; and Stephen G. Xydis, "The
Secret Anglo-Soviet Agreement on the Balkans of October
9th, 1944", Journal of Central European Affairs,
15(1955), 248-71.

1682. Sovietskii Soyuz na mezhdunarodnykh konferentsiakh
perioda velikoi otechestvenoi voiny, 1941-1945. Vol.
1-, Moscow, 1984-.

A collection of documents; vol. 1 for the foreign
ministers' conference in Moscow, 1943; subsequent volumes
to cover the Teheran, Dumbarton Oaks, Crimean and San
Francisco conferences.

Coalition Warfare and Diplomacy

1683. Stone, Glyn A. "The Official British Attitude to the Anglo-Portuguese Alliance, 1910-1945." Journal of Contemporary History, 10(1975), 729-46.

1684. Thorne, Christopher. Allies of a Kind: The United States, Britain and the War Against Japan, 1941-1945. London, 1978.

The setting of Anglo-American relations in the entirety of the Far East conflict; massively researched with extensive bibliography; see also his "Chatham House, Whitehall, and Far Eastern Issues, 1941-1945", International Affairs, 54(1978), 1-29; "MacArthur, Australia and the British, 1942-1943: The Secret Journal of MacArthur's British Liaison Officer", Australian Outlook, 29(1975), 53-67; and "Britain and the Black G.I.s: Racial Issues and Anglo-American Relations in 1942", New Community, 3(1974), 262-71.

1685. Wheeler, Mark C. Britain and the War for Yugoslavia, 1940-1943. Boulder, CO, 1980.

Based on British and Yugoslav archival sources; see also Stevan K. Pavlowitch, "Yugoslav-British Relations, 1939-1941, as seen from British Sources", East European Quarterly, 12(1978), 309-39, 425-41; F.W.D. Deakin, "Britanija i Jugoslavija, 1941-1945", Jugosolovenski istorijski casopis, 2(1963), 43-58; Elisabeth Barker, "Fresh Sidelights on British Policy in Yugoslavia, 1942-1943", Slavonic and East European Review, 54(1976), 572-85; and her "British Wartime Policy towards Yugoslavia", South Slav Journal, 2(1979), 3-9.

1686. Williams, J.E. "The Joint Declarations on the Colonies: An Issue in Anglo-American Relations, 1942-1944." British Journal of International Studies, 2(1976), 267-92.

1687. Woodhouse, C.M. The Struggle for Greece, 1941-1949. London, 1976.

In command of allied military mission to Greek guerillas, 1943; see also his Something Ventured: The Autobiography of C.M. Woodhouse (London, 1982); and Apple of Discord (London, 1948).

1688. Zieger, Gottfried. Alliierte Kriegskonferenzen, 1941-1943. Hannover, 1964.

Coalition Warfare and Diplomacy

See also his Die Teheran Konferenz (Hannover, 1967); and Die Atlantic Charter (Hannover, 1967).

1945: Before and After

1689. Alexander, G.M. The Prelude to the Truman Doctrine: British Policy in Greece, 1944-1947. London, 1983.

For the background see Procopis Papastratis, British Policy towards Greece during the Second World War, 1941-1944 (London, 1984); and Stephen G. Xydis, Greece and the Great Powers, 1944-1947: Prelude to the 'Truman Doctrine' (Thessaloniki, 1963).

1690. Anderson, Terry H. The United States, Great Britain, and the Cold War, 1944-1947. Columbia, MO, 1981.

On "the evolution of Anglo-American relations toward the Soviet Union from wartime cooperation to the Truman Doctrine" (Preface); for the related background, see among numerous studies Daniel Yergin, Shattered Peace: The Origins of the Cold War and the National Security State (Boston, MA, 1977); Martin J. Sherwin, A World Destroyed: The Atomic Bomb and the Grand Alliance (New York, 1975); George C. Herring, Aid to Russia, 1941-1946: Strategy, Diplomacy, the Origins of the Cold War (New York, 1973); John Lewis Gaddis, The United States and the Origins of the Cold War, 1941-1947 (New York, 1972); Gabriel Kolko, The Politics of War: The World and United States Foreign Policy, 1943-1945 (New York, 1968); Gar Alperovitz, Atomic Diplomacy: Hiroshima and Potsdam (New York, 1965); and Denna Frank Fleming, The Cold War and Its Origins, 1917-1960, 2 vols. (London, 1961).

1691. Balfour, Michael. The Adversaries: America, Russia and the Open World, 1941-1962. London, 1981.

More an interpretive essay than a diplomatic history; bibliography but no footnotes.

1692. Clemens, Diane Shaver. Yalta. New York, 1970.

With extensive use of published Soviet sources; of the many analyses of this conference see Arthur Conte, Yalta, ou le partage du monde (Paris, 1966); Richard F. Fenno, ed., The Yalta Conference (Boston, MA, 1955); G.F. Hudson, "The Lesson of Yalta", Commentary, 17(1954), 373-80; William D. Leahy, "Notes on the Yalta Conference", Wisconsin Magazine of History, 38(1954),

1945: Before and After

67-72, 110-13; Rudolph A. Winnacker, "Yalta - Another Munich?", *Virginia Quarterly Review*, 24(1948), 521-37; and Cyrus Leo Sulzberger, *Such a Peace: The Roots and Ashes of Yalta* (New York, 1982).

1693. Cox, Sir Geoffrey Sandford. *The Road to Trieste*. London, 1947.

Foreign and war correspondent, *News Chronicle*, 1935-37; *Daily Express*, 1937-40; served world war two, 1940-43.

1694. Douglas, Roy. *From War to Cold War, 1942-1948*. London, 1981.

Based on British and American documents.

1695. Eubank, Keith. *The Summit Conferences, 1919-1960*. Norman, OK, 1966.

Including Versailles, Munich, Teheran, Yalta and Potsdam.

1696. Garson, Robert. "The Atlantic Alliance, Eastern Europe and the Origins of the Cold War: From Pearl Harbor to Yalta", in *Contrast and Contention: Bicentennial Essays in Anglo-American History*. Edited by H.C. Allen and Roger Thompson. London, 1976.

1697. Hathaway, Robert M. *Ambiguous Partnership: Britain and America, 1944-1947*. New York, 1981.

1698. Kuniholm, Bruce R. *The Origins of the Cold War in the Near East: Great Power Conflict and Diplomacy in Iran, Turkey and Greece*. Princeton, NJ, 1980.

Explores the historical context of the cold war from a regional perspective; based on American archives and interviews.

1699. Lukacs, John. *1945: Year Zero*. New York, 1978.

Essentially a collection of essays, including a study of Winston Churchill; no bibliography; see also Brian Gardner, *The Wasted Hour: The Tragedy of 1945* (London, 1963).

1700. Mee, Charles L. *Meeting at Potsdam*. New York, 1975.

Among the numerous other studies see Jens Hacker, "Das Potsdamer Abkommen vom 2. August 1945", *Aus Politik und*

1945: Before and After

      Zeitgeschichte, supplement to Das Parlament, 6(1970),
      1-30; Klemens Keplicz, Potsdam: Twenty Years After
      (Warsaw, 1965); Wenzel Jaksch, Europe's Road to Potsdam
      (New York, 1963); Alfons Klafkowski, The Potsdam Agree-
      ment (Warsaw, 1963); Helmut Sündermann, Potsdam 1945:
      Ein kritischer Bericht (Leoni am Starnberger See, 1963);
      and Herbert Feis, Between War and Peace: The Potsdam
      Conference (Princeton, NJ, 1960).

1701. Miscamble, Wilson D. "Anthony Eden and the Truman-
      Molotov Conversations, April 1945." Diplomatic
      History, 2(1978), 167-80.

1702. Mosely, Philip E. "Dismemberment of Germany: The
      Allied Negotiations from Yalta to Potsdam." Foreign
      Affairs, 28(1950), 487-98.

1703. Nagai, Yonosuke, and Iriye, Akira, eds. The Origins of
      the Cold War in Asia. Tokyo, 1977.

      Sixteen papers presented at a symposium in Kyoto in 1975.

1704. Ovendale, Ritchie. "Britain, the U.S.A. and the European
      Cold War, 1945-1948." History, 67(1982), 217-35.

1705. Polonsky, Antony, ed. The Great Powers and the Polish
      Question, 1941-1945: A Documentary Study in Cold War
      Origins. London, 1976.

      149 documents, many from the Public Record Office, with
      introductory essay, footnotes but no bibliography; see
      also Edward J. Rozek, Allied Wartime Diplomacy: A
      Pattern in Poland (New York, 1958); and Roman
      Umiastowski, Poland, Russia and Great Britain, 1941-1945:
      A Study of Evidence (London, 1946).

1706. Rothwell, Victor. Britain and the Cold War, 1941-1947.
      London, 1982.

      Examines Britain's role in the origins of the cold war,
      mainly on the basis of Foreign Office documents.

1707. Rubin, Barry. The Great Powers in the Middle East,
      1941-1947: The Road to the Cold War. London, 1980.

      Explores "the role of great power relations in the Middle
      East in the breakdown of the wartime alliance and in the
      origins of the Cold War" (Preface); see also his

DIPLOMACY AT WAR

1945: Before and After

"Anglo-American Relations in Saudi Arabia, 1941-1945",
Journal of Contemporary History, 14(1979), 253-67; and
Harold G. Marcus, _Ethiopia, Great Britain and the United
States, 1941-1974: The Politics of Empire_ (Berkeley, CA,
1983).

1708. Sainsbury, Keith. "British Policy and German Unity at
the End of the Second World War." _English Historical
Review_, 94(1979), 786-804.

1709. Shlaim, Avi. _Britain and the Origins of European Unity,
1940-1951_. Reading, 1978.

1710. Sipols, V.Y., and Chelyshev, I.A. _Krymskaia konferentsia
1945 goda_. Moscow, 1984.

1711. Smith, Arthur L. _Churchill's German Army: Wartime
Strategy and Cold War Politics, 1943-1947_. London,
1977.

See also his _Churchill and the German Army, 1945: Some
Speculations on the Origins of the Cold War_ (Los Angeles,
CA, 1974); Center for the Study of Armament and
Disarmament, Occasional Paper, no. 2.

1712. Snell, John, ed. _The Meaning of Yalta: Big Three
Diplomacy and the New Balance of Power_. Baton Rouge,
LA, 1956.

See also his _Wartime Origins of the East-West Dilemma
over Germany_ (New Orleans, LA, 1959).

1713. Strang, Lord. "Prelude to Potsdam: Reflections on War
and Foreign Policy." _International Affairs_, 46(1970),
441-54.

Other contributors to this twenty-fifth anniversary of
Potsdam issue were historians Robert Cecil, André
Fontaine and Walter C. Clemens.

1714. Vloyantes, John. "The Significance of Pre-Yalta Policies
Regarding the Liberated Countries in Europe." _Western
Political Quarterly_, 11(1958), 209-28.

1715. Watt, D.C. "Every War Must End: War-Time Planning for
Post-War Security, in Britain and America in the Wars
of 1914-1918 and 1939-1945." _Transactions of the Royal
Historical Society_, 28(1978) 159-73.

1945: Before and After

1716. Wheeler-Bennett, John W., and Nicholls, Anthony. The Semblance of Peace: The Political Settlement after the Second World War. London, 1972.

1717. Wright, Michael. "British Foreign Policy in Europe." Annals of the American Academy of Political and Social Science, 240(1945), 73-78.

Entered diplomatic service, 1926; served Washington, Paris and Cairo, 1926-43; counsellor, British embassy at Washington, 1943-46.

V. INDEX

This index covers entries in chapters III-IV. It is an index of authors, editors and compilers, both personal and institutional. Numerical references are to entries in the guide rather than to pages.

Schmitthener, W., 1527
Schoenfeld, M.P., 1597
Schofield, B.B., 855
School of Oriental and
  African Studies, 15e
School of Slavonic and East
  European Studies, 15f
Schroeder, P.W., 1137
Schuker, S.A., 1243
Schuster, G., 544
Schuster, P., 1206
Schützler, H., 1471
Schweppenburg, L.G.v., 637
Schwoebel, J., 1018
Schwoerer, L.G., 1416
SCOLMA, 60
Scott, C.P., 545
Scott, G., 1042
Scott, H.R., 546
Scott, J.D., 331
Scott, W., 1432
Scottish Record Office, 28
Screen, J.E.O., 15f
Seale, P., 742
Seaman, L.C.B., 783
Seaton, J.R., 19
Seeland, R., 1138
Selby, W.H.M., 547, 994
Seldon, A., 15a
Selous, G.H., 548
Selsam, J.P., 1244
Sencourt, R., 1395
Senn, A.E., 1082
Seth, R., 223, 1444
Seton, R., 9a
Seton-Watson, C., 1175
Seton-Watson, H., 1175
Seton-Watson, R.W., 808
Seton-Williams, M.V., 1085
Seydoux, J., 1153
Seymour, C., 1184
Seymour, S., 1063
Shai, A., 1318
Shakespeare, G.H., 549
Shamir, H., 1477
Sharf, A., 956
Sharma, S.K., 1038
Sharp, A.J., 995
Sharp, T., 163, 1680

Shaw, M.A., 238
Shay, R.P., 856
Shearman, H., 1052
Sheehy, E.P., 109
Sheffer, G., 1039
Sheppard, J., 15d, 72
Sherman, A.J., 1538
Sherwin, M.J., 1690
Shigemitsu, M., 638
Shinwell, Baron, 550, 897
Shlaim, A., 1649, 1709
Shulman, F.J., 164
Sidebotham, P., 1009
Sillitoe, P., 551
Silverlight, J., 1076
Silverman, P., 857
Simon, Viscount, 552
Simpson, C., 647
Simpson, D.H., 26
Simpson, J.H., 1539
Sims, J., 293
Sims, N.A., 142
Sipols, V.Y., 1471, 1710
Sipple, C.E., 793
Siracusa, J.M., 1681
Siriex, P.-H., 1343
Skeat, T.C., 5
Sked, A., 1141
Skidelsky, R., 707, 761, 892,
  1139
Skop, A.L., 918
Skrine, C.P., 553
Slessor, J., 554
Slim, Viscount, 555
Slocum, R.B., 126
Sloman, A., 227
Sluglett, P., 164, 1040
Smith, A.L., 1492, 1711
Smith, B.L., 148
Smith, C., 712
Smith, C., 1636
Smith, C.M., 148
Smith, D., 1240
Smith, D.M., 1334
Smith, H., 131
Smith, J.A., 668
Smith, M., 858
Smith, M.J., 128, 149
Smith, M.L., 1182

320

INDEX

Villmow, D., 99
Vincent, J.E., 225
Vinson, J.C., 1240
Visscher, C.d., 309
Vital, D., 1437
Vloyantes, J., 1714
Vogel, G., 643
Vogel, R., 307
Voigt, J.H., 1616
Volkmann, H.-E., 828, 848, 895
Volkov, F.D., 1077

Wainwright, M.D., 85
Waites, N., 1068
Walder, D., 1248
Waley, D.P., 1343
Walford, A.J., 110
Walker, D., 9a
Walker, G., 63
Walker, S.G., 1140
Walker-Smith, D., 691
Wallace, L.P., 1169, 1353, 1475
Wallace, W.V., 1404, 1438
Walne, P., 95
Walsh, S.P., 126
Walters, F.P., 1042
Wambaugh, S., 1028
Wank, S., 1289
Wanty, E., 1651
Ward, A., 973
Wark, W.K., 1587
Warman, R.M., 1000
Warner, G., 1372
Warner, P., 771
Warth, R.D., 1216, 1260
Warwick, W.H., 698
Warwick University Library, 32
Wasserstein, B., 1043, 1547
Waterfield, G., 772
Waterlow, S.P., 1300
Watkins, K.W., 1379
Watson, C.A., 152
Watt, D.C., 207, 861, 1001, 1014, 1069, 1141, 1240, 1351, 1364, 1389, 1400, 1403, 1404, 1439, 1482, 1548, 1715

Wavell, A.P., 586, 696
Webber, R., 210
Weber, F.G., 1617
Weber, H.H., 128
Webster, C.K., 332, 587, 1440
Wedgwood, C.V., 773
Wedgwood, J.C., 588
Weidenfeld, W., 1249
Weikardt, C.R., 1250
Weill-Raynal, E., 1157
Weinberg, G.L., 1301, 1404, 1618
Weir, L.M., 733
Weisband, E., 1617
Weisbord, R.G., 1325
Welchman, G., 1560
Wellesley, V., 589
Wells, Anthony, 1588
Wells, Audrey, 1079
Wemyss, Baroness, 774
Wendt, B.J., 895, 1142, 1549
Werner, O., 1384
Wesley-Smith, P., 1111
West, N., 1589
Whates, H.R.G., 942
Whealey, R.H., 1377
Wheatcroft, A., 194
Wheeler, G.E., 1322
Wheeler, K.V., 11
Wheeler, L.J., 126
Wheeler, M.C., 1685
Wheeler-Bennett, J.W., 207, 590, 720, 775, 1044, 1158, 1276, 1435, 1597, 1716
White, C.M., 109
White, R., 1537
White, S., 1084
Whittemore, B.R., 1647
Whyte, A.F., 1323
Wiener, J.H., 812
Wiener Library, 33, 279
Wigley, P.G., 1053
Wilding, N.W., 211
Wile, A.N., 248
Willcox, T., 926
Willert, A., 591, 962, 1002, 1048
Williams, Aneurin, 1251
Williams, Ann, 1093
Williams, J.E., 1686

323